Clinical Psychology

This new edition of *Clinical Psychology* offers an expansive and up-to-date introduction to the field. Written by clinical practitioners and researchers, and supported by the personal stories of service users themselves, it provides a uniquely balanced view of contemporary clinical psychology.

Extensively revised throughout, the book explains the core principles of clinical practice, as well as outlining the role of a clinical psychologist within a healthcare team. It covers issues involved in working with children and families, adult mental health problems, people with disabilities and physical health issues, and the use of neuro-psychology. The final part of the book looks at both the history and future of the discipline, as well as professional issues in the field, and career options for those wishing to pursue their interest further.

Its integrated and interactive approach, combining the perspectives of professionals with the people they treat, make this book the ideal companion not only for under-graduate courses in clinical psychology, but also for anyone interested in a career in this field, including a range of healthcare professionals.

Graham Davey is Professor of Psychology at the University of Sussex and former President of the British Psychological Society, UK.

Nick Lake is Senior Clinical Director and a Consultant Clinical Psychologist at Sussex Partnership NHS Foundation Trust, UK.

Adrian Whittington is Director of Education and Training and a Consultant Clinical Psychologist at Sussex Partnership NHS Foundation Trust, UK.

Clinical Psychology

Second edition

Edited by

**Graham Davey,
Nick Lake and
Adrian Whittington**

Routledge
Taylor & Francis Group

LONDON AND NEW YORK

Second edition published 2015
by Routledge
27 Church Road, Hove, East Sussex BN3 2FA

and by Routledge
711 Third Avenue, New York, NY 10017

Routledge is an imprint of the Taylor & Francis Group, an informa business

First edition published by Hodder Education 2008

British Library Cataloguing in Publication Data
A catalogue record for this book is available from the British Library

Library of Congress Cataloging in Publication Data
Clinical psychology / edited by Graham Davey, Adrian Whittington,
    Nick Lake. — Second edition.
    pages cm. -- (Topics in applied psychology) 1. Clinical psychology.
    I. Davey, Graham, editor. II. Whittington, Adrian, editor. III. Lake,
    Nick (Clinical psychologist) editor.
    RC467.C5868 2015
    616.89--dc23
    2014035042

ISBN: 978–1–84872–222–4 (hbk)
ISBN: 978–1–84872–221–7 (pbk)
ISBN: 978–1–31572–356–3 (ebk)

Typeset in Bembo and Univers
by Florence Production Ltd, Stoodleigh, Devon, UK

Printed and bound in the United States of America
by Edwards Brothers Malloy on sustainably sourced paper

Contents

Contributors

Jan Burns, Professor of Clinical Psychology, Canterbury Christ Church University.

Angela Busuttil, Consultant Clinical Psychologist, Sussex Partnership NHS Foundation Trust.

Philippa Casares, Consultant Clinical Psychologist, Sussex Partnership NHS Foundation Trust.

Kate Cavanagh, Senior Lecturer, University of Sussex.

Melissa Chinery, Expert by Experience, Sussex Partnership NHS Foundation Trust.

Maeve Crowley, Consultant Clinical Psychologist, Sussex Partnership NHS Foundation Trust.

Jo Harris, Expert by Experience, Sussex Partnership NHS Foundation Trust.

Charlotte Hartley, Clinical Psychologist, formerly at Canterbury Christ Church University.

Renee Harvey, Consultant Clinical Psychologist, Sussex Partnership NHS Foundation Trust.

Mark Hayward, Director of Research and Consultant Clinical Psychologist, University of Sussex.

Anna Healey, Clinical Psychologist, Sussex Partnership NHS Foundation Trust.

Maureen Jeal, Expert by Experience, Sussex Partnership NHS Foundation Trust.

Mary John, Programme Director, Doctorate in Clinical Psychology, University of Surrey and Consultant Clinical Psychologist, Sussex Partnership NHS Foundation Trust.

Fergal Jones, Clinical Psychologist, Sussex Partnership NHS Foundation Trust and Senior Lecturer, Canterbury Christ Church University.

Neil Joughin, Consultant Psychiatrist, Sussex Partnership NHS Foundation Trust.

Nick Lake, Senior Clinical Director and Consultant Clinical Psychologist, Sussex Partnership NHS Foundation Trust.

Graham Lee, Principal Family and Systemic Psychotherapist, Sussex Partnership NHS Foundation Trust.

Sara Meddings, Consultant Clinical Psychologist, Sussex Partnership NHS Foundation Trust.

Alesia Moulton–Perkins, Principal Clinical Psychologist and CBT Therapist, Sussex Partnership NHS Foundation Trust.

Renate Pantke, Consultant Clinical Psychologist, Sussex Partnership NHS Foundation Trust.

Angela Reason, Principal Clinical Psychologist, Sussex Partnership NHS Foundation Trust.

Jan Rich, Principal Clinical Psychologist, Sussex Partnership NHS Foundation Trust.

Ines Santos, Senior Clinical Psychologist, Sussex Partnership NHS Foundation Trust.

Jane Shepherd, Consultant Clinical Psychologist, Sussex Partnership NHS Foundation Trust.

Rosey Singh, Clinical Director for Children and Young People's Services and Consultant Clinical Psychologist, Sussex Partnership NHS Foundation Trust.

Brian Solts, Complex Care Pathways Director and Consultant Clinical Psychologist, Sussex Partnership NHS Foundation Trust.

Sally Stapleton, Principal Clinical Psychologist, Sussex Partnership NHS Foundation Trust.

Clara Strauss, Consultant Clinical Psychologist, Sussex Partnership NHS Foundation Trust, and Honorary Lecturer, University of Sussex.

Monika Tuite, Principal Clinical Psychologist, Sussex Partnership NHS Foundation Trust.

Adrian Whittington, Director of Education and Training and Consultant Clinical Psychologist, Sussex Partnership NHS Foundation Trust.

Series preface

Psychology is still one of the most popular subjects for study at undergraduate degree level. As well as providing the student with a range of academic and applied skills that are valued by a broad range of employers, a psychology degree also serves as the basis for subsequent training and a career in professional psychology. A substantial proportion of students entering a degree programme in psychology do so with a subsequent career in applied psychology firmly in mind, and as a result the number of applied psychology courses available at undergraduate level has significantly increased over recent years. In some cases these courses supplement core academic areas and in others they provide the student with a flavour of what they might experience as a professional psychologist.

The original series of *Texts in Applied Psychology* consisted of six textbooks designed to provide a comprehensive academic and professional insight into specific areas of professional psychology. The texts covered the areas of *Clinical Psychology, Criminal and Investigative Psychology, Educational Psychology, Health Psychology, Sports and Exercise Psychology*, and *Work and Organizational Psychology*, and each text was written and edited by the foremost professional and academic figures in each of these areas.

These texts were so successful that we are now able to provide you with a second edition of this series. All texts have been updated with details of recent professional developments as well as relevant research, and we have responded to the requests of teachers and reviewers to include new material, and new approaches to this material. Perhaps most significantly, all texts in the series will now have back-up web resources.

Just as in the first series, each textbook is based on a similar academic formula that combines a comprehensive review of cutting-edge research and professional knowledge with accessible teaching and learning features. The books are also structured so that they may be used as an integrated teaching support for a one-term or one-semester course in each of their relevant areas of applied psychology. Given the increasing importance of applying psychological knowledge across a growing range of areas of practice, we feel this series is timely and comprehensive. We hope you find each book in the series readable, enlightening, accessible and instructive.

Graham Davey
University of Sussex, Brighton, UK
August 2014

Preface

This book sets out to offer a modern introduction to clinical psychology as it is operating on the ground – delivering clinical interventions, supervision, consultation, leadership, training and research in changing mental health services. The book places the voice of the users of these services at its heart, and it is their voices in this text that speak perhaps loudest for effective and artful psychological mental health care as a core feature of services. The content of the book also represents the best of the partnership work between lead clinicians (at Sussex Partnership NHS Foundation Trust) and clinical researchers (at the University of Sussex, University of Surrey and Canterbury Christ Church University), together with people who have experience of using our services. It is the strength of this three-way partnership, and the richness of the knowledge and understanding that may be gained from it, that lies at the core of our professional practice, now and in the future. We hope that many of you who read this book will become part of this future as practitioners or researchers in clinical psychology.

We know through careful trial evidence and qualitative analysis that psychology can offer a great deal to improve people's lives by aiding understanding of difficulties, delivering psychological therapies, and informing the wider service system with psychological knowledge. The profession of clinical psychology developed as a way of deploying competences to apply psychology to health care in the NHS. In the final decade of the twentieth century it also saw the growth of a multiplicity of professional groupings working with related aims – multiple varieties of psychological therapists and psychological well-being practitioners have flourished and developed, supported through unprecedented levels of public investment in adult and child psychological services as part of the Improving Access to Psychological Therapies programme in England, and related programmes across the UK.

All of this leaves us at a pivotal moment – with psychology in the public consciousness as never before and with ongoing public investment in services that have dramatically increased access to proven psychological therapies during the past decade. Some have interpreted the growth of other groups applying psychology in health care as a threat to the profession of clinical psychology. This fear is ironic because clinical psychologists have been leading the charge to develop the new services, train the new staff and deliver evidence-based psychological therapy to more people than ever before. In fact the public needs clinical psychology more than ever. This is because the science of psychology does not stand still: developing and delivering the best care requires those with competences in research, teaching, supervision and consultation to drive the next phase of change, as well as those able to deliver psychological therapies and interventions. The users of mental health services are telling us clearly that talking therapies and psychologically aware services are what they want and need, and research evidence offers us a clear mandate to expand the availability of psychological interventions. This will involve developing and researching new ones, as well as applying the ones we already have.

In addition to the value that clinical psychology offers as a health profession, it is also an important topic of interest for many undergraduate and graduate students studying psychology. Because of this, the contents of this text have been designed around teaching and learning features that may be used as the basis for an intermediate or advanced-level course that will allow students to learn in both breadth and depth about clinical psychology. Given the large numbers of undergraduate psychology students who aspire to a career in applied psychology, we hope that this book will be a valuable resource in the pursuit of that aim.

Graham Davey
Nick Lake
Adrian Whittington
June 2014

1 | What is clinical psychology?

1 What does a clinical psychologist do?

Fergal Jones and Charlotte Hartley

SUMMARY

Right across the world, as you are reading these words, millions of people are experiencing profound distress as a result of a wide range of psychological and mental health difficulties. Rigorous research studies demonstrate that clinical psychologists have the ability to aid recovery and alleviate suffering in relation to many of these difficulties, and yet their work is often poorly understood, and may seem mysterious. This chapter begins to demystify this work by providing detailed examples of the working weeks of two clinical psychologists. These examples illustrate how clinical psychologists apply psychological theory and research to understand and alleviate human distress, and introduce the key concepts of assessment, formulation, treatment and evaluation. The chapter offers an overview of the different types of specialities that clinical psychologist work in and the range of work that they do, including providing one-to-one interventions, group-based interventions, indirect work, consultation and teaching/training, and being involved with applied research, organisational development and leadership.

INTRODUCTION

Meet Ahmed and Susan.[1] Ahmed qualified as a clinical psychologist by completing his doctorate in clinical psychology two and a half years ago. After working in a number of temporary posts in the National Health Service (NHS) for his first-year post-qualification, he successfully applied for a permanent post as a clinical psychologist in an NHS service that provides health care to adults with intellectual disabilities. In contrast, Susan qualified eight years prior to Ahmed and worked in a number of varied posts. She is now a consultant clinical psychologist, the highest clinical grade in the profession, and is the most senior clinician in an NHS service for adults with common mental health problems, such as depression and anxiety. She provides leadership in this service on all clinical matters.

By reading about Ahmed's and Susan's working weeks, you'll come to see how the difficulties that people present with in clinical settings can have a psychological component, how clinical psychologists use psychological theories to help understand these difficulties, and how they then try to alleviate them by applying psychological approaches. In some instances the clinical psychologist will work directly with client(s), while in others the clinical psychologist will support family members, carers or other staff to use psychological ideas. Clinical psychologists may also be involved in a range of other activities that draw on their psychological knowledge and skills; a number of these will be illustrated. We begin with Ahmed's week.

FOCUS 1.1

'Patients', 'clients' and 'service-users': the implications of language

The terms 'client' and 'service-user' are frequently used to refer to the people with whom clinical psychologists work. These words are usually preferred to the more traditional label of 'patient'. This is because the latter can carry an implication that the person is a passive recipient of treatment, whereas psychological approaches usually involve the client adopting an active, collaborative role, as will become apparent throughout this book.

EXAMPLE WEEK FOR AHMED: CLINICAL PSYCHOLOGIST IN AN NHS LEARNING DISABILITY SERVICE

People with intellectual disabilities (sometimes also referred to as learning disabilities) have an intellectual impairment that is apparent from childhood, which means that they struggle to manage daily living tasks; for example, paying bills, reading letters, attending hospital appointments. The extent of the challenges they face may depend both upon the severity of their intellectual impairment and the degree to which their environment, social networks and living conditions help or hinder them. Ahmed was particularly drawn to working with this group of people after having a placement in a community learning disability team during his clinical training. He explained:

'The disability placement I had during training really changed my perspective. I hadn't given much thought before to working with this group of people but it opened my eyes to how easily people with intellectual disabilities can become vulnerable and socially excluded. I realised how the work we do as clinical psychologists has the potential to make real improvements to quality of life.'

You can read more about intellectual disabilities in Chapter 12.

Ahmed works four days a week in the NHS learning disabilities service, and spends the fifth day at home caring for his young daughter while his partner works. Ahmed's diary for a typical working week is shown in Table 1.1. The main activities outlined in his diary are described in more detail later. Sometimes Ahmed's diary may change at the last minute, when appointments are cancelled, extra meetings and emergency appointments are slotted in, people do not turn up to meetings, or unscheduled telephone calls or emails need to be dealt with urgently.

Let us now consider in more detail what some of the key activities in Ahmed's diary involve.

REFERRAL INFORMATION

Ahmed starts the week by reading some 'referral information' about a client, Jacob, who he has been asked to help. This explains that Jacob has a moderate intellectual disability and that his carers are concerned because he has started self-harming by banging his head against a wall. The carers and Jacob find this distressing and the carers hope that a psychological intervention might help stop this behaviour.

Irrespective of the setting and client group, like Ahmed, a clinical psychologist will usually receive referral information about the client(s) before she or he meets them. In some instances this may just be a letter from a psychiatrist or another clinician. In other cases a client may have been receiving support from the health services for a number of years and so have several volumes of clinical notes, which the clinical psychologist may be able to read if they are seeing the client as part of their NHS work. When reading the referral information clinical psychologists ask themselves whether it seems likely that psychological approaches could be used to understand and address the problems described. Often the referral information may not contain enough detail to make a decision on this, so the psychologist may try to speak with the referrer, if they are available, and conduct an assessment to investigate further. To this end, Ahmed speaks to the referrers by telephone and arranges an assessment meeting for Jacob later in the week.

Assessment

During the assessment, Ahmed meets with Jacob and his carers to gain both of their perspectives. He attempts to understand more about the problem, including why Jacob is banging his head. Jacob's moderate intellectual disability means that he is unable to explain this and his carers also do not have an explanation. Therefore Ahmed explores how often the head banging occurs, whether there are any events that occur immediately prior to each bout of head banging that seem to trigger it, and whether there were any changes in Jacob's environment around the time the head banging episodes first started. He also arranges to return the following week to spend some time observing at Jacob's care home, in case that provides further useful information.

As in this example, clinical work usually begins with an assessment. This information-gathering process can last one or more sessions and takes a variety of forms, depending upon the client group and the type of intervention the clinical psychologist plans to use. It is common for clinical psychologists to draw from a range of information

TABLE 1.1 A typical week from Ahmed's diary

Monday	Tuesday	Wednesday	Thursday	Friday
8.30–9.00 Email catch-up.	**9.00–1.00** Team 'away morning' at the team's base in large meeting room. Time is spent brainstorming ways to communicate better and discussing recent changes to management structure.	**9.00–9.30** Respond to emails and messages.	**9.00–9.30** Discuss recent referrals with a colleague and decide which clinicians to allocate them to.	Day at home looking after daughter.
9.00–9.20 Reading referral information on a new client (Jacob).		**9.30–11.30** Cognitive assessment with a client.	**9.30–12.30** Consultation clinic with two colleagues and three new clients.	
9.20–9.30 Telephone call to Jacob's carers to get more detailed information and to arrange an assessment for Thursday.	[Away mornings only happen occasionally; on other weeks Ahmed's morning might be as follows]:	**11.30–12.00** Write up clinical notes and score cognitive tests.	**12.30–1.30** Write up reports from consultation clinic.	
9.30–12 noon Two individual therapy sessions, including time to write up clinical notes.	**9.00–10.30** Supervision on case work.	**12.00–12.30** Lunch.		
	10.30–12.30 Continuing Professional Development (CPD) time to read up on the research evidence around the provision of group work for people with mild intellectual disabilities who are struggling with anxiety.	**12.30–1.00** Travel		
12.00–12.30 Prepare for afternoon visits by reading clients' clinical notes.				
12.30–1.00 Drive to a day centre. Eat lunch in car when arrive.				

Monday	Tuesday	Wednesday	Thursday	Friday
1.00–1.50 Session with an ongoing client (Jodi) who is being supported through the emotional impact of having her child taken into foster care.	**1.00–1.15** Read up on notes for next client and speak to his social worker.	**1.00–2.30** Meet care staff at new care home, to discuss a new referral and to meet the client (Cleo).	**1.30–2.00** Travel to Jacob's care home.	
1.50–2.00 Write up notes from session.	**1.15–1.30** Travel to care home.	**2.30–4.00** Individual session at the care home to complete an assessment of whether someone has an intellectual disability using psychological tests.	**2.00–3.30** Discuss care staff's concerns and meet Jacob. Complete a behavioural assessment and formulation. Start to make a behavioural intervention.	
2.00–3.00 Client 'does not attend'. Cannot access computer at this centre so use the time to read up on Down's syndrome and dementia for work tomorrow.	**1.30–3.00** Meet client (Freddie) who is showing early signs of dementia. Carry out the initial part of an assessment with him and his key worker.	**4.00–5.00** Finish early to pick up daughter from nursery.	**3.30–4.30** Travel to new community disability day centre and discuss potential evaluation project to be carried out jointly with staff.	
3.00–4.00 Meeting with a speech and language therapist to provide consultation and advice on a piece of clinical work the therapist is doing with someone who exhibits challenging behaviour.	**3.00–4.30** Continue the second part of a behavioural assessment with another client.		**4.30–5.30** Back to base to make sure notes are written up and filed away.	
4.00–5.15 Return to base. Finish writing up a cognitive assessment report from last week. Check emails and messages.	**4.30–6.00** Return to base to write up notes and score the psychological measures used in the assessments.			

sources, and sometimes they may interview clients, relatives and carers in order to obtain a range of perspectives. While the majority of information is usually collected at the beginning of clinical work, new information often comes to light in later sessions as people's trust in the clinical psychologist grows.

Sometimes clinical psychologists will use psychological tests as part of an assessment. For example, on Wednesday Ahmed conducts an assessment to determine whether someone has an intellectual disability and, if so, the severity of this disability. As part of this, he administers an IQ test to obtain an estimate of the client's level of intellectual functioning and a profile of the client's cognitive strengths and limitations. He uses other psychological measures to gain a sense of the client's ability to function in everyday life. As well as determining whether this person has an intellectual disability and the severity of it, this assessment enables Ahmed to provide feedback to the client and his support workers regarding his cognitive profile and its implications.

Another key task for the clinical psychologist, which starts during the assessment, is to develop good working alliances with the people involved. Without this it is more likely that these people will terminate the work prematurely, and even if they don't, that the work will be less effective. See Focus 1.2 for further discussion.

FOCUS 1.2

The role of relationship skills

A key part of clinical psychologists' work is being able to build and maintain relationships with people, including clients, clients' relatives and colleagues. In some cases clinical psychologists will need to build relationships with clients who have significant difficulties trusting people, as a result of previous breaches of trust, such as child abuse. Research suggests that one of the predictors of good outcomes in face-to-face psychological interventions with clients is the strength of *therapeutic relationship* that the clinical psychologist is able to foster with the client.

When thinking about the relationship-building skills that clinical psychologists need, it can be helpful to start from your own experience. If you wish, try to recall a time when you felt listened to and understood by someone. Replay this event in your mind and then write down what that person did that helped you to feel understood. You may want to think about what attitude they brought to the discussion, what they said and how they said it, and what their body language was like. You could repeat this process for some other occasions during which you felt listened to and understood. Are there any commonalities in the lists you have drawn up? Now, as a contrast, if you wish, consider some times when you have not felt understood by people to whom you were talking. What was it that these people were doing differently?

Based on these reflections, what do you think are the key skills and attitudes a clinical psychologist needs to bring to meetings with people in order to try to build positive relationships with them?

Formulation

A defining aspect of the clinical psychologist's role is their application of psychological theory and research findings to understanding the problems with which they are presented. Clinical psychologists combine the information they have gained from an assessment with relevant psychological theory and research findings, in order to create a 'formulation'. A formulation may be thought of as a psychological understanding of a client's problems, and provides a basis on which decisions about helpful interventions can be made. The process of making connections between assessment information and psychological theory (which is essential to creating a formulation) is referred to as developing 'theory–practice' links.

For example, Ahmed draws links between behavioural theory and the information he has gained during the assessment to develop an initial formulation of Jacob's head banging. Part of Ahmed's formulation is that Jacob tends to bang his head when he is by himself and seemingly bored. His head banging attracts the attention and care of staff. Therefore, the head-banging behaviour appears to be communicating Jacob's wish for more contact with care staff, and seems to be reinforced by the attention they give to Jacob when he bangs his head. Furthermore, this formulation suggests a possible helpful intervention: Jacob could be provided with more human contact and stimulating things to do when he isn't head banging, which should reduce the chances of him becoming bored and feeling lonely.

Sometimes clinical psychologists structure their formulations around *predisposing*, *precipitating* and *maintaining* factors. In creating a formulation, the clinical psychologist may be thought of as acting as a *scientist-practitioner*, since they are applying psychology theories to clinical practice. Furthermore, like scientists, clinical psychologists will tend to view their formulations as a series of hypotheses that can be confirmed or disconfirmed by information that may come to light at a later date. Therefore, the formulation is frequently modified and refined as the intervention progresses.

There are a variety of different approaches to formulation, including behavioural, cognitive-behavioural, systemic and psychodynamic, among others. As will be discussed in more detail in Chapter 2, each of these approaches offers a different way of understanding clients' difficulties and a different view on what the intervention should involve. In brief, behavioural therapy considers people's behaviours, the function they serve and the environmental factors that may reinforce them. Cognitive-behavioural therapy is particularly concerned with the interactions between thoughts (cognitions), behaviours and emotions. Psychodynamic psychotherapy emphasises the importance of early relationships and unresolved unconscious conflicts, and systemic therapy focuses on the systems of which the person is part, such as their family. Therefore, the nature of the formulation will depend upon the approach adopted by the clinical psychologist. Some clinical psychologists stick mainly to one approach, while others work in a more *integrative* way by drawing upon ideas from different approaches.

While many health and social care professionals draw upon psychological ideas in their work, the breadth and depth of their training enables clinical psychologists to draw upon and formulate, using a wide range of psychological theory, in a flexible manner, across a range of different clinical settings.

Communication

The ability to communicate clearly with people, including colleagues, clients and carers, is crucial to being an effective clinical psychologist. For example, in order for his work to be effective, Ahmed needs to be able to communicate clearly with people with varying degrees of intellectual disability, care staff and fellow health care professionals, and in each case pitch what he is saying in an appropriate way that is likely to be understood.

Before communicating, clinical psychologists will usually consider what information needs to be conveyed, what emotional impact it may have, and what the most effective way of conveying it will be. Often clinical psychologists will ask for feedback to gauge how information is received and understood. Sometimes communicating effectively with clients or staff can be difficult; for example, when a clinical psychologist is providing information that a client does not wish to hear or that does not fit with their worldview.

Intervention

Clinical psychologists are trained to provide a variety of psychological interventions. The intervention is based on the formulation and depends heavily upon the approach that a clinical psychologist decides to take. As already discussed, the main classes of psychological approach are *behavioural therapy*, *cognitive-behavioural therapy*, *psychodynamic therapy* and *systemic therapy*, and sometimes clinical psychologists choose to work in an *integrative* manner by drawing upon a variety of models/approaches. During the intervention the clinical psychologist pays attention to the quality of their relationships with the people involved, and to whether changes need to be made to the formulation in light of new information that becomes available. In some approaches, the clinical psychologist works collaboratively with the client to shape the course of the intervention.

Sometimes a clinical psychologist may offer a psychological intervention in *one-to-one sessions* with the client. For example, Ahmed meets weekly with Jodi on Monday afternoons to offer her psychological therapy to help her process and adjust to the loss of her child, who was taken into foster care, because Jodi had been assessed as being unable to safely parent him. In other cases they may work *indirectly* through significant people in the client's life; for example, Ahmed encourages Jacob's carers to provide him with more human contact and stimulating things to do when he isn't head banging, in order to reduce the chances of him becoming bored and feeling lonely and so starting to head bang. Interventions can also be offered in groups. *Group work* can have a number of advantages. For example, clients can find it valuable to meet other people who are struggling with similar difficulties, since this can help them feel less alone and offer them a way to provide mutual support. Groups can be a relatively safe space for clients to build confidence in social situations and explore how they relate to others. They can also be more cost-effective than individual work. That said, groups are not suitable for all clients and some clients find it too daunting to attend a group. Sometimes the clinical psychologist will find it helpful to consider the group as an entity in its own right, and so they may formulate both their understanding about an individual group member's difficulties as well as the dynamics or difficulties within the group as a whole.

Clinical psychologists may also offer *interventions to teams and organisations*. For example, during the 'away morning' Ahmed helps his team think about intra-team communication difficulties and this helps stimulate a useful discussion, out of which emerges an action plan to improve their communication. In other cases it may be that clinical psychologists take on a more formal consultation role to teams of which they are not a member (thus offering an outsider perspective and enabling the team or organisation the space to think differently).

Regardless of its format, an intervention is nearly always preceded by an assessment and guided by a formulation that makes connections between the assessment information and psychological theory. Further examples of interventions are provided throughout this book.

Evaluation

It is important to *evaluate* the effectiveness of an intervention, both during its course and after it is complete. This enables the clinical psychologist to gain a sense of whether the intervention seems to be having the desired effect. Both quantitative and qualitative information may be used to evaluate interventions. *Quantitative* measures assign a number or numbers to the desired outcomes; for example, to evaluate the intervention for Jacob's head banging, Ahmed asks Jacob's care staff to record how often he bangs his head each day. A reduction in this daily frequency over time would be consistent with the intervention being helpful. Quantitative information may also be obtained from more formal psychological measures and tests; for instance, there are well-respected questionnaires that measure potential targets for psychological interventions, including depression, anxiety, anger, quality of life, well-being, etc. Sometimes measures are self-report (i.e. the client completes them) and sometimes they are completed by people who know the client well; the latter may be more appropriate where the client has little insight into their difficulties or where their comprehension skills may make measure completion difficult. As part of his training, Ahmed was taught how to access and interpret the research literature on psychological tests and questionnaires in order to select the best available questionnaire for the evaluation task in hand.

Just as important is *qualitative* evaluation information. This includes clients' and carers' impressions of whether the intervention seems to be helping and their sense of what has and has not changed. Usually, clinical psychologists will want to collect both quantitative and qualitative evaluation information in order to obtain a rounded picture.

However, when interpreting such information, clinical psychologists will be mindful of factors that may bias it. For example, some clients may want to please their clinical psychologist and so give overly positive answers, while others may not want the work to finish and so over-emphasise their problems. If an evaluation suggests that an intervention is not helping, the clinical psychologist, often in conjunction with the client or carers, will try understand why this is the case. Once hypotheses have been developed as to the reasons why the intervention is failing, then the formulation can be modified and a new way forward planned. This is another example of how clinical psychologists behave as scientist-practitioners.

In addition, clinical psychologists may also be involved in evaluating interventions on a wider scale. For example, on Thursday afternoon, Ahmed travels to a new community disabilities day centre to speak with staff there who want to establish a programme to evaluate the service they offer. Ahmed helps the staff to crystallise their evaluation aims and agrees to return the following week, to allow him time to consult the research literature to see what evaluation tools might be helpful in this instance.

As an aside, it is perhaps worth adding that the degree of travel that clinical psychologists undertake as part of their role can vary substantially depending upon the setting in which they work and how geographically spread (or otherwise) the services are into which they provide input.

SUMMARY: STAGE OF CLINICAL WORK

The stages of assessment, formulation, intervention and evaluation are present in the majority of clinical psychologists' clinical work. Typically these do not occur as discrete stages, but rather overlap and blend into each other. Given their importance, they will be returned to throughout this book.

MULTI-DISCIPLINARY TEAM (MDT) WORKING

Clinical psychologists, like Ahmed, frequently work as members of MDTs. Part of the rationale for MDTs is that they can provide clients with more holistic care, since they include workers from a range of disciplines that specialise in different aspects of health and social care.

Clinical psychologists often provide psychological advice and consultation to MDT colleagues, to help them develop a psychological understanding of their clinical work. In addition, clinical psychologists see clients jointly with MDT colleagues when it seems helpful to do so. For example, fortnightly on Thursdays Ahmed facilitates a consultation clinic with MDT colleagues, during which he meets with clients together with colleagues. Team working is discussed in more detail in Chapter 3.

REFLECTIVE PRACTICE

In addition to following the scientist-practitioner model in his clinical work, Ahmed, like other clinical psychologists, behaves as a *reflective-practitioner*. For example, during his work with clients he reflects on the assumptions that he is making, and how his cultural background and life experiences influenced these assumptions. He also uses his monthly meetings with his clinical *supervisor* (a more senior clinical psychologist) to reflect on his work and assumptions, and to gain his supervisor's perspective. In addition, he attends a fortnightly MDT 'reflective-practice meeting', which provides the team with space to reflect together upon clinical work and team issues.

We all have beliefs and perspectives about our self, other people and the world. These will have been influenced by our cultural background and previous life experiences. We may be aware of some of the beliefs that we hold, and thus be able to examine their validity. However, it is likely that we have a number of beliefs which we automatically assume to be true but have not critically examined.

Clinical psychologists reflect on their own beliefs in order to try to reduce the impact of unexamined assumptions on their work with clients. Supervision meetings with a more experienced colleague can play an important role in this process because the psychologist may be blind to some of their own assumptions. Supervision plays a number of other key roles, including supporting the clinical psychologist's *continuing professional development* and monitoring their work. All practising clinical psychologists should receive some form of supervision. Some clinical psychologists also choose to have their own psychological therapy, in order to increase their self-awareness and understanding of how they relate to others.

EXAMPLE WEEK FOR SUSAN, CONSULTANT CLINICAL PSYCHOLOGIST IN MENTAL HEALTH SERVICES

Let us now consider the working week of the more senior clinical psychologist, Susan, who has reached the highest clinical grading in the profession: 'consultant clinical psychologist'. She is the most senior clinical psychologist in an NHS service for adults with common mental health problems, such as depression and anxiety, and provides leadership in this service on all clinical matters.

As with Ahmed, during her 'clinical day' on Fridays, Susan follows the stages of *assessment, formulation, intervention* and *evaluation*, with *communication* playing a vital role throughout. However, given her relative seniority and experience, she tends to see clients with some of the highest degrees of severity and complexity in the service.

Senior clinical psychologists will often do less 'hands-on' clinical work than their more junior colleagues due to the other demands on their time. However, usually they will still make the time to do some regular clinical work in order to retain their clinical skills and to be able to offer clinical supervision and management to others that remains based in personal clinical competence.

LEADERSHIP

Consultant clinical psychologists in clinical lead roles are typically responsible for providing clinical leadership to their service and for advising the service director on clinical matters relating to psychological approaches. For example, as part of her leadership role, Susan attends the service's 'leadership group meeting', where the majority of decisions about the service are made or ratified. At the leadership group and when speaking with the service director, Susan draws upon both her extensive clinical experience and her knowledge of the research evidence base. For instance, when the leadership group was reviewing the psychological group-based interventions the service offered to people struggling with depression, she advised them as to which interventions had been found to be most effective in research and also about the staff training and supervision changes that would need to be made to enable these to be safely and effectively offered by the service.

In leadership roles, consultant clinical psychologists also draw upon their *formulation* skills to apply psychological theories of organisational processes to understand the

TABLE 1.2 A typical week from Susan's diary

Monday	Tuesday	Wednesday	Thursday	Friday
9.00–10.00 Peer supervision with other senior psychologist in the NHS Trust.	**9.00–10.00** Appearance on a local radio show to help raise public awareness of the effects of anxiety and depression and how people can access local services.	**9.00–10.00** Meeting with a client who has made a complaint about the service to hear more about their concerns and respond to these.	**9.00–5.00** Teach on a local clinical psychology training programme.	**9.00–5.00** Clinical day: assessment or intervention sessions with five clients.
10.00–10.30 Travel.	**10.00–10.30** Travel.	**10.00–11.00** Provide supervision to a psychotherapist in the service.		
10.30–12.30 Service leadership group meeting.	**10.30–11.30** Performance contract review with the local Mental Health Commissioner.	**11.00–1.00** Review the service's performance with the service director and develop a plan to improve this.		
12.30–1.00 Meet with team psychiatrist to agree local referral pathways between medics and psychologists.	**11.30–12.00** Travel, using the time to make several calls to work colleagues on both clinical and service-related issues.	**1.00–1.30** Lunch.		
1.00–1.30 Lunch.	**12.00–2.00** Review and redraft a service policy on how to respond to clients who do not attend sessions. Eat sandwich while doing the work.	**1.30–2.30** Prepare for coroner's court appearance.		
1.30–3.30 Supervise a trainee clinical psychologist.	**2.00–3.00** Provide supervision to a more junior clinical psychologist.	**2.30–3.00** Travel.		
3.30–4.00 Write up trainee evaluation form.	**3.30–5.00** Chair the service's audit and evaluation group.	**3.00–5.00** Appear in coroner's court to outline the input that the service provided to a client who subsequently committed suicide.		
4.00–5.30 Admin, including emails.	**5.00–6.00** Admin and emails.	**5.00–7.00** Return to base to check emails and prepare for teaching tomorrow.		

challenging interpersonal dynamics that sometimes arise within services. For example, when a restructuring of Susan's service was planned, many of the staff within the service started to feel understandably anxious about this, and it seemed that this feeling was being increased by the anxious interactions among staff. Susan was able to formulate an understanding of this by drawing on theories of organisational change. On the basis of this formulation she offered the leadership group advice on helpful ways to work with this anxiety, including ensuring clear communication with staff, being transparent, helping staff to feel that their concerns had been heard and helping them to have ownership in the change process.

As part of their leadership role, consultant clinical psychologists may also be involved in developing or reviewing policies and procedures. This is another way in which they can influence the services that are offered and, as previously, they make use of their psychological knowledge and experience during this process. For example, on Tuesday, Susan reviews and redrafts a service policy on how to respond to clients who stop attending their appointments, drawing on her psychological understanding of why this may happen.

As with Ahmed, good *communication* skills are a vital part of Susan's armoury. For example, not all her colleagues in the leadership group have the same understanding of psychological approaches or placed the same value on them as Susan does. Therefore, she needs to be able to provide clear, succinct and convincing arguments in relation to them. Overall, Susan attempts to act with integrity, sensitivity and fairness in her leadership role. This helps her to earn the trust of other staff members within the team and means that they are more willing to listen to her advice and recommendations.

It is important not to underestimate the powerful effect that competent, trusted leadership can have on the effective functioning of teams and services, and senior clinical psychologists can play an influential role in this respect. For completeness, it is also worth adding that, as part of their leadership role, consultant clinical psychologists may need to carry out some more emotionally draining but nevertheless important activities. These may include meeting service users who have made complaints about the service and responding to these complaints, and attending the coroner's court when a user of the service has taken their own life.

SUPERVISION AND CONSULTATION

Like their more junior colleagues, consultant clinical psychologists continue to receive supervision of their work. Sometimes this may be provided by even more senior and experienced clinical psychologists. However, more experienced colleagues may not be available, and so consultant psychologists may instead participate in *peer-group supervision*, during which they meet colleagues of a similar level of experience and seniority, usually from other services within the NHS Trust, to reflect upon and formulate the challenges they are each facing in their work. Susan participates in a peer-group supervision once a month on a Monday, with consultant clinical psychologists from other services.

In addition, consultant clinical psychologists will usually spend some of their time offering supervision to more junior colleagues. This may range from supervising people who are training to become clinical psychologists, to supervising junior clinical psychologists and other professionals who use psychological approaches (e.g. psychotherapists). Susan supervises one trainee clinical psychologist, three psychotherapists and one junior clinical psychologist. Susan is able to supervise the psychotherapists because, following her clinical psychology training, she completed further training in the form of psychotherapy they use.

Sometimes colleagues from other health professions may not need ongoing supervision from a clinical psychologist, but may nevertheless wish to receive advice on the psychological aspects of their work. To this end, clinical psychologists and consultant clinical psychologists may provide psychological *consultation* to their colleagues. This involves the psychologist helping their colleague to formulate psychologically aspects of a specific piece of clinical work. The aim of consultation is two-fold: to help the colleague develop a psychological formulation that may aid the specific piece of clinical work, and to help them develop their ability to think psychologically about their work more generally. Susan is no exception to this: she provides consultation to colleagues when they request it and when her diary allows.

TEACHING AND TRAINING

Arguably, fostering psychological ways of thinking among the wider health care workforce is a key part of the clinical psychologist's and consultant clinical psychologist's role. One way to contribute to this may be through the provision of training events to health care colleagues. In addition, clinical psychologists may contribute to the teaching of people training to be clinical psychologists. For example, on Thursday, Susan visits a nearby university and spends the day facilitating a workshop on providing consultation and supervision for students on a clinical psychology training course. (See Chapter 17 for more information about training to be a clinical psychologist.) Sometimes clinical psychologists may also seek to educate the public more widely through media work, such as Susan's appearance on local radio on Tuesday to increase public awareness of the effects of anxiety and depression and how people can access local services.

RESEARCH AND SERVICE EVALUATION

As scientist-practitioners, clinical psychologists draw upon psychological theory and psychologist research. Therefore, the future improvement of the services that clinical psychologists offer is in a large way dependent upon ensuring that research continues to occur that helps to improve psychological theory and develop more effective and efficient psychological interventions. Clinical psychologists' research training means that they are in a good position to contribute to this. Some clinical psychologists work in universities and are heavily involved in such research. Others working in clinical settings may help research, for example, by facilitating recruitment of participants to research studies.

Most clinical psychologists working in clinical settings are also involved in audit and service evaluation; that is, using research methods to examine whether the service is meeting its targets, for example, in terms of waiting times, and evaluating the quality and effectiveness of the interventions that are offered. Every month on a Tuesday, Susan chairs the service's audit and service-evaluation group, because she has the most research training of all the clinicians in the service. Audit and service evaluation can provide important information to services about what they are doing well and where they need to make improvements.

DIFFERENT CLIENT GROUPS, SETTINGS AND PSYCHOLOGICAL APPROACHES

Generally, clinical psychologists and consultant clinical psychologists specialise in working with one, or sometimes two, client groups. This is in part influenced by the fact that services in the NHS are frequently organised by client group. If a clinical psychologist wants to work with more than one client group then they will usually need to have a 'split post', which involves being a part-time employee in two different services. Some of the main client groups are as follows.

- Children with mental health problems or physical problems and their families (see Chapters 4 and 5).
- Adults with mental health problems (see Chapters 6 to 11).
- Adults with physical health problems (see Chapter 13).
- People with an intellectual disability (see Chapter 12).
- People with brain injuries or progressive degenerative conditions, such as dementia (see Chapters 14 and 15).
- People with substance misuse difficulties (not covered specifically in this book).

Furthermore, for some client groups there are a range of different settings and sub-specialities within which clinical psychologists can work. For example, in adult mental health, clinical psychologists can work in services including, among others, assessment and treatment services, inpatient units, primary care mental health teams, specialist units for people with particular difficulties, and forensic services. In addition, clinical psychologists may choose to specialise in adopting a particular psychological approach (e.g. cognitive-behavioural, systemic or psychodynamic), or they may choose to work in an integrative manner by drawing upon a variety of models.

CONCLUSIONS

Clinical psychologists draw upon psychological theory to try to understand the difficulties their clients are struggling with and then apply psychological approaches to try to manage or alleviate these difficulties. In general, they act as scientist-practitioners and reflective-practitioners. Usually, clinical work includes assessment, formulation, communication, intervention and evaluation. Clinical psychologists are often members of MDTs and frequently offer consultation and advice to colleagues. Moreover, they work within a range of different settings and with a variety of different client groups. Finally, senior clinical psychologists can play influential leadership roles in services.

KEY CONCEPTS AND TERMS

- Assessment
- Formulation
- Communication
- Intervention
- Evaluation
- Scientist-practitioner
- Reflective-practitioner

- Multi-disciplinary team
- Behavioural therapy
- Cognitive-behavioural therapy
- Psychodynamic therapy

- Systemic therapy
- Supervision, leadership
- Teaching
- Audit
- Research

LEARNING OUTCOMES

When you have completed this chapter you should be able to:

1 Describe the core elements of the work of a clinical psychologist.
2 Understand how psychological knowledge and research is applied to the treatment of people in psychological distress.
3 Understand the different types of interventions that clinical psychologists employ.
4 Understand the role of assessment, formulation, treatment and evaluation.
5 Have an understanding of the range of specialities in which psychologists work.

SAMPLE ESSAY TITLES

- What are the key stages of clinical work and what does each stage comprise?
- Describe the range of activities that clinical psychologists engage in. How does psychological theory inform how clinical psychologists carry out these activities?
- What are the similarities and differences between the roles of a junior and a senior clinical psychologist?

NOTE

1   Ahmed and Susan are composites created by drawing on the experiences of a range of different clinical psychologists and, as such, provide representative examples of the roles clinical psychologists can take, without violating confidentiality.

FURTHER READING

Beinart, H., Kennedy, P. and Llewelyn, S. (2009). *Clinical Psychology in Practice*. Oxford: Wiley-Blackwell.

Cheshire, K. and Pilgrim, D. (2004). *A Short Introduction to Clinical Psychology*. London: Sage.

Johnstone, L. and Dallos, R. (eds) (2006). *Formulation in Psychology and Psychotherapy: Making Sense of People's Problems*. Abingdon: Routledge.

2 The art and science of psychological practice

Nick Lake and Adrian Whittington

SUMMARY

We are still at an early stage in developing our understanding of the human mind. This makes the practice of clinical psychology challenging. There is still so much that we don't know and not knowing can be anxiety-provoking for a professional. However, clinical psychology practice is also enormously rewarding. No two pieces of clinical work are ever the same, the science is constantly developing, and there is room for real creativity in what we do. In the end we also help people to get better – and that can feel very rewarding indeed.

Despite the complexity of our subject, psychological science has made some significant progress and the profession of clinical psychology grounds itself in this science and plays a key role in advancing this science. However, clinical psychology practice is also an 'art', and our psychological knowledge often has to be applied creatively to help address the types of psychological difficulties psychologists face in their everyday practice.

This chapter reviews the principles behind the 'science' of clinical psychology, including the role of the empirically supported treatments, evidence-based practice and practice-based evidence. It also looks at the 'art' of psychological practice; in other words, how a psychologist applies their psychological knowledge in creative and sometimes unique ways to help address the complex array of factors that may underpin any one person's (or couple, family, group or team's) particular set of emotional or psychological difficulties. It requires both rigour to the approach (if we know from the research that this works) and a flexibility to adapt to the circumstances.

In order to help us navigate this science and art, three overarching frameworks of psychological practice are introduced: the scientist-practitioner, the reflective-practitioner and the critical practitioner. The chapter will also give an introduction to the types of psychological models and theories used in practice, focusing on four of the most influential: behaviour therapy, cognitive-behavioural therapy, short-term psychodynamic therapy and systemic therapy.

We will argue that the 'science' and 'art' of psychological practice should not be seen as opposing principles. There must be artistry in the application of science, and greater scientific examination of the 'art' of practice, if we are to further develop our capacity to treat the most complex of human attributes – the mind – and the thoughts, emotions and behaviour connected to it.

INTRODUCTION TO THE 'SCIENCE' AND 'ART' OF PRACTICE

We will begin by introducing three models of psychological practice that are taught at the start of most clinical psychology professional training programmes and which help navigate the science and art of clinical practice. These emphasise the roles of science (the scientist-practitioner), reflection (the reflective-practitioner) and critique (the critical-practitioner) in the application of psychology into practice. While they sometimes appear to be in tension with one another, the three frameworks should be complementary in enabling effective practice.

The scientist-practitioner

The scientist-practitioner model is in essence about applying the rigour and knowledge obtained from science to the practical problems faced by the practitioner in everyday life (see Lane and Corrie, 2006). For clinical psychologists, it is the practical application of the scientific study of psychology to the alleviation of psychological distress that underpins what we do. The scientist practitioner model is partly about applying what we know from research evidence obtained from the following sources:

- *Randomised controlled trials*, which examine how well interventions work in carefully controlled conditions (the *efficacy* of the intervention).
- *Effectiveness trials*, which examine how well interventions work in routine care environments (the *effectiveness* of the intervention).
- *Case series*, which examine possibilities of effects, typically for new interventions, by examining a number of cases in detail.
- *Experimental research*, which tests the underpinning principles or psychological theory behind interventions.

It is also about embedding the scientific principles of hypothesis testing, empirically grounded psychological theory and careful outcome evaluation in all the work we do.

The scientist-practitioner model has been very important in enabling the development of effective psychological practice, with significant advances having been made through rigorous research since the 1950s. The scientific process has led to the development of effective psychological treatments for a whole range of difficulties across the lifespan. For example, we know that CBT for depression is effective for the majority of people who receive it and has more long-lasting effect than anti-depressant medication (Hollon *et al.*, 2006). Consistently drawing upon evidence-based practice has helped establish the credibility and value of the profession of clinical psychology.

In the UK, the National Institute for Health and Care Excellence (NICE) provides guidance on what psychological treatments are known to be effective for which conditions (see Focus 2.1). These recommendations for particular 'empirically supported treatments' (ESTs) are based on the best evidence we have available – usually outcome research from at least two randomised controlled trials (see Focus 2.2 for details).

NICE recommended treatments for different mental health diagnoses for adults

Depression

Cognitive behaviour-therapy (CBT), interpersonal therapy (IPT) and behavioural couples therapy. Mindfulness-based cognitive therapy (MBCT) for people who have suffered repeated episodes of depression.

Where these treatments have been unsuccessful then also choose from: short-term psychodynamic psychotherapy and counselling.

Bipolar disorder

CBT.

Generalised anxiety, panic, agoraphobia, OCD, social phobia

CBT.

PTSD

CBT and eye movement desensitisation and reprocessing (EMDR).

Eating disorders

Anorexia: family therapy, psychodynamic psychotherapy and cognitive-analytic therapy (CAT).

Bulimia: CBT and IPT.

Borderline personality disorder

Extended psychological therapy (model not specified). Consider dialectical behaviour therapy (DBT) for self-harm.

Schizophrenia

CBT and family interventions.

Randomised controlled trials (RCTs)

RCTs are considered the 'gold standard' in outcome research. The key elements are as follows:

- Clients with the same type of emotional difficulty (e.g. agoraphobia) are selected from a wider patient group and then divided randomly into different treatment groups. There must be enough people in each group to achieve an appropriate effect size; in other words, to ensure that the effects are big and significant enough not to have happened by chance.
- One group receives the therapy to be evaluated. Other groups may receive a different therapy, a different intervention (e.g. a drug), or a control-based procedure (e.g. active monitoring) which attempts to control for the general effects of receiving care and attention.
- There is often a waiting list or 'treatment as usual' control group to see whether the patient group may have got better even if they had not received the intervention.
- An assessment is made of the severity of the person's condition at different points during the intervention using a well-established measure.
- There are clear protocols for each of the interventions to ensure that the interventions are applied consistently.
- The people taking part in the trials are selected, and certain exclusion criteria applied. These may include the presence of some co-morbid conditions (e.g. drug or alcohol abuse).
- Some trials are 'blind', meaning that people assessing the effects of the intervention should not be aware of what intervention the person has had.
- Participants are sometimes followed up for some time after the intervention to determine whether the effects of the intervention are maintained.

A powerful technique called 'meta-analysis' has been used to draw together results from across several high-quality RCTs studying the same type of treatment, in order to make an overall analysis of the efficacy of that treatment.

Limitations in interpreting the evidence base

While the use of empirically supported treatments should underpin the work of a clinical psychologist, there are some limitations to the research base which psychologists need to remain aware of when applying findings to clinical practice. The limitations are as follows:

- Most ESTs are based largely on RCTs which themselves have limitations:
  - o They typically focus on one focal problem, whereas people often suffer with more than one type of emotional difficulty. Much less research has been done on determining what types of approaches are best for people with multiple problems.
  - o Because RCTs look at the general effects of a particular therapy across a number of people, they offer less insight into more specific questions about what type of therapy may best suit a particular individual at a particular point in time.
  - o RCTs include significant attention to fidelity to a specific treatment protocol, usually based on a manual. Critics have suggested that a manual-based approach is 'mechanistic' and unsuitable for routine care settings, although others have highlighted that manual-based approaches can and should be applied flexibly.
- Far more research has been conducted with some therapy models than others, and this may be partly responsible for the greater recommendation of some therapies than others in treatment guidance.
- There is strong evidence that the qualities of the individual therapist are as important, if not more important, than the specific type of intervention given (Okiishi *et al.*, 2003).
- The tools used to assess 'outcome' will vary according to the values and aims of the approach taken, so some measures (e.g. symptom reduction versus change in family dynamics) suit some therapeutic interventions better than others.

Given these limitations to the application of *empirically supported treatments*, it is also important to introduce the concept of *evidence-based practice*. This is an approach to clinical decision making where a psychologist makes a judgement about the best

---

FOCUS 2.3

Choice of therapy

Once we know that a particular intervention has proven effectiveness there would need to be a good reason for choosing an alternative intervention that has a weaker evidence base. Good reasons include the following:

- The client making an informed choice to start with a different intervention.
- Target problems that are of greater concern may best be addressed by a different therapy (different therapies emphasise different target problems (e.g. emotional/cognitive/behavioural 'symptoms' in CBT, repeated relationship dynamics in short-term dynamic psychotherapy, or patterns of 'stuck' or unhelpful dynamics in a group or family that may be the focus of treatment in systemic therapy).
- Good-quality previous attempts at an empirically supported treatment have been unsuccessful.

treatment by drawing on the 'three-leg stool' of research evidence (the science), clinical expertise (the art), and client preferences (Spring, 2007). Where there is no research evidence at all that directly relates to a clinical issue faced, the skills of the scientist-practitioner may still be applied by ensuring that we use scientific principles in the design, implementation and evaluation of the intervention so that we can assess its impact and effectiveness.

The reflective-practitioner

Expert practitioners can be identified and research trials have suggested that they have better results than other therapists no matter what form of therapy they are following (Okiishi *et al.*, 2003). This further reinforces what we already know: that skilled psychological practice consists of far more than just simply following prescribed techniques. What it requires is the ability to bring together potentially conflicting ideas and difficulties into a defined explanation of problems (the formulation) and then flexibly to apply psychological knowledge to generate solutions to the issue raised. This is another component of the 'art' of practice. The usual attributes used to define these skills include wisdom and intuition.

Traditionally, these qualities have been seen as being less open to scientific understanding or evaluation. However, models have been developed which attempt to describe how psychologists (and others) may go about developing these 'clinical expert' skills in practice and become more consciously aware of them. Schon (1987) describes two key elements:

1   Reflection in action: this involves reflecting upon learning within sessions themselves, connecting with our emotions and what this tells us, and attending to the theories that guide our thoughts and actions. This process enables us to build new understandings to inform our actions in the situation as it is unfolding.
2   Reflection on action: reflecting after the event to analyse and review the situation to gain insight for improved action in the future.

Unfortunately, while a useful framework for highlighting good practice, the lack of specificity in Schon's work about exactly what 'reflection on and in action' entails means that the model still fails to open up these qualities to more scientific exploration. This lack of specificity is a problem for those who emphasise the 'artistry' of psychological practice over the science. Few question the importance of these high-level skills but if we don't evaluate the effectiveness of these skills, how can we know which are the most important, and how can we demonstrate their value in a modern health care environment that demands evidence?

More recently there has been an attempt to define more clearly the *metacompetences* that underpin expert practice *within* specific therapy models (e.g. Roth and Pilling, 2007). These metacompetences consist of procedural rules for adapting and flexing the therapy appropriately in different situations and they provide a framework for navigating a path between the science and art of effective practice. However, to date, there has still been relatively little research that has examined how these meta-competences influence outcome.

Clinical psychology often sells itself on the ability of practitioners to integrate the best of different therapy models in practice. However, the truth is that there has been very little research conducted to evaluate the value of an integrative approach compared to single model therapies. We need to apply more science to the 'artistry' of practice.

The critical practitioner

With the development of *postmodernism* (Lyotard, 1984) and our increasing understanding of how 'knowledge' can often be constructed and maintained by those with a vested interest in promoting that type of knowledge, it has become increasingly important for clinical psychologists also to apply a 'critical lens' to their practice in an attempt to ensure their practice does not unintentionally contribute to continuing social inequalities and injustice.

Let us take a well-known example. Medicine is sometimes criticised for overly 'medicalising' the language of human emotions and distress, applying diagnosis (labels of illness) to human experiences, thus bringing them under the 'expertise' and 'influence' of the profession of medicine. A critical practitioner would reflect on how this use of language may have served to maintain the power and authority of the medical profession and justify the medical 'treatment' of human distress (labelled mental illness) – historically in large asylums. They might evaluate the strengths and weaknesses of using this constructed knowledge or language and challenge it where it contributes to continuing social injustice or poor care.

Applying this critical lens to our understanding of human distress has already led to some very important changes in our way of conceptualising emotional distress in mental health and well-being services. We no longer label someone as being 'a depressive' – rather we say that someone has depression. We no longer unquestioningly apply diagnosis when this isn't helpful to a person in understanding their difficulties. There has also been a move away from an 'illness model' in mental health towards 'recovery-orientated practice' that emphasises personal choice, empowerment and helping people improve their quality of life rather than focusing only on the treatment of specific psychiatric symptoms. This has helped to significantly improve the quality of mental health services and the experiences of people receiving care within them.

It is also important that we question our own practice as psychologists. For example, a critical practitioner may argue that the dominance of one-to-one therapy has resulted in psychological distress usually being seen as a result of a 'fault' within the individual (e.g. they are thinking unhelpfully, they keep repeating certain relation-ship patterns, etc.) – so it is an individual who carries responsibility for it and who must work on improving their life through therapy. A critical practitioner might argue that this view overlooks the fact that much human distress is a result of societal problems that we all have a responsibility to address. For example, is a single, unemployed, socially isolated, lone parent depressed because she is thinking unhelpfully, or is she depressed because she never had a real opportunity to learn skills, she lives in extremely poor housing on a violent estate, and as an Asian woman she experiences racial abuse within a largely white neighbourhood? In these types of situations a community psychologist might argue that psychology would have a much greater impact if resources were targeted at community level to address sources of inequality and injustice. This may include societal problems and processes such as poverty, unemployment, poor health, poor education, poor housing, poor community infrastructure, social stigma and discriminatory attitudes in society. This approach to psychological work is known in the UK as *community psychology* (Orford, 2008).

DRAWING UPON THE THREE FRAMEWORKS IN CLINICAL PRACTICE

In clinical practice, a psychologist will usually make a decision about treatment approach with an understanding of the evidence base and a knowledge of what works for whom (Roth and Fonagy, 2005). However, this decision must be negotiated with the client, indeed the final decision should always be theirs, and there may be times when it is appropriate to follow an alternative course (see Focus box 2.3). Whatever the starting point, the skills of the reflective-practitioner, the perspective of the critical practitioner and the rigour of the scientist-practitioner are all required to ensure that:

- we start with a good understanding of what can work and the evidence base for this;
- we are able to tailor our work appropriately to the unique circumstances facing each individual client;
- we avoid imposing our own cultural norms or worldview on our client;
- we incorporate our wisdom and intuition in ways that help inform our clinical practice;
- we create the space to reflect upon what we are doing and learn from that reflection;
- we evaluate the work we do on an ongoing basis using valid assessment tools and scientific principles.

This enables the practitioner to draw on the best of the 'science' and 'art' of practice.

CORE MODELS OF PSYCHOLOGICAL THERAPY IN CLINICAL PSYCHOLOGY PRACTICE

We will now turn our attention to how the science and artistry of practice are applied through the use of four core models of *psychological therapy*. All clinical psychologists undertake significant training in at least two models of psychological therapy, of which one must be CBT (BPS, 2013). There are many different models of psychological therapy, but there are four that have been particularly influential and are likely to be drawn upon by clinical psychologists. These are behaviour therapy, cognitive-behavioural therapy, short-term psychodynamic therapy and systemic therapy. We will illustrate the key concepts and features of each of these models and describe how they may be applied in clinical work.

CASE STUDY: ANNA

Anna was a 24-year-old general nurse who was referred by her general practitioner (GP) suffering from panic disorder, agoraphobia and symptoms of depression. The panic disorder and agoraphobia had started six months previously when Anna experienced a panic attack in her local shopping centre. The panic attack had been very intense and she had been rushed to hospital. Anna initially believed that she must have been suffering from a heart attack although investigations subsequently revealed that there was nothing physically wrong with her. She had been due to meet her biological mother that day whom she had not seen since she was 6 years of age. Anna had been very anxious about the meeting. Since the panic attack, Anna had struggled to go out alone – suffering from severe anxiety whenever she made an attempt and which would lead her to rush home again. She could manage short trips – especially by car – if accompanied by her boyfriend whom she had been with since she was 16 years of age. Anna was also suffering from symptoms of low mood and depression. She scored 17 on the GAD-7 (a questionnaire measure of anxiety) and 16 on the PHQ-9 (a questionnaire measure of depression) – scores in the severe and moderately severe range respectively.

Anna had been taken into foster care when she was 6 years old due to neglect that she experienced at the hands of her biological mother who was suffering from the effects of severe alcohol abuse. After various foster placements, Anna was eventually adopted at the age of 8 and reported developing a close relationship with both adoptive parents – particularly over time. She said she had also suffered a period of depression (seeing a psychotherapist in the Child and Adolescent Mental Health Service) when she was 13. Apart from that, Anna had experienced a happy childhood with her foster parents, doing reasonably well at school – although she said she could get anxious at times – and said that she worried more than she felt she should at the possibility of her boyfriend leaving her. She felt she was overly dependent on him and wanted to be more self-confident and assertive. She had been contacted by her biological mother a year previously and had eventually, and somewhat reluctantly, agreed to the meeting, despite feeling very anxious about what it could bring up for her.

BEHAVIOUR THERAPY

Behaviour therapy has its roots in academic psychology and draws upon learning theory – the science of increasing or decreasing certain behaviours through changing what is paired with or follows these behaviours. The most famous set of experiments that inform behaviour therapy were by Pavlov (1927), who found that by pairing an initially neutral stimulus (a bell) with a naturally occurring unconditioned stimulus (e.g. the smell of food) that produces salivation (the unconditioned response), the bell (becoming a conditioned stimulus) could eventually on its own produce a conditioned response (salivation) even in the absence of food. This process has been called *classical conditioning*.

The second important process is *operant conditioning* (Thorndike, 1911). This is based on the principle that behaviour can be increased and decreased depending on the consequences associated with the behaviour. By manipulating the consequences the behaviour can be changed. Specific processes include the following:

*   positive reinforcement (behaviour increasing when paired with a positive consequence);
*   negative reinforcement (behaviour increasing when it allows avoidance of a negative event);
*   punishment (behaviour reducing as a result of negative consequences).

The behavioural view of psychological distress

The principles of operant and classical conditioning were used by behavioural psychologists to explain what causes and maintains a wide variety of emotional difficulties. The principles of behaviour therapy are that:

*   All human behaviour is determined by classical and operant conditioning.
*   Establishment of maladaptive anxiety is through the process of classical conditioning, maintenance through the process of operant conditioning.
*   Mental health symptoms are discrete pieces of behaviour which have arisen through faulty or unhelpful learning.
*   Maladaptive behaviour can be altered by means of unlearning.
*   The focus of therapy isn't on the past – it is on how the behaviour can be changed in the here and now through the application of behavioural interventions.

Behaviour therapy draws upon its understanding of what causes and maintains symptoms, and uses a range of techniques including exposure therapy (supporting someone to stay in the feared situation to enable them to learn that it isn't threatening), stress inoculation training (including relaxation training and mental rehearsal), behavioural activation (helping people who are depressed to gradually increase activities which can be rewarding and which break the behavioural cycles that maintain depression), operant conditioning (e.g. giving rewards, providing praise for children) and structured problem solving.

There is a strong body of empirical support for the effectiveness of behaviour therapy (Spiegler and Guevremont, 2009).

A behavioural view of Anna's difficulties

Anna was initially referred to a clinical psychologist, Paul, who took a largely behavioural approach to his work. Paul was interested in Anna's behaviour – her avoidance of going out alone – and how this was linked to the maintenance of her panic and fear. He also paid attention to the fact that Anna now avoided all activities she had previously enjoyed and began to explore with her the role this played in maintaining her depression.

Towards the end of the first session, Paul developed a behavioural formulation collaboratively with Anna. Anna's agoraphobia had originally been triggered on the day she was due to meet her biological mother. The initially neutral stimulus (being away from home in a crowded space) became associated with intense anxiety (originally the intense anxiety she felt about the upcoming meeting with her mother) through the process of classical conditioning (albeit just through a single event). Being away from home alone then became associated with intense fear. The association was maintained by the fact that Anna subsequently avoided going out so that the association between fear and going out failed to be desensitised. Instead, the association was negatively reinforced by the avoidance behaviour (i.e. Anna believed that the only reason she didn't experience intense fear was because she was successfully avoiding going out alone).

This formulation led to Paul and Anna agreeing to take forward a course of behaviour therapy, which would initially aim to address the agoraphobic avoidance through exposure work. There is a good evidence base for this approach. The therapy would involve helping Anna take a graded approach to gradually increasing the amount of time she spent outside the home on her own, managing the anxiety in the situation through applying relaxation strategies, and by making sure her anxiety had reduced significantly before returning home.

Anna engaged well in therapy and over time the treatment helped her reduce the association between being away from home and fear and to increasingly go out further and further away from home alone. Anna was discharged after eight sessions of therapy.

COGNITIVE-BEHAVIOURAL THERAPY

Behavioural therapy is often criticised for the fact that it largely focuses on overt, measurable behaviour and is generally less interested in internal subjective experiences, such as cognition or emotion. Cognitive therapy in contrast stems from the viewpoint that our subjective thoughts or perceptions about something have a direct impact upon our behavioural or emotional state (Beck *et al.*, 1979). According to the cognitive model:

- Psychological disturbance comes from unhelpful ways of viewing the self, the world and the future.
- Emotions and behaviour are shaped directly by cognitive processes.
- Cognitive processes are accessible to consciousness in the form of thoughts and images, and so the person has the potential to change them.
- The meaning we give to a situation will be determined by our beliefs or 'schemas' that we bring to it. These are also accessible and may be altered.
- By learning to identify unhelpful beliefs and schemas, and by reviewing and testing out alternative beliefs, it is possible to change the unhelpful beliefs that are serving to maintain or trigger someone's symptoms.

There is considerable evidence for the effectiveness of cognitive and cognitive-behavioural treatment approaches (Stewart and Chambless, 2009; NICE, 2009, 2011).

A cognitive-behavioural approach to Anna's difficulties

Anna was re-referred to the service six months later as her anxiety had returned. Paul had left for another job, so Clare (another clinical psychologist) began seeing her. Clare used a cognitive-behavioural formulation to generate a further understanding of Anna's difficulties. Together, they began to identify a vicious cycle that was serving to sustain Anna's difficulties with panic attacks and agoraphobia. This vicious cycle for Anna consisted of the *physical sensations* of anxiety that she had come to experience in outside spaces, which she was misinterpreting, *thinking* they might be signs of an impending heart attack. Understandably this led to the *emotion* of fear. In response to this meaning she was ascribing to the sensations, Anna's *behaviour* in these situations consisted of avoiding or escaping from these situations as soon as the sensations occurred.

In the background, the formulation also began to identify more long-standing beliefs of relevance to Anna's difficulties. For Anna, this included a set of beliefs based in her early experience that had been activated by her current situation. Her early experiences of struggling to bond with her biological mother had left her with a deep vulnerability and a set of core beliefs around being 'unlovable, inadequate and helpless'. While her later positive protective experiences with her adoptive parents had served to foster an alternative set of more positive core beliefs, getting back in touch with her biological mother had served to reactivate these negative core beliefs.

Clare began to work with Anna by helping her to break the vicious cycle of panic, by testing out whether her misinterpretations of physical sensations of anxiety as a sign of imminent physical disaster were actually true. This included providing information about the body's normal response to anxiety (the 'fight-flight response' caused by a surge in adrenaline), and testing out what happens if these sensations are allowed to run their course without intervening. This enabled Anna to discover for herself that the sensations were not actually signs of a heart attack but benign and normal responses to stress. Knowing this in turn reduced the intensity of the fear response, and therefore the sensations. These tests of what happens to the sensations are known as 'behavioural experiments'.

Towards the end of the work, Clare also began to help Anna re-examine her troublesome core beliefs to see if they were really useful and relevant to her life now. This enabled Anna to develop a capacity to hold on firmly to the more positive set of beliefs she had about herself that had been active before her biological mother got back in contact.

PSYCHODYNAMIC THERAPY

Psychodynamic therapy has its roots in the medical profession which helped to provide it with legitimacy. It was established in a white European middle-class social context and was traditionally applied to 'neurotic problems'. However, more recently it has been extended to provide treatments for more severe forms of emotional distress including psychosis.

There are many forms of delivery of psychodynamic therapy including several short-term dynamic psychotherapies such as time-limited dynamic psychotherapy (Levenson, 1995), short-term dynamic psychotherapy (Malan, 1979) and brief dynamic interpersonal therapy (Lemma *et al.*, 2011). Most short-term approaches focus on the ways in which emotional and relationship dynamics that are set up early in life come to be replayed in later life in ways which may be unhelpful for the person and in ways that give rise to psychological symptoms. The core principles behind these models are that early life experiences – usually with early caregivers – give rise to internalised models and behaviours about what it takes to remain connected emotionally to that caregiver. While these models and behaviours may have been adaptive in childhood, enabling the child to survive psychologically and maintain as close a connection as possible to the caregiver, in adulthood these internalised models of relationships can lead the person into repeated relationship patterns which are unhelpful and distressing. They may also give rise to psychological symptoms.

Short-term psychodynamic therapy does not focus on the reduction of symptoms per se (although there is an expectation that these will be alleviated by treatment) but instead focuses on changing these ingrained patterns of interpersonal relating (or personality style). Therapy aims to achieve this by bringing these patterns into consciousness, by focusing on particular relationship themes or issues, by giving clients new experiences of relationships and by enabling them to understand and integrate these experiences into their conscious awareness (developing new understandings). Helping the client to recognise and work through the repeated dynamics (emotions and behaviour) from the past that are being repeated in the client's experience of the therapy relationship as well as in other current relationships are central to the work.

A short-term psychodynamic perspective on Anna's difficulties

Clare primarily took a cognitive-behavioural approach in her one-to-one therapy work. However, she had also received further training in short-term psychodynamic therapy, which she would sometimes use when CBT hadn't been successful previously for a client and where the origins of a person's difficulties had a strong interpersonal focus (as recommended by NICE depression guidance: NICE, 2009). While Anna avoided changing treatment approach in the middle of CBT, particularly when this was going well, she did at times find it useful to draw upon other models of therapy to help inform her work, although remaining centred in a CBT-based framework.

After the fifth session, Clare became increasingly aware that Anna had become more sensitive about perceived rejection from Clare. Anna also began to swing between being quite off hand and dismissive of therapy and then subsequently being very apologetic and extremely compliant, voicing her anxiety about not being a good enough client with fears that the therapist might stop working with her because she was failing to make enough progress. Clare also recognised that she was, at times, feeling increasingly worthless as a therapist despite the progress they were making and that she had an urge to try to finish therapy sooner rather than later.

Clare gave herself time to reflect on what she was feeling and brought this to supervision. This helped her to develop an understanding of how Anna's early experiences of her relationship with her mother might be being replayed in the therapy relationship (because this was Anna's internal model of all close relationships) and that Anna's feelings about her mother might be being 'transferred' on to Clare (this is known as the *transference* in dynamic therapy). She also reflected on the fact that Anna's early ways of coping with the anxiety of being rejected by her mother (moving between a rejection of her mother when she was drinking to the attempt to create a close, dependent relationship at other times – both ways of trying to *defend* against the anxiety of being rejected herself) was also replaying itself in Anna's relationship with her. Her supervisor helped Clare to reflect on the fact that her own feelings (an urge to be rejecting) might also be a result of these dynamics. Clare made sure that she noticed these feelings but didn't act on them directly.

Clare felt that it was important to maintain a CBT approach to treatment and did not move to a short-term psychodynamic approach. However, using the themes of rejection of others/dependency on others, the therapist used what was being played out in the therapy relationship (transference) to help Anna become conscious of the patterns she repeated in relationships and to test out a new way of relating through the therapy relationship – one where she could be more assertive without feeling rejected or abandoned by the psychologist. The psychologist also helped Anna to be more conscious of the relationship dynamics she was repeating with other important people in her life, particularly her boyfriend, and how she might work on changing these dynamics.

Anna was able to develop an understanding about how this way of relating kept her in an unassertive position and reinforced her sense of neediness and dependency. Through the therapeutic relationship initially, Anna discovered a new way of relating which gradually generalised to her other relationships. She began to feel more confident, more assertive and less distressed.

SYSTEMIC THERAPY

There are a variety of models of systemic therapy including the structural systems approach, the Milan model, strategic systemic therapy and post-constructionist therapies including narrative therapy (see Dallos and Draper, 2010).

Although there are key differences between these approaches, the common element to all systemically orientated therapies is that they tend not to focus on individual problems but rather on the role of the system (e.g. couple, family, group or organisation) in which the individual problem is located. The focus of the treatment isn't on the individual themselves, or directly on their symptoms, but rather on the 'stuckness' in the system (usually the family) that is giving rise to these symptoms. The assumption is that you must work with the stuck system to promote change.

A systemic perspective on Anna's difficulties

After the twelfth session, Anna began to talk about the way in which her adoptive parents had reacted when she had told them about the contact made by her biological mother. They had become very cross with Anna for even thinking about agreeing to see her biological mother and Anna had felt extremely anxious about either letting them down or letting her mother down. At a deeper level, she feared that her worthlessness might be reinforced in the minds of either her biological mother or her adoptive parents, depending on whether she decided to see her biological mother or not. This tension had played a significant part in her original anxiety. Becoming agoraphobic had enabled Anna to avoid making a decision on this and she had told her biological mother that she was too unwell to meet her – at least for the time being.

From a systemic perspective, the psychologist wondered whether Anna's difficulties might be being maintained by the fact that her emotional difficulties were helping to resolve a relationship dilemma in the family system in that it enabled the family to avoid the possibility of rejection being enacted between Anna, her biological mother or her adoptive parents. If this were the case, it could be making it difficult for Anna to make progress in treatment. The psychologist decided to gently explore this possibility with Anna and to use this hypothesis as a way of opening up a conversation about how Anna might address the tensions with both her adoptive family and biological mother in a different way. Anna responded very positively to this exploration and she decided that she would try to share her own views and concerns with her adoptive parents. They met, and her adoptive parents reacted very warmly to Anna when she talked about the dilemma she was in. They said that they would be okay with her meeting her biological mother. Soon after, Anna began to make much more significant steps forward in her CBT treatment.

Anna was discharged after 20 sessions of therapy. At the end of therapy, depression and anxiety had both fallen significantly to the 'not depressed' and 'mild anxiety' ranges on questionnaire measures (PHQ-9 = 3; GAD-7 = 5). Anna and Clare produced a written summary 'blueprint' together of what had been learned in therapy and identified ways of recognising and tackling any future difficulties. Anna was very pleased with the progress she had made and the ending of therapy went well.

REFLECTING ON THE THERAPY

Clare was aware that she had to carefully monitor why she was moving away at times from the CBT treatment model for panic and agoraphobia. She did not take a short-term dynamic or systemic approach – remaining largely cognitive in focus – but she did use her psychodynamic and systemic understanding of the work to flex the way she applied CBT. She based this work on a clearly developed *psychological formulation* that she had shared with Anna, and she brought the case regularly to supervision. Her work could be described as an *integrative* approach based within a largely CBT framework. She brought her psychodynamic understanding of the work to help her address and work through tensions and difficulties developed within the therapy relationship that might have interfered with therapy had they not been explored and made conscious. This helped Anna not only in therapy but also in recognising patterns of relating that had become generally unhelpful in her life. A systemic perspective, shared with Anna, helped Anna begin to have important conversations with her adoptive parents that she had previously been avoiding and which may have been contributing to her feelings of stuckness.

CONCLUSION

We hope we have demonstrated the key role of both science and artistry in the practice of clinical psychology. As our profession continues to grow and develop we will need to continue to use 'artistry' in our application of the 'science', balancing the need for rigour in the skilled application of the treatment with the need to remain sufficiently flexible and creative to ensure that we meet the specific needs of each individual client. However, it will be just as important to undertake a greater scientific examination of the 'art' of practice, including developing a greater understanding of the therapist factors (e.g. empathy, genuineness and positive regard) that seem to play such an important role in outcome. By combining the art and science of practice in this way we will be able to generate a more sophisticated understanding of human distress and an ever-growing knowledge of what we can do to alleviate it.

KEY CONCEPTS AND TERMS

- Clinical psychology: art and science
- Psychological practice
- Psychological therapy
- Empirically supported treatment
- Evidenced-based practice
- Randomised controlled trial

- Scientist-practitioner
- Reflective-practitioner
- Critical practitioner
- Community psychology
- National Institute of Health and Care Excellence
- Behaviour therapy

- Cognitive-behavioural therapy
- Short-term psychodynamic therapy
- Systemic/family therapy

LEARNING OUTCOMES

By the end of the chapter the reader should have:

- An understanding of the necessity of both science and artistry in the delivery of psychological treatment.
- A critical appreciation of three frameworks of practice that inform the work of clinical psychologists:

  o the scientist-practitioner model
  o the reflective-practitioner model
  o the critical practitioner model.

- An awareness of the core principles underpinning four of the most influential models of psychological practice:

  o behavioural therapy
  o cognitive-behavioural therapy
  o psychodynamic therapy
  o systemic therapy.

- Through the use of a case study, an understanding of how these different psychological models may be used to help alleviate psychological distress.

SAMPLE ESSAY TITLES

- What are the key components of the 'science' of clinical psychology practice?
- Is clinical psychology practice an art, a science, or both?
- What role does evidenced-based practice play in psychological treatment?
- What are the common psychological therapy models applied in clinical psychology practice and what evidence base is there for these models?

REFERENCES

Beck, A., Rush, A., Shaw, B. and Emory, G. (1979). *Cognitive Therapy of Depression*. New York: Guilford Press.

British Psychological Society (2013). *Accreditation through Partnership Handbook: Guidance for Clinical Psychology Programmes*. Leicester: BPS.

Dallos, R. and Draper, R. (2010). *An Introduction to Family Therapy: Systemic Theory and Practice*. Oxford: Oxford University Press.

Hollon, S., Stewart, M. and Strunk, D. (2006). Enduring effects for cognitive behaviour therapy in the treatment of depression and anxiety. *Annual Review of Psychology, 57,* 285–315.

Lane, D.A. and Corrie, S. (2006). *The Modern Scientist-practitioner: A Guide to Practice in Psychology*. Oxford: Routledge.

Lemma, A., Target, M. and Fonagy, P. (2011). *Brief Dynamic Interpersonal Therapy: A Clinician's Guide*. Oxford: Oxford University Press.

Levenson, H. (1995) *Time-limited Dynamic Psychotherapy: A Guide to Clinical Practice*. New York: Basic Books.

Lyotard, J-F. (1984). *The Postmodern Condition: A Report on Knowledge*. Manchester: Manchester University Press.

Malan, D.H. (1979). *Individual Psychotherapy and the Science of Psychodynamics*. Oxford: Butterworth-Heinemann.

NICE (2009). Depression: the treatment and management of depression in adults. NICE Clinical Guidelines CG 90.

—— (2011). Common mental health disorders: identification and pathways to care. NICE Clinical Guidelines CG 123.

Okiishi, J., Lambert, M.J., Nielsen, S.L. and Ogles, B.M. (2003). Waiting for supershrink: an empirical analysis of therapist effects. *Clinical Psychology and Psychotherapy, 10,* 361–373.

Orford, J. (2008). *Community Psychology: Challenges, Controversies and Emerging Consensus*. Chichester: John Wiley & Sons.

Pavlov, I.P. (1927). *Conditioned Reflexes: An Investigation of the Physiological Activity of the Cerebral Cortex*. Oxford: Oxford University Press.

Roth, A. and Fonagy, P. (2005). *What Works for Whom? A Critical Review of Psychotherapy Research* (2nd edn). New York: Guilford Press.

Roth, A.D. and Pilling, S. (2007). Clinical practice and the CBT competence framework: an update for clinical and counselling psychologists. *Clinical Psychology Forum, 179,* 53–55.

Schon, D.A. (1987). *Educating the Reflective Practitioner*. San Francisco, CA: Jossey-Bass.

Spiegler, M. and Guevremont, D. (2009). *Contemporary Behavior Therapy* (5th edn). Belmont, CA: Wadsworth.

Spring, B. (2007). Evidenced-based practice in clinical psychology. What it is, why it matters; what you need to know. *Journal of Clinical Psychology, 63*(7), 611–631.

Stewart, R. and Chambless. D. (2009). Cognitive-behavioral therapy for adult anxiety disorders in clinical practice: a meta-analysis of effectiveness studies. *Journal of Consulting and Clinical Psychology, 77*, 595–606.

Thorndike, E.L. (1911). *Animal Intelligence*. New York: Hafner.

3 Working in teams

Different professions, different models of care and the role of the clinical psychologist

Philippa Casares and Nick Lake

SUMMARY

In health care, and in the NHS in particular, it is rare for clinical psychologists to work alone. They usually work as part of a multi-disciplinary team, i.e. a group of individuals with different training and skills who come together to offer the best care they can to an individual client. The rationale for multi-disciplinary work is simple. No one professional can hold expertise in the assessment and treatment of the wide range of biological (e.g. low serotonin), psychological (e.g. poor attachment history) and social (e.g. unemployment) factors that result in mental illness. By drawing on the knowledge of different professionals we can ensure that the client receives the right treatment based on a comprehensive understanding of their difficulties.

Because team working is so central to the work of an NHS clinical psychologist, this chapter focuses explicitly on the nature of team work in mental health and what enables these teams to be effective. We will review the roles of the different professionals and the models of care they traditionally draw upon in their practice. We focus in particular on the roles clinical psychologists play in these teams that take them beyond their direct clinical work with clients. This includes staff support, training and supervision, team development, team formulation, the development of reflective practice sessions and clinical leadership.

OVERVIEW

The effectiveness of multi-disciplinary working in mental health stems from the rich mix of professionals within these teams, each with different backgrounds and training, and the different perspectives they bring to our ability to understand and offer treatment to people in distress. Unfortunately, bringing a group of different professionals together doesn't necessarily mean that they will work as a functional team. Team dynamics, competition between individuals, professional rivalries, different approaches to understanding and treating emotional distress, and a struggle to understand and value the different perspectives which different professionals can bring can all result in teams that struggle to make creative use of the different viewpoints and skills of the people within it.

So what does help teams to work effectively? We know that role clarity – people knowing and respecting their roles and other people's roles in the team – is one important element (BPS, 2007). The chapter will therefore begin by giving the reader an overview of the work done by the different professionals who work within a mental health team.

We also know that clear purposes and goals (including a common philosophy and culture of care) are also important for teams. The chapter will therefore explore some of the key differences in the 'knowledge' brought by these different professional groups to the understanding of human distress, focusing in particular on the role of the medical model (and diagnosis), the psychological model (including formulation) and the biopsychosocial model which attempts to integrate each of these perspectives with an understanding of how the social context impacts upon mental health. We will also review the very significant impact of the 'recovery model' (increasingly now referred to as recovery-orientated practice), which emphasises human growth and the maximisation of human potential over a specific focus on the alleviation of symptoms. We will review the potential strengths of each perspective as well as illustrate, through a case study, how these are brought together, often very creatively, to help clients in our care.

The final part of this chapter will focus in more depth on the particular roles that clinical psychologists have within these multi-disciplinary teams.

INTRODUCTION TO PROFESSIONAL ROLES WITHIN MENTAL HEALTH MULTI-DISCIPLINARY TEAMS

A number of different professions work collaboratively together in mental health multi-disciplinary teams. The success of the team will depend on the extent to which the team can effectively harness the different skills and perspective which each profession brings. It is therefore vital that every member of the team has a detailed and comprehensive understanding of the knowledge and skills of each professional group. An overview of these roles is provided here in Focus 3.1.

Service managers

In NHS Mental Health Services, service managers usually come from a nursing, social work or occupational therapy background (although some people enter management without a core clinical training through NHS management schemes) and have progressed through their careers to management. They provide leadership to teams, ensuring safe practice of the team as a whole, and coordinating the work of the professionals within it. They also work closely with more senior managers to ensure

Professions and roles in mental health teams

- Managers
- Psychiatrists (doctors)
- Psychologists (usually clinical or counselling psychologists)
- Mental health nurses
- Occupational therapists
- Social workers
- Psychological therapists
- Speech therapists (in learning disabilities teams)
- Health care or nursing assistants
- Support workers
- Peer recovery workers (people who draw on their experiences of using mental health services to support others)
- Administrators.

that the service is developing in line with NHS Trust policy, is meeting NHS Trust targets, and is maintaining appropriate standards of care.

Psychiatrists

Psychiatrists are medically trained doctors who have specialised in the field of mental health. They will have trained for a minimum of nine years with a three-year undergraduate medical degree followed by a three-year basic specialist training and three-year higher specialist training. They tend to offer specialist mental health assessments, diagnoses (see below), and oversee and monitor the prescription of psychiatric drug treatments. Some psychiatrists also undergo additional training in psychotherapy but due to the demands on their time they will more often refer to psychology or other staff for specific psychotherapeutic treatments. They are usually one of the most senior clinicians within the team and they provide clinical leadership to these teams, helping to coordinate and oversee the work of other professionals.

Clinical psychologists, counselling psychologists and psychological therapists

Clinical and counselling psychologists have usually trained for a minimum of seven years, with an undergraduate psychology degree followed by work experience and then a three-year in-service training, usually at doctorate level. Psychotherapy training now takes place over a minimum of four years and often requires degree-level qualifications before commencement. Together, these professionals tend to offer the mainstay of psychotherapy treatments within community mental health teams. They also provide support and supervision to other staff members offering psychotherapy or psycho-therapeutically informed treatments.

Clinical and counselling psychologists also tend to be senior members of the clinical team and many provide a clinical leadership role within these teams. Clinical directors (clinicians who occupy a senior clinical leadership role in an organisation) tend to be from either a psychiatric or clinical/counselling psychology background.

Community mental health nurses (CMHNs)

CMHNs have usually trained for three to four years for a nursing diploma or degree to provide general nursing care including mental health assessments, supportive therapeutic relationships and psycho-educational treatments (e.g. explaining what it means to experience anxiety and what might help), as well as to advise on and administer medical interventions (such as regular 'depot' injections of psychiatric medication that avoids someone having to remember to take their medication daily). Some CMHNs do further training in psychotherapeutic interventions including cognitive-behaviour therapy (CBT) or family interventions training. Some now also prescribe a limited range of medications.

Because of their broad-based training, CMHNs commonly take on the role of care coordinators within mental health teams, coordinating the care of the various different professionals and organisations involved in providing services to people with particularly complex and high-risk needs (e.g. someone who is homeless, suffers from schizophrenia, abuses alcohol, and who is vulnerable to abuse and exploitation by others). They may also play a particular role in helping people to manage periods of crises where a person may be particularly vulnerable to self-harm or suicide.

Occupational therapists (OTs)

Most occupational therapists have completed a three-year degree in OT. If they specialise in mental health their role tends to focus on skills development and supporting service users' recovery by helping them to develop meaningful activities of daily living which may include returning to work or learning to live independently. OTs often offer psycho-educational groups to support recovery. Some OTs will also have further training in psychological or psychotherapeutic interventions such as behavioural activation and graded exposure, which are recognised therapeutic approaches to depression and anxiety.

Social workers

Most social workers are trained to degree or Masters level in specialist social work courses. The main focus of the work is on the social care needs of service-users. This means that social workers will be involved in supporting housing needs and helping service-users to manage their benefits, know their rights, and they will protect them appropriately when they are vulnerable. Social workers often get involved in supporting carers of those with mental health problems and many of them are further trained as approved mental health professionals (AMHPs), which means that they can carry out specialist Mental Health Act assessments when a service-user may need compulsory treatment (sectioned). Like many of the other mental health professionals, some social workers will also have undergone further training in specialist psychotherapies.

Nursing assistants, support workers and peer support workers

Nursing assistants and support workers do not hold a core professional training, although some are looking for experience of working with people with mental health problems prior to going on to further professional training. Peer support workers also don't normally have a professional training but they do have direct experience of their own mental health problems and recovery which they will then use to support and help service-users manage theirs. Both tend to use practical and supportive methods to encourage service-users to develop and maintain meaningful and satisfying lives. This may include taking service-users out to a support group or other activity, or helping them to learn the skills of independent living.

Administrative staff

Secretarial staff continue to support the work of the team by organising appointments, sending out letters and coordinating much of the day-to-day running of the office base. They can be a great support to the professionals and, as the front door to the service, they set a key first impression for people entering our services.

DIFFERENT PERSPECTIVES BROUGHT TO THE UNDERSTANDING OF HUMAN DISTRESS

Mental health is perhaps unique in the fact that the different training received by the different professions means that different professional groups can take different perspectives in how they come to view and understand emotional distress. When a team works well together, these different perspectives enable a rich understanding to be developed of the various factors that contribute to any one person's difficulties. However, these differences can also lead to tension and rivalry when individuals and teams struggle to integrate and harness these differences. Some of these 'perspectives' are reviewed here.

The medical model: diagnosis

At its simplest, the medical model views many forms of human distress as conditions or illnesses. These 'illnesses' tend to be 'diagnosed' when a person exhibits a certain cluster of emotional and behavioural characteristics that have become associated with a particular condition. The conditions tend to be linked to particular biological, genetic or neurological difficulties. It is important not to confuse the 'medical model' with general psychiatric assessment, as most psychiatrists nowadays take a much broader approach to the understanding of mental illness.

Diagnosis is used within mental health services to identify and 'label' the types of problems that a service-user is struggling with and to help inform what might therefore be the most appropriate treatment. To date, mental health services have tended to be configured around diagnoses. Psychiatric diagnosis also tends to be used for the majority of research trials in mental health so that most of our evidence base for medical and psychological treatments is related to psychiatric diagnosis. There are currently two widely established systems for classifying mental disorders: The ICD–10 (International Classification of Diseases, WHO, 1992), which tends to be used in the UK, and the more recently published DSM V (Diagnostic and Statistical Manual of Mental Disorders, APA, 2013), which tends to be used more in America.

There is no doubt that psychiatric diagnosis can be very reassuring for some service-users who feel safer having a label for what they are experiencing and to have some idea of what to expect given the diagnosis they have. They can also feel empowered by knowing what treatments are recommended by NICE (National Institute for Care and Health Excellence, the NHS body that makes recommendations about particular treatments) for their particular diagnosis. Diagnosis is also a convenient way of labelling certain collections of symptoms and helps services to organise themselves around these labels. However, there is a considerable amount of controversy that still surrounds the activity of labelling or diagnosing human distress as discrete forms of 'mental illness', with many arguing that this over-medicalises their condition. The argument is further strengthened by the fact that many diagnoses have little reliability or validity in the way they are applied, many have little explanatory power, and many (e.g. schizophrenia) collect together such a broad range of symptoms and human experiences that the label itself tells us very little.

Some service-users clearly experience diagnostic 'labelling' as demeaning and stigmatising, and do not feel that the label helps them to make sense of their symptoms or understand why they are struggling in the way that they are. Clinical psychologists and other professionals must remain very sensitive to these issues. This is particularly the case for possible diagnoses of 'personality disorders'.

The controversy around diagnosis has heightened over the past year with the publication of DSM V and the subsequent publication by the DCP (Division of Clinical Psychology, the professional body that regulates clinical psychology) of its controversial 'Position statement on the classification of behaviour and experience in relation to functional psychiatric diagnosis: Time for a paradigm shift' (DCP, 2013). The DCP is looking for a more holistic, less categorical approach to understanding mental health problems to allow for a more balanced view of the biological, psychological and social determinants of emotional distress. One of the ways forward, proposed by the DCP, is a greater emphasis on formulation.

Formulation

A formulation is essentially a working hypothesis about the nature of an individual's problems that attempts to explain why this person has developed this type of problem at this point in time and what may be maintaining it. A formulation is less categorical than a diagnosis and attempts to deal with the question 'what has happened to you' rather than 'what is wrong with you'. Clinical psychologists are trained to formulate every case that they work with. This may be according to a single modality therapy (e.g. CBT) or it may be integrative, drawing upon a range of psychological theories in order to provide the most holistic understanding of the issues the individual is facing. Johnstone and Dallos' (2013) book on formulation gives a full guide to all the approaches. A comprehensive formulation should draw on bio-psychosocial theories and be consistent with a recovery approach. Understanding a given diagnosis may be

The changing use of language in mental health

Language fundamentally shapes how we see the world, and as we have gradually changed the framework we have used to understand emotional distress and mental health problems, we have had to change the way we talk about people with mental health problems. The following are examples of currently unacceptable and acceptable language in mental health.

Unacceptable	Acceptable
He is crazy/mad/insane	He has a mental health condition
She is a schizophrenic	She has a diagnosis of schizophrenia
He is normal/sane	He doesn't have a mental health condition
She went crazy	She felt very emotionally disturbed
Patient (in some settings)	Service-user/expert by experience
He committed suicide	He took his own life
Mentally handicapped	She has a learning disability
Lunatic asylum	Acute inpatient unit

FOCUS 3.2

an important part of the formulation – but a formulation should encompass more than that. The formulation may then be used to determine the most appropriate treatment plan. The British Psychological Society Division of Clinical Psychology has developed 'Good Practice Guidelines on the use of psychological formulation' (DCP, 2011).

The bio-psychosocial model

When developing an understanding of the causes of mental health problems, the bio-psychosocial model of mental illness now provides the most consistently accepted framework. This model was first described by Engel (1977) as an attempt to move beyond a purely biological approach to the understanding of all illness. Quite simply, the model when applied to mental illness requires biological, psychological and social factors to all be considered in understanding why someone is presenting with particular symptoms at any point in time. The bio-psychosocial model will include an exploration of biological factors/diagnosis and may be drawn upon as part of a formulation. The different aspects of the framework are depicted in Figure 3.1.

It is easy to see how this model fits well within a multi-disciplinary approach, as it helps to place equal value on the knowledge and skills of the different professions working together in community mental health teams.

Recovery-orientated practice

Over the past 50 years we have seen a shift away from institutionalised care in large psychiatric hospitals, to models of community care, and most recently to the adoption of recovery-orientated practice.

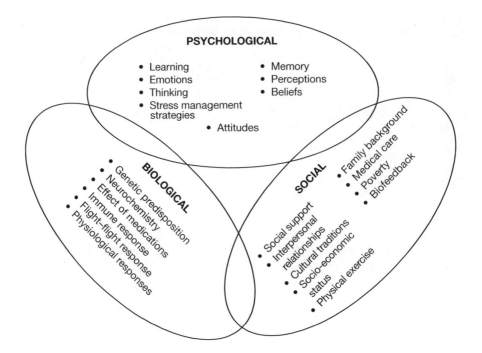

FIGURE 3.1 The bio-psychosocial model

The idea of recovery has its roots in the civil rights movements of the 1960s and 1970s and the service-user/survivor movement of the 1980s and 1990s. It is derived from an acknowledgement of the right to health and well-being combined with the realisation that institutionalised care and psychiatric practices were failing to support a person to have a satisfying and fulfilling life *alongside* any mental health condition.

At the core of recovery-orientated practice is the assumption that people need to be supported to develop a meaningful and satisfying life, as defined by the person themselves, whether or not there are ongoing or recurring symptoms or problems. Recovery, as defined in the recovery model, is not centrally about 'getting well' but is rather about maintaining the highest quality of life in spite of any ongoing symptoms or difficulties faced. It represents a significant shift in approach for mental health services and requires a focus on strengths, hope, empowerment, and the development of meaningful and satisfying roles rather than an exclusive focus on symptom reduction or management. It has become a key driver in the improvement of the quality of services to people with severe and enduring conditions.

As part of the adoption of the recovery model within mental health services, service users are encouraged to develop their own Wellness Recovery Action Plan (WRAP) as a way of having mastery over their own crises and symptoms, and making sure that services are meeting their needs rather than overpowering them at those critical times (see www.mentalhealthrecovery.com for examples). A good summary of the recovery approach may be found in the Sainsbury Centre for Mental Health Document *Making Recovery a Reality* (Shepherd *et al.*, 2008).

The latest development in recovery approaches is the introduction of recovery colleges which are now beginning to offer a wide range of courses to people with mental health problems and their carers. The idea is to encourage people to take control over their own well-being and recovery through peer-supported learning within these classes or educational workshops. Although still in their early stages, recovery colleges are seen as extremely empowering.

A CLINICAL PSYCHOLOGIST'S ROLE IN MULTI-DISCIPLINARY TEAMS (MDT)

The role of the clinical psychologist in a MDT is not only to provide high-quality psychological assessment, formulation and intervention to individuals and groups accessing the help of that team. It is also about supporting and enhancing the development of good psychological skills and thinking within the team as a whole. This can be done through the following:

- supervision of staff individually or in groups;
- consultation for staff around complex cases;
- education and training sessions for the team;
- formulation and team formulation sessions;
- reflective practice groups for staff;
- team development sessions;
- supporting high-quality psychologically informed service development.

In this respect, therapy is only one element of the work conducted by a clinical psychologist. The full range of skills that psychologists are trained in – assessment and therapy skills, teaching, supervision, consultation, research and audit, clinical leadership and psychometric assessment combined with a high level of analytical ability – can and should be used to good effect to support the development of a highly effective mental health team.

While these indirect ways of working are highly valued by staff (see examples below), this broad range of work is time consuming and one of the current issues facing clinical psychology is how to demonstrate the effectiveness and value of indirect ways of working in the face of increasing demands for individual treatments. This is particularly the case as services move towards the system of Payment by Results (www.gov.uk). The document *New Ways of Working for Applied Psychologists in Health and Social Care: Working Psychologically in Teams* (BPS, 2007) provides a full description of all the ways in which psychologists can and should contribute towards effective team working.

Team formulation

One of the increasingly common ways in which psychologists are contributing to skills development in teams, and to effective team functioning, is through team formulation (Lake, 2008). 'Team formulation is the process of facilitating a group or team of professionals to construct a shared understanding of a service user's difficulties' (Johnstone in Johnstone and Dallos, 2013). In developing a team formulation, team members are encouraged to think together about the service user and to develop a shared understanding derived from all of their experiences. This information may then be used to develop a comprehensive care plan where each professional is clear about their role and how their work contributes towards the treatment package as a whole. To date there has not been much formal research on the impact of team formulation, but some of the predicted benefits are: achieving a consistent team approach to intervention; helping team, service user and carers to work together; generating new ways of thinking; drawing on and valuing the expertise of all team members; reducing negative staff perceptions; raising staff morale, and facilitating culture change in teams and organisations.

In our services we have been supporting clinical psychologists to facilitate team formulation with the aim of improving the quality of team working and the care provided to our service-users. The value of this work is best illustrated by the following quotes:

'My experience of the formulation space has been very good and it's really exciting for me to see the approach spreading gradually into our culture and general practice. I think the space itself gives us an excellent framework for establishing (or re-establishing) the client's story and background, which allows us to develop a much more conceivable account of what might be happening for them on a deeper psychological level. I've found it to be a very holistic and person-centred process. It's non-stigmatising and I like that it is fluid and open to change/ adjustment. I like that it helps me, as a member of staff, to feel like I know why things are happening as they are. This not only helps me to feel a much deeper sense of empathy, it gives me/the team a much more credible basis for establishing the best form of treatment or intervention for that person. In a nutshell, I think it raises the standard of care we are able to offer to people and to my mind is what services should have been doing all along!'

Alex, Support Worker

'A navigational psychological and clinical compass when you are lost in the emotional maze created by the chaos of the patient's past hurts and rejections and losing your own sense of direction with them. It helps regain perspective and clinical effectiveness.'

Gail, CMHN

Clinical leadership

New Ways of Working for Applied Psychologists in Health and Social Care (BPS, 2007) is a document produced by the British Psychological Society that aimed to fully describe the types of roles and work that a clinical psychologist should be taking on in a modern NHS. It re-emphasised the importance and value of good, clear clinical leadership in community mental health services and argued that, as senior members of the MDT, psychologists should be taking on these clinical leadership roles (e.g. ensuring safe practice, leading on clinical improvements, negotiating with clinical commissioners, etc.). As a consequence, developing leadership skills has increasingly been seen as important for the profession even in initial clinical training. The British Psychological Society has developed a leadership framework that sets out clearly what is expected in terms of leadership at all levels (Skinner and Toogood, 2010).

Staff support

Work in MDTs in mental health care can be rich and rewarding but also challenging and complex. Staff must hold and contain the highly complex and often challenging difficulties faced by their clients, manage high levels of risk and deal with the consequences of suicide and high workload levels, and cope with an ever-changing and highly complex organisational context due to constant ongoing change within the NHS. Sometimes these pressures can result in fractious relationships and conflict among professionals, both within and sometimes between different teams. Understanding this reality from a psychological perspective in order to support staff and build staff resilience is another important element of a clinical psychologist's role. Sometimes psychologists will provide support and advice to their own team, although a psychologist must always be wary of offering team support to a team of which they are a part. More often, a psychologist will be asked to provide support to other teams and services, acting in a consultant capacity, supporting team building and development, and providing psychological support to individuals within the team as required. We must bear in mind that some staff members who are drawn to work in mental health may be attracted because of relevant personal or family experiences (Casares and Leiper, 2000). For example, they may have been drawn into caring roles within their own families earlier in life or they may have suffered from their own traumas and difficulties, leading to a desire to support others through these experiences. This can make them highly effective as caregivers but also vulnerable to certain stressors, such as experiencing a particularly high sense of personal failure if someone decides to end their life, a deep sense of frustration and anger at not feeling cared for themselves in a particular organisational context (such as another NHS reorganisation), or from burn-out because of a failure to set boundaries around their caring role.

Clinical psychologists are encouraged through training and beyond to reflect upon their own processes and to understand and work with their vulnerabilities. They are increasingly being encouraged to use this knowledge and understanding to help staff thrive and function in a resilient way in the face of high stress and demand. A good understanding of attachment theory in relation to work and an appreciation of how decreasing fear can increase vitality (in the same way that a child who feels safe is able to play and explore) can be really helpful with understanding and supporting staff under stress. There is a wealth of literature on resilience and developing team resilience as services have come to appreciate the importance of keeping staff well and motivated in order to maintain quality and enhance productivity: see McCluskey (2005) and Frost (2003).

CASE STUDY: SARAH

Referral

Sarah, a 46-year-old art teacher, was referred to one of our local community assessment, treatment and recovery services following discharge from a three-month stay in the local acute (inpatient) mental health hospital. She had previously been diagnosed with bipolar disorder (a condition where someone fluctuates between very depressed mood to periods of elevated mood and manic behaviour) and had become extremely depressed and unmotivated in the months leading up to her admission. Sarah was married with no children. She had struggled with depression over the past five years and hadn't worked for the past four years. Prior to her admission she had been talking about the possibility of suicide, as she did not feel that life was worth continuing. Her husband acted as her advocate and full-time carer, and always accompanied her at appointments to offer his support. She and her husband were unhappy with the diagnosis and had requested a second opinion. Based on previous experience, they were both anxious that they would not receive the support they needed.

Initial assessment

Sarah was seen for a joint initial assessment by a psychiatrist and a female community mental health nurse. One aim was to review diagnosis and medication but there was also a recognition that the acute staff had struggled to get close to Sarah and to develop a shared understanding about what might be contributing to her current depression. Sarah said initially that she did not believe that talking about her problems was helpful. However, during the meeting she began to talk about the four miscarriages she had suffered since her late thirties. She had not talked about this before with any mental health professional and she became quite emotional during the meeting.

Despite both members of staff feeling that they had engaged well with Sarah, Sarah became critical towards the end of the meeting, expressing her feeling that they had not listened properly and that that they didn't really seem to care about what she was experiencing. Both members of staff felt hurt and a little defensive initially, although both also tried to use her complaint to try to tease out what Sarah felt wasn't being heard or understood. Despite this, by the end of the meeting both members of staff felt unclear about what intervention would best help Sarah. To help them with this, Sarah's case was discussed in the team clinical meeting. The team felt that a further assessment was important to tease out the psychological issues that might be relevant, and it was agreed that the team psychologist (one of the authors) would meet her for three further assessment/formulation sessions and that this would be followed by a team formulation meeting so that the team could share their knowledge and experience of being with Sarah. Both Sarah and her husband were happy with this proposal when it was raised in a subsequent telephone call. The psychiatrist thought that the diagnosis might more reasonably be reactive depression and altered her medication accordingly.

Further assessment/formulation sessions

I met with Sarah for three sessions. Sarah talked about being the third daughter of two high-achieving doctors. Her mother had suffered with postnatal depression following her birth and had left Sarah in the care of her grandmother for much of her first year. Sarah described the relationship she had with her mother growing up as critical, absent and cold. She was closer to her father but he was extremely busy and often away on call. He also had high expectations of Sarah. Sarah felt that she was a disappointment to her parents, believing that they had really wanted a son and someone who was more academic. When she was 13 she discovered that her father was having an affair with her mother's best friend. This was a secret that she was unable to share with anyone. Her two elder sisters followed in her parents' footsteps and became doctors, leaving Sarah increasingly feeling like the odd one out. Sarah, however, had learned from her family not to complain and keep a 'stiff upper lip'. At 18 Sarah met David, her current husband, who was training to be a doctor. He never completed his training and they subsequently moved to Australia. Six years ago, Sarah's mother died of a heart attack and Sarah and David returned to live in England after the funeral. It was not long after this that Sarah started to struggle with intense feelings of depression.

Team formulation meeting

The meeting was attended by the psychiatrist, the psychologist (me), the CMHN, an OT and a support worker. I facilitated the meeting and everyone had a chance to share their experience of working with Sarah. I seemed to feel more empathy with Sarah, perhaps because I had heard her whole story, while the psychiatrist and CMHN had been left feeling somewhat inadequate and rejected by her after their first meeting. The whole team felt that despite our good intentions, we might struggle to meet Sarah's expectations and we were aware that she had a tendency to use formal complaints when she felt her needs weren't being met. The team reflected on how, if they weren't careful, this could result in the team taking an overly defensive stance in relation to Sarah's care. The team began to reflect on what might be going on for Sarah. The following formulation emerged from the discussions.

The formulation

Sarah was abandoned by her mother very early in life and she subsequently struggled to develop a warm and loving relationship with her. The team reflected on the fact that this had probably left her feeling that she was not that lovable, that she wasn't good enough and that she was possibly the wrong gender. The anxiety, anger and depression that she would have felt about this as a child would have needed to be suppressed (defended against) in order to maintain some emotional connection to her parents and to avoid the overwhelming anxiety of being abandoned. Moving abroad and maintaining a long physical distance from her parents probably helped to keep these negative emotions suppressed.

Unfortunately, losing four babies again exposed deep feelings of loss and exacerbated the awful feeling from childhood of not being good enough. When her own mother died Sarah's grief was prolonged and complicated because of the unresolved issues in that relationship, on top of having to manage the loss of her own unborn children. Having not yet discovered a way to express or process these negative emotions, Sarah found herself overwhelmed by uncomfortable feelings of anger and grief with no expectation that they could be understood, held or soothed. In fact, her expectation was the opposite and she expected criticism and neglect. The team reflected on the fact that she was probably projecting her expectation of abandonment on to the members of the team who were trying to offer her support. In order to manage the awful feelings of unworthiness and unlovability which underpinned these expectations, the team also felt that she might be unconsciously defending against these feelings by rejecting those people, and undermining their efforts to care for her, before they had a chance to reject her.

The psychiatrist reflected that it was interesting that Sarah initially ended up with a very medical approach to her care in hospital, perhaps paralleling the fact that describing medical illnesses was one of the few ways of communicating and meeting needs in her family of origin. Her anger towards the staff could also be seen as a representation of her anger with both her medical parents and medical siblings who failed to 'emotionally care' for her. It is often the case that it is easier for service users to express their anger towards staff than towards the original caregivers upon whom they have been so dependent.

The care plan

Developing a greater understanding of Sarah's depression, and in particular how her early attachment relationships and care-seeking behaviour were being replayed in her interactions with the team, enabled the team to develop a care plan that was responsive to her individual needs and issues. The key component was to offer Sarah the opportunity to engage in a psychological therapy that would enable her to develop an emotional and intellectual understanding of the factors underlying her depression. One element of this was to help Sarah identify how her early relationship patterns set up with her parents had contributed to repeated relationship patterns in the present (i.e. seeing others as rejecting and therefore sabotaging any connection she might develop to avoid this feared rejection). These relationship patterns were serving to further maintain her underlying feelings of inadequacy, her lack of connection to others, and resulted in further experiences of loss.

A number of other issues were also contributing to her depression, including isolation, unemployment, and a lack of meaning and purpose in life. The care plan therefore included the following components:

1 Sixteen sessions of CAT (cognitive-analytic therapy) conducted by the clinical psychologist.
2 Six sessions of OT interventions to enable Sarah to begin to reconnect with her local community.
3 A support worker offered to help Sarah with her WRAP plan. Sarah was encouraged to attend whatever course she liked from the local recovery college. She chose a mindfulness course and a 'coping with your depression' course. The longer term plan was to support her return to work. The support worker offered to take her along to a local art group.
4 Her husband was offered a carer's assessment by the social worker and some support.

In addition, this case was highlighted by the psychologist in an education session for the team. It enabled the psychologist to explore the impact of early attachment failures, how that may impact upon a client's care-seeking behaviours, and how we can use this understanding to meet that person's needs rather than repeat and play out an old, unhelpful dynamic (McCluskey, 2005).

Outcome

Sarah engaged in the therapy and after three months began tentatively to create art pieces again. Her husband felt confident that she was progressing enough to go back to work himself. Sarah decided to use her teaching skills by becoming a peer teacher at the local recovery college. She had a brief relapse around the time of the anniversary of her mother's death, but with extra support from the support worker at that time and by using her WRAP plan she was able to avoid a further admission and get herself back on track. The team began to view Sarah much more positively and she developed good working relationships with the staff. Sarah was discharged from the service after eight months of treatment.

Reflections

By understanding the causes of Sarah's depression and understanding how her early attachment relationships and care-seeking behaviour were being replayed in her interactions with the team, the team were able to be more empathic to Sarah's distress and provide a comprehensive package of care that was genuinely responsive to her individual needs and issues. Sarah learned how she unintentionally pushed people away because of her expectation that she would not be good enough for them and how she in turn could be quite critical of other people. This enabled her to shift her style of relating and to find new ways of coping when under stress. She also learned to be much more comfortable with knowing and expressing her emotions which reduced her anger towards herself and others.

CONCLUSION

We do the best for our clients when we can successfully harness the knowledge, skills and experience of the broad range of professionals who work within multi-disciplinary mental health teams. We hope this chapter has given you a good introduction to what these different professionals do and what perspectives they bring to the understanding and treatment of human distress. We also hope you will have gained an insight into the particular roles psychologists play in these teams and that help these teams to be effective. These roles are just as important as our direct clinical work with clients. While occasionally challenging and stressful, we have found working as a psychologist in multi-disciplinary team settings to be a hugely enriching and stimulating experience.

LEARNING OUTCOMES

When you have completed this chapter you should:

1 Have an understanding of the role of different professional groups in treating human distress.
2 Understand the principles underpinning the 'recovery model'.
3 Understand the principles underpinning a bio-psychosocial formulation of distress.
4 Understand what diagnosis and formulation contribute to the care and treatment of people with mental health problems.
5 Have an understanding of how clinical psychologists work with teams and organisations.

SAMPLE ESSAY TITLES

- Describe the principles of recovery.
- Describe the pros and cons of diagnosis versus formulation. Does one approach preclude the other?
- How might a psychologist contribute towards effective team functioning?
- What roles do psychologists play in multi-disciplinary mental health teams?

REFERENCES

American Psychiatric Organisation (2013). *Diagnostic and Statistical Manual of Mental Disorders, Fifth Edition.* DSM 5.

British Psychological Society (2007). *New Ways of Working for Applied Psychologists in Health and Social Care: Working Psychologically in Teams.* Leicester: BPS.

Casares, P. and Leiper, R. (2000). An investigation of the attachment organisation of clinical psychologists and its relationship to clinical practice. *British Journal of Medical Psychology, 73*(4), 449–464.

Division of Clinical Psychology (2011). *Good Practice Guidelines on the Use of Psychological Formulation*. Leicester: BPS.

—— (2013). *Position Statement on the Classification Behaviour and Experience in Relation to Functional Psychiatric Diagnosis: Time for a Paradigm Shift*. Leicester: BPS.

Department of Health (2007). *New Ways of Working for Everyone. A Best Practice Implementation Guide*. DOH, Care Improvement Services.

Engel, G.L. (1977). The need for a new medical model: A challenge for biomedicine. *Science, 196*, 129–136.

Frost, P.J. (2003). *Toxic Emotions at Work. How Compassionate Managers Handle Pain and Conflict*. Boston, MA: Harvard Business School Press.

Johnstone, L. and Dallos, R. (2013) *Formulation in Psychology and Psychotherapy. Making Sense of People's Problems* (2nd edn). Abingdon, Oxon: Routledge.

Lake, N. (2008). Developing skills in Consultation 2. A team formulation approach. *Clinical Psychology Forum* No. 186. BPS.

McCluskey, U. (2005). *To Be Met as a Person: The Dynamics of Attachment in Professional Encounters*. London: Karnac.

Shepherd, G., Boardman, J. and Slade, M. (2008). *Making Recovery a Reality*. Sainsbury Centre for Mental Health.

Skinner, P. and Toogood, R. (2010). *Clinical Psychology Clinical Leadership Development Framework*. Leicester: BPS.

World Health Organisation (1992). *ICD-10 Classifications of Mental and Behavioural Disorder: Clinical Descriptions and Diagnostic Guidelines*. Geneva: World Health Organisation.

2 | **Working with children and families**

4 Working with children

Mary John

RACHEL'S STORY

My name is Rachel and I am 15 years old and live with my mother and father and two brothers who are out all the time, into sport and their girlfriends. My parents, irritatingly, have become very worried about my weight. They have forced me to see a number of doctors privately as well as my local GP and now as a last resort they have demanded that I meet with people at Child and Adolescent Mental Health Services. I don't want to be doing this. I am happy going to school part time and being able to avoid doing PE and games. They say it is not safe for me to do any activity now as my weight is too low.

My parents keep making a fuss about me and keep on about my weight, wanting to talk to me about why I have lost so much weight and why I have stopped seeing my friends. They seem to forget that friendship is two-way and they need to contact me too. I think it's nice to look great. When one of my so-called friends said I was fat I thought it was time to lose some weight and now I just want to keep it off. How you look is really important at our school. If you don't measure up then you are excluded from being in the 'in' groups and I don't want to be in any of the others. They are just odd [people]. I do see that as I have only been at school for lessons and then immediately go home I have lost touch and they have made new friends, which means that there is little to talk about. New people have joined the year group and I don't know them and don't want to get to know them, as they will see what a dull and boring person I am. I used to have friends in my previous school where I was a bit of a rebel and was always in the middle of things. I used to listen to everyone's problems and sort them out but since I moved to this school when I was 13 it all changed.

At school the teachers are okay but don't really do much to help as I am only in half the lessons, so it feels as if I have to do all the work outside myself. Mum and Dad have organised for me to see a tutor to help with the work and I go and see them once a week or talk to them on the phone. I have always done well at school and want to get 3 A*s for my A levels so that I can become a vet, so when I am not watching TV or a DVD then I am working or worrying about it.

Over the last year my weight has dropped which I am pleased about and I have managed to get my parents to see that it is easier for me to cook my own food so that I can make sure that I only eat what I want and that the food is clean and not infected with other people's bugs. If this doesn't happen then I start to worry about it and cannot stop thinking about it.

SUMMARY

Growing up is a time of learning, physical and emotional development and quite a few challenges, even if everything goes well. It is normal for children and young people to be distressed at times along this journey. For some children, however, distress becomes more extreme or long-lasting. This chapter sets the scene by highlighting normal psychological and social development, then describes a range of common psychological difficulties that may be experienced by children including depression, anxiety, conduct disorders, attention-deficit hyperactivity disorder (ADHD) and eating disorders. Clinical psychologists can help as part of a network of services available for children and young people across the age span and in different settings. The task of the clinical psychologist working with children is to understand what has caused the distress and what is keeping it going, then to find a way with the child and their family or other caregivers to improve things. The chapter highlights theory and evidence that they can draw upon in addressing some of the most common problems, and illustrates their application in practice with a case example of a clinical psychologist working with a 12-year-old girl with depression linked to her experience of diabetes.

INTRODUCTION

Children and young people's mental health is incredibly important because successful intervention in early life can prevent a whole lifetime of further psychological difficulties (Kim-Cohen *et al.*, 2003). This is not only important for the individuals themselves, but for families' effective functioning and for society as a whole. It even makes sense economically, as early intervention could save an enormous amount of tax payers' money on helping people later in life with ongoing mental health difficulties (Centre for Economic Performance, 2012). Clinical psychologists work with children and young people in a wide range of ways across a large number of different settings in the community, hospital and residential care. These include working with young children with physical health problems, children experiencing difficulties with school, or children who have been traumatised by abuse.

Across all of these lines of work, it is important to understand normal development and how what is happening for a child or young person is interacting with this. For example, when a teenager becomes socially anxious, it may be understood as relating to a difficulty within the normal developmental stage of finding their own identity as they grow through adolescence. It is usually also important to involve the family, other carers and members of the 'system' around the young person, such as teachers or other professionals. This is because this 'system' can sometimes inadvertently be keeping difficulties going and also because it can be so influential in helping to resolve difficulties.

Working with children can be very challenging, particularly when dealing with abuse or neglect, but it is also fun, creative and very rewarding because of the dramatic difference it can make to people's lives.

NORMAL CHILDHOOD DEVELOPMENT AND ITS PITFALLS

Psychological difficulties in childhood always need to be understood in the context of normal cognitive, linguistic and physical development (see Smith *et al.* (2011) for an overview), as well as influences such as culture and gender. This complex interaction of factors shapes how children and young people express distress and how families respond. Infants and toddlers typically show their unhappiness through changes in behaviour; for example, running away, shouting and having temper outbursts, or refusing to go to sleep. It is difficult for very young children to voice emotional distress through speech, as the necessary language has not yet been sufficiently developed. As the child matures, emotional distress becomes expressed in more complex ways as they are able to communicate through verbal and non-verbal means and to make choices about when and how to alert others to their distress.

Alongside cognitive, linguistic and physical development, children develop in terms of their identity and relationships with others. Erik Erikson's theory of psychosocial development provides a helpful map to understand this (Erikson, 1950; 1995). Erikson considered that our beliefs, ideals and values, which form our identity, are constantly changing and are dependent on social interactions. For psychological well-being, an individual's personal identity should be well integrated and coherent across all areas of their life. He defined a series of developmental stages to be negotiated in order to increase psychosocial competence and avoid self-doubt and anxiety. Parents or guardians are critical in the early stages for these foundations to be successfully navigated. Erikson conceived of eight stages across the lifespan with five stages focused upon childhood and adolescence (See Table 4.1).

If these stages are not negotiated satisfactorily, young people tend to become isolated and are less able to manage new relationships and challenging situations. How parents or other carers respond to children as they approach each new life experience provides them with specific life lessons. Parents can provide support and encouragement, frame feedback in constructive and positive ways to support the successful negotiation of challenges and in so doing develop a child's resilience. Alternatively, they can inadvertently undermine this process by being overprotective and conveying a sense of the world as a scary and dangerous place that is best avoided.

Besides parents and carers, peers provide learning opportunities to manage new situations and new levels of intimacy in adolescence. However, vicious cycles may occur which inhibit development. For example if a young person sees themselves as less socially competent than others; they may not take up opportunities for healthy experimentation and therefore become more isolated. These sorts of challenges then can lead to emotional distress, including low mood, depression and anxiety.

TABLE 4.1 Erikson's five stages of psychosocial development from birth to adolescence

Stage	Function	Successful resolution Outcome	Unsuccessful resolution
Trust vs. mistrust (0–2 years)	Development of 'trust' in those caring for him or her	Sense of safety and security	The world is perceived as inconsistent and unpredictable
Autonomy vs. shame and doubt (2–4 years)	Greater sense of control, and independence over bodily functions and choices (e.g. food and clothing)	Confidence when acting autonomously	Sense of inadequacy and self-doubt
Initiative vs. guilt (typically 4–5 years)	Ability to assert influence over one another through play and other social interactions	Confidence to make choices and exert influence	Self-doubt, lack of initiative and guilt
Industry vs. inferiority (5–12 years)	Gaining a sense of competence which is secured through the positive and constructive feedback about abilities and achievements	Self-worth and discovery of own talents and abilities	Lack of motivation, low self-esteem, inactivity
Identity vs. role confusion (13–19 years)	Transition to adulthood Developing sense of own identity in relation to others	Form effective relationships and sense of own place in society	Unable to form relationships with varied levels of intimacy and unsure about own place in the world

Source: Erikson (1950, 1959).

WHAT PSYCHOLOGICAL DIFFICULTIES CAN OCCUR FOR CHILDREN AND YOUNG PEOPLE?

In infancy psychological concerns about children tend to be linked to sleep, feeding, gaining urinary and bowel control or disruptive behaviour. Between 5 and 26 per cent of 0- to 3-year-olds have been found to meet diagnostic criteria for some form of emotional or behavioural difficulty, depending on population sampled and definitions used (Skovgard, 2010).

Approximately one in ten children and young people aged 5 to 16 suffer from a diagnosable mental health disorder (Green *et al.*, 2005). This equates to about three children in every school class. Some of the most common diagnoses, their key characteristics and prevalence, as found in a 2004 community survey of families in Great Britain, are shown in Table 4.2.

Prevalence estimates for the different types of difficulty vary significantly according to methodology and the criteria for identifying problems. For example, pooling all studies from 1965 to 1996 that used structured diagnostic interviews showed a much higher prevalence of depression, at 2.8 per cent for children under 13 and 5.6 per cent for those aged 13 to 18 (Costello *et al.*, 2006).

Self-harm is common across depression and other difficulties, with one in twelve children and one in fifteen young people deliberately self-harming, for example, by

TABLE 4.2 Key features and prevalence of common psychiatric diagnoses in children and young people in Great Britain, 2004

Diagnosis	Key features	Percentage of 10- to 16-year-olds meeting diagnostic criteria
Conduct disorders	Persistent hostility, defiance and disobedience	5.8
Anxiety disorders	Persistent and disabling fears and phobias including the anxiety disorders listed in Chapter 7, plus separation anxiety (fear when separated from parents or caregivers)	3.3
Attention-deficit and hyperactivity disorder (ADHD)	Disabling difficulties with concentration, attention and/or impulsivity	1.5
Depression	Persistent and disabling low mood or irritability, loss of pleasure, fatigue, sleep disturbance and thoughts of death	0.9
Eating disorder	Determined weight loss or recurrent binges and food restriction, accompanied by preoccupation with body weight, shape or control	0.3
One or more disorders		9.6

Source: Green et al. (2005).

taking an overdose or cutting their arms (Mental Health Foundation, 2006). Some groups of children and young people are especially vulnerable to emotional difficulty, with 72 per cent of looked-after children (e.g. in care homes or foster homes) and 95 per cent of imprisoned young offenders having a diagnosable mental health disorder (Green *et al.*, 2004).

While many emotional difficulties resolve themselves naturally, more severe or persistent conditions can remain stable over time if young people are not provided with the appropriate interventions. More than half of all adults with mental health problems were diagnosed in childhood with less than half treated appropriately at the time (Green *et al.*, 2004).

FOCUS 4.1

Diagnosis

For many children and young people, being assigned a diagnostic label can be unhelpful as it may remain with them even when they grow and change, shaping expectations over a number of years, and may become a self-fulfilling prophesy in other contacts with services. Some of the labels associated with mental health difficulties can lead to prejudice and stigma in the wider community. Children and young people have less chance to influence the process of whether they are given a diagnostic label than adults, and diagnostic labels can unhelpfully detract attention from social and environmental factors that may have contributed to the development and maintenance of the problem. For example, a child diagnosed with conduct disorder may be seen as requiring 'treatment' themselves, rather than highlighting domestic violence which may be contributing to the problem. For some families however, diagnosis can be helpful, as it offers access to certain educational benefits and social services, or gives the family a way of uniting against the difficulty rather than blaming problems on an individual's character or intent.

AETIOLOGY

The causes of emotional and behavioural difficulties in children may be understood as the interaction of biological, psychological and social factors.

Biologically, genetic predisposition to some difficulties and development of the brain both play a role. Many mental health conditions have a genetic component, although this is a rather general risk factor rather than specific problems being directly inherited (Rutter, 2002). There is also a clear association between the occurrence of adverse events in childhood (such as emotional, physical or sexual abuse or neglect) and the development of the brain in areas that enable abilities to manage one's own behaviour and emotions (Stien and Kendall, 2004).

Psychologically, there is good evidence that the quality of bonds between children and caregivers has a significant impact upon later relationships and psychological welfare. The nature and impact of these bonds are highlighted by *attachment theory* (Bowlby, 1969, 1973). According to this theory, if the primary caregiver is not consistently emotionally available (e.g. owing to ill health) bonding experienced by the child is likely to be 'insecure'. This particular form of interpersonal relationship between carer and child is likely to have a significant, negative impact upon subsequent relationships in childhood, adolescence, and even adulthood (Sroufe *et al.*, 2005). Parents and caregivers play a crucial role in enabling children to process emotions and respond to them. If, however, children are exposed to trauma, and negative parenting behaviours such as indifference, rejection and abandonment, this development can be severely inhibited. This can make mental health difficulties more likely.

Social relationships are also very important to young people's well-being. Young people become increasingly influenced by the culture and behaviour of their peers as they grow up and exposure to negative social experiences such as bullying can have lasting effects upon psychological well-being.

FOCUS 4.2

Whose problem is it anyway?

It is usually a parent's idea that their child needs to come for psychological help. Children are often brought along reluctantly to appointments, for example, because they are behaving in ways that are difficult for others, such as being withdrawn or aggressive. Parents sometimes see the issues as being centred on the young person, while the young person themselves may hold a different view, perhaps seeing the problem as how others are acting towards them. This process is very different to what occurs for the majority of adults who decide themselves when they want to seek help. It is essential that all family member voices are heard when children and young people meet a clinical psychologist. In resolving the problem these viewpoints need to be understood in order to develop a collaborative way forward for the entire family.

PSYCHOLOGICAL HELP FOR CHILDREN AND YOUNG PEOPLE

When a child or young person is experiencing psychological difficulty, help may be available from a range of sources, including family, school, social services or health services. Some of the professionals and services that provide help are described in this section, including health visitors, school counsellors and Children and Young People's Mental Health Services (CYPMHS) – the most usual settings for clinical psychologists to work with children.

All babies come into contact with a health visitor soon after birth, who has a responsibility to establish that they are thriving and have basic needs met for love, food and warmth. Health visitors may typically be involved in families' lives up to and until a child is 7 years old, monitoring well-being and facilitating access to health, social and educational services if a need is identified. However, due to the potential demands on services only the most vulnerable families are seen and supported by these professionals for an extended period.

Many schools and colleges have chosen to employ a school counsellor who is available to young people to provide psychosocial education as well as psychological interventions. Typically, young people will access these services if they have concerns about family, peer relationships, educational performance, appearance, identity and bullying. However, if the counsellor or school nurse is concerned that the presenting problems need a more intensive intervention a referral will be made to specialist Children and Young People's Mental Health Services (CYPMHS) following discussion with both the young person and their parents or carers (McDougal and Crocker, 2001). School staff members are important in identifying and supporting young people at times of emotional distress (Salomon and Kirby, 2008).

Most referrals to CYPMHS are initiated by parents via their child's general practitioner or other professionals. CYPMHS' purpose is to ensure that a comprehensive assessment is undertaken to help the family understand the causes of the distress and to try to reach solutions together. CYPMHS teams include social workers, nurses, child psychotherapists, art therapists, play therapists, clinical psychologists and psychiatrists. Within these teams clinical psychologists offer direct assessment and therapeutic work with children and families, but also work as consultants and supervisors offering a psychological perspective to others involved in the young person's care.

FOCUS 4.3

Consent for psychological treatment

It is really important that children and young people understand the help they are being offered and are fully involved in decisions about that help. For most psychological interventions it is reasonably easy to describe what the assessment and intervention process entails and easy for an individual to grasp the consequences of deciding whether to take part or not in this process. Under UK law children under the age of 16 can decline an intervention if they understand what is being proposed and the consequences of their decision. They can also veto the involvement of their parents or guardians in an intervention, although if this veto is considered life threatening, professionals can override this.

THE USE OF THEORY AND EVIDENCE IN PSYCHOLOGICAL PRACTICE

Clinical psychologists draw upon a formulation-based approach in working with children and young people, constructing a map of factors contributing to the difficulties of the individual and/or family to help guide intervention (Johnstone and Dallos, 2013;

Manassis, 2014). In particular, working with children and young people requires clinical psychologists to consider multiple perspectives on problems, as there will almost always be both an individual child's perspective and parents' and other family members' views to consider. This may mean drawing upon a combination of systemic, developmental and individual psychological theories.

Some specific intervention approaches have strong evidence to support their effectiveness across each of the main diagnostic areas. The evidence base for psychological interventions in conduct disorder, anxiety disorders, ADHD, depression and eating disorders is reviewed briefly below. For a more comprehensive review, see Fonagy et al. (2005).

Conduct disorder

The role of a clinical psychologist in working with children with conduct problems will often be to offer a formulation-based perspective that allows the behaviour to be understood in the context of multiple psychological and social factors, including family or carer attachments, trauma, underlying neuro-behavioural problems (e.g. ADHD) and learning difficulties. There are also a number of specific skills-based group interventions that have been found to help parents and carers be more effective in preventing and managing the child's behaviour. For older children group or individual social and cognitive problem-solving programmes are often offered alongside the groups to build parents' skills (NICE, 2013). For the most complex and entrenched problems, family therapy often involving extended networks of school, social services, criminal justice and other professionals can be helpful in allowing a coordinated approach to tackling difficulties (Borduin et al., 2003).

Anxiety

The dominant approach for treating anxiety in children and young people is the 'Coping Cat' programme (Kendall and Hedtke, 2006). This 16-session CBT-based intervention can be delivered to individuals or small groups and is designed to enable children aged 7 to 13 experiencing generalised anxiety disorder, separation anxiety disorder or social anxiety disorder to recognise, cope with and reduce their anxiety in real-life situations. Two sessions for parents are also provided. Explanations are tailored to the linguistic, emotional and cognitive level of the children receiving the intervention. Two randomised controlled trials have produced promising results for the intervention (Kendall, 1994; Kendall et al.4, 1997). A later trial appeared to show that adding a family intervention to the CBT-based intervention enhanced its effectiveness (Barrett et al., 1996).

Attention-deficit hyperactivity disorder (ADHD)

Psychological interventions for ADHD are based on skills training principles, aimed at minimising and adapting to difficulties with inattentiveness, hyperactivity and impulsiveness, to reduce their impact on relationships and educational achievement. For younger children with ADHD, helping parents to manage and shape the child's behaviour has been found to be helpful, through group-based parent education programmes (Montoya *et al.*, 2011). For school-aged children this has been augmented by group or individual CBT or social skills training, with promising results (NICE, 2008; Hirvikoski *et al.*, 2011). For those with the most severe ADHD these interventions are often offered alongside drug treatment.

Depression

The psychological approaches with the strongest empirical support for depression in children and young people are cognitive-behavioural therapy (CBT), interpersonal psychotherapy (IPT) and family therapy. NICE guidance for treatment of depression in children and young people recommends that these approaches are offered for moderate to severe depression and should last for at least three months (NICE, 2005). Milder depression may be treated with non-directive supportive psychotherapy, group CBT or guided self-help. CBT for young people has tended to be based on Beck's model of depression, exploring and re-evaluating an overly negative view of self, world and other people while also scheduling activities likely to give a sense of accomplishment and pleasure (Beck *et al.*, 1976; Verduyn *et al.*, 2009). Interpersonal psychotherapy attends to the relationships young people have and how they are meeting their needs. Typically, depression in young people is considered to be a manifestation of the conflict between what they hope for in a relationship and the reality; this affects mood in a negative way and can lead to depression. Therapy considers how to change relationships in ways that will impact positively upon how the young person views themselves and their social world (Mufson *et al.*, 2011). CBT and IPT are usually delivered on a one-to-one basis with young people but some family involvement is common alongside this, providing opportunities to challenge beliefs or change relationships. Family therapy provides families with the opportunity to explore unspoken issues which may be maintaining the depression for an individual family member. This is described in more detail in Chapter 6. Recent innovations include the adaptation of mindfulness-based cognitive therapy (MBCT) for children and young people. This group intervention is based on cultivating a non-judgemental attention to present moment experiences, using methods based on Buddhist meditation practices. A small number of studies have explored its utility to relieve symptoms of depression in children, with promising results (e.g. Lau and Hue, 2011).

Eating disorders

Both individual and family interventions for eating disorders have shown evidence of effectiveness. For anorexia nervosa, individual treatments for adolescents based on CBT, IPT and cognitive analytic therapy (a brief therapy with its roots in psychodynamic and cognitive theory) have shown promising effects, although further research is needed (NICE, 2004). These interventions must be delivered alongside interventions focused specifically on ensuring weight gain, as the severe weight loss associated with this condition can be fatal. For adolescents with anorexia nervosa, the strongest evidence supports a specific form of family therapy known as the Maudsley model, which involves 10 to 20 family sessions over 6 to 12 months, during which time parents are coached to enforce eating and weight gain in their child. Later, the adolescent's move towards a level of autonomy appropriate for their age is promoted as an explicit consequence of the resolution of eating problems (Lock *et al.*, 2001). For bulimia nervosa a specific form of CBT (CBT-BN) has the strongest evidence of success. IPT has also shown success over a longer time frame, but with some indications that it may reduce risk of relapse (Wilson *et al.*, 2002).

FOCUS 4.4

Communication and creativity in working with children

Children and young people tend to talk about things in different ways to their parents and other adults, using different language. Clinical psychologists therefore need to listen very carefully to the young person to establish which words they use to describe their distress and to follow this lead rather than use adult-determined words. Young people also tend to have less developed abstract thinking than adults, so psychological ideas in therapy need to be made concrete by grounding them in the young person's life experience. The pattern of communication within sessions as a consequence tends to be more irreverent and contain more humour than in adult therapy. Clinical psychologists have to be creative, linking psychological ideas with everyday situations to bring the ideas alive for the child or teenager. This will often mean using a variety of art materials, magazines or websites. For example, engaging a young person to do something differently may involve discussing how a film character who faced a similar challenge went about resolving it.

CASE STUDY

Sian was a 12-year-old girl, referred to the Children and Young People's Mental Health Service by her school because of concerns about her well-being. The pastoral head of her school was perturbed about Sian's attendance levels, which had dropped to 82 per cent. Sian lived with her mother Jessica and father John. By the time of the assessment, a further letter had been received from the diabetic service expressing concern about Sian's ability to control her diabetes. Her glycogen levels were elevated to dangerous levels, suggesting that she was not keeping to her insulin injections and food controls, which could result in long-term physical consequences.

Assessment

Sarah, one of the clinical psychologists on the team, offered an initial appointment to Sian and her family. At the outset of the meeting it was evident that Sian was angry about having to attend. Her mother, although polite, was upset that the school had made the referral. Her father and sister sat quietly, appearing to be unsure about the reasons for the appointment. Sian reported that she had been diagnosed with diabetes when she was 11, just after starting secondary school. This had been an upsetting time. She said she had enjoyed primary school and had many friends there, had been working well academically and was enrolled in a range of after-school activities. She had felt happy and was appropriately independent. Sarah also established that the family had no previous history of physical or psychological difficulties.

Being diagnosed with diabetes had led to Sian needing to manage her activity levels, eat sensibly, and inject herself with insulin twice per day. Her mother said that Sian was worried about 'getting fat' and confirmed that she had put on some weight over the past year. Sarah asked the family how Sian felt about all of this, and Sian was able to reply that she felt upset and angry and did not see the point of living in this way. John commented that he thought Sian found her mother's concern about her health intrusive and annoying, and Sian confirmed that she did not like her mum 'fussing' over her blood tests, insulin dosage and diet. However, she was also able to see that she had become increasingly dependent on her mum's support to stick to her diabetes management. Socially, she had become isolated from her previous friends as they had formed new friendships and although she had tried to join new after-school activities she was unable to keep these up because she felt exhausted at the end of the school day.

During the meeting Sian told her family that she had been truanting from school as she was fed up with her peers who called her names and were making negative comments about her appearance and weight. She had begun a cycle of eating very little during the day and then eating excessively when she got home from school. When talking about this behaviour she became highly critical of herself and stated that she was useless and that she was ashamed of the fact that she could not eat sensibly. She was also drinking alcohol when she met up with a male friend. She described her mood as low, frequently being in tears and finding it difficult to sleep. Before the first session both Sian and her parents had completed versions of the Strengths and Difficulties Questionnaire (SDQ), a 25-item self-report measure of emotional, behavioural and social experiences. Sian and her parents' responses showed significant social and emotional difficulties.

Consent was gained to contact the school and the diabetic service to gain further information. The school reported that Sian was sullen, uncommunicative and reluctant to join in activities. Their perception was that Sian was constantly breaking the school rules, flouting the dress code, and was rude and disrespectful to staff. Academically she was under-performing but her form teacher said she had the capability of performing within the average range. The diabetic service staff members were concerned at the enduring nature of her poor diabetes management, despite significant input from the nursing team. They thought she understood what she needed to do but that she was resistant to making the necessary changes. The diabetic nurse involved was perturbed about the school's response to Sian's specific needs.

Formulation

Developing an understanding with the family of what might be happening required the integration of a number of theoretical models; a developmental perspective, with a systemic and cognitive behavioural understanding of the presenting distress and dilemmas.

Sian appeared to have a secure attachment with her mother and father, but the family had not faced any challenges of a similar scale to Sian's diagnosis and treatment, which ironically predisposed them to struggle with these challenges – there was no map for the family of how to get through it together. The main precipitant of the current difficulties was the onset of Sian's diabetes, but the impact of this was amplified by the fact that she was at a critical developmental point in her life; at the outset of adolescence, exploring her identity and independence. The sudden constraint on her life owing to the necessary medical self-care routines and the current dependence on her mum to help her with this had a significant impact on her self-esteem and confidence. All of this, coupled with some of the physical effects of poor diabetes management, had led to a vicious cycle of withdrawal, truanting, and thinking she was fat and ugly and that no one liked her, which further hindered her diabetes management and led to further withdrawal from school and her peers. This vicious cycle amounted to depression.

Unfortunately, the teaching and pastoral teams within the school had not been able to provide a supportive framework for Sian to manage the medical and social consequences of her condition. Her mother's reassurance and control of her diabetes had an unwitting impact of making Sian feel less capable and more dependent. A formulation diagram showing the multiple interactions of cognitive, behavioural and physiological factors that were keeping the problem going, in the context of the critical incident of the diabetes onset, developmental and systemic factors is shown in Figure 4.1.

Action plan

Sarah developed an intervention plan with Sian and her family. She offered Sian 12 sessions of cognitive-behavioural therapy to tackle her low mood and to facilitate her managing her diabetes. She also offered the family a series of family meetings to facilitate a new way of communicating and supporting each other at this transition point. The diabetic nurse and clinical psychologist agreed together, with Sian's consent, to meet with Sian's personal tutor and pastoral head at the school to discuss ways to help the teaching staff become more aware of her psychological and medical needs.

Intervention

In the individual CBT sessions Sarah and Sian drew a basic formulation diagram together, identifying the specific negative thoughts that had come up in the first family meeting and their links to withdrawal, poor management of her diabetes, low

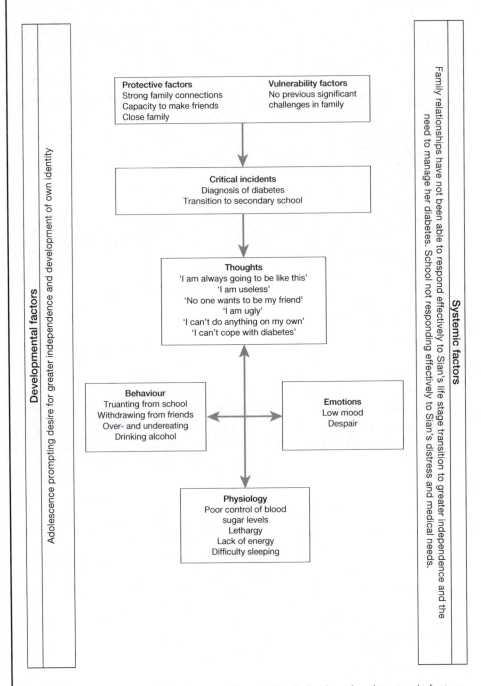

FIGURE 4.1 Formulation of developmental, cognitive-behavioural and systemic factors contributing to the onset and maintenance of Sian's depression

mood and lethargy. Sian agreed that it would be a good idea if she could work out a way to break this vicious cycle. Although Sarah found Sian rather reluctant to engage at first, they developed a good rapport and worked through part of a workbook called *Think Good – Feel Good* together (Stallard, 2002). Sian liked the practical approach of using drawings and worksheets and discovered that she was overlooking the fact that the diabetes had not really altered many of her qualities that she felt had made her popular in the past – friends had liked her because she was caring and funny and not because of how she looked. She thought she could still be caring and funny even with diabetes. Sian started to see that it might be worth trying to stop diabetes getting in the way of her friendships and her life. Sian and Sarah designed a diary of her blood tests and worked out what helped and hindered her in doing the blood tests. Sian was concerned that she would miss out on her friendship group's activities if she went to the 'sick-room' to do the blood tests. She had not told her friends that she needed to do this regularly. Sarah helped Sian to think through how she would tell them and what they could do to help in the process. Informing her friends had a positive impact upon Sian's view of herself because they stuck by her and one friend in particular started coming to the sick-room with her. Sian and Sarah completed 12 sessions. Each month they met with her parents and fed back on how this was progressing. This gave Sian the opportunity to show how she had a careful plan for monitoring and maintaining healthy blood sugar levels and, over time, her mum was able to step back and allow Sian to manage this more independently. The school meetings led to an agreement for the diabetic nursing team to offer some training to staff at their next training day.

Outcome

After three months, Sian's mood was much improved and she had been inviting friends over after school. Her parents commented that Sian was more like her old self. Scores on the SDQ had improved significantly from before intervention. Sian wondered if all her experience of injections might help her if she decided to work as a nurse in the future.

CRITICAL ISSUES

Multi-agency working

Effective and safe work with young people requires good communication and collaboration among agencies, including schools, social services, health and charities involved in the young person's life. A number of tragic child deaths (such as the murders of Victoria Climbié and Peter Conelly) have led to investigations to see how services might have acted more effectively to step in and prevent them. These investigations have often criticised poor collaboration and communication between agencies, leading to warning signs being missed or not passed on (e.g. Department of Health and the Home Office, 2003). A *Common Assessment Framework* (Department for Education, 2013) has been developed to facilitate better communication. This provides a common process to be followed by any practitioner when a concern is raised about a child, and leads to the identification of a lead professional to coordinate integrated care where several agencies become involved.

Person-centred recovery

The concept of 'recovery' for most people means the loss of symptoms. For some mental and physical health difficulties however, complete loss of symptoms may never occur. In these instances the concepts of *person-centred recovery, or social recovery,* can be helpful. These promote a broader idea of recovery as meaning a young person being able to function and engage with life while still having to manage some ongoing symptoms (Simonds *et al.*, 2013). This can offer a more achievable way forward for children and young people with the most disabling difficulties, reducing a sense of failure that may occur through not meeting traditional recovery criteria.

This chapter has shown how clinical psychologists can contribute to work with children, their families, schools and other agencies, drawing together multiple perspectives on problems and finding shared ways forward based on psychological theory and evidence. It is a field that includes tears and anger, but also fun, laughter and creativity. Success in helping a young person overcome difficulties can free them from a lifetime of future difficulties, and nothing can give you more job satisfaction as a clinical psychologist than that.

CONCLUSION TO RACHEL'S STORY

After I met with the psychologist I decided that I could work with her as long as my parents were not involved in the sessions. I could see that I had to put weight on to avoid going into hospital but I did not want to work on this. We spent a lot of time discussing what the goals were going to be and eventually agreed that we would have two goals: one for me to re-engage with my friends and a second for me to understand what it would mean if I was to put some weight on. A year later I have been able to meet up with friends and have started a college course, and am working part time in a shop. I do feel happier and my weight has gone up a little but I still feel in control. I have agreed to join my parents in some family therapy sessions, which has been much more helpful than I thought it would be. It gave us all the chance to talk and say things without one of us getting in a rage and it has made home life much better.

KEY CONCEPTS AND TERMS

- Erikson psychosocial development
- Anxiety
- Coping cat
- Communication with young people
- Depression
- Shame
- Recovery
- Ethics
- Team working

LEARNING OUTCOMES

On completion of this chapter the reader will be able to:

1 Recognise the features of some common mental health conditions experienced by children and young people.
2 Describe how children access psychological help.
3 Understand the development of emotional distress in children and the psychological factors that contribute.
4 Understand how theory and evidence are used to help children with some of the most common emotional and behavioural difficulties.

SAMPLE ESSAY TITLES

- What factors need to be considered when understanding how young people present with emotional distress?
- What are the implications for young people in how they access mental health services?
- What factors do practitioners need to think about when seeing a young person in specialist CYPMHS? Give consideration to the developmental issues associated with childhood and adolescence in your answer.

REFERENCES

Barrett, P.M., Dadds, M.R. and Rapee, R.M. (1996). Family treatment of childhood anxiety: A controlled trial. *Journal of Consultant Clinical Psychology*, 64(2), 333–342.

Beck, A.T. (1967). *Depression: Clinical, Experimental, and Theoretical Aspects*. New York: Harper & Row.

—— (1976). *Cognitive Therapy and the Emotional Disorders*. New York: International Universities Press.

Beck, A.T., Rush, A. J., Shaw, B.F. and Emery, G. (1979). *Cognitive Therapy of Depression*. New York: Guilford Press.

Beck, J. (1995). *Cognitive Therapy: Basics and Beyond*. New York: Guilford Press.

Borduin, C., Schaeffer, C. and Ronis, S. (2003). Multisystemic treatment of serious antisocial behaviour in adolescents. In C. Essau (ed.), *Conduct and Oppositional Defiant Disorders: Epidemiology, Risk Factors and Treatment*. New Jersey: Taylor and Francis, pp. 299–218.

Bowlby, J. (1969/1982). *Attachment and Loss*, Vol. 1, *Attachment*. New York: Basic Books.

—— (1973). *Attachment and Loss*, Vol. 2, *Separation: Anxiety and Anger*. New York: Basic Books.

—— (1980). *Attachment and Loss*, Vol. 3, *Loss: Sadness and Depression*. New York: Basic Books.

Carr, A. (2012). *Family Therapy: Concepts, Process and Practice*. Chichester: Wiley Blackwell.

Cartwright-Hatton, S., McNicol, K. and Doubleday, E. (2006). Anxiety in a neglected population: Prevalence of anxiety. *Clinical Psychology Review, 26*(7), 817–833.

Centre for Economic Performance (2012). *How Mental Health Loses Out.* A Report by the Centre for Economic Performance's Mental Health Policy Group. London: London School of Economics. http://cep.lse.ac.uk/pubs/download/special/cepsp26.pdf (accessed 21 January 2014).

Costello, J., Erkanli, A. and Angold, A. (2006). Is there an epidemic of child or adolescent depression? *Journal of Child Psychology and Psychiatry, 47*(12), 1263–1271.

Department for Education (2013). *Common Assessment Framework.* http://www.education.gov.uk/childrenandyoungpeople/strategy/integratedworking/caf (accessed 21 January 2014).

Department of Health and The Home Office (2003). *The Victoria Climbie Inquiry, Report of an Inquiry by Lord Laming.* Cm 5730, January.

Erikson, E. (1950; 1995). *Childhood and Society.* London: Vintage Books.

Fonagy, P., Target, M. and Phillips, J. (2005). *What Works for Whom? A Critical Review of Treatments for Children and Adolescents.* New York: Guilford Press.

Green, H., McGinnity, A. and Meltzer, H. (2005). *Mental Health of Children and Young People in Great Britain 2004.* London: Palgrave.

Hirvikoski, T., Waaler, E., Alfredsson, J., Pihlgren, C., Holmström, A., Johnson, A., Rück, J., Wiwe, C., Bothén, P. and Nordström, A. (2011). Reduced ADHD symptoms in adults with ADHD after structured skills training group: Results from a randomized controlled trial. *Behaviour Research and Therapy, 2011, 49(3),* 175–185.

Johnstone, L. and Dallos, R. (2013). *Formulation in Psychology and Psychotherapy: Making Sense of Peoples' Problems.* Hove: Routledge.

Kendall, P. (1994). Treating anxiety disorders in children: Results of a randomised clinical trial. *Journal of Consulting and Clinical Psychology, 62*(1), 100–110.

Kendall, P.C. and Hedtke, K.A. (2006) *Cognitive-behavioural Therapy for Anxious Children: Therapist Manual* (3rd edn). Ardmore: Workbook Publishing.

Kendall, P., Flannery-Schroeder, E., Panichelli-Mindel, S., Southam-Gerow, M., Henin, A. and Warman, M. (1997). Therapy for youths with anxiety disorders: A second randomised clinical trial. *Journal of Consulting and Clinical Psychology, 65(3),* 366–380.

Kim-Cohen, J., Caspi, A., Moffitt, T.E., Harrington, H., Milne, B.J. and Poulton, R. (2003). Prior juvenile diagnoses in adults with mental disorder: Developmental follow-back of a prospective-longitudinal cohort. *Archives of General Psychiatry, 60,* 709–717.

Lock, J., le Grange, D., Agras, W.S. and Dare, C. (2001). *Treatment Manual for Anorexia Nervosa: A Family-based Approach.* New York: Guilford Press.

Manassis, K. (2014). *Case Formulation with Children and Adolescents.* New York: Guilford Press.

McDougal and Crocker (2001). Referral pathways through a child mental health service: The role of the specialist practitioner. *Mental Health Practice, 5(1),* 15–20.

Mental Health Foundation (2006). *Truth Hurts: Report of the National Inquiry into Self-harm among Young People.* London: Mental Health Foundation.

Montoya, A., Colom, F. and Ferrin, M. (2011). Is psychoeducation for parents and teachers of children and adolescents with ADHD efficacious? A systematic literature review. *European Psychiatry, 26*(3), 166–175.

Mufson, L., Pollack, D.K., Moreau, D. and Weissman, M. (2011). *Interpersonal Psychotherapy for Depressed Adolescents* (2nd edn). New York: Guilford Press.

NICE (2004). *Eating Disorders: Core Interventions in the Treatment and Management of Anorexia Nervosa, Bulimia Nervosa and Related Eating Disorders.* http://www.nice.org.uk/nicemedia/live/10932/29218/29218.pdf (accessed 16 January 2014).

—— (2005). *Depression in Children and Young People: Identification and Management in Primary, Community and Secondary Care.* http://www.nice.org.uk/nicemedia/live/10970/29856/29856.pdf (accessed 16 January 2014).

—— (2008). *Diagnosis and Management of ADHD in Children, Young People and Adults.* http://www.nice.org.uk/nicemedia/live/12061/42059/42059.pdf (accessed 16 January 2014).

—— (2013). *Antisocial Behaviour and Conduct Disorders in Children and Young People: Recognition, Intervention and Management.* http://www.nice.org.uk/nicemedia/live/14116/63310/63310.pdf (accessed 16 January 2014).

Rutter, M. (2002). The interplay of nature, nurture, and developmental influences: The challenge ahead for mental health. *Archives of General Psychiatry, 59*(11), 996.

Salomon, G. and Kirby, A. (2008). Schools: Central to providing comprehensive CAMH services in the future? *Child and Adolescent Mental Health, 13*(3), 107–114.

Shonkoff, J.P. and Phillips, D.A. (2000). *From Neurons to Neighborhoods: The Science of Early Childhood Development.* Washington, DC: National Academy Press.

Simonds, L.M., Pons, R.A., Stone, N.J., Warren, F. and John, M. (2013). Adolescents with anxiety and depression: Is social recovery relevant? *Clinical Psychology and Psychotherapy.* doi: 10.1002/cpp.1841.

Skovgard, A. (2010). Mental health problems and psychopathology in infancy and early childhood. An epidemiological study. *Danish Medical Bulletin, 57*(10), 1–30.

Smith, P., Cowie, H. and Blades, M. (2011). *Understanding Children's Development.* Chichester: Wiley.

Sroufe, L.A., Egeland, B., Carlson, E. and Collins, W.A. (2005). Placing early attachment experiences in developmental context. In K.E. Grossmann, K. Grossmann and E. Waters (eds), *Attachment from Infancy to Adulthood: The Major Longitudinal Studies.* New York: Guilford Publications (pp. 48–70).

Stallard, P. (2002). *Think Good – Feel Good. A Cognitive Behaviour Therapy Workbook for Children and Young People.* Chichester: John Wiley & Sons.

Stien, P.T. and Kendall, J. (2004). *Psychological Trauma and the Developing Brain: Neurologically Based Interventions for Troubled Children.* New York: The Haworth Maltreatment and Trauma Press.

Verduyn, C., Rogers, J. and Wood, A. (2009). *Depression: Cognitive Behaviour Therapy with Children and Young People (CBT with Children, Adolescents and Families).* Hove: Routledge.

Wilson, G., Fairburn, C., Agras, W., Walsh, B. and Kraemer, H. (2002). Cognitive-behavioral therapy for bulimia nervosa. *Journal of Consulting and Clinical Psychology, 70*(2), 267–274.

5 Working with families

Graham Lee and Rosey Singh

D'S STORY

We are a family of four: Father (F, 47), Mother (M, 43), Daughter (D, 14) and Son (S, 10). D had a long history of poorly controlled diabetes and hospitalisation, was self-harming, had difficulty attending school regularly and had been receiving treatment from CAMHS. M suffers from depression and anxiety and S has become withdrawn. We came to family therapy having reconciled after a period of six months' parental separation with D and S dividing their time equally between parents. D was starting GCSEs and S had just entered secondary school.

Our family therapy sessions usually involved the family therapist, F, M and D, with S attending occasionally. These generally took the form of questions and discussions of historical or present issues, a conversation between two observers who were watching from another room and a summary at the end. We would often discuss D's problems with managing her diabetes and its impact upon the rest of the family, as well as individual relationships within the family unit and how we communicated with one another. For example, D was hospitalised and this resulted in an investigation by Social Services into potential neglect. In turn, this raised questions within the family about how we should deal with the diabetes centre managing D's condition as well as the deleterious impact this has on M's depression and anxiety. It helped a great deal to know that we would have a safe place in which to raise our fears and worries without them becoming a source of confrontation at home. The sessions and observers' conversations were valuable in helping us understand one another's perspective, identifying underlying issues we had not vocalised and also to bring out positives that we had overlooked.

SUMMARY

Family relationships are very important to our well-being, all the more so when we are children and entirely dependent upon these relationships. It is not surprising therefore that when children experience distress and psychological difficulty the solutions will often be found within their families. Systemic practice is a way of working with the 'system' of relationships around and including an individual in a family in order to tackle problems that may be affecting everyone. In some ways it is a very different way of working from other therapies with individuals. It sees distress and symptoms as emerging from relationship dilemmas rather than being located with individuals. It is a form of therapy that is adopted, usually after further training, by some clinical psychologists and by practitioners from other professional backgrounds. This chapter describes the core features of systemic therapy and the evidence regarding its effects with children and adults. The approach is illustrated with a detailed case study where complex difficulties for several children in a family were addressed by family therapy and systemic work with other professionals involved with the family.

INTRODUCTION

We live our lives in and through our relationships, and evidence highlights the value and priority we place on close family relationships. They define who we are and what matters most to us. We derive strength and resilience from these relationships and they closely affect and influence our sense of well-being and our health. When problems in close relationships occur that are experienced as insoluble or unspeakable dilemmas, psychological distress is the result. This effect may be seen across all age groups, but it is particularly pronounced for children and young people, who are largely dependent upon family to meet their emotional and physical needs.

When working with families, symptomatic behaviours in individual children or adults such as depression, anxiety or eating disorders are understood as attempts at a self-cure to a relational dilemma experienced by the sufferer as insoluble or too frightening for them to speak about. Working with 'yet-to-be-said' is a cornerstone of systemic therapy practice in terms of working collaboratively with families. The therapist and family thus work together to create the relational conditions in which family members can feel safe enough to take the 'risk' of saying the unsayable. Enabling

---

FOCUS 5.1

Diagnosis

Diagnostic categories, such as those found in DSM V and ICD-10, with their emphasis on locating the problem within the individual, have pros and cons. When working with families, diagnoses can sometimes be an unproductive way to understand distress, which may inappropriately label the individual as having some kind of personal deficit. In addition to this, diagnostic categories can have an unhelpful censoring effect on curiosity beyond the diagnosis. Because of this, systemic therapists will often use diagnoses only as a starting point to enable the family to explore what role or function the symptoms play in the family.

families to take the risk of saying the unsayable inevitably changes the meaning of the symptoms as well as resulting in shifts in the way family members position themselves and each other in their relationships. It is as a result of these underlying changes in the family that the relational issues are resolved and symptoms of distress become increasingly redundant. For example, a child refusing to go to school may do so because of an intense fear that their parents will fight and therefore separate while they are away. Enabling discussion about this in the family can allow the underlying problem to be dealt with appropriately by the parents, and the apparent need for refusing to go to school may therefore disappear.

WHAT IS SYSTEMIC PRACTICE?

> Systemic family therapy is an approach to helping people with psychological difficulties which is radically different from other therapies. It does not see its work as to cure mental illnesses that reside within individuals, but to help people mobilise the strengths of their relationships so as to make disturbing symptoms unnecessary or less problematic.
>
> (Stratton, 2010: 5)

Systemic family and couples psychotherapy is an approach that began to develop in the 1940s. Its parentage was an unlikely alliance of influences that included psychoanalysts, cyberneticists (who study regulatory systems, both mechanical and biological, to explore patterns and connections in communication systems, based on theory derived from mathematics), anthropologists, linguists, communication theorists and philosophers. Since these early days systemic family therapy and couple therapy has continued to evolve into a range of 'stand-alone' models which although different from each other are still based on the same underlying principles. The fundamental assumption of all of these models is that the context in which psychological difficulties emerge is the unique constellation of relationships within the family and that the meanings that are given to these 'difficulties' are a function of this context. The primary focus of systemic family and couples therapy is, together with the family or couple, to create a therapeutic context in which changes in the nature, patterns and functions of relationships can take place. When achieved, it is these 'second-order' changes, in the personal meaning the problem has for each family member, that effectively dis-solve or render redundant the psychological problems that brought the family or couple into therapy.

Systemic practice involves a broad view of interconnected social systems at a range of levels. Attention is paid to the role of power, diversity and culturally constructed notions of difference. The psychological impact of life experiences upon families and systems such as adversity and hardship (employment, poverty, migration, racism) as well as privilege is actively incorporated into subsequent ongoing formulations within the work.

Systemic practitioners work flexibly with a wide constellation of people, from individuals, siblings, couples and families to groups of families, professional networks and wider organisational systems. Individuals are not viewed as having a monopoly on understanding their life and experiences. Others in relationship with them are viewed as a resource and will inevitably have a different version of them, seeing and understanding them in ways that the individual may be blind to. Whoever is worked with, the systemic practitioner always keeps in mind the impact of change and its effects on and how it is affected by the broader system and sub-systems.

Common features of the systemic therapies are summarised below:

- Sharing knowledge and expertise with family members about how family systems and processes operate.
- Working with each family member in relationship to other family members (e.g. children in relation to their siblings; children's relationships with parents; couples in relation to each other, and families' relationships with members of their wider family: grandparents, uncles, aunts, nieces and nephews).
- Working with family members to understand their family culture – their stories, beliefs and traditions. Working alongside family members to productively enable them to examine and understand the influence of these narratives upon each of their lives and their family as a whole.
- Highly skilled question construction and therapeutic actions which aim to help family members notice potential resources, strengths and options which they may not have recognised or been harnessing.

FOCUS 5.2

Relationships and the brain

Neuroscience research has demonstrated that interpersonal relationships affect the physiological development of our brain biochemistry, from development in the womb through to old age. In turn, this physiological development influences how we engage in relationships with others.

Siegal (1999) outlines how patterns in relationships across our lives interact with brain biochemistry and thus brain development to shape who we are. He summarises fundamental principles regarding the plasticity of neurological development that rest on the two-way influence of patterns of energy and information flow within the brain and between brains. This seminal work described in detail how the mind is created from an interaction of internal neuro-physiological processes and interpersonal experience. Genetically programmed maturational processes within the nervous system are shaped by experience, especially interpersonal human interactions, to impact upon the structure and functioning of the developing brain. He states succinctly that 'human connections shape the neural connections from which the mind emerges ' (p. 2).

For example, disruption to early attachment relationships with caregivers has been shown to influence a wide range of biological markers in the brain, including hormone levels and epigenetic changes, which in turn may impact upon ability to cope with stressful events in the future.

HELP FOR FAMILIES: FAMILY NEEDS AND SERVICE RESPONSES

The fabric of family life involves a rich array of emotional experience, from joy and pain to the mundane experiences of day-to-day living. Families love, nurture, squabble, argue and care for their members, often processing, containing and coping together with huge pressures, stressors and strains from both within the family and from external sources. Therefore family life requires members to adapt to new situations, roles and relationship patterns. Focusing on these relationship patterns at times of transition and change is often useful in developing shared understandings of distress.

Particular difficulties, distress and symptoms may arise at transition points in the family life cycle, i.e. entries and exits to and from the family, children entering school or moving to secondary school, as well as later life changes related to older age and increased dependency. At these life-cycle transition points, family members are required to negotiate significant changes in relation to each other – new expectations and new roles begin to evolve in families' relationships; for example, upon becoming a new parent, a couple's relationship, to being part of a triangular relationship. This demands that the couple construct a *parenting relationship* in order to effectively meet the needs of an infant. At the same time the couple's own parents acquire the new role of grandparents. Changes in familial relationships are required throughout the family life cycle in order to negotiate successfully the developmental tasks involved in meeting each family member's needs. Difficulties for individuals and families as a whole arise when families are unable to make the necessary relational changes needed to meet one or other family member's developmental needs.

The first port of call when seeking help for distressing relationship dilemmas, and the consequent emerging problems for individuals, will often be the family itself, the wider family network, and the family's social and friendship groups. The majority of families with children with significant psychosocial problems do not seek professional help, or, if they do seek help, they are unlikely to be able to access it (Offord *et al.*, 1987; Eyberg *et al.*, 2008). A number of barriers to seeking help from specialist mental health services have been identified. These barriers are often associated with the perceived stigma of mental health problems, negative beliefs about provider services, overly complex referral routes to services, as well as lack of capacity from specialist services to meet demand (Day *et al.*, 2012).

Psychological and psychotherapeutic help for families is provided in a range of different settings – within a family's own home, community services such as GP practices, child and adolescent mental health settings, Social Services departments and within specialist services such as psychiatric inpatient units and eating disorder units. Help for families aims to be family centred and embedded in culturally relevant practice (Beckman *et al.*,1994; Hanson and Carta,1995). McWilliam *et al.* (1995) defined family-centred practice as: responding to family priorities; empowering family members; adopting an ecological approach to family work; and showing sensitivity and insight with families.

Many different types of community interventions have been delivered by psychologists and family and systemic psychotherapists. Peer-led interventions (where parents experiencing similar needs are trained and supported to support other parents) have been piloted with the specific intention of increasing helping capacity and acceptability for families. An example of this type of approach is the Enabling Parents Enabling Communities project (Day *et al.*, 2012) where local parents were trained to provide group workshops to help other parents in their own communities. Family and systemic psychotherapists have developed multi-family groups where multiple families join a series of groups to seek help about a shared difficulty (e.g. eating disorders) (Fairbairn and Eisler, 2007).

Some more intensive family-based psychosocial interventions have been developed, such as functional family therapy, multi-systemic therapy and multi-dimensional treatment foster care. These interventions have been designed to help families where a young person presents with a conduct disorder (a pervasive, persistent pattern of antisocial behaviour). These intensive interventions are on a continuum of intensity often provided in community settings and family homes. The emphasis is on developing positive strength-based family alliances, family problem-solving skills, parenting strategies and working with the wider network to achieve behavioural change.

Recent initiatives in the UK have set out to expand the availability and improve the acceptability of psychological help for children and families. These include the Children and Young People's Increasing Access to Psychological Therapies (CYP-IAPT) initiative, which aims to improve access to help for children experiencing anxiety and depression by training service staff in cognitive-behavioural therapy and to support parents, and You're Welcome (Department of Health, 2011), a set of quality criteria to ensure that services are welcoming to young people.

USE OF THEORY AND EVIDENCE IN PRACTICE

Effectiveness and different types of systemic therapy

The evidence base for the efficacy of systemic interventions for a range of child- and adult-focused problems is building. General conclusions from meta-analyses indicate that for many child and adult mental health problems and relationship difficulties, families who receive couples or family therapy have better outcomes than families in control groups receiving a range of 'usual care' (Shadish and Baldwin, 2003).

A wide range of different systemically informed interventions have been developed.

Many systemic approaches reviewed by Carr (2009a, 2009b) have integrated ideas from other theoretical models such as behavioural and cognitive-behavioural approaches into the work with families. Others, such as Flaskas (2002), have intersected systemic thinking with psychoanalytic thinking to produce a model that draws on both modalities.

Currently there are limited studies comparing the efficacy of different forms of systemic intervention with each other. Initial evidence (Henggeler and Sheidow, 2003) suggests that there is more similarity and shared practice than difference between the various treatment approaches. Henggeler and Sheidlow (2003) found similarities in 'conceptualisation, delivery and procedures' when they reviewed three different approaches to adolescent conduct disorder: functional family therapy, multi-systemic therapy and Oregon treatment foster care.

Stratton (2010), who identified 22 stand-alone models of family therapy, refers to the similarities between systemic approaches as 'common ground', writing that reviews comparing different approaches find much similarity in practice and little difference in outcome. An overview of the efficacy of family therapy and systemic practice as it applies to children and adolescents follows.

The effectiveness of family therapy in children's and young people's services

Carr (2009a) reviewed the literature (selecting meta-analyses, RCTs and experimental single case studies) for the efficacy of family therapy and systemic interventions for children and adolescents. The review adopted a broad-based definition of systemic interventions, including cognitive-behavioural, structural and strategic approaches to working with families. Parenting interventions as well as interventions involving family members and members of the child or young person's wider network were included. His review indicates evidence of the effectiveness of family therapy or systemic interventions either as a stand-alone treatment or in combination with other treatment modalities for the following:

- Problems in infancy such as sleeping, feeding and attachment.
- Childhood adversity problems such as abuse and neglect.
- Conduct problems, including childhood behavioural difficulties and problems with substance misuse, and attention-deficit and hyperactivity disorder (ADHD).
- Emotion, mood and risk problems, including anxiety, depression, grief, bipolar disorder and suicidality.
- Eating disorders such as anorexia nervosa, bulimia and obesity.
- Somatic and developmental difficulties such as enuresis, encopresis (soiling), recurrent abdominal pain, poorly controlled asthma and diabetes.

The following conclusions may be drawn regarding the current evidence (Carr, 2009a, 2009b: Sydow et al., 2010):

1   Systemic interventions encompassing a broad range of approaches are effective for a wide range of child- and adult-focused problems.
2   These interventions are relatively brief, usually involving no more than 20 sessions, and can be offered by a wide range of professionals in community-based settings.
3   Treatment manuals have been developed for many systemic interventions and these may be used by clinicians with appropriate training and supervision.
4   The majority of systemic interventions evaluated in controlled conditions have been developed within cognitive-behavioural, structural and strategic models. More research is needed on social constructionist and narrative approaches which are widely used in systemic clinical practice.
5   Carr's review is consistent overall with the role which systemic interventions and family involvement have had within NICE guidelines for a range of disorders in childhood and adolescence, including: depression (NICE, 2004a), eating disorders (NICE, 2004b), attempted suicide/self-harm (NICE, 2004c), bipolar disorder

(NICE, 2006), OCD (NICE, 2005a), PTSD (NICE, 2005b) and diabetes (NICE, 2004d).

6   Future research needs to clearly define the intervention used, and common outcome tools (e.g. SCORE: Stratton *et al.*, 2010) should be adopted to enable clear comparisons. Research should prioritise evaluations of systemic interventions for child abuse and neglect, emotional problems and psychosis in young people.

CASE STUDY

The referral

Joshua (12), Kyle (10), Wayne (8), Charlie (6) and Amber (4 months) were all referred to Child and Adolescent Mental Health Services (CAMHS) by Social and Caring Services. All the children, who lived with both parents, Mr and Mrs Smith, were on the Child Protection Register under the categories of neglect and emotional abuse. In addition to this, Joshua was displaying aggressive behaviours at school towards teachers, often spilling into violent outbursts towards his peers. Predictably these behaviours resulted in an emerging pattern of exclusions. Wayne was reported as displaying aggressive behaviours at school and at home and was also struggling with nocturnal enuresis (bed wetting) and diurnal encopresis (daytime soiling). Charlie was described by the local authority as often displaying a frozen watchfulness when social workers visited the family home. Amber was described as thriving. All five children were the subjects of care orders. The local authority plan was to remove all five children from their parents and find permanent homes for them elsewhere. At a recent hearing the judge had ordered that both parents and their five children be referred to CAMHS for family therapy to provide one last attempt to establish whether any further work could be done to prevent the breakup of this family.

Formulation

The first meeting at CAMHS was challenging and difficult to manage insofar as Mr Smith (who had mild learning difficulties) and Mrs Smith were openly hostile, rude and contemptuous towards the therapist, the process of therapy and the service as a whole. The children sat in silence, presenting as sullen and uncommunicative, and giving the impression that they had been instructed not to say anything. Mr and Mrs Smith made it plain that they were attending as a result of coercion.

Systemic therapists are trained to develop and maintain an acute level of curiosity towards whatever their clients may be showing them in the words they use, the tone used to deliver the words, their body language – facial expressions, gestures, use of space, etc. – and not work to a pre-set professional or clinical agenda. A key question for the therapist was therefore 'Why is it important to these parents that they show this level of hostility and open contempt – what function might it be serving for them?' The presenting themes of hostility, contempt for professionals and a deep mistrust of authority were explored with them over two separate sessions. What emerged from this was a long and painful history of both parents having been brought up in family contexts characterised by alcohol abuse, drug abuse, neglect and physical abuse, punctuated by frequent extended periods in the care of the local authority.

Mr and Mrs Smith both conceded that their deep mistrust and angry feelings towards Social Services and social workers had very long roots going all the way back to their early childhoods. As the discussions progressed it also became clear that it was not just their own personal experiences of being in and out of local authority care but also that their families of origin all had similar strongly held feelings and beliefs about the local authority, and so there were issues of loyalty to their families of origin. Mr and Mrs Smith felt that the local authority's decision to seek to remove all of their children was a fait accompli which they were totally impotent to influence. Being sent for family therapy was to them simply the latest example of the authorities' attempts to humiliate them further and to demonstrate conclusively that they were unfit parents. Mr and Mrs Smith's hostility, anger and contempt, displayed so openly and unambiguously in the sessions, could now be tentatively reframed as their last-ditch attempts at preserving some self-respect and dignity in the face of what they perceived as an overwhelming hostile force.

Intervention

In the two initial sessions it had become clear that family therapy in the way it had been envisaged would not be possible without addressing the relational issues between the family and the local authority. The idea of putting the family, the local authority social worker, the family's sessional worker, and key staff at the local family centre into a therapeutic process felt risky to say the least. However, from a systemic perspective individuals and families inevitably develop 'relationships' with larger and more powerful institutions and organisations and, like any other relationship, they can become stuck in negative, unproductive patterns of interaction. Mr and Mrs Smith and the local authority professionals were very reluctant to engage in this process. However, despite their mutual scepticism they agreed to give it a go. The court was consulted and they agreed, so long as the original work they envisaged took place afterwards.

We had five sessions altogether attended by Mr and Mrs Smith, the key worker from the Family Centre, the children's social worker and the family's sessional worker. The emergent themes in the first two sessions that had to be explored were mistrust and scepticism of the process, and a belief that this was a complete waste of time. However, as the sessions progressed a stark interactional pattern began to emerge characterised by a close mirroring of emotions, cognitions and beliefs between Mr and Mrs Smith and the professionals. Both sides felt deeply misunderstood by the other. Both sides experienced the other as hostile and contemptuous. Both sides experienced the other as mistrustful. Both sides experienced the other as uncooperative. Both sides felt demoralised following their encounters with each other. Both sides experienced a lack of respect from the other. Both sides experienced feelings of impotence to influence the other.

After the five meetings involving the family and the professionals, the family went on to attend a series of ten family therapy sessions roughly a month apart. Perhaps unusually, the family began the programme of family therapy with a pre-existing level of trust due to the work done with them and the local authority. Trust facilitates risk-taking and one of the early major themes to emerge in the therapy with the whole family was the impact of the cot death of Jade at 8 months, four years previously. Joshua and Kyle spoke about this in ways that suggested a significant conflict – on the one hand, both boys continued to experience strong grief reactions connected to the loss of their sister; on the other hand, they felt angry feelings towards her, believing that her death robbed them of their mother. Jade's death had become unspeakable in the family and Mrs Smith conceded that she had never spoken to anyone about this, not even to her husband. Mr Smith confirmed this. It transpired that this silent prohibitive message that Jade was unspeakable had constrained all the children from speaking about her and thus appropriately mourning her loss. It appeared that Mrs Smith had become locked into her traumatic grief at the loss of her (at the time) only daughter, effectively rendering her emotionally unavailable to her children and her husband. Mr Smith, who had taken his cue from his wife that Jade had become unspeakable, spoke tearfully of his bewilderment and confusion at feeling so disconnected from his wife and children around the death of Jade. The family used a significant number of subsequent therapy sessions to begin the painful process of reconnecting with each other around the death of their daughter and sister. The level of trust in the process had now reached a level whereby the children in the family, in particular Joshua and Kyle, began to take the risk of expressing their anger and rage towards their parents. At one point Joshua accused his mother of caring more about someone who was dead than about either him or his siblings. At this point Mrs Smith stormed out of the room in floods of tears. To her immense credit she returned a few minutes later and re-engaged with what was being said for the first time. The therapist had no need to touch explicitly upon the issue of neglect or emotional abuse given that the children had found a voice and a sense of enough safety to confront their parents with the reality of their situation.

Outcome

As the previously unsayable issues began to be voiced and explored, both professionals and the family experienced a sense of shock as they started to become detached from their construction of the other and began to develop new and different understandings of each other's behaviour. This recognition of the destructive patterns of mutual influence they had all become locked into created the conditions for the emergence of a more productive style of relationship between the family and a larger, more powerful system. Previously Mr and Mrs Smith had effectively refused to cooperate with either the family centre or the children's social worker. With improved mutual understanding between everyone, Mr and Mrs Smith agreed to regular meetings with the social worker, to attend the family centre regularly and to begin the family therapy work with themselves and their children.

Throughout the programme of family therapy we had regular liaison meetings with the local authority staff involved together with the family. The main themes of these meetings focused on the continuing positive developments in the relationship between the family and the local authority, and, for the first time, the emergence of a dynamic of mutual trust in this relationship.

The family remained in therapy for 12 months, during which time their relationship with the local authority professionals continued to thrive. Joshua's aggressive behaviours at home and at school fell away – his school reported a transformed boy who was doing well. Wayne's aggressive behaviours also fell away, as did his enuresis and encopresis, and Charlie had been reported as having become a chatterbox.

Shortly before the ending of therapy all five children's names were removed from the child protection register, and some eight months after this the care orders on all of the children were rescinded.

Two years later we heard from the local authority that the family had moved home and all were continuing to do well.

CRITICAL ISSUES

Culturally sensitive practice

Working with families in ways that are culturally sensitive is extremely important. However, adopting a sensitive approach to working with families from a different cultural origin from one's own is complex. As a therapist, understanding your own positioning and connection within your own culture and how this differs from other cultures is vital. For example, in many families from Eastern or Middle Eastern cultures the primary social unit is the family, whereas in Western cultures it tends to be the individual – for some cultures patriarchal gendered practices are considered the norm, whereas in Western cultures such practices tend to be frowned upon and have been the subject of much feminist critical analysis. When confronted by a family whose beliefs, thoughts and behaviours pose a challenge to a therapist's own beliefs and arouse strong conflicting feelings and thoughts in the mind of the therapist, the therapist needs to know how to use such challenges to good therapeutic effect. Efforts to be respectful of the other culture can risk the therapist becoming too passive and feeling overly anxious about what to say or do next. When this happens the therapist may become ineffectual or even be experienced as disrespectful.

Expert or reflective-practitioner

Achieving a state of what is called collaborative practice is an outcome of co-creating the conditions in which a process of authentic *co-labouring* between therapist and family can take place. Achieving this requires a shift from being an expert practitioner to being a reflective-practitioner. An expert practitioner is presumed to know regardless of their felt uncertainties. A reflective-practitioner is also presumed to know but is keenly aware that they are not the only one with important knowledge. A reflective-practitioner is also aware that their feelings of uncertainty are a source of learning for themselves as well as their clients. An expert practitioner tends to hold on to the 'expert role' and works at giving their clients a sense of their expertise. A reflective-practitioner seeks out connections with their clients' thoughts and feelings, allowing their client to develop respect for their knowledge from its evidence in their working relationship. At the extreme, a practitioner who identifies themselves too strongly as 'expert' may look for deference and status in their clients' responses to their professional persona, whereas a reflective-practitioner looks for a sense of real connection with their clients.

CONCLUSION

Working with families using a systemic approach can enable them to become free from symptoms of distress by broadening what is talked about and dealt with, the relevant issues becoming shared family problems with shared family solutions.

Families and children can be helped by a wide range of different types of systemic practice by clinical psychologists and others. This practice draws upon a range of theoretical perspectives from cognitive-behavioural, social learning theory, narrative and social constructionist approaches. There is a need for a better understanding of which types of help are most useful for which types of difficulty a family is experiencing. Future service-related clinical research needs to clearly define the intervention that is being used, and common outcome tools need to be widely adopted to allow systematic comparisons of outcomes. This knowledge needs to inform practitioner training, to be translated into increased access to therapies, and to ensure that these therapies are acceptable to young people and their families.

D'S STORY: THE CONCLUSION

A particular benefit was the interaction of the family therapy with other care providers, including a diabetes clinic, social services and school. For example, by signing D off from school the cycle of unwelcome correspondence and other pressures had been removed, making the immediate circumstances more manageable.

At times the sessions were difficult for us, both individually and collectively, but these sessions were probably the most valuable. The process has helped each of us find our voice and express ourselves more effectively, particularly D and S.

Conflicts still exist between us as a family; we again live in two separate homes. However, we are better able to resolve these conflicts and many of our original problems are now resolved. D has markedly improved diabetes control and is now studying A levels full time, and S has developed a wide circle of friends. We are all in a better place for family therapy, and value its positive effects upon us as a family and individually.

LEARNING OUTCOMES

When you have read this chapter you will be able to:

1 Understand that although someone in the family may be diagnosed with a mental health condition (e.g. depression, OCD, anxiety), in working with families such diagnoses are used as a starting point for exploring the meaning and function of the associated behaviours in the context of the family.

2 Appreciate that there are different approaches to the same mental health difficulties which often work in tandem with one another. Thus the use of medication can work alongside work with families by providing a window of relief or partial relief from symptoms, enabling therapeutic work to take place more easily.

3 Understand that any patterns of behaviours, thoughts or feelings have to be viewed in context in order to be understood. People live in and through a complex web of relationships throughout their lives. The constitutive power of this web to forge and shape identities is fundamental to systemic thinking and therapeutic practice with families.

4 Understand that the processes involved in achieving a collaborative relationship between family and therapist rely on the skills of the therapist to pay attention to the views and beliefs of all family members, especially when they are in conflict with one another.

5 Appreciate that when working with families, 'symptoms' emerging in one or more individual family members tend to be understood as an attempt at a 'self-cure' to an unvoiced or unspeakable relational dilemma.

REFERENCES

Ackerman, N.W. (1958). *The Psychodynamics of Family Life*. New York: Norton.

Bateson, G. (1972). *Steps to an Ecology of Mind. Collected Essays in Anthropology, Psychiatry, Evolution and Epistemology*. London: Jason Aronson.

Beckman, P.J., Robinson, C.C., Rosenberg, S. and Filer, J. (1994). Family involvement in early intervention: the evolution of family–centred services.

Bronfenbrenner, U. (1979). *The Ecology of Human Development*. Cambridge, MA: Harvard University Press.

Burnham, J. (2012) Developments in social GRRRAAACCEEESSS: Visible-invisible and voiced-unvoiced. In I.B. Krause, *Culture and Reflexivity in Systemic Psychotherapy: Mutual Perspectives*. London: Karnac.

Carr, A. (2009a) The effectiveness of family therapy and systemic interventions for child-focussed problems. *Journal of Family Therapy, 31*, 3–45.

—— (2009b) The effectiveness of family therapy and systemic interventions for adult-focussed problems. *Journal of Family Therapy, 31*, 46–74.

Dallos, R. and Stedman, J. (2006) Systemic formulation: Mapping the family dance. In L. Johnstone and R. Dallos (eds), *Formulation in Psychology and Psychotherapy: Making Sense of People's Problems*. London and New York: Routledge.

Day, C., Michelson, D., Thomson, S., Penney, C. and Draper, L. (2012). Innovations in practice: Empowering parents, empowering communities: A pilot evaluation of a peer-led parenting programme. *Child and Adolescent Mental Health*, *17*(1), 52–57.

Eyberg, S.M., Nelson, M.M. and Boggs, S.R. (2008). Evidence-based psychosocial treatments for children and adolescents with disruptive behaviour. *Journal of Clinical Child and Adolescent Psychology*, *37*, 215–237.

Fairbairn, P. and Eisler, I. (2007) Intensive multiple family day treatment: Clinical training perspectives. In S. Cook-Darzens and A. Almosnino (eds), *Therapies Multi Familiales Agents Therapeutiques* (Multiple Family Therapy: Groups as Therapeutic Change). Paris: Eres.

Flaskas, C. (2002) *Family Therapy Beyond Postmodernism: Practice Challenges Theory*. Hove and New York: Brunner-Routledge.

Hanson, M.J. and Carta, C.J. (1995). Addressing the challenges of families with multiple risks. *Exceptional Children*, *62*, 201–212.

Henggeler, S.W. and Sheidow, A.J. (2003). Conduct disorder and delinquency. In D.H. Sprenkle (ed.), *Effectiveness Research in Marriage and Family Therapy*. Washington, DC: AAMFT.

Lidz, R.W. and Lidz, T. (1949). The family environment of schizophrenic patients. *American Journal of Psychiatry*, *106*, 332–345.

Lyotard, J-F. (1979). *The Postmodern Condition: A Report on Knowledge*, trans. G. Bennington and B. Massumi. Manchester: Manchester University Press.

McWilliam, R.A. and Strain, P.A. (1993). *DEC recommended practices: Indicators of quality in programs for young children with special needs and their families*, S.L. Odom and M. McClean (co-chair persons). Council for Exceptional Children, DEC Task Force on Recommended Practices.

McWilliam, R.A., Tocci, L. and Harbin, G. (1995). *Services are Child Oriented and Families Like It That Way But Why?* Chapel Hill, NC: Early Childhood Research Institute: Service Utilization, Frank Porter Graham Child Development Center, University of North Carolina at Chapel Hill.

Midelfort, C. (1957) *The Family in Psychotherapy*. New York: McGraw Hill.

NICE (2004a) *Depression: Management of Depression in Primary and Secondary Care*. London: National Institute of Clinical Excellence.

—— (2004b) *Eating Disorders: Core Interventions in the Treatment and Management of Anorexia Nervosa, Bulimia Nervosa and Related Eating Disorders. A National Clinical Practice Guideline*. London: National Institute of Clinical Excellence.

—— (2004c) *Self Harm. The Short Term Physical and Psychological Management and Secondary Prevention of Self Harm in Primary and Secondary Care. A National Clinical Practice Guideline*. London: National Institute of Clinical Excellence.

—— (2004d). *Type 1 Diabetes. Diagnosis and Management of Type Diabetes in Children and Young People. A National Clinical Practice Guideline*. London: National Institute of Clinical Excellence.

—— (2005a). *Obsessive Compulsive Disorder: Core Interventions in the Treatment of Obsessive Compulsive Disorder and Body Dysmorphic Disorder*. London: National Institute of Clinical Excellence.

—— (2005b). *Post Traumatic Stress Disorder: The Management of PTSD in Adults and Children in Primary and Secondary Care*. London: Gaskell and the British Psychological Society.

—— (2006). *Bipolar Disorder: The Management of Bipolar Disorder in Adults, Children and Adolescents in Primary and Secondary Care*. London: National Institute of Clinical Excellence.

Offord, D., Boyle, M., Szatmari, P., Rae-Grant, N., Links, P., Cadman, D., Byles, J., Crawford, J., Blum, H., Bryne, C., Thomas, H. and Woodward, C. (1987). Ontario Child Health Study: II. Six month prevalence of disorder and rates of service utilization. *Archives of General Psychiatry, 44*, 832–836.

Olds, D., Eckenrose, J., Henderson, C. Jr., Kitzman, H., Powers, J. and Cole, R. (1997). Long term effects of home visitation on maternal lifecourse and child abuse and neglect: 15-year follow-up of randomized control trial. *Journal of the American Medical Association, 278*, 637–643.

Sameroff, A.F. and Fiese, B. (2000). Transactional regulation: The developmental ecology of human development. In J.P. Shonkoff and S.J. Meisels (eds), *Handbook of Early Childhood Intervention* (2nd edn). Cambridge: Cambridge University Press.

Shadish, W.R. and Baldwin, S.A. (2003). Meta-analysis of MFT interventions. *Journal of Marital and Family Therapy, 29*, 547.

Siegal, D.J. (1999). *The Developing Mind: How Relationships and the Brain Interact to Shape Who We Are*. New York and London: Guilford Press.

Stratton, P. (2010). *The Evidence Base of Systemic Family and Couples Therapy*. Association of Family Therapy, UK. The report is available at www.aft.org.uk.

Stratton, P., Bland, J., Janes, E. and Lask, J. (2010). Developing an indicator of family function and a practicable outcome measure for systemic family and couple therapy: The SCORE. *Journal of Family Therapy, 32*(3), 232–258.

Sydow, K., Beher, S., Schweitzer, J. and Retzlaff, R. (2010). The efficacy of systemic therapy with adult patients: A meta contact analysis of 38 randomized controlled trials. *Family Process, 49*(4), 457–485.

Watzlawick, P., Weakland, J. and Fisch, R. (1974) *Change: Principles of Problem Formulation and Problem Resolution*. New York: Norton.

Wynne, L.C., Ryckoff, I., Day, J. and Hirsch, S. (1958) Pseudomutuality in the family relations of schizophrenics. *Psychiatry, 21*, 205–220.

3 | Working with adults in psychological difficulty

6 Working with depression

Kate Cavanagh and Clara Strauss

SALLY'S STORY

My name is Sally; I am 36 and live with my partner and two young children in a small village. Georgia, my daughter, is 3 and has just started pre-school, and Archie is 18 months. Before having children I worked full time as an administrator. I enjoyed my job and got on well with people at work.

I grew up with my mum, dad and younger brother Toby in a nearby town. When I was little I was a bit clumsy and didn't do really well at school. Toby was brilliant at football and usually got all As in his exams. I was always thinking that I was not as good as him. My mum used to be really critical of me, saying I should be doing better at school and be more like Toby.

A few weeks after I started university I began to feel really down and saw my GP, who prescribed antidepressants. I soon began to feel better, but about six months after Georgia was born I started to feel really low again and was crying all the time. I stopped eating and stopped going to the local parent and baby group or meeting up with my friends. I thought I wasn't a good enough mum and I would sit at home and dwell on all the reasons why I wasn't doing a good enough job. Although my mood improved after a few months, it has recently become much worse and I am finding it difficult to cope. Everyone else is coping well and I feel that I am completely useless.

SUMMARY

Depression is one of the most common mental health problems — as many as one in ten people may suffer from an episode of depression during their lifetime. Depression can affect anyone, young or old, male or female. Episodes of depression sometimes follow significant life events or a series of more day-to-day difficulties, but can also emerge for no obvious reason. Some people experience a single episode of depression and then recover fully; for others chronic or recurrent episodes of depression may cause difficulties over the life course. Fortunately, there are a number of effective treatments available for depression. Clinical psychologists often work with people with depression to help them make sense of their experiences, improve their mood and help them re-engage with their activities and goals.

This chapter will explore the nature of depression and describe the major psychological theories and evidence-based psychological interventions for this disorder. We will illustrate the journey through depression using Sally's story – a woman struggling with the transition into motherhood.

INTRODUCTION: WHAT IS DEPRESSION?

Depression is characterised by persistent low mood and a loss of interest or pleasure in activities. However, it is also experienced differently by different people. While some describe depression as a feeling of deep sadness, for others feeling irritable, anxious or agitated are more common experiences. Some people describe depression as an absence of emotions such as feeling empty or 'feeling nothing at all'.

The common psychological symptoms of depression include feeling worthless, hopeless, guilty and tearful. When experiencing depression people often describe themselves (e.g. 'I am useless'), their world (e.g. 'other people see me as a failure') and the future (e.g. 'nothing good will happen') in negative terms, and tend to see these things as fixed, all-encompassing and uncontrollable. This bleak view may be exacerbated by a tendency towards thinking styles that focus on and maximise the importance of negative events while ignoring positive experiences. Common thinking errors in depression include the following:

- Filtering: taking in all the negative details while filtering out any positive aspects of a situation (for example, dwelling on critical feedback while ignoring compliments).
- Over-generalisation: drawing general conclusions from minimal evidence (for example, thinking that 'I am a useless student' if you get a bad mark on one test).
- All-or-nothing thinking: seeing things as extremes and missing the middle ground (for example, if your performance isn't 100 per cent perfect, you see yourself as a total failure).
- Personalisation: believing that everything is somehow directly related to you (for example, taking things personally, and taking responsibility for things that are beyond your control).

People with depression often struggle to recall specific positive memories about themselves or their experiences which may impair both problem-solving and mood repair. In addition, depression is associated with over-general recollection of both positive and negative events, which may have a negative impact upon a person's sense of self and their ability to overcome future challenges.

Cognitive difficulties such as a loss of concentration, dwelling on past events and perceived failings and indecisiveness are also common in depression. These characteristic thinking processes may place a heavy burden on a person's psychological resources and make it difficult to keep up with vocational or leisure activities, and may also impair social and interpersonal relationships.

Physical changes such as a loss of energy, motivation and sex drive are also common in depression. Changes in appetite are also common. For some people depression is characterised by a loss of appetite and associated weight loss; for others increased appetite, which paired with decreased activities may lead to weight gain. Changes in sleep patterns are also typical of depression. In some cases people find it more difficult

Medicalisation of the human experience

We all experience low mood and negative automatic thoughts, at least from time to time, and most of us probably hold some negative core beliefs. Does this mean that we all have a depressive 'illness'? There is increasing controversy about the medicalisation of what some see as a normal part of the human condition. For example, in the most recent edition of the *Diagnostic and Statistical Manual* (DSM-V, APA, 2013) bereavement is no longer an exclusion criterion for a diagnosis of major depressive disorder. Some argue that it is natural and expected to be depressed after the death of a loved one, and that while we should be caring and compassionate to those experiencing bereavement it is not helpful to see this as a psychiatric illness in need of treatment.

It is also the case that depressive symptoms lie on a continuum in the general population and symptoms tend to fluctuate from day to day. That is, there is not a clear and neatly defined cut-off between those 'with depression' and those 'without depression'. This is not to deny the fact that that some people struggle almost daily with extremely low mood, loss of pleasure and self-critical thinking. However, it suggests that considering depression as part of the human experience may be more accurate. Psychological theories such as those underlying MBCT (see p. 108) do not distinguish between people with 'mental illnesses' and those without. Rather, these approaches acknowledge that difficult experiences are there for all of us and that what might be particularly helpful is if we can all learn to kindly notice, accept and not judge these experiences.

Some clinical psychologists are critical of psychological therapies such as CBT, as they can locate the problem (depression) in the individual rather than in the wider society. There is good evidence that levels of social and wealth inequality are associated with mental health problems such as depression. That is, communities with a wider discrepancy between the richest and the poorest tend to have higher rates of depression than more equal societies. This has led to the development of community psychology which suggests, among other things, that we should be treating depression through reducing wealth and social inequality rather than through treating the individual.

FOCUS 6.1

to fall asleep or stay asleep (insomnia), while others feel very fatigued or lethargic and spend more time asleep than usual (hypersomnia).

For some people depression can lead to recurring thoughts of death or suicide, and people with depression are at higher risk of taking their own life than other people in the general population.

Diagnosis

DSM-V recognises a number of different mood disorders which are characterised by episodes of depressed mood or irritability and a loss of interest or pleasure in activities. A range of additional psychological, motivational, physical and interpersonal or social difficulties are also associated with depression.

Symptoms of a major depressive disorder include the following:

- low or irritable mood for most of the day, nearly every day;
- loss of interest or pleasure in activities;
- changes in appetite or weight;
- changes in sleep patterns;
- changes in motor functioning, such as psychomotor retardation or agitation;
- loss of energy or fatigue;
- loss of concentration or decisiveness;
- feeling worthless or guilty;
- feeling hopeless or helpless about the future;
- thoughts of death or suicidal ideation.

A formal diagnosis of depression may be given if you are experiencing five or more symptoms of depression that are not improving for more than two weeks and this is affecting your work, study, other interests or relationships with other people. Severity of depression can vary. A greater number of symptoms, more severe functional impairment and specific suicidal plans or attempts are associated with more severe depression.

Episodes of depression may co-occur with episodes of heightened mood and behavior sometimes termed 'mania'. In this case a diagnosis of bipolar disorder may be considered.

EPIDEMIOLOGY

One in ten adults may suffer from an episode of depression during their lifetime (NCCMH, 2010). Children can experience depression, although this is less common than depression in adolescence and adulthood. Women are around twice as likely to be diagnosed with depression than men (NCCMH, 2010). Other risk factors for depression include a family or personal history of mental health problems including mood disorders, early adversity, economic and educational disadvantage, negative life events, ongoing life stress and low levels of close social support (NCCMH, 2010). Depression often co-occurs with anxiety disorders, personality disorders and substance misuse (Kessler et al., 2005).

AETIOLOGY

There is no single cause of depression. Biological, psychological, social and environmental factors can all influence an individual's vulnerability to, and resilience against, the development of depression. Episodes of depression may sometimes follow life-changing events, or a series of day-to-day difficulties, but may also emerge with no obvious trigger. A bio-psychosocial model of the aetiology of depression attempts to describe how these factors affect vulnerability to depression and how they interact (Engel, 1977; see Figure 6.1).

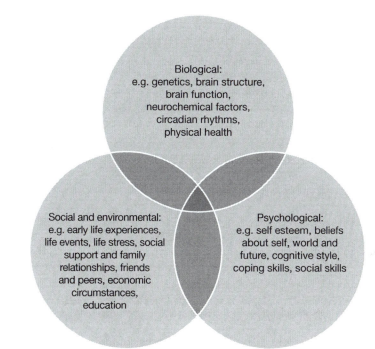

FIGURE 6.1 A bio-psychosocial model of depression

Biological theories

There is evidence from twin, adoption and family studies that genetic factors may play a role in the development of depression. While findings among studies vary, recent estimates suggest that around 30 to 40 per cent of the variance in depressive symptomatology may be accounted for by inherited factors (Agrawal *et al.*, 2004). The efficiency of neurotransmitter systems in brain areas may also be associated with depression. For example, abnormalities in serotonin metabolism are implicated in depression. Both structural and functional differences in the brains of depressed and non-depressed study participants have also been noted. For example, depression may be associated with lower levels of activation in brain areas (e.g. pre-frontal cortex, anterior cingulate cortex) associated with emotional regulation and goal attainment, and abnormalities in other areas associated with emotional contextualisation and processing (e.g. hippocampus, amygdala) (Davey, 2008).

Psychological theories

There are a number of different psychological models of depression which propose that our experiences and how we interpret and react to them play an important role in the development of depression. Psychological models consider both conscious and unconscious influences. Psychodynamic models view depression as a largely unconscious process which unfolds as a response to loss (Freud, 1917). Cognitive models of depression emphasise the role of negative beliefs and thinking patterns which maintain low mood and disengagement from meaningful activity (Beck *et al.*, 1979). Behavioural theories suggest that depression results from a lack of positive reinforcement of pleasurable and meaningful activities (Lewinsohn, 1974). Attachment theories highlight the role of early relationships with caregivers as paving the way for patterns of relationships throughout the lifespan, which may be depressogenic (Bowlby, 1980). Systemic theories of depression suggest that individuals' experiences cannot be understood in isolation, and view depression as a problem within the wider family system (Dallos and Draper, 2010).

Social and environmental factors

Social and environmental factors may also play an important role in the development of depression. In early life, traumatic experiences (e.g. abuse, neglect and maltreatment) may be associated with increased vulnerability to depression, and challenging early life circumstances such as economic and educational disadvantage are also associated with increased risk (Kessler *et al.*, 1997). In adulthood, both life events and ongoing life stress may be the catalyst for depression. Limited relationships with family and friends can increase the risk of developing depression in adverse circumstances (Teo *et al.*, 2013).

The bio-psychosocial model of depression suggests that it is psychological responses to adverse life circumstances in the context of a biological vulnerability to low mood that best explains depression, rather than any one factor alone (Kinderman *et al.*, 2013).

It is important to note that as well as a wealth of research aimed at understanding the factors that put individuals at risk of depression, a complementary body of work aims to understand what factors help people to remain depression free despite adversity (Haeffel and Grigorenko, 2007). Protective factors such as secure parenting, close-confiding relationships, well-developed social and problem-solving skills, and engagement in meaningful activities and goals may buffer against depression even in difficult circumstances.

THEORY AND EVIDENCE FOR PSYCHOLOGICAL INTERVENTIONS

Fortunately, clinical psychologists can offer a range of different options when working with people experiencing depression. These include one-to-one psychological therapies, group therapy and supported use of self-help materials. While a wide range of options are available, much of the work psychologists do is guided by evidence-based guidelines such as those offered by the National Institute of Health and Care Excellence (NICE) in the UK. For depression (see Figure 6.2), NICE recommends a choice between cognitive-behavioural therapy (CBT), interpersonal therapy, behavioural activation and behavioural couples therapy (National Collaborating Centre for Mental Health [NCCMH], 2010). For people who decline these options counselling or short-term psychodynamic therapy may also be considered. When it comes to relapse prevention, NICE recommend mindfulness-based cognitive therapy for people who are currently well but who have had three or more previous episodes of depression (see critical issues section, p. 108). Some of these therapies are described below.

Cognitive-behavioural therapy

Cognitive-behavioural therapy (CBT) is a psychological therapy based on the principle that how we think about a situation has a powerful effect on how we feel and how

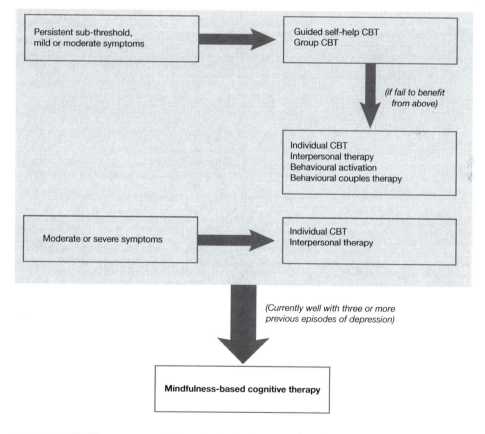

FIGURE 6.2 NICE recommended psychological interventions for depression

Source: NCCMH (2010).

we act, and in turn that what we do can affect our thoughts and feelings. This approach to depression was originally popularised by Aaron Beck in the 1970s. There is evidence that CBT for depression is helpful when offered one-to-one, in groups or in a supported self-help format.

In CBT the therapist and client work together to understand the client's experiences and to overcome overwhelming problems by breaking them down into smaller parts. Clients learn to identify unrealistic and unhelpful thinking patterns and processes that may be maintaining their depression, and are taught techniques to challenge and change these habits in daily life. During therapy clients develop more adaptive ways of thinking about themselves and their world and learn practical ways to improve their state of mind on a daily basis.

Behavioural activation

Behavioural activation (BA) is a psychological therapy based on the principle that when people become depressed many of their activities function as avoidance or escape from unpleasant thoughts, feelings or situations. The BA approach was developed by Peter Lewinsohn, and it focuses on activity scheduling to help clients with depression re-engage in pleasurable and meaningful activities, so that these can be positively reinforced. Planned timetables of activity are developed that promote engagement with both pleasurable and challenging experiences and reduce behavioural and cognitive avoidance. The client is encouraged to introduce small changes and build up the level of activity gradually towards long-term goals.

Interpersonal therapy

Interpersonal psychotherapy (IPT) was developed by Gerald Klerman and Myrna Weissman, based on the idea that psychological symptoms, such as depressed mood, may be understood as a response to current difficulties in relationships which may in turn affect the quality of those relationships. Typically, IPT focuses on current relationship themes such as conflict with another person, life changes that affect how the person feels about themselves and others, grief and loss, or difficulty in starting or keeping relationships going. During therapy the client works with the therapist to understand the reciprocal relationship between interpersonal factors and depression, and seeks to reduce symptoms by learning to cope with or resolve interpersonal problem areas.

Behavioural couples therapy

Behavioural couples therapy (BCT) is based on the principle that in some cases unhelpful patterns of relating within a romantic relationship can cause and maintain depression. This therapy is offered to couples where one of the partners is experiencing depression and there is relationship distress. The intervention, developed by Andrew Christensen and Neil Jacobson, aims to help couples understand how their interactions may affect one another in order to change and develop more helpful interactions which may reduce stress and increase support within the couple. The focus of the treatment is on relieving stress and improving communication; managing feelings and changing behaviour; solving problems and promoting acceptance; and revising perceptions.

Counselling

Sometimes, the term 'counselling' is used to refer to talking therapies in general, but counselling is also a specific type of therapy in its own right. It was developed by Carl Rogers, who believed that depression could be alleviated through the provision of a genuine and empathic therapeutic relationship in which the therapist demonstrates unconditional positive regard for the client.

Short-term psychodynamic therapies

Brief psychodynamic therapy is a psychological intervention where the emphasis is on gaining insight into conscious and unconscious psychic conflicts which are believed to contribute to depression. The therapy sessions are unstructured and do not involve an emphasis on skills attainment. The therapeutic relationship is foregrounded as a vehicle of change, and therapy is non-directive.

Indirect working

As well as offering therapies themselves, it is becoming increasingly common for clinical psychologists to support other mental health practitioners. This includes training and supervising psychological therapists (such as CBT therapists) and teaching and supporting non-therapists (such as community mental health nurses, social workers and doctors) to use psychological principles in their work.

FOCUS 6.2

Improving access to psychological therapies

The Improving Access to Psychological Therapies (IAPT) programme is a large-scale initiative to extend the reach of evidence-based psychological therapies and to increase patient choice via investment in the training of thousands of new therapists in England, alongside a fundamental restructuring of therapy services and the kinds of interventions they offer. NICE (2009) recommends a stepped-care approach to the management of depression; this means that as well as offering traditional one-to-one therapies for people with depression, these services also offer guided self-help interventions based on the principles of CBT as a first-line treatment to many people experiencing mild to moderate symptoms. To date, 3600 new IAPT therapists have been trained by the IAPT programme and many new high-volume services targeting common mental health problems such as depression have been established which, in their first three years, have seen one million patients. There is a current expansion of IAPT services to increase service-user choice from among the range of evidence-based therapies such as CBT and IPT.

CASE STUDY

About a year ago, Sally went to her GP to talk about how she was feeling. Her GP referred Sally to her local Improving Access to Psychological Therapies (IAPT) service. Sally met with a clinical psychologist, Fiona, who started by asking Sally about her current difficulties and her life history.

Assessment

Fiona wanted to have a good understanding of Sally's difficulties and of her upbringing. This would help when drawing upon psychological theories to develop a shared formulation with Sally. At the time of the assessment Sally said she was feeling low in mood almost every day but what bothered her more was that she never felt any pleasure, even about the things that once made her feel happy or excited. She said it was as if someone had switched off her happiness button. Sally was very self-critical and would lie awake at night, finding it difficult to sleep, thinking about why she felt so bad and why she was not a better mother. These thoughts would just go round and round in her head. Sally felt tired most of the time and tended to stay at home with her children. She would avoid seeing friends, as she would then compare herself to them unfavourably.

Her relationship with her partner was good, Sally said, and he was loving and supportive, but his job involved working long hours and sometimes travelling away from home. Sally saw her parents about once a week and tried to keep how she was feeling a secret from them, as she was worried that it would make her seem more of a failure in their eyes than she thought she was already. Sally's mother helped with childcare and shopping but Sally says she tended to be critical of Sally's parenting style, often telling her how she should be looking after Georgia and Archie differently.

Sally completed some self-report questionnaires during the assessment. This included the Patient Health Questionnaire (PHQ-9), a self-report measure of depressive symptoms. Sally's score of 22 suggested that she was experiencing severe depression.

Formulation

Fiona drew upon Beck's cognitive theory of depression (1979) to help make sense of Sally's difficulties (see Figure 6.3). According to Beck's theory of depression, we all develop core beliefs early in our lives as a way of making sense of our life experiences. Core beliefs therefore always make perfect sense when we consider them in light of someone's early life experiences. Core beliefs are subconscious, deeply rooted, fact-like beliefs. They include beliefs about ourselves (e.g. 'I am unlovable'), other people (e.g. 'other people are untrustworthy') and the world (e.g. 'the world is dangerous').

Together, Sally and Fiona identified some of Sally's core beliefs. In particular Sally held a core belief that she was useless and not as good as other people. When we look back at Sally's early life experiences, this makes sense from Sally's perspective. She remembers not doing as well at sport or at school as her younger brother and she remembers her parents telling her she should be doing better. According to Beck's theory, we develop rules in order to cope with our core beliefs. These rules will often be written in an 'if . . . then . . .' format. Sally realised she had developed a rule 'If I am successful then I am not useless'. Before having her children, Sally enjoyed her job as an administrator and performed very well. While she was working, Sally was therefore able to successfully apply this rule and cope with her negative core beliefs, keeping them at bay. Beck suggests that rules can help keep core beliefs dormant in this way for many years, while the rules are working. However, problems can arise when rules stop working. Life events may happen that prevent our rules from working effectively (so-called 'critical incidents') and it is at this point that negative core beliefs may be reactivated.

Sally could see that giving up her job was a critical incident that stopped her rules working. As a parent she did not see herself as successful and so the core beliefs that had been dormant for many years became activated. Once activated, Beck suggested that negative core beliefs would give rise to a stream of negative automatic thoughts. We all experience a stream of automatic thoughts that are often outside of our conscious awareness ('where did I leave my keys?', 'I like that song'). When negative core beliefs are activated however, the content of automatic thoughts can reflect the content of our core beliefs, giving rise to a stream of subconscious, negative automatic thoughts. Sally could easily see how this applied to her and could identify a long list of negative automatic thoughts. According to Beck, in depression these thoughts are seen to trigger and then maintain feelings of low mood and can lead to changes in behaviour, such as Sally avoiding seeing her friends as she thought she was not as good as them. More recent research suggests that there is a reciprocal relationship between negative automatic thoughts and low mood, whereby low mood can increase the frequency of negative thoughts and then negative thoughts can maintain low mood. In this way a vicious cycle may be established between low mood and negative thinking.

Fiona and Sally drew up a diagram to try to show how all of these aspects fitted together (Figure 6.3).

Action plan

According to Beck's cognitive theory of depression, negative automatic thoughts and negative core beliefs are seen to cause and then maintain depression. Cognitive therapy for depression therefore aims to improve mood and well-being through re-evaluating negative thoughts, rules and core beliefs, and to establish more accurate and helpful core beliefs in their place. Fiona and Sally drew up a therapy action plan that began with an initial phase of monitoring negative automatic thoughts, then re-evaluating their accuracy, then moving on to re-evaluating underlying negative core beliefs before finally identifying and strengthening alternative, more accurate and balanced core beliefs.

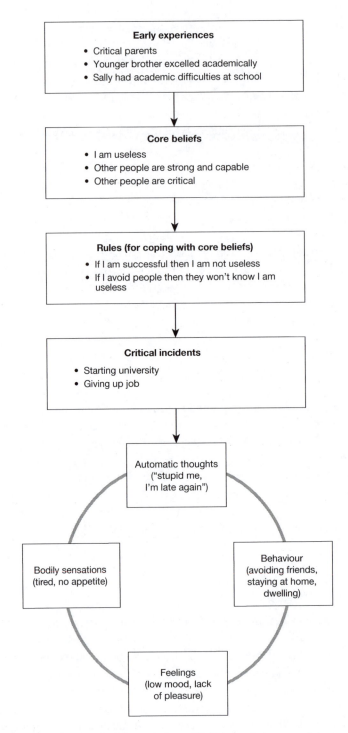

FIGURE 6.3 Beckian longitudinal formulation of Sally's experiences of depression

Source: Adapted from Fennel (1989).

Intervention

The National Institute of Health and Care Excellence recommend between 16 and 20 sessions of cognitive-behavioural therapy for depression (NICE, 2009). Fiona and Sally agreed to meet for 16 sessions.

Sessions 1 to 3

During the first three sessions Fiona and Sally used thought records to help Sally recognise the stream of negative automatic thoughts that she had previously not always been aware of. Thought records are diaries that encourage us to notice and write down our thoughts and feelings. An example of a thought record is shown in Figure 6.4.

1. Situation	2. Moods	3. Automatic thoughts (images)
Who? What? When? Where?	What did you feel? Rate each mood (0–100%)	What was going through your mind just before you started to feel this way?
At home with Georgia and Archie on Tuesday afternoon. I put them in front of the TV for a couple of hours so I could get on with some housework.	Guilty (80%) Low (70%)	I shouldn't let them watch so much TV I'm a really bad mum for letting them watch TV I bet none of my friends would do this

FIGURE 6.4 Three-column thought record

Source: Greenberger and Padesky (1995).

The thought record allowed Sally to write down the day and time when she noticed a change in her mood, to make a note of her feelings and their intensity, and to write down automatic thoughts that were in her mind just before or at the time of the mood change. Sally completed these records between therapy sessions and Sally and Fiona would discuss the records during their sessions.

Sessions 4 to 6

In the next three sessions Sally used a longer thought record (see Figure 6.5) that allowed her to identify the automatic thought that was most strongly associated with the change in mood (often called a 'hot thought') and then to carefully consider and write down evidence supporting and not supporting her hot thought (see Greenberger and Padesky (1995) for examples). It is interesting to see that Sally was encouraged to write down evidence *supporting* her hot thought. This is because we can think that our hot thoughts are based on good evidence and so it is only by closely examining this evidence that we can really see if the evidence supports our thoughts. After carefully writing down evidence for and against a hot thought, Sally

1. Situation	2. Moods	3. Automatic thoughts (images)	4. Evidence that supports the hot thought	5. Evidence that does not support the thought	6. Alternative/ balanced thoughts	7. Rate moods now
Who? What? When? Where?	What did you feel? Rate each mood (0–100%)	What was going through your mind just before you started to feel this way? Circle hot thought			Write an alternative or balanced thought. Rate how much you believe the alternative or balanced thought (0–100%)	Re-rate moods listed in column 2 as well as any new moods (0–100%)
On Wednesday I was late dropping Georgia at playgroup	Embarrassed (90%) Guilty (70%)	I'm always late No one else is ever late I bet they think I'm useless	Georgia's keyworker didn't smile at me	The playgroup leader was really friendly and said not to worry about being late Last week I saw another mum was late dropping off her son	They are used to people being late and don't really mind (40%)	Embarrassed (20%) Guilty (20%)

FIGURE 6.5 Seven-column thought record

Source: Greenberger and Padesky (1995).

was encouraged to identify an alternative, balanced thought that fitted the evidence. Here we can see that Sally is not simply encouraged to 'think positive'; rather she is encouraged to identify a thought that accurately reflects all the evidence. Once she had identified an alternative thought Sally was encouraged to undertake behavioural experiments to test out the accuracy of these new thoughts. A behavioural experiment is a way to test out the accuracy of our thoughts and beliefs by predicting what will happen if our thoughts/beliefs are true, and then reviewing what really happens and what this means about the accuracy of our thoughts and beliefs. Sally asked her partner to help her conduct behavioural experiments.

Sessions 7 to 12

In these sessions Sally began to work with her rules and core beliefs. Initially this involved using techniques to more fully identify core beliefs and rules. Sally used a record form similar to the thought record, but this time she wrote down experiences and evidence that did not support each of her negative core beliefs. Because core beliefs are often held as fact-like beliefs and have been in place since childhood, it can be difficult to notice evidence that does not support them. So Sally asked her partner and a close friend to help her recognise evidence. As well as looking at evidence not supporting her negative core beliefs in the present Sally was also encouraged to look for evidence throughout her life going back to childhood, and to conduct behavioural experiments to test out the accuracy of these beliefs.

Sessions 13 to 15

During sessions 13 to 15 Sally considered all the evidence on her core belief records and together with Fiona used this to explore alternative perspectives that accurately reflected the evidence. These new ideas about herself were that Sally was as good as other people and that she was competent and respected. During these sessions Sally began to notice and write down evidence supporting these new perspectives.

Throughout sessions 7 to 15 Sally was encouraged to undertake behavioural experiments to test out the accuracy of her old, negative core beliefs and of her newly emerging core beliefs. Her husband supported Sally in conducting the experiments and in reviewing the evidence from these experiments. In their therapy sessions Fiona and Sally would carefully review the outcome of these experiments and consider what they meant. Sally started meeting up with old friends, rejoined the parent and baby group, and started making enquiries at her old place of work about part-time admin assistant jobs.

Session 16

In the final session Sally and Fiona reflected upon Sally's progress through therapy and drew up a therapy blueprint to act as a quick reminder for Sally of everything she had learned during the therapy so that she could refer to it in the future. Sally's PHQ-9 score at the end of therapy was 14, which is in the mild clinical range. Although showing an improvement from the initial assessment, it suggested that Sally was still experiencing some symptoms of depression. Sally confirmed that she felt less low in mood and was beginning to enjoy things she had enjoyed in the past, such as being with friends. However, she said that she still sometimes felt low and found herself caught up in dwelling on her negative automatic thoughts and low mood.

Team working/indirect work

During the course of therapy, Sally had a number of meetings with Steve, an employment specialist in the IAPT service. Steve's job was to support clients in the service in returning to work. One day Steve asked to speak to Fiona to say he was puzzled that although Sally seemed keen to return to work she seemed to reject all of his suggestions and that he was beginning to feel frustrated.

With Sally's permission, Fiona arranged to meet with Steve the following week to share the formulation they had developed and to consider why Sally might be reluctant to follow Steve's suggestions. Steve found this very useful and it helped him to understand that Sally might be ambivalent about returning to work because she was worried that she would not succeed in a new job, which would confirm her core belief that she was useless.

Sally then had a joint meeting with Fiona and Steve to consider her job seeking in light of the formulation. This helped them all to see Sally's job seeking as a behavioural experiment to test out her newly emerging core beliefs that she was competent, respected and as good as other people. From this point forward Sally was able to follow Steve's advice and she attended a couple of job interviews, one of them resulting in a job offer for a part-time administrator. Sally was delighted and surprised with this offer, and in their next therapy session Fiona and Sally were able to review what this meant in relation to Sally's core beliefs. The job offer became evidence for Sally to strengthen her newly emerging core beliefs.

CRITICAL ISSUES

Relapse and depression

While many people who experience an episode of depression will recover fully and never experience depression again, for some people depression may present difficulties over the life course. As the number of episodes of depression increases so does the risk of subsequent episodes so that once someone has experienced two episodes of depression they have an 80 per cent risk of experiencing another episode.

While both psychological and pharmacological interventions can be helpful for depression in the short term, studies usually do not follow participants up beyond a few months after the intervention has ended. Therefore it is not at all clear how effective psychological interventions are at protecting people from relapse in the long term. There is some evidence that CBT is more effective than medication at reducing the risk of relapse, although more research is needed.

Mindfulness-based cognitive therapy (MBCT)

Mindfulness-based cognitive therapy (MBCT; Segal *et al.*, 2002) is a therapy that incorporates mindfulness practice and principles with cognitive therapy. Mindfulness refers to the ability to fully notice our current experiences (thoughts, feelings, bodily sensations) while being kind, accepting and non-judgemental of these experiences (Bishop *et al.*, 2004). MBCT was designed as a relapse prevention intervention for depression for people who are currently well but who are at risk of relapse.

MBCT differs from cognitive therapy in that while cognitive therapy is interested in identifying and changing the content of thoughts and beliefs, MBCT is interested in developing a different way of relating to this content. The theory underlying MBCT is that it is not the content of negative thoughts and beliefs that is distressing; rather it is how we respond to these experiences. Rumination is the tendency to think about negative thoughts, feelings and their consequences over and over again; to get lost in the content and to be attached to the content (Nolen-Hoeksema, 2000). MBCT sees rumination as the problem rather than the content itself. During MBCT people engage in mindfulness meditation practices and learn through practice to take a step back and to observe all experiences (including thoughts) at a distance, to not judge these experiences as good or bad or as right or wrong and to mindfully make decisions about how best to respond, rather than responding in potentially unhelpful ways. In this way, MBCT can help people to let go of ruminative ways of responding to negative thoughts.

There is evidence from randomised controlled trials that MBCT in comparison to usual care is effective at reducing the risk of relapse for people who are currently well and who have experienced three or more previous episodes of depression (Kuyken *et al.*, 2008; Ma and Teasdale, 2004; Teasdale *et al.*, 2000). It is also becoming increasingly clear that the benefits of MBCT extend beyond preventing relapse in that it can help to reduce symptoms of a current depressive episode (Van Aalderen *et al.*, 2012).

CONCLUSION TO SALLY'S STORY

After I finished working with Fiona we agreed that I would try a mindfulness-based cognitive therapy (MBCT) group. Fiona said that this can help to keep people well who have been depressed. During the course I learned to take a step back from my negative thoughts and I learned to just observe these thoughts as thoughts, rather than as facts. This meant that I was more able to accept negative thoughts and not to get caught up in worrying about them or what they meant. I am now more able to let thoughts pass into my mind and pass out again, without getting lost in my thoughts. I have also become more aware of making choices about what I do, so that if I notice thoughts such as 'Emma won't want to see me so I'll call and cancel' I can now let go of the thought and meet up with my friend. Although I still have negative thoughts and can sometimes feel low this doesn't have the power over me it once had and I can just get on with my life. I am now back at work, which I find really rewarding, and spending more time with my family and friends.

KEY CONCEPTS AND TERMS

- MBCT
- Mindfulness
- Cognitive therapy

- Core beliefs
- Negative automatic thoughts

- Relapse prevention
- Diagnosis
- DSM V

LEARNING OUTCOMES

When you have completed this chapter you should be able to:

1. Know what features or symptoms are characteristic of depression and have an awareness of the types of psychological difficulties suffered by people experiencing depression.
2. Have an understanding of the psychological and societal impact of depression.
3. Have an understanding of the psychological theories or models that are relevant to depression.
4. Have an understanding of the treatment approaches used by clinical psychologists to treat depression – and the evidence base for these approaches.
5. Have an understanding of how assessment, formulation, intervention and evaluation may be used in a psychologist's work with a specific case of depression.
6. Be able to provide a critical appraisal of the different intervention approaches for depression.

SAMPLE ESSAY TITLES

- Compare and contrast Beck's cognitive theory of depression with the principles underlying mindfulness-based cognitive therapy.
- Describe the stress vulnerability model of depression.
- Mindfulness-based cognitive therapy should be offered to everyone with depression. Discuss.
- It is helpful to think of depression as an illness. Discuss.

REFERENCES

Agrawal, A., Jacobson, K.C., Prescott, C.A. and Kendler, K.S. (2004). A population based twin study of sex differences in depressive symptoms. *Twin Research, 7,* 176–181.

American Psychiatric Association (APA) (2013). *Diagnostic and Statistical Manual of Mental Disorders* (5th edn). Arlington, VA: American Psychiatric Publishing.

Beck, A.T., Rush, A.J., Shaw, B.F. and Emery, G. (1979). *Cognitive Therapy of Depression.* New York: Guilford Press.

Bishop, S.R., Lau, M., Shapiro, S., Carlson, L., Anderson, N.D., Carmody, J. and Devins, G. (2004). Mindfulness: A proposed operational definition. *Clinical Psychology: Science and Practice, 11,* 230–241.

Bowlby, J. (1980). *Attachment and Loss, Volume 3: Loss; Sadness and Depression.* London: Random House.

Brown, T.A., Campbell, L.A. and Lehman, C.L. (2001). Current and lifetime comorbidity of the DSM–IV anxiety and mood disorders in a large clinical sample. *Journal of Abnormal Psychology, 110,* 585–599.

Dallos, R. and Draper, R. (2010). *An Introduction to Family Therapy* (3rd edn). Buckingham: Open University Press.

Davey, G.C.L. (2008). *Psychopathology.* Chichester: Blackwell.

Engel, G.L. (1977). The need for a new medical model: A challenge for biomedicine. *Science, 196*(4286), 129–136.

Fennel, M. (1989). Depression. In K. Hawton, P.M. Salkovskis, J. Kirk and D.M. Clark (eds), *Cognitive Behaviour Therapy for Psychiatric Problems: A Practical Guide* (pp. 169–234). Oxford: Oxford University Press.

Freud, S. (1917). Mourning and melancholia. *Standard Edition, 14*(239), 1957–1961.

Greenberger, D. and Padesky, C.A. (1995). *Mind over Mood: Change How You Feel by Changing the Way You Think.* London: Guilford Press.

Haeffel, G.J. and Grigorenko, E.L. (2007). Cognitive vulnerability to depression: Exploring risk and resilience. *Child and Adolescent Psychiatric Clinics of North America, 16,* 435–448.

Kessler, R.C., Davis, C.G. and Kendler, K.S. (1997). Childhood adversity and adult psychiatric disorder in the US National Comorbodity Survey. *Psychological Medicine, 27,* 1101–1119.

Kessler, R.C., Chiu, W.T., Demler, O. and Walters, E.E. (2005). Prevalence, severity, and comorbidity of 12-month DSM-IV disorders in the National Comorbidity Survey Replication. *Archives of General Psychiatry, 62*(6), 617.

Kinderman, P., Schwannauer, M., Pontin, E. and Tai, S. (2013). Psychological processes mediate the impact of familial risk, social circumstances and life events on mental health. *PLoS ONE, 8(10)*: e76564. doi:10.1371/journal.pone.0076564.

Kuyken, W., Byford, S., Taylor, R.S., Watkins, E., Holden, E. and White, K. (2008). Mindfulness-based cognitive therapy to prevent relapse in recurrent depression. *Journal of Consulting and Clinical Psychology, 76*, 966–978.

Lewinsohn, P.M. (1974). A behavioral approach to depression. In R.J. Friedman and M.M. Katz (eds), *The Psychology of Depression: Contemporary Theory and Research* (pp. 157–178). Washington, DC: Winston-Wiley.

Ma, S.H. and Teasdale, J.D. (2004). Mindfulness-based cognitive therapy for depression: Replication and exploration of differential relapse prevention effects. *Journal of Consulting and Clinical Psychology, 72*, 31–40.

NCCMH (2010). *Depression: The Treatment and Management of Depression in Adults (Update)* (updated edn). Leicester and London: The British Psychological Society and the Royal College of Psychiatrists.

NICE (2009). *Depression: The Treatment and Management of Depression in Adults (Update)*. NICE clinical guideline 90. Available at www.nice.org.uk/CG90.

Nolen-Hoeksema, S. (2000). The role of rumination in depressive disorders and mixed anxiety/depressive symptoms. *Journal of Abnormal Psychology, 109*, 504–511.

Segal, Z.V., Williams, J.M.G. and Teasdale, J.D. (2002). *Mindfulness-based Cognitive Therapy for Depression*. New York: Guilford Press.

Teasdale, J.D., Segal, Z.V., Williams, J.M.G., Ridgeway, V.A., Soulsby, J.M. and Lau, M.A. (2000). Prevention of relapse/recurrence in major depression by mindfulness-based cognitive therapy. *Journal of Consulting and Clinical Psychology, 68*, 615–623.

Teo A.R., Choi, H. and Valenstein, M. (2013). Social relationships and depression: Ten-year follow-up from a nationally representative study. *PLoS One, 8*(4): e62396.

Van Aalderen, J.R., Donders, A.R.T., Giommi, F., Spinhoven, P., Barendregt, H.P. and Speckens, A.E.M. (2012). The efficacy of mindfulness-based cognitive therapy in recurrent depressed patients with and without a current depressive episode: A randomized controlled trial. *Psychological Medicine, 42*, 989–1001.

7 Working with people with anxiety disorders

Alesia Moulton-Perkins, Adrian Whittington and Melissa Chinery

MILLIE'S STORY

My name is Millie. I'm 42 and have worked as a hospital radiographer since 1998. This is when my washing problems started and I became aware of the obsessive compulsive disorder (OCD) that was to rule my life for the next thirteen years.

The first time it happened was in the operating theatres. Going for my break I went to the scrub room, washed my hands and opened the door. In the kitchen I washed my hands again because I had touched the door. I made my tea and washed again because I had touched the fridge and kettle.

It felt like something was hanging off my thumb and forefinger. Until I had wet 'it' (whatever 'it' was!) I couldn't use them because I felt like everything I touched would be contaminated. I never had to scrub: simply touching something wet and rubbing them together would remove the 'thing'. Getting a parking ticket from the machine at work was an issue, I was happy if it had rained as I could wipe my finger and thumb on the machine to wet them. One day I used snow.

It wasn't the wiping but more the thought processes involved and the time wasted trying to avoid touching things. Working in a busy department was tricky, watching colleagues touching everyday objects that had dropped on the floor and not cleaning their fingers. Eventually I wasn't comfortable touching patients' beds, or door handles – I would kick the doors open to save touching them! The rituals became relentless.

SUMMARY

Anxiety is a normal and useful part of life, helping guide us to avoid danger. However, anxiety becomes a problem if it persists when we are not in situations that present real threat. If this continues for some months we think of the anxiety as having become an 'anxiety disorder'. There are lots of different types of anxiety disorder but they all have in common that they are linked to a persistent perception of threat or danger that is exaggerated beyond the actual level of danger. Anxiety disorders are the most common mental health problems, with more than one in ten people suffering from an anxiety disorder at any moment in time. Anxiety disorders can be very persistent if not treated, and most people never receive any treatment. However, there are psychological treatments that can be delivered by clinical psychologists and others, which have a very good track record of success.

This chapter outlines the nature of anxiety disorders and the main evidence-based treatments. It then presents an example of how a clinical psychologist helped one client, Jim, to make significant progress in overcoming the difficulties he was experiencing as a result of generalised anxiety disorder.

INTRODUCTION: WHAT ARE THE TYPES OF PSYCHOLOGICAL DIFFICULTIES THAT MAY OCCUR IN ANXIETY DISORDERS?

Everyone experiences anxiety at times. It is a normal reaction to threatening events or circumstances and its presence has obvious survival and therefore evolutionary advantages, driving organisms to escape or avoid real danger. People who are moderately anxious tend to perform better than those with very low or very high anxiety, for example, when giving a talk or attending an interview (Yerkes and Dodson, 1908). However, anxiety can become a problem when it is persistent, interferes significantly with daily life and is out of proportion to the actual danger in a situation. This sort of trouble with anxiety is often a sign of an anxiety 'disorder'.

What is it like to have an anxiety disorder? Clark and Beck's (2010) cognitive-behavioural model of anxiety describes anxiety in terms of four response systems: cognition, affect, physiology and behaviour.

Cognitions

Cognitions may take the form of thoughts (persistent or fleeting) or mental images. People with anxiety disorders tend to be troubled by cognitions that are focused on present or future threat. For example, someone with panic disorder may have the thought 'If I keep breathing this fast I will pass out'. Someone with OCD may fleetingly think 'If I touch this door handle I could catch a disease and pass it on to my daughter' – a thought that may be accompanied by a mental image of the daughter in a hospital bed. These thoughts and images are often highly believable to the person experiencing them, even though they are not accurate representations of the true degree of threat.

Affect

Thinking this way it is easy to see how someone may feel fearful, apprehensive, stressed or agitated. This would be a healthy and useful response if the thoughts were true.

Physiology

Anxiety can trigger the bodily 'fight–or–flight response' where a release of the hormone adrenaline leads to body sensations such as fast breathing, racing heart or sweating. All of these reactions prepare the body to fight or flee the source of perceived danger and are themselves harmless.

Behaviours

When anxious, people often try to avoid, escape from or neutralise the perceived threats. For example, someone with agoraphobia may avoid crowded shops because once before they had a panic attack in one. Staying at home and doing internet shopping feels safer. If forced to stay in the situation they may do something that makes them feel safer (e.g. checking where the escape route is or taking deep breaths).

DIAGNOSIS

DSM-V and ICD-10 list numerous different anxiety disorders, each with specific signs and symptoms. Table 7.1 lists seven of the most common anxiety problems and highlights key symptoms. Typically, diagnosis of any of these disorders requires the presence of a defined number of symptoms, on more days than not, across a defined period of time (usually six months).

EPIDEMIOLOGY

Anxiety disorders are the most common of all mental disorders. The British Psychiatric Morbidity Survey measured prevalence of mental disorders in adult households (McManus *et al.*, 2009), finding that 13 per cent of the population met diagnostic criteria for an anxiety disorder during the past seven days. The same survey showed that 43 to 75 per cent of those with an anxiety disorder received no treatment at all,

---

FOCUS 7.1

Co-morbidity and anxiety disorders

It is commonplace for people to have more than one anxiety disorder at the same time and for people with anxiety disorders also to be depressed. Assessment at a large US outpatient clinic showed that 64 per cent of people with depression attending the clinic also had an anxiety disorder and that 43 per cent had more than one anxiety disorder (Brown *et al.*, 2001). Anxiety disorder can also co-occur with severe mental health difficulties like personality disorder, psychosis, dementia or alcohol and drug misuse. Those with co-morbid conditions tend to have more severe difficulties and these may require adaptations to treatment.

TABLE 7.1 Common anxiety disorders with key symptoms

Specific phobia	• Excessive anxiety triggered by specific objects or situations (e.g. spiders or flying).
Social anxiety disorder	• Excessive fear of being judged negatively by others in social or performance situations.
Panic disorder	• Recurrent unexpected panic attacks (rapidly surging bodily sensations of anxiety).
	• Anxiety about the perceived implications of the attack or its consequences (e.g. a concern that a racing heart means that a heart attack is imminent).
Agoraphobia	• Anxiety about and avoidance of being in places or situations where escape is difficult/embarrassing or where help is unavailable (e.g. travelling on public transport). Often the core fear is that a panic attack will occur in these situations.
Generalised anxiety disorder	• Excessive worry about a variety of everyday events and problems (e.g. work, money, relationships).
	• Physical tension and difficulty relaxing.

Obsessive compulsive disorder	• The presence of obsessions, compulsions or both:
	  o Obsessions: recurrent and persistent thoughts, impulses or images experienced as intrusive and inappropriate (e.g. contamination by germs, harming a loved one).
	  o Compulsions: repetitive behaviours (e.g. hand washing, ordering, checking) or mental acts (e.g. praying, counting, repeating words silently) that the person feels driven to perform (typically thematically linked to obsessions (e.g. hand washing to avoid contamination with germs)) and that are aimed at reducing anxiety.

Post-traumatic stress disorder	• Exposure to a traumatic (often life-threatening) event where the person's response involves intense fear, helplessness or horror.
	• Re-experiencing symptoms (e.g. flashbacks and nightmares).
	• Avoidance/numbing symptoms (e.g. trying not to think about what happened).
	• Hyper-arousal symptoms (e.g. difficulty sleeping, very alert to potential danger).

and of those who did only 2 per cent received CBT, the psychological therapy with the strongest evidence base for treating anxiety disorders.

Anxiety disorders can begin at any age, with most people developing them between 7 and 31 years old (Kessler *et al.*, 2005). Being female or of low socio-economic status significantly increases the risk of developing anxiety disorder (Michael *et al.*, 2007). Table 7.2 shows prevalence of the main disorders during one-week and one-year periods.

TABLE 7.2 Prevalence of anxiety disorders

	Prevalence (%)		
	7 days	*12 months*	
	UK	*USA*	*Europe*
Specific phobias		8.7	3.5
Social phobia		6.8	1.2
GAD	4.4	3.1	1.0
PTSD	3.0	3.5	0.9
Panic disorder	1.1	2.7	0.8
All phobias	1.1		
OCD	1.1	1.0	
Any anxiety disorder		18.1	6.4

Source: McManus *et al.* (2009); Kessler *et al.* (2005); Alonso *et al.* (2004)

AETIOLOGY

Understanding what leads to the onset of anxiety disorders has lagged behind the development of effective psychological treatments, which usually tackle processes maintaining the problem rather than attending in detail to its origins. While different theorists have stressed different factors in aetiology, it is likely that biogenetic vulnerability, combined with environmental stressors, creates the context for the development of troublesome anxiety, which may persist and become a disorder through the interplay of behavioural and cognitive psychological factors.

Biological factors

Anxiety disorders usually occur in the absence of any identifiable biological cause. However, there appears to be a genetic vulnerability to anxiety disorders. For example, twin studies show that monozygotic twins, sharing identical genetic make-up, are much more likely to both develop specific phobia than dizygotic twins (49 per cent compared to 4 per cent) (Marks, 1987). The processes underlying this are unclear, but natural variation in anxiety responses within a species is likely to confer an evolutionary survival advantage.

Environmental factors

Exposure to repeated unpredictable and uncontrollable negative life events, or grow-ing up in an over-protective, over-controlling family environment, increases risk of later anxiety disorder compared to sensitive, consistent caregiving (Barlow, 2002). Some anxiety disorders are clearly triggered by a particular traumatic event or events, notably PTSD, and sometimes social phobia and specific phobias (e.g. driving phobia after a car accident). However, anxiety disorder also commonly occurs in the absence of any history of this sort, and many who have experienced such adversity do not go on to develop anxiety disorder.

Psychological factors

Behavioural theory

Behavioural theory proposes that fears are learned. Three learning processes have been proposed:

- Classical conditioning (Watson and Rayner, 1920): where previously neutral stimuli become feared as a result of being paired with stimuli that induce an anxiety reaction. For example, if you have a frightening car accident on a particular stretch of road, you may feel anxious weeks later when you pass that area again.
- Operant conditioning (Mowrer, 1948): where anxious avoidance is said to persist through negative reinforcement of avoidance behaviours, through the repeated pairing of avoidance and the relief of anxiety. For example, avoiding the stretch of road where you had the accident becomes a habit because this means you don't get anxious.
- Social learning theory (Bandura, 1977): which proposes that fears can be acquired vicariously through observational learning. For example, your child may start to get anxious too when you pass the feared stretch of road, because they see you are scared.

Behavioural theories of aetiology represent useful explanations of some aspects of anxiety disorder, and have been influential in the design of some successful treatments.

Cognitive theory

Cognitive theory proposes that people develop anxiety disorders when they misinterpret the true level of threat or danger associated with particular stimuli (Beck *et al.*, 1985; Clark and Beck, 2010). The phenomenon of the overestimation of threat has been robustly tested experimentally and is a feature of persistent anxiety disorder. Reversal of these misperceptions of threat has become a focus of successful treatment across anxiety disorders.

Cognitive-behavioural theory proposes that anxiety disorders arise as a result of a complex interplay of cognitive and behavioural factors. For example, someone who has had a car accident may develop a belief that driving along a certain stretch of road will have catastrophic consequences, and therefore avoid it. The avoidant behaviour is negatively reinforced, their negative predictions remain intact, habituation is prevented and therefore subsequent presentation with the feared stimulus evokes intense anxious arousal.

THEORY AND EVIDENCE FOR PSYCHOLOGICAL INTERVENTION

Therapies based on cognitive or behavioural principles are effective in treating anxiety disorders according to evidenced-based guidelines (e.g. National Institute of Clinical Excellence (NICE), 2004; see also Focus 2.1). Each anxiety disorder has one or more recognised specific cognitive-behavioural treatments with good evidence of effectiveness. Therapy is typically brief (2 to 16 hours), collaborative and structured around reversing key behavioural or cognitive maintaining processes associated with the particular anxiety disorder(s) being treated. Left untreated, anxiety disorders often persist, but with psychological therapy between 50 and 85 per cent of people completely recover (Roth and Fonagy, 2005).

Behaviourally based exposure therapies

Exposure therapies are based on learning theory, and focus on prolonged and deliberate exposure to feared stimuli. The therapist guides the person to place themselves into the feared situation and through a process of habituation anxiety gradually drops. As a consequence the feared stimulus becomes paired with lack of fear so that 'extinction' of the fear is achieved. Exposure therapy is often used with specific phobias, PTSD and OCD. For example, in PTSD prolonged exposure to the detail of traumatic memories has been shown to reduce their impact (Foa *et al.*, 2007).

Cognitive-behavioural therapy (CBT)

CBT extends behavioural therapy by additionally tackling the cognitions that drive anxiety (as illustrated by the detailed case study later in this chapter). Cognitive theory suggests that anxiety is maintained when people perceive things to be more threatening than they objectively are. If we think it is very likely that bad things will happen, or very awful if they do, then we will feel more anxious. However, if we think that we will be able to cope, or that at least somebody or something may help us, then our anxiety will be lower. Beck *et al.* (1985) summarised these ideas in the anxiety equation:

$$\text{Degree of anxiety} \ = \ \frac{\text{Perceived \textbf{probability} of threat} \times \text{Perceived cost/\textbf{awfulness} of danger}}{\text{Perceived ability to \textbf{cope} with the danger} + \text{Perceived \textbf{rescue} factors}}$$

CBT for anxiety disorders aims to strengthen coping appraisals and weaken threat appraisals, in other words making the denominator larger than the numerator. This is done by reversing key maintaining cognitive and behavioural processes. For example, someone with panic disorder may avoid supermarkets fearing an attack, but because they need to buy food for dinner they are forced to enter the supermarket. Standing in the check-out queue they experience a slight dizzy feeling (the normal result of fight–flight physiology). Failing to understand that fainting is not caused by panic,[1] they catastrophically misinterpret their physical symptoms as evidence of imminent collapse.

They employ the 'safety behaviour' of stiffening their legs. Ironically this makes their legs even shakier, which raises their anxiety still further. They do not faint, and the panic gradually subsides, with the catastrophic misinterpretation intact: 'Thank goodness I tensed my legs, otherwise I really would have collapsed!'

CBT breaks the vicious cycle by reversing these processes: challenging exaggerated threat appraisals, teaching approach rather than avoidance, and dropping safety behaviours. The therapist helps the individual look objectively at how likely and how awful their feared catastrophe would be, evaluating and challenging cognitive distortions (see Focus 7.2). In order to gather more objective evidence, the patient is taught to attend to both positive and negative stimuli, rather than only 'looking for trouble' (thus reducing the anxiety equation numerator). Perception of coping ability and access to rescue factors is increased by a similar process of rational examination of the evidence, and thus their self-efficacy and perceived sense of control is improved (denominator thereby increasing). Alongside this cognitive restructuring process, the individual is assisted to approach the things they are afraid of and have been avoiding. This may be through conducting behavioural experiments, where they test out their anxious predictions by dropping safety-seeking behaviours, or by progressing through

---

FOCUS 7.2

Cognitive distortions

Burns (1999) proposed that certain unhelpful thinking styles or 'cognitive distortions' cause us to look at the world through distorted lenses, and therefore not see things as they actually are but as we fear them to be. While originally developed for depression (see Chapter 6), several are particularly relevant to anxiety:

- *Jumping to conclusions*: (a) Mind reading – you assume that people are reacting negatively to you when there's a lack of evidence for this. 'The people at the party will think I'm boring and reject me' (social anxiety); (b) Fortune-telling – you arbitrarily predict that things will turn out badly. 'If I get on a bus I won't be able to cope and I'll humiliate myself by having a panic attack and losing control of my bladder' (panic and agoraphobia).
- *Magnification or minimisation*: You blow things way out of proportion or you shrink their importance inappropriately. 'Touching this toilet seat means I will be contaminated by a life-threatening illness' (OCD).
- *Emotional reasoning*: You reason from how you feel: 'I feel terrified when I see this spider, so it must be dangerous' (specific phobia).
- *'Should' statements*: You criticise yourself or other people with 'shoulds' or 'shouldn'ts'. 'Musts', 'oughts' and 'have-tos' are similar offenders. 'Strong men should control their minds and eradicate worries' (GAD).
- *Labelling*: You identify with your shortcomings. Instead of saying, 'I had a serious attack and many people would be frightened after that', you say, 'I'm pathetic and weak because I can't get over this' (PTSD).

exposure and habituation. These exposures may be 'in vivo' (direct or live) or 'imaginal' (indirect or imagined). Facing the feared situation and discovering that no catastrophe occurs provides further evidence to erode the original exaggerated threat appraisal, thus reducing anxiety and physiological arousal.

Eye movement desensitisation and reprocessing

This approach to treatment originated with a chance observation by Shapiro (1995) who observed that moving her eyes from side to side repeatedly while reviewing distressing memories appeared to lead to relief from distress. A short–term treatment (typically 8 to 18 hours) was developed and trialled for PTSD based on reviewing trauma memories and meanings while making these eye movements, tracking movements of the therapist's fingers. This treatment has proved as effective as trauma–focused CBT for the treatment of PTSD, although the active ingredients of the treatment remain a subject of debate and investigation (e.g. van den Hout and Engelhard, 2012).

CASE STUDY

Jim was a 54-year-old man who went to see his GP because he had become very anxious and depressed. He was unable to shake off worries about several topics, including family relationships, housing and health issues. Jim's GP used some questionnaire measures which showed that he was experiencing severe anxiety and moderately severe depressive symptoms. Antidepressant medication was proving ineffective and she decided to refer Jim to the local Primary Care Mental Health Team. Jim met with a clinical psychologist, Theresa.

Assessment

At the first session, Jim described various recent negative life events starting two years previously with a stressful time in his job as a senior accountant. Following this he started to feel depressed and anxious. He also injured his back, and after developing mobility difficulties was medically retired. His wife left him, and their teenage daughter reacted badly by avoiding school work, consequently failing an important exam.

Jim told Theresa that he had always been 'a worrier', but had never been depressed before. Since the separation he had felt especially low, withdrawing from socialising and finding decision making tortuous as he over-analysed and worried over every eventuality: his health and whether he should manage his mobility problems by moving to a bungalow or building a downstairs extension, how to repair the relationship with his wife, how to occupy his time now that he was retired, and how to encourage his daughter to start studying for her exam resits. He felt unable to stop these worry bouts, fearing they would send him mad or damage his health. All this worrying left him exhausted and depressed.

Theresa suspected that Jim had developed generalised anxiety disorder (GAD) and investigated this further by asking him to complete the Penn State Worry Questionnaire (PSWQ). This is a validated 16-item measure of trait worry. Jim scored 63/80, clearly above the cut-off score for GAD of 45.

Formulation

Theresa and Jim worked together to come to a shared understanding of how his problems began and were then maintained.

How the problems developed

- *Predisposing factors:* Theresa made use of Judy Beck's (Beck, 1995) developmental CBT model, which highlights how early life experiences can lead to particular negative beliefs, assumptions and unhelpful coping strategies. Relevant aspects of Jim's early life included an unaffectionate father who only praised him when he achieved perfect performance at school, and an anxious mother who saw potential disaster everywhere. Jim developed beliefs about himself as unlovable, others as critical, and the world as a difficult and dangerous place. He lived according to certain rules and assumptions such as 'If I excel in everything, I'll be a worthwhile person' and 'I must foresee and prepare for all potential problems'. As long as he could follow his rules and use his preferred coping strategies like overworking, appeasing others or over-analysing decisions he felt in control and OK.
- *Precipitating factors:* A series of negative events around Jim's job, health, marriage and daughter pitched his life into chaos. Jim's normal coping strategies did not work and he struggled to maintain control. His difficulty in tolerating the unknown and failure to meet his expectations of himself as a man meant he judged himself cruelly for not coping and therefore he tried even harder to solve his problems by analysing every eventuality. Incessant worry about work, and his failing marriage, led to chronic generalised anxiety and depression.

How the problems were maintained

Theresa and Jim drew a diagram based on Dugas and Robichaud's (2007) GAD model. This diagram was built up in stages over a series of sessions to explain how specific cognitive and behavioural factors were maintaining his worry and eventually leading him to become demoralised, exhausted and depressed. Maintaining factors in the model include the following:

- *Intolerance of uncertainty:* Jim was clearly intolerant of uncertainty as a result of his early experiences and was always grappling to arrive at a perfect conclusion to his concerns.
- *Beliefs about worry being a helpful strategy:* Jim described a number of 'positive' beliefs about worry, including 'worrying helps me to problem solve and prove I'm a good parent'.

- *Negative orientation to problem solving:* Jim tended to catastrophise when faced with a decision, and increasingly doubted his problem-solving abilities.
- *Cognitive avoidance:* Jim avoided thinking about the real losses he had suffered over recent months, inhibiting emotional processing and further maintaining his anxiety.

These factors together led to persistent worry processes. He tended to pose himself a series of 'what if?' questions: 'What if my wife meets someone else . . . my daughter fails her resits . . . my back gets worse . . . the builders I choose to build my house extension swindle me?'

Jim ceased pursuing previously enjoyed sports like bowls and avoided friends. He became depressed which in turn maintained his anxiety further because inactivity left more time for worry, and more things to worry about. He started to 'worry about worry', thinking his anxiety could further damage his health.

The final diagram, which shows the main factors maintaining GAD, illustrated by the way this specifically applied to Jim, in his own words, is shown in Figure 7.1.

Action plan

Theresa offered Jim 16 sessions of CBT in line with NICE (2004) guidelines. Theresa explained that the therapy would follow the formulation they had made together, and they agreed the following aims:

1   To help decrease Jim's worry by increasing *tolerance* of uncertainty, re-evaluating the usefulness of worry, and enhancing problem-solving ability.
2   To reduce depressive symptoms by problem-solving difficulties with interpersonal relationships and increasing activities likely to improve Jim's mood.

Jim identified specific goals, including the following:

- Reducing stress and anger with his daughter around her lack of studying by letting go of worries about this.
- Making decisions more easily, reducing stress levels so that he could enjoy his retirement more.
- In the longer term finding greater acceptance of his health problems and changed professional identity and status.

Intervention

Decreasing Jim's worry

Theresa introduced various cognitive and behavioural methods to target each of the main maintenance factors from the formulation:

- *Using exposure to increase tolerance of uncertainty:* Jim and Theresa made a list of situations he was facing involving uncertainty, especially those requiring a decision, and their potential to trigger worry bouts was related to the formulation.

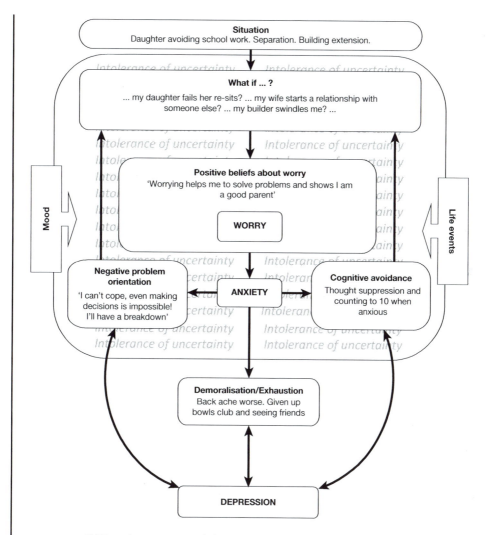

FIGURE 7.1 GAD maintenance model

Source: Based on Dugas and Robichaud (2007).

For example, Jim was worrying about building a house extension, becoming increasingly anxious as he tried to choose between various designs and builders. He imagined cowboy builders swindling him and leaving a crumbling wreck. 'Fortune-telling/catastrophisation' and 'magnification/minimisation' cognitive distortions trapped him in a never-ending chain of 'what-ifs' which paralysed his decision-making ability. He was encouraged to face the uncertainty of whether his chosen builder would be perfect by dropping his usual safety behaviour of over-planning and instead make a timely decision. The builder was chosen and the work completed, not perfectly but adequately.

Jim learned that he could tolerate the uncertainty and tension, and that, even when things do not turn out perfectly, he could cope.

- *Cognitively restructuring beliefs about worry being helpful:* Theresa asked Jim to think of his 'positive' beliefs about worry when they were discussing his concerns about his daughter's lack of studying. Theresa and Jim explored the effect of Jim's worry upon his relationship with his daughter. Jim realised that worry had led him to become over-controlling, much as his father had been with him. Rather than work harder as Jim had done as a boy, his daughter had become defiant and less studious. Jim finally accepted that he could not 'make' his daughter work, and that it was indeed uncertain whether she would pass her resits. Jim started to 'let go' a little of his worries and instead focused more on engaging in fun activities with her. Thus, Jim was able to re-evaluate the usefulness of his beliefs that worrying assists problem solving and demonstrates good parenting.
- *Helping Jim to have a more positive orientation to problem solving:* Theresa and Jim discussed the difference between hypothetical problems ('what if . . .') and real current problems. Real current problems demanded a problem-solving approach whereas hypothetical worries required an acceptance-based approach. In order to raise his awareness of these two types of worries Jim agreed to complete a worry diary for homework. Theresa then introduced Jim to a structured method of problem solving for real current problems, and acceptance-based techniques for hypothetical worries.
- *Using exposure to address cognitive avoidance:* Several sessions into the therapy, Jim told Theresa that he had been avoiding anxious and painful feelings by trying to think about other things (thought suppression) and counting to ten to distract himself (a safety behaviour). He feared that not doing these things would eventually lead to a breakdown. Theresa asked Jim to picture the scene he dreaded most: his wife walking along hand in hand with another man. While doing this 'imaginal exposure' he was invited to drop his safety behaviours, and instead allow himself to feel and think whatever came to mind. Jim became initially very upset, but as he emotionally processed and habituated to these core fears he gradually calmed down.

These interventions collectively helped Jim realise that his anxious thinking styles had distorted reality: exaggerating threats and underestimating his coping ability.

Decreasing Jim's depression

- *Challenging cognitive distortions and behavioural avoidance:* As treatment progressed and Jim's anxiety reduced, there was an increasing emphasis on overcoming depression and identifying his interpersonal needs. His wife's departure had triggered painful beliefs about worthlessness. These beliefs were identified and then re-examined, allowing him to arrive at a more balanced view. Planning pleasurable activities like visiting friends, and re-engaging in gentle physical exercise like playing bowls, helped Jim manage his low mood.

Towards the end of therapy a relapse prevention plan was collaboratively constructed. Triggers and early warning signs of relapse for worry and low mood were identified and an action plan was outlined.

Outcome

Jim made good progress in reducing his worry and depression, as his scores on questionnaire measures testified. His emotional resilience and perception of coping skills increased. Jim's belief in the usefulness of worry decreased and he was more confident in solving problems in more effective ways. His greatest worry had been that if his wife started a relationship with another man, he would break down into severe depression. Towards the end of therapy he discovered that she had indeed started a new relationship. Instead of having a breakdown, he was understandably upset but found he was able to cope.

Jim's relationship with his daughter improved as he ceased to allow worries about her studying to dominate. Jim started meeting up with friends and engaging in sport once more. He began to enjoy his retirement, and achieved greater peace and acceptance over his changed health and professional status.

TEAM WORKING/INDIRECT WORK

Clients with problems like Jim's are generally seen in settings where most of the work is direct and conducted by a single professional (clinical psychologist or psychological therapist) at any one time. However, with severe and enduring anxiety disorders (e.g. if house-bound or self-neglecting) or where there are significant co-morbid mental health difficulties, such as psychosis, personality disorder or severe depression, a multi-disciplinary team approach is likely to be helpful. The work of clinical psychologists in these multi-disciplinary settings tends to include a range of indirect work, such as the following:

- *Supervision of multi-professional colleagues:* For example, a psychologist may be seeing a client with severe agoraphobia for CBT, but also supervising a support worker who visits the client in the community, providing practical assistance with completing exposure tasks, such as travelling on public transport.
- *Providing in-house training to non-psychologist colleagues:* This could, for example, cover the use of manualised psychological interventions, such as psycho-educational anxiety management groups.

CRITICAL ISSUES

Low- and high-intensity treatments

There has been much interest in 'low-intensity' interventions for anxiety disorders and depression. These tend to be based on very brief contact with practitioners who are not trained as therapists but who support the use of online or paper-based self-help materials (Clark *et al.*, 2009). These therapies are distinguished from 'high-intensity' CBT or other psychological therapies. Some low-intensity therapies have been found to be just as effective as their high-intensity equivalents. For example, an internet-delivered cognitive therapy for social anxiety disorder succeeded in achieving comparable results to face-to-face therapy in one-fifth of the time (Stott *et al.*, 2013). Low-intensity treatments are of interest because they can allow greater numbers of people to be treated for the same cost, and have shown some promising results compared to no-therapy control groups. However, in most cases it is not known how the effectiveness of low-intensity and high-intensity treatments compare. The 'high-intensity' individual therapy format therefore remains the treatment of choice for most people with more persistent anxiety disorders.

Trans-diagnostic treatments

Specific CBT treatments have been developed to tackle certain maintaining factors for each of the main anxiety disorders, resulting in a number of distinct treatments for different disorders. Each one has been evaluated and therapists are trained to deliver it. However, having lots of different specialist treatments presents some problems. First, it is very common to have more than one type of problem and the specific treatments are less clear about how this should be tackled. Second, it means that therapists need to learn and stay skilled at many different forms of treatment, which can be difficult if they are only using each one infrequently. There is growing interest in 'trans-diagnostic' treatments for anxiety or mood disorders, which may help to tackle these issues. Trans-diagnostic approaches are based on a set of modules of therapy, each designed to tackle a problem that occurs across several different conditions (e.g. avoidance). Modules may then be chosen and joined together to tailor the therapy to individual need (e.g. Barlow *et al.*, 2010). There are some promising early results, but the effectiveness of trans-diagnostic treatments is still relatively unknown (Farchione *et al.*, 2012).

MILLIE'S STORY: THE CONCLUSION

I went to Occupational Health at the hospital and was referred to a clinical psychologist for ten sessions of cognitive-behavioural therapy. During our sessions we discussed situations that arose regularly for me and came up with ways of overcoming them. We set goals, sometimes pushing me to do things I never believed possible. I actually spoke to the OCD in my head, telling it to leave me alone. I had to stop myself wetting my fingers, which sometimes seemed almost impossible. I knew I was winning when I made myself touch my fingers on the floor and not wipe them. It felt good. My psychologist taught me that I was allowed to be in control. I do have days when it controls me but they don't last. On these days I remember those sessions, think what we did at the time and get back on track.

KEY CONCEPTS AND TERMS

- Post-traumatic stress disorder
- Panic disorder
- Agoraphobia
- Specific phobia
- Obsessive compulsive disorder

- Generalised anxiety disorder
- Social anxiety disorder
- Exposure therapy
- Graded hierarchy
- Worry
- CBT

- Fight-or-flight response
- Classical conditioning
- Operant conditioning
- Eye movement desensitisation and reprocessing

LEARNING OUTCOMES

When you have completed this chapter you should be able to:

1 Know what features or symptoms are characteristic of the anxiety disorders.
2 Understand the psychological impact of the anxiety disorders.
3 Understand the psychological theories or models that are relevant to the anxiety disorders.
4 Understand the treatment approaches used by clinical psychologists, and the evidence base for these approaches.
5 Understand how assessment, formulation, intervention and evaluation may be used by a psychologist working on a specific case.

SAMPLE ESSAY TITLES

- What are the key maintaining factors across anxiety disorders and what strategies are helpful in their treatment?
- Describe the main theories of how anxiety disorders develop. What are their relative strengths and limitations?
- Describe the phenomenology, aetiology and epidemiology of two common anxiety disorders.
- How can psychologists work individually and in teams to help people with anxiety disorders?

NOTE

1   Blood pressure rises with panic/anxiety. Fainting is associated with low blood pressure. The only anxiety disorder associated with fainting is blood injury phobia when blood pressure drops suddenly.

FURTHER READING

Davey, G.C., Cavanagh, K., Jones, F., Turner, L. and Whittington, A. (2012). *Managing Anxiety with CBT for Dummies.* New York: John Wiley & Sons.

Wells, A. (2013). *Cognitive Therapy of Anxiety Disorders: A practice manual and conceptual guide.* New York: John Wiley & Sons.

REFERENCES

Alonso, J., Angermeyer, M.C., Bernert, S., Bruffaerts, R., Brugha, T.S., Bryson, H. and Vollebergh, W.A.M. (2004). Prevalence of mental disorders in Europe: Results from the European Study of the Epidemiology of Mental Disorders (ESEMeD) project. *Acta Psychiatrica Scandinavica, 109,* 21–27.

Bandura, A. (1977). *Social Learning Theory.* Englewood Cliffs, NJ: Prentice-Hall.

Barlow, D.H. (2002). *Anxiety and its Disorders: The nature and treatment of anxiety and panic (2nd edn).* New York: The Guilford Press.

Barlow, D.H., Farchione, T.J., Fairholme, C.P., Ellard, K.K., Boisseau, C.L., Allen, L.B. and May, J.T.E. (2010). *Unified Protocol for Transdiagnostic Treatment of Emotional Disorders: Therapist Guide (Treatments That Work).* New York: Oxford University Press.

Beck, A.T., Emery, G. and Greenberg, R.L. (1985). *Anxiety Disorders and Phobias: A cognitive perspective.* New York: Basic Books.

Beck, J. (1995). *Cognitive Therapy: Basics and beyond.* New York: The Guilford Press.

Brown, T.A., Campbell, L.A., Lehman, C.L., Grisham, J.R. and Mancill, R.B. (2001). Current and lifetime comorbidity of the DSM-IV anxiety and mood disorders in a large clinical sample. *Journal of Abnormal Psychology, 110*(4), 585–599.

Burns, D.D. (1999). *The Feeling Good Handbook.* New York: Plume.

Clark, D.A. and Beck, A.T. (2010). *Cognitive Therapy of Anxiety Disorders: Science and practice.* New York: The Guilford Press.

Clark, D.M., Layard, R., Smithies, R., Richards, D.A., Suckling, R. and Wright, B. (2009). Improving access to psychological therapy: Initial evaluation of two UK demonstration sites. *Behaviour Research and Therapy, 47*(11), 910–920.

Dugas, M.J. and Robichaud, M. (2007). *Cognitive-behavioral Treatment for Generalized Anxiety Disorder: From science to practice.* New York: Brunner-Routledge.

Farchione, T.J., Fairholme, C.P., Ellard, K.K., Boisseau, C.L., Thompson-Hollands, J., Carl, J.R. and Barlow, D.H. (2012). Unified protocol for transdiagnostic treatment of emotional disorders: A randomized controlled trial. *Behavior Therapy, 43*(3), 666–678.

Foa, E.B., Hembree, E.A. and Rothbaum, B.O. (2007). *Prolonged Exposure Therapy for PTSD: Emotional processing of traumatic experiences (Therapist Guide).* New York: Oxford University Press.

Kessler, R.C., Berglund, P., Demler, O. and Robert, J. (2005a). Lifetime prevalence and age-of-onset distributions of DSM-V disorders in the National Comorbidity Survey replication. *Archives of General Psychiatry, 62*(6), 593–602.

Kessler, R.C., Chiu, W.T., Demler, O. and Walters, E.E. (2005b). Prevalence, severity, and comorbidity of 12-month DSM-IV disorders in the National Comorbidity Survey replication. *Archives of General Psychiatry, 62*(6), 617–627.

Marks, I.M. (1987). *Fears, Phobias, and Rituals: Panic, anxiety, and their disorders.* Oxford: Oxford University Press.

McManus, S., Bebbington, P., Meltzer, H., Brugha, T., Bebbington, P. and Jenkins, R. (2009). *Adult Psychiatric Morbidity in England, 2007: Results of a household survey.* National Centre for Social Research.

Michael, T., Zetsche, U. and Margraf, J. (2007). Epidemiology of anxiety disorders. *Psychiatry, 6*(4), 136–142.

Mowrer, O.H. (1948). Learning theory and the neurotic paradox. *American Journal of Orthopsychiatry, 18*(4), 571–610.

National Institute of Clinical Excellence (NICE) (2004). *Management of Anxiety (Panic Disorder, with or without Agoraphobia, and Generalised Anxiety Disorder) in Adults in Primary, Secondary and Community Care.* London: NICE.

Roth, A. and Fonagy, P. (2005). *What Works for Whom? A critical review of psychotherapy research* (2nd edn). New York: The Guilford Press.

Shapiro, F. (1995). *Eye Movement Desensitization and Reprocessing: Basic principles, protocols, and procedures.* New York: The Guilford Press.

Stott, R., Wild, J., Grey, N., Liness, S., Warnock-Parkes, E., Commins, S. and Clark, D.M. (2013). Internet-delivered cognitive therapy for social anxiety disorder: A development pilot series. *Behavioural and Cognitive Psychotherapy, 41*(4), 383–397.

van den Hout, M.A. and Engelhard, I.M. (2012). How does EMDR work? *Journal of Experimental Psychopathology, 3*(5), 724–738.

Watson, J.B. and Rayner, R. (1920). Conditioned emotional reactions. *Journal of Experimental Psychology, 3*(1), 1.

Yerkes, R.M. and Dodson, J.D. (1908). The relation of strength of stimulus to rapidity of habit formation. *Journal of Comparative Neurology, 18*, 459–482.

8 Working with people with psychosis

Mark Hayward, Sara Meddings and Jo Harris

JO'S STORY

Looking back, I had a lot of factors that contributed to my psychosis. I was a quiet child, lacking in confidence. My parents divorced when I was 8 years old and my father was treated for depression so it seems to run in the family. My father was a disinterested one, reinforcing my feelings of worthlessness.

I found it hard at secondary school to make friends and not having a lot of money meant I was singled out. While it wasn't physical, mainly name calling and being spat at, it reinforced the feeling that I didn't deserve to be here. By now I was hearing 'inside' voices in my head telling me I was useless, shouting words like 'Bitch!' and 'Die!' I was having severe mood swings. I thought about self-harming and became controlling about my food intake. At age 14 I started taking drugs and drinking alcohol. Between 14 and 21 I had a cannabis and cocaine addiction which I overcame. At age 24 I was planning my suicide when my father died. Within three days I was having extreme audio and visual hallucinations such as whispering and people calling my name and seeing deceased people, dead bodies and shadows as well as everyday objects. People also transformed into other people in front of me, leading me to believe they were possessed by the dead. I also heard menacing voices issuing commands. I experienced strange smells, tasting poison in my food and on one occasion felt someone stroking my hair. I thought that my mind was being controlled, that I could communicate with the dead and that, because of this, the government was spying on me and plotting to kill me.

SUMMARY

What is it like to experience the range of distressing experiences that Jo describes in her story? Hearing a voice criticising you and calling you names; believing other people are controlling you; having few friendships; using alcohol and street drugs to control your feelings; and to feel so hopeless about the future that you want to die? These are common experiences of people who struggle with psychosis. We will draw upon our personal, clinical and academic experience to offer insights into how clinical psychologists understand these experiences and work alongside people experiencing psychosis to alleviate distress, build hope and enhance quality of life. We have chosen to focus upon psychotic experiences and associated problems, rather than confine their exploration to any particular diagnosis. However, the value of diagnosis is acknowledged, as is the dominance of the diagnostic category of schizophrenia when considering psychotic experiences.

WHAT ARE THE TYPES OF PSYCHOLOGICAL DIFFICULTIES THAT CAN OCCUR WITH PSYCHOSIS?

People with psychosis make up the largest group of people with serious mental health problems seen by secondary mental health services in the UK National Health Service. Psychosis refers to a range of unusual or frightening experiences often associated with a detachment from reality, such as paranoia or hearing voices. People who experience psychosis face many of the same life and psychological challenges as anyone else. They also have the same range of aspirations – getting a job, having a decent life with friends and family, somewhere to live. Their main psychological challenges may be about how to live a meaningful life with a positive self-identity, while their unusual and frightening experiences continue. They also experience above-average levels of depression, trauma and anxiety, and some people experience significant highs and lows of mood.

The kinds of challenges faced by people with psychosis relate both to the psychosis itself as well as to pre-existing challenges and traumas which may have made the person more vulnerable to the psychosis initially and the psychological and social challenges resulting from and possibly maintaining the psychosis.

Distressing psychotic experiences include the following:

- *Hearing voices, seeing visions, tasting, feeling or smelling things* which other people do not hear, see, taste, feel or smell. These are sometimes described as 'hallucinations' and are experienced as real. For example, Pete heard the voice of a man telling him 'you are dirty – you are worthless' and felt the sensation of insects crawling over his body. Jane heard a voice saying 'Jane is a useless mother, her daughter hates her'. Often these voices seem all-knowing and all-powerful and may relate to a person's previous experiences or to worries they may have. Some people view voices and visions as a spiritual gift – the experiences are more likely to be seen as psychosis when outside of cultural norms and when they are distressing and disabling.
- *Holding strong beliefs* which other people do not share. For example, Pete used to feel paranoid that a researcher was filming him and was going to harm him. John thought that he was a top spy working for MI5. Where such thoughts are about

other people trying to hurt you they are sometimes described as 'paranoid delu-sions', and where they are about being special as 'grandiose delusions'. Delusional beliefs and voice hearing are sometimes described as 'positive symptoms', as they are experiences that are additional to usual functioning – not because they are enjoyable!

- *Cognitive difficulties with thinking or concentrating.* These may include making unusual connections between ideas or talking in ways that other people cannot follow – sometimes referred to as 'thought disorder'. People may also have difficulties with remembering and learning; with being easily distracted; and with executive functioning about planning and problem solving. They may struggle to motivate themselves, withdraw from social activity and feel emotionally flat. Some but not all of these difficulties may be partially attributed to the challenges of coping with the delusional beliefs and voices. For example, Greg hears voices and finds it hard to concentrate – he copes by withdrawing into his bedroom and not going out very much. He easily forgets appointments and so likes someone to text him to remind him. These difficulties are sometimes described as negative symptoms, as they represent a loss of usual functioning.

- *Psychological difficulties.* Stresses and challenges in life such as abuse and trauma increase vulnerability to psychosis or may lead to psychosis. Making sense of and dealing with these challenges aids recovery from the psychosis itself. Depression, trauma, social anxiety, insomnia, low self-esteem and social withdrawal may result from life challenges or from the psychosis. Often they precede and exacerbate the psychosis in a vicious maintaining cycle. Psychosis is also associated with a number of losses, including loss of your idea about who you are, loss of meaning in life, loss of control (often exacerbated by stigma and disempowering effects of services), and loss of hope for the future. Parallel losses may also be experienced by the person's relatives. People often need to grieve for and work on acceptance of these losses as part of moving on in order to take back control and find hope.

- *Social and practical difficulties.* People with psychosis may be more likely than other groups of people to have small social networks and be unemployed – both because of the psychotic symptoms themselves and also pre-existing social anxiety which may be exacerbated after diagnosis by reduced expectations and workplace discrimination.

- *Physical health problems.* People with psychosis also experience increased physical health problems such as diabetes and have a life expectancy of 15 years less than the general population.

- *Safety issues.* Issues of safety are also a challenge for people with psychosis and those around them. People with psychosis are *not* at a higher risk than the general population of committing violence against other people, contrary to popular perceptions often conveyed in the media. However, people with psychosis are more likely than others to be victims of violence. They are also more likely than others to kill themselves – suicide is especially related to being unemployed, concurrent physical health problems, feelings of hopelessness and the availability of methods of suicide.

For further reading about the issues discussed in this section see the British Psychological Society (2014) and Repper and Perkins (2003).

DIAGNOSIS

Psychosis is associated with a number of diagnoses which have historically been grouped together and differentiated from mood disorders. Psychotic experiences are a key feature of a number of diagnoses within DSM-V (APA, 2013), including the following:

- Schizophrenia – characterised by significant distortions of thinking and perception, and inappropriate or blunted emotions.
- Schizoaffective disorder – characterised by prominent psychotic experiences and less prominent disturbance of mood, and for which a diagnosis of schizophrenia or a mood disorder is not justified.
- Bipolar affective disorder – characterised by significant disturbance of affect and activity levels. Episodes of elevated mood and increased energy and activity occur intermittently, as do contrasting episodes of low mood and decreased energy and activity.
- Severe depression with psychotic symptoms – characterised by lowering of mood, reduced self-esteem, ideas of worthlessness or guilt, and delusions and hallucinations.

Note: Schizophrenia and schizoaffective disorder are part of a broader classification of schizophrenia spectrum disorders. Psychosis with organic origins is seen as separate from the above categories.

This chapter focuses on psychotic experiences rather than on the diagnostic groups or the mood difficulties that often go with psychosis (especially with psychotic depression, bipolar affective disorder, schizoaffective disorder and severe depression). The scientific validity of separable diagnoses has been questioned (Bentall, 2003) on a number of grounds:

- The symptoms may be understood in the context of life challenges not requiring a disease explanation and which are seen on a continuum.
- There is no common aetiology for a specific diagnosis and overlap between different ones.
- There is no evidence of specific genetic disease markers.
- Clinically there is often disagreement between clinicians about an individual's diagnosis.

It may therefore be preferable to focus on the symptoms, behaviours and experiences which people have rather than broad classifications. Effective treatments seem to relate to these or to the broader spectrum of psychosis as a whole and not to specific diagnostic groups. Nevertheless, diagnosis can be a useful shorthand, and some of the research we cite in this chapter relates to specific diagnostic categories.

EPIDEMIOLOGY

About 1 per cent (0.5 to 2%) of the general population will be diagnosed with schizophrenia spectrum or bipolar disorders at any time and the lifetime prevalence for psychosis is 3 per cent (van Os *et al*, 2009; Schizophrenia Commission, 2012; NICE, 2014). Rates are similar worldwide. However, there is a continuum of experience: about 15 per cent of the general population sometimes hear voices (Tien, 1991), and 15 to 20 per cent have regular paranoid thoughts (Freeman and Garety, 2006). Psychosis can develop at any age, but most commonly starts in adolescence and young adulthood.

AETIOLOGY

Biological, psychological, social and environmental factors all contribute to vulnerability towards and resilience against the onset and maintenance of psychosis. One way of understanding how these factors interrelate is through a stress vulnerability model (Zubin and Spring, 1977). Early life experiences, current environment and biological factors can make people more vulnerable to psychosis when faced with stresses. People who are particularly vulnerable for any of these reasons may experience psychosis after a relatively minor stress (point 'c' in Figure 8.1). Even the most resilient of people

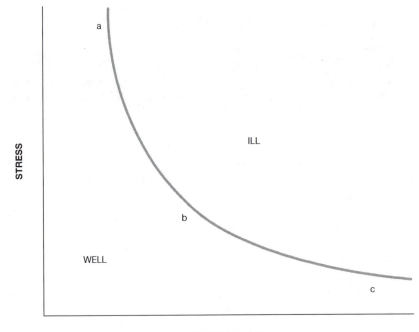

FIGURE 8.1 The stress–vulnerability model of mental illness and well-being

Source: From Zubin and Spring (1977). Copyright © American Psychological Association.

could experience psychosis if subjected to the highest levels of stress (point 'a' in Figure 8.1) (see Kingdon and Turkington (1994) for a review of the associations between stress and 'normal' circumstances in which psychotic experiences may occur).

Biological factors

Neuro-chemical imbalances in the brain increase the likelihood of someone developing psychosis. This is most notable in terms of the impact of cannabis use which can be predictive of psychosis for some people – particularly if they have a predisposing vulnerability (Henquet et al., 2004). Brain studies show that neuro-transmitters such as dopamine seem to act differently in people with psychosis. Medication which targets such chemical pathways does lead to improvement for some people. In recent years there has been significant criticism of earlier twin and adoption studies of the genetic basis of psychosis. Nevertheless, there does seem to be a genetic component which may make some people more vulnerable to experiencing psychosis (see Bentall (2003) for a review of the debates about biological factors).

Psychological factors

Self-esteem

Low self-esteem (feelings of limited worth and value) may play a causal and maintaining role in a range of mental health problems, including psychotic experiences (Garety et al., 2001). This cognitive vulnerability is characterised by negative beliefs about who one is as a person (e.g. 'I am weak/stupid/unlovable'). These beliefs seem true, generate high levels of emotional distress and are often long-standing due to their roots in early experiences of social adversity and trauma. Low self-esteem may also be a product of an individual's experience of psychosis and its negative social context, including hospitalisation and exposure to prejudice.

Information processing

Biases in information processing also play a key role in the maintenance of psychotic experiences – particularly paranoid beliefs.

People with paranoid beliefs have a 'jumping to conclusions' reasoning style that leads them to make quick decisions based on limited information (Garety and Freeman, 1999). This makes sense in relation to our survival instinct. If I am in a situation where I feel suspicious and unsafe, it is logical for me to make a quick decision about the intentions of other people if someone behaves towards me in a way that could be interpreted as threatening. Of course, I could be wrong about those intentions – but if I am right I get a chance to escape. The fact that I *feel* threatened when entering a situation may lead me to conclude that I am under threat – 'emotional reasoning'. But these feelings are likely to result from my expectations which set up a vicious cycle.

Within this scenario the confirmatory bias is also likely to play a role - environmental information that is consistent with and confirms existing beliefs is noticed preferentially, whereas disconfirmatory information is filtered out and essentially ignored. In the scenario described above, I will be hyper-vigilant for and notice the (possibly) threatening behaviour of others, but will pay little or no attention to the behaviour of people which suggests otherwise.

Social and environmental factors

The majority of people who come into contact with mental health services due to psychosis have experienced some form of abuse or trauma in childhood or adolescence. Sixty-nine per cent of women and 59 per cent of men with psychosis have been physically or sexually abused as children and over half as adults (Read *et al.*, 2005).

People with psychosis have typically experienced higher than average levels of childhood social deprivation, social isolation and other forms of social exclusion (Bentall *et al.*, 2012). Unemployment, poverty in adulthood and inequality and relative deprivation also make people more vulnerable to psychosis. Recovery rates are better during periods of full employment than of economic recession and in developing countries than in industrialised ones (Warner, 1994), perhaps due to closer family cohesion, work opportunities and social inclusion. Being valued by others, having control over one's own life, and work, family and community relationships are important (Tew *et al.*, 2012).

The above review of aetiology suggests that a full understanding of the variables that may influence the cause and maintenance of psychosis needs to embrace a holistic biological, psychological and social approach – a *bio-psychosocial* approach. The formulation shown in Figure 8.2 uses a bio-psychosocial approach to understand Jo's experiences.

PROGNOSIS

About half of people who have psychosis and might be diagnosed with schizophrenia spectrum disorder have only one episode and then recover completely. About a quarter have ongoing symptoms and a quarter have a fluctuating condition with periods of wellness and illness.

However, prognosis may be considered in a broader sense, not just in terms of symptoms. People with psychosis have a wide variety of needs and priorities for recovery. They may want to focus upon reducing symptoms, or upon improving relationships, confidence or getting a job. Therefore practitioners need to focus upon those outcomes which an individual sees as important – their personal goals. 'Recovery is about building a meaningful and satisfying life, as defined by the person themselves, whether or not there are ongoing or recurring symptoms or problems' (Shepherd *et al.*, 2008). Many people with psychosis live full and meaningful lives.

USE OF THEORY AND EVIDENCE IN PSYCHOLOGICAL PRACTICE

There is evidence for the efficacy of cognitive-behavioural therapy and family interventions for psychosis as well as anti-psychotic medication and employment interventions – all are recommended by the National Institute of Health and Clinical Excellence (NICE, 2014).

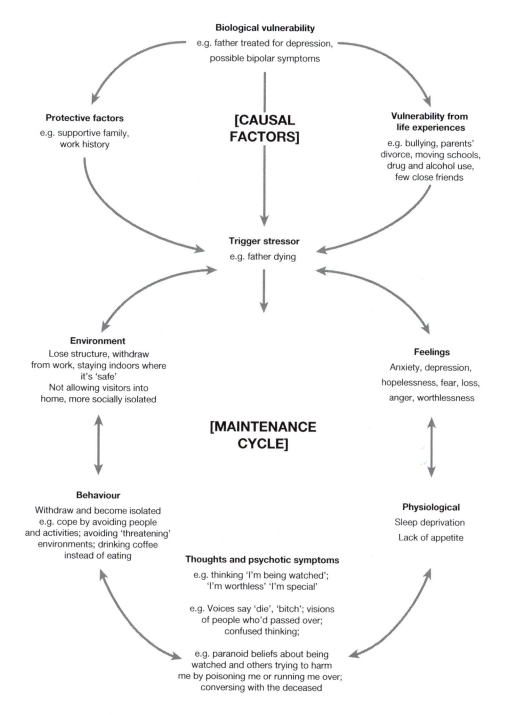

Biological vulnerability
e.g. father treated for depression,
possible bipolar symptoms

Protective factors
e.g. supportive family,
work history

**[CAUSAL
FACTORS]**

**Vulnerability from
life experiences**

e.g. bullying, parents'
divorce, moving schools,
drug and alcohol use,
few close friends

Trigger stressor
e.g. father dying

Environment
Lose structure, withdraw
from work, staying indoors where
it's 'safe'
Not allowing visitors into
home, more socially isolated

Feelings
Anxiety, depression,
hopelessness, fear, loss,
anger, worthlessness

**[MAINTENANCE
CYCLE]**

Behaviour
Withdraw and become isolated
e.g. cope by avoiding people
and activities; avoiding 'threatening'
environments; drinking coffee
instead of eating

Physiological
Sleep deprivation
Lack of appetite

Thoughts and psychotic symptoms
e.g. thinking 'I'm being watched';
'I'm worthless' 'I'm special'

e.g. Voices say 'die', 'bitch'; visions
of people who'd passed over;
confused thinking;

e.g. paranoid beliefs about being
watched and others trying to harm
me by poisoning me or running me over;
conversing with the deceased

FIGURE 8.2 Jo's formulation

Source: Adapted from Beckian longitudinal CBT formulation discussed in Chadwick (2006); systemic
formulating discussed in Meddings *et al.* (2010); and Lake's team formulation (2008).

Cognitive-behavioural therapy for psychosis (CBTp)

CBTp focuses primarily upon positive symptoms (voice hearing and delusional beliefs). Its basic premise is that the beliefs a person develops about themselves (I am worthless or I am very special and important), other people (they can't be trusted and want to harm me) and voices (have great power and know everything) may not be totally accurate. These beliefs represent 'best guesses', but may be inaccurate due to the biases in information processing that are common to everyone. CBT helps people make sense of psychotic experiences and thoughts in the light of their life experience, and how these experiences impact upon their lives.

During CBTp the therapist will encourage the client to review the evidence for and against a particular belief. For example, if the client believes the voices they hear are all powerful and can make bad things happen, evidence will be reviewed that supports and does not support this belief. If there are times when the voice has said bad things will happen but they have not happened, the therapist will help the client reflect upon the meaning of such a contradiction. The client may realise that although the thoughts had previously been a helpful adaptation to life's challenges they may no longer be helpful or accurate in the current context – they start to question the belief and what the voice says, and the therapist and client may together identify an alternative belief; for example, that voices don't always tell the truth. Evidence for this alternative belief may then be gathered and its accuracy assessed (for a step-by-step guide to these interventions see Hayward *et al.* (2012; voices hearing), and Freeman *et al.* (2006; paranoid beliefs).

Throughout CBTp the therapist and client work together to test the accuracy of strongly held beliefs. This is called 'collaborative empiricism'. The therapist is not trying to persuade the client to revise or give up their beliefs. Rather, the therapist is enabling the client to disengage from biases in information processing that restrict the range of information available, and to consider a wider array of information before making decisions. At the end of this process the client may decide that their strongly held (delusional) belief fits accurately with the evidence, or they may decide that an alternative explanation has some credibility.

Family interventions for psychosis

About half of those people who experience serious mental health problems live with family or friends. For those living independently, family, friends and house mates remain important. Living with someone with psychosis is a multi-faceted experience – people with psychosis contribute positively to such relationships (Coldwell *et al.*, 2010); yet it can also be stressful and feel burdensome (Fadden, 1998). People who have supportive relationships do better than those who have less support, or more stressful, critical or over-protective ones (Kavanagh, 1992). It is vital that mental health services offer information and support to friends and family as well as to the person experiencing psychosis.

There is long-established evidence for the effectiveness of family interventions for psychosis, especially schizophrenia spectrum disorders (Burbach, 1996; Fadden, 1998). Family intervention meetings focus on improving relationships and reducing any perceived criticism or hostility; developing a shared understanding of the psychosis, how it affects everyone, and that the problems are not anyone's fault; developing coping strategies and ways of dealing with practical challenges; coping with life–cycle issues such as losses or people leaving home; separating the problems from the person and separating each member of the family so that they can live their own lives; appreciating each other's strengths; and exploring 'vicious circles' that may be keeping problems going. For example, Ben copes with voices which persecute him and his mother by withdrawing to his room and shouting at them. His mother finds this stressful as she has heard that it is better for him to remain active, so she tries to cajole him but he experiences this as criticism and this makes the voices worse. The family intervention may help them make sense of this and to appreciate how each of them is trying to do their best for the other; how Ben is trying to protect his mother and how she is trying to do what the clinical team have suggested. For further reading and case examples, see Meddings *et al.* (2010) or Burbach *et al.* (2007).

CASE EXAMPLE[1]

This case example provides an overview of one kind of psychological intervention – group person-based cognitive therapy (PBCT) for people who hear distressing voices (see Focus 8.1 for a brief description of PBCT), and follows the progress of one particular client through a group process.

Group PBCT was offered to eight people who heard distressing voices over 12 90-minute sessions. The group was facilitated by two clinical psychologists. Jessica was referred to the group by a member of the clinical team that cared for her. She heard voices which told her to harm herself and made critical and abusive comments. Jessica responded by cutting her arms and trying to hide from the voices. She rarely left her home and felt very anxious about attending the group.

FOCUS 8.1

Acceptance, mindfulness and psychotic experiences

Mindfulness is increasingly being used with positive effect across a range of health conditions. Mindfulness is an approach based on practising a particular form of non-judgemental attention to present moment experiences, drawn originally from methods in Buddhist meditation. Brief mindfulness practices are being used within therapies that encourage people to accept their psychotic experiences rather than battle against them, and focus instead upon valued activities and goals. Person-based cognitive therapy (PBCT) is one such approach, building on the strengths of CBTp by combining cognitive and behavioural approaches with brief mindfulness practices. PBCT can be syndrome (psychosis) or symptom (delusional beliefs or distressing voices) focused (Chadwick, 2006).

Description of therapy through its phases

Mindfulness practices (every session)

One of the therapists led the ten-minute mindfulness practice and verbally guided members through a 'body scan' (scanning the body from head to toe, paying attention to what is happening in each part) and a focus upon the breath (paying attention to the in-and-out breath without trying to change it in any way). The guidance included instruction to bring awareness to the full range of cognitive and emotional experience – thoughts, feelings, voices, images – and invited group members to notice their minds wandering and bring their attention back to the breath if they wished to do so. In this respect, noticing was emphasised as the first part of a two-part process – and one that created a choice about whether to allow oneself to be caught up in an internal (voice-hearing) experience, or to bring attention back to the breath. This conceptualisation encouraged group members to exercise agency and make their own decisions about how to relate to voices.

Group members engaged well with the practices from the outset, and readily accepted the central role of mindfulness within the therapy. The initial practices offered a novel experience to Jessica and she became concerned about not practising 'properly' or 'not getting it'. These concerns were reflected upon during the sessions and normalised. Jessica's voices were often active during practices and she was invited to describe the process of noticing voices and her subsequent response. On some occasions Jessica was able to focus her attention on her breathing during the mindfulness practice and she noticed her voices fading into the background. This was accompanied by feelings of calm and peacefulness.

ABC model (sessions 2 to 3)

During sessions 2 and 3, there was a focus upon collaborative discussion of feelings and behaviours that are commonly associated with hearing voices, including the impact of beliefs about voices and beliefs about self. This was discussed using the ABC model. An example is given in Table 8.1.

Subsequent discussion then focused upon how different beliefs and thoughts about the same experience (i.e. hearing a voice) could result in different consequences. This was again formulated using the ABC model and an example is given in Table 8.2.

TABLE 8.1 *The ABC model: an example*

Activating event A	Beliefs and thoughts B	Consequences C
Voice comments	Beliefs about voices	Feelings
'You are a bad mother, if you go out I will hurt your daughter'	'Voices are powerful' 'Voices have control'	Anxious Low in mood
	Beliefs about me	Behaviour
	'I have no control' 'I am weak' 'I am bad'	Stop doing the things I want to do

TABLE 8.2 The ABC model: an example

Activating event A	Beliefs and thoughts B	Consequences C
Voice comments	Beliefs about voices	Feelings
'You are a bad mother, if you go out I will hurt your daughter'	'Voices are lying again' 'Voices don't have total control'	Proud of myself Enjoyment
	Beliefs about me	Behaviour
	'I am strong' 'I have some control'	Go to work Spend time with friends Read a good book

As members began to talk about their voice-hearing experiences the sense of universality (I'm not the only person who hears voices) became apparent. This is a common and powerful experience in groups and was particularly striking for Jessica who had only ever spoken to mental health workers about her voices.

Personal control (sessions 4 to 6)

The focus during sessions 4 to 6 was upon collaborative discussion of the belief that voices have control over us. Discussions sought to assess the accuracy of this belief, using questions such as:

1   What is the evidence that the voices have control over us?
2   Is there any evidence that the voices do *not* have control over us (Table 8.3)?

All the evidence gathered was reviewed and group members were asked to reflect on what this evidence said about themselves and the voices. Members were particularly struck by Jessica's courage as she resisted voice commands to cut herself. Through collaborative reviewing of the evidence, participants developed the insight that they had some personal control, even when voices were around. This was subsequently

TABLE 8.3 'Voices have control over us'

Evidence supporting this idea	Evidence not supporting this idea
Last week voices told me to harm myself and I cut my arms.	Yesterday voices told me to cut myself and I refused to obey them.
Voices told me not to ring my friend last night and I didn't.	Voices made threats that something bad would happen if I went out on Tuesday but I went out anyway and nothing bad happened.
Voices told me I was stupid and should stop reading my book, and I stopped reading it.	Voices told me that my friend didn't like me and not to bother calling them, but I picked up the phone and called them. They seemed really pleased to hear from me and we met up for a coffee.

TABLE 8.4 The ABC framework: an example

Antecedent event A	Beliefs and thoughts B	Consequences C
Voices are around and tell me to cut myself.	'I have some personal control even when the voices are around.'	*Feelings* Pride, enjoyment. *Behaviours* Don't cut. Go out. See friends. Do things I enjoy.
Voices are around and tell me to cut myself.	'Voices have control over me.'	*Feelings* Anxious, depressed, angry. *Behaviours* Cut myself. Stay at home. Avoid seeing people. Hide in bed.

used to examine the difference between believing that voices had total control, and believing that members themselves had some control, which was again illustrated using the ABC framework (Table 8.4).

Members were guided to consider how their day-to-day lives might be different if they began to believe they had some personal control, and acted in accordance with this belief. Individuals were encouraged to plan enjoyable activities to do outside of the therapy (e.g. going to the shops, seeing friends) which supported the belief that they had some personal control even when the voices were around. Jessica chose not to hide from the voices by staying in bed, and would try to go out and see friends instead.

Positive self-beliefs (sessions 7 to 10)

Sessions 7 to 10 focused upon individuals' views of themselves. Members were introduced to some of the cognitive biases that can maintain negative self-beliefs (described in the aetiology section above), and were encouraged to notice, and reflect upon, examples based on their own experiences. Jessica recalled the way her parents neglected her and criticised her whatever she did – leaving her feeling like a worthless failure.

Members were also encouraged to recollect positive beliefs about themselves, or times when they had felt okay about themselves. This was very difficult for members, as their views of themselves were dominated by negative self-beliefs. Consequently, when asking members to reflect upon times when they felt okay about themselves, it was helpful to ask:

- What was happening? (e.g. helping a friend with something)
- How did you feel? (e.g. feeling proud)
- What did this experience mean about you as a person? (e.g. 'I am a good person', 'I am valued', 'I am helpful').

This facilitated the development of, and reflection on, positive experiences of self. Jessica spoke of the care that she was able to provide for her partner and children, and how much they appreciated this. In addition, mindfulness was used to bring full awareness to positive experiences, even though such experiences were perceived to be infrequent. This process became easier and more fluid as members gained experience of noticing positive experiences of self. When Jessica reflected on a positive experience of herself, there was a sense of her visually growing in stature and confidence – sitting upright, smiling and seeming 'bigger'. These changes were highlighted to the group and reflected back to Jessica.

Looking back and forward (session 11 to 12)

During the final two sessions, individuals were invited to discuss what they each learned from therapy and what they planned to take forward into their daily lives. Jessica spoke of trying to do the following:

- Practise mindfulness every day or as often as seems helpful.
- Remind myself of the evidence from my own life that I sometimes have control even when voices are around.
- Do what I want to do and not what the voices tell me to do.
- Regularly remember a positive experience when I felt okay about myself as a person.

At the end of the group Jessica still heard voices that told her what to do and criticised her. She still cut herself occasionally and tried to hide from the voices by going to bed. However, these instances occurred less frequently as Jessica believed she had some control and was able to resist the commands of the voices when she felt strong enough. This personal control helped Jessica feel okay about herself and she was able to notice and reflect upon experiences that were positive. Jessica was able to leave the house occasionally and enjoyed spending time with friends whom she had not seen for a long time.

TEAM WORKING

Most people with psychosis who need to access mental health services are seen by multi-disciplinary teams. Outcomes are better when professionals work together in such teams. Jo worked with a community psychiatric nurse (CPN) in an Early Intervention in Psychosis Team. She coordinated Jo's care, arranged for her to see a psychiatrist who prescribed medication and referred her to a support group. It was she who realised that Jo had been experiencing bipolar affective disorder for a while and that her dad dying had triggered this episode. The team psychologist met with the CPN and the rest of the team and helped them develop a formulation about how to make sense of what was going on for Jo and what might help (see Figure 8.2). The psychologist also consulted with the CPN working with Jo about how she could use psychological approaches in their weekly meetings.

After about a year, Jo met with peer support workers who used their personal experience of mental health problems to help others with similar difficulties. She saw a vocational specialist who helped her to decide to get a job in mental health – she helped with job search, put her in touch with other peer support workers and helped her write her CV. Work gave Jo a sense of purpose, structured her time and kept her updated on different ways of keeping well.

Modern medication and meaningful work are as effective as CBTp and family interventions in improving recovery with psychosis. Evidence is growing about how working with a peer who has personal experience of psychosis is also effective, improving empowerment, confidence and self-esteem and reducing time spent in hospital (Schizophrenia Commission, 2012). Jo now works as a peer trainer with Sussex Recovery College and as a peer support worker. Peer support workers help people identify and follow their own goals, sometimes using psychological and recovery-oriented techniques. For example Jo recently supported someone to achieve their goal of going to London through problem-solving, grading activity whereby they started with a short train journey, and keeping a diary of achievement. She helped them develop a personal recovery plan to monitor their wellness and take actions to stay well. She finds the Recovery College a good setting to experience the equality of clinicians working with peers to co-produce and co-deliver trainings about mental health to people with mental health challenges, their relatives and friends and other staff.

CRITICAL ISSUES

Research is currently being undertaken to try to enhance the effectiveness of CBTp. A further body of research relates to the availability of CBTp, as it is currently offered to only a minority of people with psychosis (APPGMH, 2010). In response to the need to enhance effectiveness and availability, a number of psychological interventions are being developed that may be beneficial for and made available to a broader range of clients. Many of these interventions have the following elements in common:

- *Positive beliefs about the self*: CBTp has tended to emphasise the need to address negative beliefs about the self. Therapies for people hearing distressing voices have recently focused not upon negative self-beliefs but upon the enhancement of positive beliefs about the self (see case study for an illustration of this approach). This work focuses upon the re-enactment of times when the client has achieved something and felt good about themselves (Dannahy *et al.*, 2011; Van der Gaag *et al.*, 2012). The aim is to strengthen positive beliefs about the self and to achieve a more balanced view of self as sometimes negative and sometimes positive.
- *Acceptance and mindfulness*: Therapies are increasingly focusing on finding ways to live satisfying and fulfilling lives in spite of psychotic experiences, rather than necessarily aiming to remove these experiences. Therapies that include mindfulness meditation such as PBCT (described in the case study) target acceptance in this way. Acceptance and commitment therapy (ACT; Morris *et al.*, 2013) is another increasingly popular therapy that uses a range of techniques (including mindfulness) to help clients accept their psychotic experiences and invest energy in alternative valued behaviours and activities.

- *What needs to change?* CBTp has typically focused upon delusional beliefs and voice-hearing experiences in order to reduce associated emotional distress. Innovative approaches are currently exploring the impact of focusing upon other problems that are experienced by people with psychosis, rather than focusing upon the psychotic experiences themselves. Daniel Freeman advocates an interventionist–causal model approach, which focuses upon one putative causal factor at a time (e.g. worry and sleep problems – see Focus 8.2), showing that an intervention can change it, and examining the subsequent effects on the delusional beliefs (Freeman, 2011). Other interventions being developed focus upon the prevention of social disability (e.g. Fowler *et al.*, 2013) and the enhancement of interpersonal relating (e.g. Hayward *et al.*, 2011).

CONCLUSION TO JO'S STORY

Since being diagnosed and getting the right medication and treatment I feel my life has turned around. My personal relationships have improved and I am now engaged to marry my partner who supported me through the psychosis. Working in mental health services gives me a sense of purpose and constantly reminds me how strong people can be and how much easier it is to get well when you feel supported.

Talking through my experience with professionals has helped me greatly as well as attending support groups, practising mindfulness and listening to others' stories. I have a recovery plan so that I make sure I eat properly, get enough sleep and avoid too much stress. I no longer suffer psychotic symptoms and using the different techniques I have learned over the last few years such as CBT, I no longer need to take medication.

FOCUS 8.2

Worry and sleep

A recent theme within the psychosis literature has been to identify key non-psychosis symptoms associated with emotional distress and to target these symptoms in treatment. Freeman and colleagues have highlighted this approach in their work on worry and sleep difficulties in people with persecutory delusions. By placing the focus of treatment on these everyday issues and utilising basic treatment strategies from the anxiety and sleep literature, a 'normalising' framework is adopted from the outset that promotes engagement and motivation. There is emerging evidence that brief high-volume interventions targeting worry and sleep not only lead to improvements in worry and sleep but also in paranoia. These brief interventions for worry and sleep have the potential to address the limited availability of psychological interventions for people experiencing psychosis. Due to their simplicity, the interventions may be delivered to individuals or groups/courses by a broad range of mental health professionals following a short period of training.

KEY CONCEPTS AND TERMS

- Hearing voices
- Delusional beliefs
- Trauma
- Stress-vulnerability
- Self-esteem
- Information processing
- Bio-psychosocial approach
- Formulation
- Cognitive-behavioural therapy
- Family interventions
- Mindfulness
- Recovery

LEARNING OUTCOMES

When you have completed this chapter you should be able to:

1. Know what features or symptoms are characteristic of psychosis and have an awareness of the types of psychological difficulties suffered by people experiencing psychosis.
2. Have an understanding of the psychological and societal impact of psychosis.
3. Have an understanding of the psychological theories or models that are relevant to psychotic experiences.
4. Have an understanding of the approaches used by clinical psychologists to treat psychotic experiences – and the evidence base for these.
5. Have an understanding of how assessment, formulation, intervention and evaluation may be used in a psychologist's work with a specific case of the positive symptoms of psychosis.
6. Be able to provide a critical appraisal of the different intervention approaches for psychosis.

SAMPLE ESSAY TITLES

- Discuss the factors which may play a role in the cause and maintenance of psychosis.
- How can the effectiveness of cognitive-behavioural therapy for psychosis be enhanced?
- How can people with psychosis be helped to recover? What role can clinical psychologists play in facilitating this recovery process?
- If someone is experiencing psychosis, how do we know whether they are getting better?

NOTE

1   Adapted from a case example in Hayward *et al.* (2015). PBCT for distressing psychosis. In B. Guardiano (Ed.). *Incorporating Acceptance and Mindfulness into the Treatment of Psychosis: Current trends and future directions.* Oxford: Oxford University Press.

FURTHER READING

British Psychological Society (2014). *Understanding Psychosis and Schizophrenia: Why people sometimes hear voices, believe things that others find strange, or appear out of touch with reality, and what can help.* A report by the British Psychological Society Division of Clinical Psychology. Leicester: BPS.

Chadwick, P. (2006). *Person-based Cognitive Therapy for Distressing Psychosis.* Chichester: Wiley.

Hayward, M., Strauss, C. and Kingdon, D. (2012). *Overcoming Distressing Voices.* London: Constable & Robinson.

Repper, J. and Perkins, R. (2003). *Social Inclusion and Recovery: A model for mental health practice.* London: Balliere Tindall.

Velleman, R., Davis, E., Smith, G. and Drage, M. (2007). *Changing Outcomes in Psychosis: Collaborative cases from practioners, users and carers.* Oxford: BPS Blackwell.

REFERENCES

All Party Parliamentary Group on Mental Health (AAPGMH) (2010). *Implementation of NICE Guideline on Schizophrenia.* London: Author.

American Psychiatric Association (2013). *Diagnostic and Statistical Manual of Mental Disorders* (5th edn). Author.

Bentall, R.P. (2003). *Madness Explained: Psychosis and human nature.* London: Penguin.

Bentall, R.P., Wickham, S., Shevlin, M. and Varese, F. (2012). Do specific early-life adversities lead to specific symptoms of psychosis? A study from the 2007 The Adult Psychiatric Morbidity Survey. *Schizophrenia Bulletin, 38*(4), 734–740.

British Psychological Society (2014). *Understanding Psychosis and Schizophrenia: Why people sometimes hear voices, believe things that others find strange, or appear out of touch with reality, and what can help.* A report by the British Psychological Society Division of Clinical Psychology. Leicester: BPS.

Burbach, F. (1996). Family based interventions in psychosis – an overview of, and comparison between, family therapy and family management approaches. *Journal of Mental Health, 5,* 111–134.

Burbach, F., Carter, J., Carter, J. and Carter, M. (2007). Assertive outreach and family work. In Velleman, R., Davis, E., Smith, G. and Drage, M. (eds), *Changing Outcomes in Psychosis: Collaborative cases from practitioners, users and carers.* Oxford: BPS Blackwell.

Chadwick, P. (2006). *Person-based Cognitive Therapy for Distressing Psychosis.* Chichester: Wiley.

Coldwell, J., Meddings, S. and Camic, P. (2010). How people with psychosis positively contribute to their family: A grounded theory analysis. *Journal of Family Therapy, 33,* 353–371.

Dannahy, L., Hayward, M., Strauss, C., Turton, W., Harding, E. and Chadwick, P. (2011). Group person-based cognitive therapy for distressing voices: Pilot data from nine groups. *Journal of Behavior Therapy and Experimental Psychiatry, 42,* 111–116.

Fadden, G. (1998). Family intervention in psychosis. *Journal of Mental Health, 7,* 115–122.

Fowler, D., French, P., Hodgekins, J., Lower, R., Turner, R. and Burton, S. (2013). Cognitive behaviour therapy to address and prevent social disability in early and emerging psychosis. In C. Steel (ed.), *Cognitive Therapy for Schizophrenia: Evidence-based interventions and future directions.* Chichester: Wiley.

Freeman, D. (2011). Improving cognitive treatments for delusions. *Schizophrenia Research, 132,* 135–139.

Freeman, D., Freeman, J. and Garety, P. (2006). *Overcoming Paranoid and Suspicious Thoughts.* London: Constable & Robinson.

Freeman, D. and Garety, P. (2006) Helping patients with paranoid thoughts. *Advances in Psychiatric Treatment, 12,* 404–415.

Garety, P. and Freeman, D. (1999). Cognitive approaches to delusions: A critical review of theories and evidence. *British Journal of Clinical Psychology, 38,* 113–154.

Garety, P.A., Kuipers, E., Fowler, D., Freeman, D. and Bebbington, P.E. (2001). A cognitive model of the positive symptoms of psychosis. *Psychological Medicine, 31,* 189–195.

Hayward, M., Berry, K. and Ashton, A. (2011). Applying interpersonal theories to the understanding of and therapy for auditory hallucinations: A review of the literature and directions for further research. *Clinical Psychology Review, 31,* 1313–1323.

Hayward, M., Ellett, L. and Strauss, C. (2015). Person-based cognitive therapy for distressing psychosis. In B.A. Guadiano, *Incorporating Acceptance and Mindfulness into the Treatment of Psychosis.* New York: Oxford University Press.

Hayward, M., Strauss, C. and Kingdon, D. (2012). *Overcoming Distressing Voices.* London: Constable & Robinson.

Henquet, C., Krabbendam, L., Spauwen, J., Kaplan, C., Lieb, R. and Wittchen, H. (2004). Prospective cohort study of cannabis use, predisposition for psychosis, and psychotic symptoms in young people. *British Medical Journal, 330,* 11.

Kavanagh, D.J. (1992). Recent developments in expressed emotion and schizophrenia. *British Journal of Psychiatry, 160,* 601–620.

Kingdon, D. and Turkington, D. (1994). *Cognitive Behaviour Therapy of Schizophrenia.* New York: The Guilford Press.

Lake, N. (2008). Developing skills in consultation 2: A team formulation approach. *Clinical Psychology Forum, 186,* 18–24.

Meddings, S. Gordon, I. and Owen, D. (2010). Family and systemic work in assertive outreach. In C. Cupitt (ed.), *Reaching Out: The Psychology of Assertive Outreach.* Hove: Routledge.

Morris, E.M.J., Johns, L.C. and Oliver, J.E. (2013). *Acceptance and Commitment Therapy and Mindfulness for Psychosis.* Chichester: Wiley.

NICE (2014). *Psychosis and schizophrenia in adults: treatment and management.* London: Author.

Read, J., van Os., J., Morrison, A.P. and Ross, C.A. (2005) 'Childhood trauma, psychosis and schizophrenia: A literature review with theoretical and clinical implications'. *Acta-Psychiatrica Scandinavica 112*, 330–350.

Repper, J. and Perkins, R. (2003). *Social Inclusion and Recovery*. London: Balliere Tindall.

Schizophrenia Commission (2012). *The Abandoned Illness: A report by the Schizophrenia Commission*. London: Author.

Shepherd, G., Boardman, J. and Slade, M. (2008). *Making Recovery a Reality*. London: Sainsbury Centre for Mental Health.

Tew, J., Ramon, S., Slade, M., Bird, V., Melton, J. and Le Boutillier, C. (2012). Social factors and recovery from mental health difficulties: A review of the evidence. *British Journal of Social Work, 42*, 443–460.

Tien, A.Y. (1991). Distribution of hallucinations in the population. *Social Psychiatry and Psychiatric Epidemiology, 26*, 287–292.

Van der Gaag, M., van Oosterhoot, B., Daalman, K., Sommer, I.E. and Korrelboom, K. (2012). Initial evaluation of the effects of competitive memory training (COMET) on depression in schizophrenia-spectrum patients with persistent verbal hallucinations: A randomised controlled trial. *British Journal of Clinical Psychology, 51*, 158–171.

van Os, J., Linscott, R.J., Myin-Germeys, I., Delespaul, P. and Krabbendam, L. (2009). A systematic review and meta-analysis of the psychosis continuum: Evidence for a psychosis proneness–persistence–impairment model of psychotic disorder. *Psychological Medicine, 39*, 179–195.

Warner, R. (1994). *Recovery from Schizophrenia: Psychiatry and political economy* (2nd edn). London: Routledge.

Zubin, J. and Spring, B. (1977). Vulnerability: A new view of schizophrenia. *Journal of Abnormal Psychology, 86*, 103–126.

9 Working with people with personality disorders

Brian Solts and Renee Harvey

JANE'S STORY

I'm 35 now and for as long as I can remember I've been involved with Services. As a child I was in and out of foster care as life at home was just one big mess. My parents drank heavily, and all my brothers and sisters – including me – were neglected, physically and emotionally. When I was 7, my mum's brother moved in, my so-called uncle, and that's when the sex abuse started. I was moved into care because no one could understand why I was so unhappy all the time, but I couldn't tell anyone, he made me promise, and anyway he was pretty controlling and scary. I should have been safe in care but there were people who hurt me and interfered with me.

I started self-harming when I was 13 or 14. It was a complete distraction from all the mess and unhappiness around me, cutting my arms, being in control of something, and letting the pressure out. Then I got pregnant by an older guy when I was 16 and he promptly dumped me. That was a terrible time. I was utterly desperate and so vulnerable, and I ended up giving my baby up for adoption. I will always feel guilty for that.

I had to leave school, though I was pretty rubbish there, and just couldn't focus or concentrate on anything, and didn't really have anyone I could call a friend, someone who really knew me and what my life was like. I ended up going from one job to the next, supermarkets, cleaning, you name it. So boring I couldn't hack it.

Then I really started hurting myself bad, so alone, so depressed, so much wanting not to exist, so needing to be dead. Drinking helped, as did smoking weed, but that feeling of nothingness, the deadened peace, never really lasted and I ended up doing some pretty stupid things with people. Don't even go there. I was 20 and going from one fella to the next. Then I started being knocked around and was hurt so badly one time I just did it, tried to kill myself, that's when I first went to the mental hospital. I was in and out of the wards, it was like a pattern, pick myself up and start all over again and then bam, I was back to square one. The shrinks and the therapists tried to help but it was useless, and I just hurt myself more and more. I think they were as close as I was to giving up, maybe more so.

SUMMARY

What does it mean to say that someone has a 'personality disorder'? Can we even use the word 'disordered' when we still cannot clearly define what 'normal' is? What we can unquestionably say, whether as a qualified professional or anyone else, is that we all know people who struggle with severe challenges to living a 'normal' life, who seem to have had more than their fair share of difficulties and personal unhappiness, and who use extreme and often very damaging ways to try to cope.

This chapter will look at approaches to understanding how the personality traits and behaviours of a person may develop from childhood to adulthood, and become increasingly entrenched and destructive in nature. We will look at how this may result in a formal diagnosis of personality disorder. There are several key debates. For example, does diagnosis provide any guidance on how we might help someone (the usual reason why diagnosis is made for any condition)? Certainly no other psychiatric category creates more controversy and negative responses in most people. Are the potentially negative consequences of the diagnosis balanced by potential benefits?

The chapter will also look at how a clinical psychologist might work within a health care system to try to facilitate directly and indirectly the process by which people with personality disorders not only merely cope but also recover. We will focus particularly upon borderline personality disorder (BPD), as this is by far the most common presenting condition in clinical services.

INTRODUCTION

We are all a unique product of our nature (i.e. our genes and innate temperament) and nurture (e.g. the environment in which we grow up), and this shapes our adult personality. This developing personality sets out who we are, our core identity, and is a result of how we have come to know ourselves, through the eyes of others, as we grow up and experience the world. It also defines how we relate to and are experienced by others. We tend not to think of personality as a 'static' state; rather it operates at the interface between our inner and outer worlds, making sense of our relational world and how best to interact with others.

Unlike many other clinical presentations you will read about in this book, personality disorders are not medical illnesses as such and do not fit neatly into a medical model. The behaviour we witness in someone with this diagnosis may be extreme, for example, impulsive dangerous behaviour or a complete shut-down from human relationships. It often represents the final common pathway of a behavioural pattern that was essential for psychological or actual survival in infancy and childhood, but is no longer an effective solution in adulthood. Working with people with this diagnosis tends to also provoke extremes of emotional response in those who try to help and we think this is because the manifest problem itself is interpersonal. For the clinical psychologist involved, their input can be vital in helping others, including the family, make better sense of the here-and-now relationship difficulties and to understand better the extremes of behaviour. A bio-psychosocial formulation enriches the medical diagnosis and enables us to think about how best to intervene without making things worse for everyone involved.

THE DEVELOPMENT OF A PERSONALITY DISORDER

So how do personality disorders come about? If we think about early infant develop-ment we are all born with unique temperaments, which will be influenced by things like our attachment relationships (the emotional bond between parent and child that mediates safety and exploratory behaviours), childhood illnesses and the environment (Ainsworth *et al.*, 1978). An early attachment to a secure caregiver who is able to respond to the emotional needs of a child, along with a fairly straightforward tempera-ment, enables a child to develop a secure sense of themselves or their personality that will help them trust others, and be trusted by others, in later life.

Children who suffer more difficult or traumatic early life experiences must learn to adapt their emotions and behaviour to maximise their connection to their caregiver (e.g. by learning not to express emotional needs that may lead to rejection) and minimise risk (e.g. never expressing anger that may lead to feared abandonment). How a child shapes their personality to cope with difficult childhood experiences will depend upon a child's temperament. Yet, while these ways of coping may be adaptive in childhood (the best way of coping in a difficult environment), people who go on to attract a diagnosis of personality disorder have usually not learned how to outgrow the early pattern of behaviour that was so crucial for psychological survival in childhood. Thus the ways of coping in childhood become rigid, inflexible and unhelpful ways of coping in adulthood. If our personality cannot flex according to the relational need, for instance, adapting our behaviour so that we can work with others or raise a child, then people end up getting stuck in patterns of relationships that are ultimately self-defeating and reinforcing of the maladaptive behaviour. This dynamic is at the core of all personality disorders and represents the 'failure to achieve adaptive solutions to life tasks' (Livesley, 2004, p.19).

One example is James, who grew up in foster care having been severely emotionally neglected and physically abused for the first few years of his life. He was a suspicious and nervous child who rarely went to others for comfort. His foster carers would try hard to get close to him, but he would push them away, so he was never seen as a rewarding child to be with. He always kept himself to himself and when he started to struggle at school he never asked anyone for help. In the playground, he often got into fights and never developed friends. As a baby, shutting off from harmful relationships may have been a good form of psychological self-protection in those early years, but in school it got him into trouble, and in foster care led to the breakdown of placements over and over again. As an adult, James still cannot sustain close relationships. Desperate to be liked and to have friends, he is overly generous and is frequently exploited for money; when he realises this, he becomes aggressive and rejecting of others, isolates himself for long periods of time, and relapses into depression. He then becomes desperate again for friendship and the cycle begins again.

MAKING A DIAGNOSIS

The issue of diagnosis is highly controversial. It is a 'sticky label' that comes with prejudice and rejection (Haigh, 2002). It thus becomes very hard for someone to escape the judgemental attitudes they sometimes encounter. This can cloud others' views of the person with a personality disorder in all its aspects, such as assuming that because someone has this label, they are not capable of being a good parent, or that any of their other difficulties could be explained by the diagnosis, including physical symptoms. People receiving the diagnosis sometimes also judge themselves, concluding, for example, that there is something deeply wrong and 'unfixable' about them. But for some, getting a diagnosis comes as a relief after years of confusion and brings a sense of knowing what one is dealing with. Pragmatically, a diagnosis should enable people to access help, and helps service providers put arguments forward to commissioning bodies to provide funds to develop services. Not diagnosing someone who needs help is arguably a worse option. There is also a growing consensus that individuals moving around mental health care systems without the right approach may actually get worse.

One controversy surrounding the diagnosis of BPD for some people is the overlap with post-traumatic stress disorder (PTSD) and particularly the notion of 'complex PTSD'. Many people prefer this as a diagnostic label for BPD. However, current opinion in the literature favours the notion that they overlap but are not the same. Some individuals fall into one camp but not the other. A clear focus on what each individual needs would hopefully prevent individuals being treated as having either one or the other, or seeing them as needing help with both if necessary.

Diagnostic methods reflect the complexities of actually reaching an accurate diagnosis: ICD-10 and DSM-5 do not overlap completely and the latter system, having recently gone through a major revision, rejected all proposed changes because of criticisms and reverted back to DSM-IV, a system many know is fraught with problems (Mullins-Sweatt et al., 2013). The diagnosis eventually given depends too often upon who is doing the diagnosing (Treloar and Lewis, 2009). One potential advantage of the new system in the Appendix of DSM-V is that it provides a *dimensional* approach, which allows for placing individuals on a continuum from 'normal' to very severely affected, and challenges the idea that there is a fixed cut-off point somewhere in the middle.

It is important that clinicians follow a sound procedure for determining the presence both of the personality disorder as well as any other problems that may exist concurrently. Clinicians can access a range of interview or questionnaire-type instruments to help with diagnosis, such as SCID-II (First et al., 1997) or the MCMI-III (Millon et al., 2009), among others. These instruments should only be interpreted within the context of a full clinical picture, and benefit from observations from people who know the person best, though this may also be fraught with difficulties if a family member or carer is known to be part of the problem. There is probably more to be gained than not in terms of having a diagnosis, as long as this is based on a number of different sources of information and reports, and is never used as shorthand for describing patients or colleagues with whom we simply do not get on.

EPIDEMIOLOGY OF PERSONALITY DISORDERS

> Research suggests that about ten per cent of people have problems that would meet the diagnostic criteria for Personality Disorder. Estimates are much higher among psychiatric patients, although they vary considerably: some studies have suggested prevalence rates among psychiatric outpatients that are in excess of 80 per cent. Between 50 per cent and 78 per cent of adult prisoners are believed to meet criteria for one or more personality disorder diagnoses, and even higher prevalence estimates have been reported among young offenders.
>
> (Alwin *et al.*, 2006, p. 1)

The epidemiology of personality disorder is fraught with problems. Unlike in medicine where pathology is often a discrete set of cellular symptoms, measuring psychological illness and marking the point at which something ceases to be normal and becomes 'disorder' is not an exact science. The tools we use to 'measure' personality disorder, such as self-report questionnaires, face-to-face interviews or behavioural indicators, will all be subject to bias.

What we see 'under the microscope' in personality disorder is essentially interpersonal, which inevitably introduces subjective bias. In order for us to accurately predict prevalence and incidence we must assume that the concepts we are studying are valid and reliable constructs, not influenced by social norms. Yet so-called deviation from cultural norms is part and parcel of how someone might come to attract this diagnosis in the first place. There aren't many disorders that, in theory, can be cured just by boarding a plane and travelling to another country. In terms of gender, it is interesting that in Western countries women are more likely to be diagnosed with BPD, whereas men tend to be diagnosed as antisocial. Is this a 'true' feature of these conditions, or further evidence of cultural and social bias?

BORDERLINE PERSONALITY DISORDER (BPD)

It is impossible to look at the characteristics of all personality disorders in one chapter, and looking in more detail at the aetiology of all personality disorders would require a whole book, so we will focus on one: borderline personality disorder (BPD). We have chosen BPD because this is by far the most common presentation in adult mental health services and has also seen the most significant advances in evidence-based approaches over the past two decades.

What are the types of psychological difficulties that may occur in BPD?

A new system has been proposed for understanding BPD in DSM-V (APA, 2013). The core diagnostic features are as follows.

A disorder of the self

This is where people have a poor self-identity and struggle with their sense of who they are and what they are like as people. Their identities may change dramatically, depending on current relationships or environments. A question such as 'Tell me about yourself' may be met with confusion and distress, such as 'I don't know what to say, I'm nothing'.

Emotional instability

People with BPD have intense, rapid and dramatic fluctuations in mood, sometimes without obvious precipitants. When stressed, individuals may become angry, severely depressed and anxious, develop paranoid thoughts and even experience dissociation and transient episodes of psychosis. In a clinical setting, an individual's mood may change dramatically within the space of a single session or even moment by moment. An important skill for the psychologist is learning to stay calm and constant in the face of highly charged affect while maintaining and communicating empathy. For example, Mary (29) began her session in a positive mood, talked about her weekend, suddenly got upset and ran from the room.

Behavioural instability

In BPD, impulsive decision making and destructive (mainly self-destructive) behaviours disrupt the individual's life and can interfere with engagement and progress in assessment and treatment. For example, four weeks into a 20-week group, Sue (25) wrote to say she wouldn't be back, as she had decided to go to America to be with a person she had met on the internet a week previously.

Interpersonal instability

For people with BPD, relationships are generally unstable, characterised by frequent chaotic upheavals. Many people with BPD suffer intense fears of abandonment and make active attempts to avoid others leaving them (whether real or imagined). In the therapeutic relationship it may take a long time for a person to develop trust in the psychologist. They may also, paradoxically, form intensely dependent relationships very quickly. They are likely to be highly sensitive to change and unpredictability in any aspect of the psychologist's behaviour or in relation to arrangements made. Any changes in the routine such as holiday breaks and especially endings, such as when a professional is leaving, should be discussed well in advance. For example, John (35) begins each meeting with his psychologist with 'Is today going to be our last session?'

Aetiology of BPD

Biology and our early environment

It is thought that people who go on to develop BPD start out in life with strong temperamental characteristics that lead to a propensity for high emotional reactivity. A particularly difficult baby will be a challenge for most parents to 'contain' and help regulate their emotional world, and without this we can speculate that there will be a reinforcing negative interplay between emotional expression of the child and the experience of being parented. Linehan (1993) and Blum *et al.* (2008) would view someone with BPD as primarily having a dysfunction of the emotion regulation system, made worse when someone grows up within an emotionally invalidating relational environment. According to Linehan, one of the most emotionally invalidating experiences a child can have is abuse, so it is no surprise that there is a strong association between a diagnosis of BPD and reports of childhood physical, emotional and/or sexual abuse. Self-harm, drug and alcohol use, dangerous risk taking, abusive later relationships, dependency: these may all be symptoms of a person who is struggling to manage intimate relationships and their internal emotional system.

Emotions in the context of insecure attachment

Bateman and Fonagy (2004), strongly influenced by the work of Bowlby and attachment theory, have focused our attention on the nature of early attachment relationships, and in particular disorganised attachment patterns and the later development of BPD. If an infant learns early on that not only is their attachment figure inconsistent and unreliable, but also a source of terror, at times of stress in adulthood (e.g. relationship breakups, managing conflict at work, being in need of help) the activation of the attachment system becomes a source in itself of destabilising and dysregulating emotions. In other words, it is not the case that people with BPD reject or will not accept help; it is that they *cannot,* and in fact at times of stress it becomes impossible to see others as a potential source of comfort and genuine help. This is what they refer to as the breakdown of mentalisation. At times of stress, other people become a source of fear. Self-harm and dangerous behaviour in this context may be seen as attempts to 'reset' the internal emotional regulatory system to more manageable levels, though this may not be how others interpret the behaviour, which is easily labelled manipulative, divisive, intentional or psychopathic. It is our view that the damaging behaviours we see in people with BPD are not conscious attempts to control or damage others, though this may be a secondary consequence.

It is hard for most of us to imagine how seeking help and being helped could lead to a temporary mental breakdown. Yet remember, people with this diagnosis may be biologically disadvantaged by having an emotional system that is quickly over-aroused, may never have learned skills to regulate their emotional system, and, on top of this, some will only have experienced attachment figures as abusive, controlling, humiliating or downright dangerous.

Alwen's (2006) bio-psychosocial model places attachment status (secure or insecure) and our internal representational models of people at the interface between the '*internal past*' experiences (psychological, social and biological) and the '*external present*' symptoms of distress (behavioural, cognitive and emotional patterns) that are played out in the *here-and-now* of everyday interpersonal relationships. In the absence of any good-enough corrective relationship experiences, the survival pathway for someone with BPD may be to look for extreme ways to manage extreme emotions that emerge when trying to deal with people (e.g. partners, friends, managers). Drugs, alcohol and self-harm, for instance, may be reframed as ways of coping with the extreme emotions that emerge at times of relationship stress. It is thus common to see a repeat of abusive relationship patterns in the *here-and-now* in response to a manager at work trying to address difficult work behaviour, or indeed with mental health professionals trying to help. If the internal working model that has developed through childhood has taught someone repeatedly that getting close to others at times of stress is humiliating, shaming and damaging, it is no surprise that people with this diagnosis can be so hard to help when they are experiencing symptoms of distress.

Theory and evidence for psychological intervention for BPD

The past provides a perspective, not an explanation. All the evidence-based therapies for BPD, even those based on psychoanalytic principles, help patients to put the past behind them and to foresee a future, in some cases, for the first time. This is why getting better requires getting a life.

(Paris, 2010, p.155)

Just as there is no single determining factor that leads to the development of BPD, equally treatment that only takes account of one aspect of the disorder is unlikely to lead to recovery (Paris, 2010). For instance, a purely medical approach may eradicate

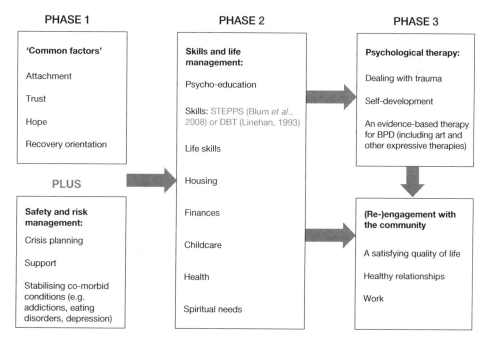

FIGURE 9.1 A proposed model for treatment

some symptoms, but increase the likelihood of impulsive self-harm by giving someone the means of really hurting themselves (overdosing). Prescribing tablets alone may also give someone the impression that they cannot develop their own internal skills for managing their difficulties. On the other hand, a purely psychological approach might reinforce victimhood and blame of others and neglect social factors such as poor education, housing and poverty that might be equally important sources of distress. In our local services we have developed a care pathway approach that breaks treatment down into three phases, and emphasises the importance of a holistic and integrated bio-psychosocial approach to recovery (see Figure 9.1 above).

Our pathway model is important, as it sets out a rationale for interventions aimed initially at stabilisation and risk management within a recovery-orientated approach. This is *prior* to undertaking psychological therapy. You would not embark upon a journey to climb Mount Everest without the appropriate gear (suitable clothing and climbing equipment) or knowledge of what to do in a crisis. Likewise, we think it is very unwise to embark upon a course of therapy if you do not know how to regulate and manage your emotions safely, or what to do when things go wrong (as they invariably do from time to time in therapy). For BPD, the goals of therapy need to be realistic and made explicit, no matter how complicated the presenting picture looks, so, if someone is not ready to give up self-harm or drug use, undertaking work on a trauma would be too premature and potentially self-defeating for both patient and therapist.

Bateman and Fonagy (2000) reviewed the literature on factors that are common for all effective treatments for BPD. Treatments that work best are well structured, devote time and effort to enhance motivation and adherence, have a clear focus upon which both sides have agreed, are theoretically coherent for both therapist and patient (i.e. everyone knows what they are meant to be doing!), are relatively long-term, and encourage a powerful attachment relationship between therapist and patient that enables the therapist to adopt an active stance. Finally, treatment needs to be well integrated with other services available for the patient. This is extremely important because of the potential for those around the patient to mirror early experiences of growing up in inconsistent, chaotic, unreliable and confusing contexts.

CASE STUDY

Karen is a 35-year-old married mother of a 10-year-old daughter and a grown-up daughter from her first marriage. She had been an inpatient on a psychiatric ward for about two months when she first met Sam the psychologist. Prior to this, she lived in staff-supported accommodation during the week, but spent weekends with her family. She was known to take regular overdoses of prescribed antidepressants and anti-anxiety medication 'to knock myself out'. She had been known to mental health services for about eight years following the death of a new-born baby. She used services intermittently, presenting initially with severe depression and intent to kill herself, but then she resisted attempts to help her and withdrew until the next crisis.

The most recent crisis in many ways followed the same pattern. However, a number of issues were destabilising the situation even further. Karen's husband was concerned that her behaviour was now beginning to affect weekends with her daughter and he was signalling a wish to end the relationship. This led to a number of aggressive outbursts from Karen followed by complete withdrawal and refusal to talk, then a very serious overdose that necessitated several days in intensive care and then admission to a psychiatric hospital. Once on the ward, the housing project began taking action to withdraw their support because of the severity of overdosing and concern that they could not manage her aggressive and suicidal behaviours. When Karen heard that they were taking action to evict her, she attempted to hang herself in her room on the ward, only to be found, and cut down, by staff. Staff began to take more and more action to stop Karen cutting or strangling herself during the day, for instance, taking away potential ligatures such as laces, belts, headphones or phone charger. Once staff got to the point where they had stripped the room of bedding during the day, Karen became even more aggressive, and complained to the authorities that she was being treated like a prisoner. In staff-reflective practice groups, people spoke about feeling controlled and manipulated by her behaviour and it was clear that trust had broken down on both sides.

This is a common dynamic when people with BPD are admitted to inpatient wards, but is usually the last resort for professionals who are trying to manage the accompanying high-risk behaviours to self (e.g. severe cutting, dangerous overdosing, threats to jump off buildings). Unfortunately an admission is rarely able to make social or psychological changes and has a tendency to become overly medically focused. Attempts at recovery-focused self-management interventions can be hampered by a tendency for people with BPD to regress into helpless dependency at points of crisis as they seek idealised care and being looked after to escape their dangerous feelings. If hospital systems do not take into account social and psychological factors throughout the admission and prior to discharge, this will further exacerbate the internal crisis for the patient, at which point there will be further escalation of dangerous behaviours. Ironically, this may be all the patient has left to survive the emotional turmoil of being cared for on the ward, or when facing the prospect of discharge (abandonment).

When Sam the ward psychologist first got involved, he worked hard to remain as neutral as possible in formulating what was going on and in thinking about the most helpful way to intervene. This was not easy: his colleagues expressed resentment at having to care for Karen, and, after sitting with the team and reflecting on events on the ward, Sam remembered feeling afraid of meeting Karen because of her anger and being overwhelmed by all the difficulties staff were worried about, something he needed to process in supervision. Sam wanted to really understand Karen, but the ward was so concerned about her behaviour that no one had reviewed her history. He thought this was a good place to start and was guided by Alwin's (2006) bio-psychosocial model to help him think about Karen in an attempt to better understand her.

External present

Karen had poor general coping abilities, a chronic depressive mindset, and an interpersonal style that made it very difficult to help her. She would reach out with desperate cries for help, only to then reject it and withdraw into a mute and angry state. Aggressive and hostile behaviour towards staff was, in Karen's mind, justified, because she felt she was being controlled and abused.

Outside of hospital, Karen led two lives. On the one hand, she was a mother and wife at weekends, but on the other hand she withdrew into a drug-induced haze the rest of the time to avoid social interactions. Her inability to get her needs met by professionals (the approach–withdrawal dynamic) probably mirrored what happened with her husband and daughter. In this way, her interpersonal style left her struggling to express or hold on to what she really wanted from life.

Karen had a very mistrustful relationship with her mother and saw her as the root of most of her problems. She saw herself as a victim of her mother's hatred and therefore a worthless human being unfit to be alive. At times of stress, she tended to locate the difficulties in other people alone, reinforcing her feelings of being victimised and bullied by others, putting her on the offensive, and then she would be experienced as victimising and bullying of others. In this way, her interpersonal pattern repeated itself within the hospital setting.

Sam identified housing as a key destabilizing issue and, rather than avoid it out of fear that she would hurt herself, Sam talked it through. He taught her skills to manage the strong feelings this evoked and reviewed her options with colleagues who were then able to present Karen with good advice. This intervention led to a breakthrough – Karen asked her primary nurse to help her talk to her husband about living arrangements, and this led to an increase in trust on both sides.

Internal past

Sam recognised the risk of forming an intense therapeutic relationship with Karen on the ward when the team were working towards discharge from hospital. Whenever staff prompted Karen to talk about her childhood, she became very distressed and this led to self-harm. Sam helped the staff understand from existing clinical reports that Karen always felt unwanted and unloved as a child, believing that her mother preferred her older sister. She spoke about a very loving relationship with her father, but this was at odds with reports that he was violent and had died when she was a young teenager as a result of his own battle with alcohol addiction.

Karen blamed her mother for her father's problems. After he died, Karen became increasingly alienated from her family, refusing to go to school, making friends with a 'bad crowd', and eventually she left home at 16 to live with an older boy, only to get pregnant and have her first child. Although she got married, this only lasted for six months as it quickly escalated into violence on both sides. After being hospitalised following one particularly violent incident, Karen left with her baby and had no further contact with her husband. After this time, she had periodic episodes of depression and anxiety, and there was a recurring pattern of emotionally intense but short-lived relationships, until she met her now second husband. Although she described him as dull, boring and everything she was not, she recognised how much stability he gave her, including financial security for the first time in her life.

Sam was able to help staff steer themselves away from talking to Karen about her past; rather he guided them towards *here-and-now* relationships and problem solving.

INTERFACE BETWEEN INTERNAL/EXTERNAL

This patterning of Karen's internal and external world suggested an insecure-ambivalent attachment style. In Ainsworth's 'strange situation' test, Karen may have been the child who would become distressed at the caregiver leaving, but then make alternate bids for contact on reunion, with signs of angry rejection and tantrums (Ainsworth *et al.*, 1978). These are children that tend not to find comfort in their parent caregiver.

Sam helped staff not to take Karen's verbal outbursts personally. He helped them see why, given her past, the process of getting close to others activated an internal working model of people who she expected to emotionally let her down, hurt or abandon her when she needed them most. With no skills to regulate her emotions, her interpersonal style puts her between a rock and a hard place. The more trapped she becomes in a system that takes control, the more out of control her emotions get, and the more her aggression kicks in as she literally fights for emotional survival.

WHERE SHOULD SAM INTERVENE?

One of the most important roles the psychologist played was to help the team develop a shared understanding of Karen that went beyond the medical diagnosis. Staff can struggle to step back and think in the face of hostile and highly charged emotion in the patient. Sam provided space to 'digest' the emotions and map out Karen's way of thinking about people to help them empathise more readily and see that her aggression was also a sign of attachment crisis. Rather than take more control during these times, staff were encouraged to back off and not get into a position of confrontation. This also applied to the self-harm. Karen often self-harmed after seeing her daughter, and so staff began to provide more emotional support at these times rather than avoid her, thinking she wanted to be alone. Karen found saying goodbye to her daughter very difficult, and so staff started to model to Karen that she could put her feelings into words rather than get angry. Once Karen developed more trust in staff, she talked about her poor parenting skills and together they thought about a service that could help her when she left hospital. Her daughter's emotional needs were also flagged up as Karen and her husband began to talk through with the team a more sustainable solution for their living arrangements after discharge.

As staff began to regain their own sense of empathy for Karen, and recognised trigger points for her anger and distress, the frequency of self-harm episodes lessened, and Sam agreed at this point to do some skills-based work with Karen that included psychoeducation about her diagnosis. The contracted work was articulated clearly in her care plan, as many people assumed that Sam would be offering a formal piece of therapy work. Importantly, Sam was able to attend review meetings and meet with her community team to ensure that everyone knew about the work that was being done. Karen understood that this would be time-limited work aimed at giving her more control over her emotions, though she was clear that she wanted the work to continue after discharge. Sam had to be boundaried and experienced a real emotional tug of war as he felt a pull to carry the work on after discharge. Supervision was essential in helping him hold on to his role as an inpatient team member, and to maintain a realistic and not devaluing view of the team in the community.

Discharge from hospital is a real danger time for this group of patients, as feelings of abandonment are triggered which further destabilise the patient and escalate risks of self-harm and suicidal feelings. At these times, staff may feel manipulated and controlled into not discharging the patients, so this point in treatment must always be well thought through with clear crisis and risk management plans. Even when all goes according to plan, patients will still feel punished and hurt at the prospect of returning to the community when they still feel chronically suicidal. The real work for Karen had only just begun as she started to make adult choices about the sort of life she wanted to live.

MANAGING BORDERLINE DYNAMICS IN THE TEAM

With this group of patients, the best work occurs when everyone involved in the care of the patient is signed up to the care plan. Support and supervision, often provided by a psychologist or psychological therapist, helps the team work through difficult feelings about the patient. If feelings are not checked, the team can end up re-enacting unhelpful dynamics that mirror for the patient his or her own uncontained and conflicted early life. Alternatively, if one member of staff goes the extra mile, they risk being vilified by another who wants the patient to be discharged, and soon the team may find itself divided and unable to make effective decisions.

A good team can work through differences of opinion and develop a boundaried but fair care plan. The experience of being emotionally contained may be quite novel for some people, and it is not uncommon for the patient to test out each staff member to look for differences in boundaries, tolerance of risk, or personal beliefs and attitudes. The role of the team is to understand and work alongside someone as they re-evaluate deeply ingrained beliefs about who they are and the sort of world in which they exist.

CRITICAL ISSUES

Psychologists are skilled in bringing together psychological theory into practice to help others understand how best to intervene at critical points in a patient's recovery. In this chapter we have outlined the limitations of diagnostic frameworks that may be quite arbitrary in determining the point along a continuum of functioning where disorders begin. At the same time diagnosis can, when combined with a bio-psychosocial formulation, help identify need and open up treatment pathways. We have presented a care pathway approach for treating people with BPD and have explored different ways in which psychologists may help. Providing individual therapy is only one of many roles the psychologist may have in this area of work.

Helping people with entrenched and risky behavioural patterns, in the context of damaging interpersonal dynamics, is not easy. Psychologists cannot do this work alone and need to locate their interventions within the context of a whole-team approach. We are all, however, human beings at the end of the day, and in this field of work personal reflection, the ability to use supervision and support well, and doing work on our own personal issues in therapy, may be just as important as learning the tools of our trade.

CONCLUSION

This chapter has explored some of the ways a clinical psychologist can contribute to the care and recovery of people diagnosed with personality disorders. Psychologists will contribute to a bio-psychosocial formulation of the presenting difficulties that will try to address the repetitive and ultimately self-defeating patterns of relating to others that make the lives of this group of people so unbearable. In psychiatric settings, it is common to work with people who have a diagnosis of BPD. Although we argue that there are pros and cons in having a personality disorder diagnosis, ultimately we think this has allowed practitioners to make arguments to commissioners about how best to develop services. We have developed a three-phase care pathway in our local services that attempts to help people manage their presenting risks (e.g. suicidality and self-harm) in the context of safe relationships; develop life skills that can help regulate their emotions; and finally use psychological therapy so that they can re-engage with life outside of professional services and make a meaningful recovery. We are very optimistic about the contribution that psychologists can make in this area.

JANE'S STORY: HOPED-FOR RECOVERY

Okay, so my life has turned a corner. I had a great care coordinator, someone who made sure I wasn't forgotten, in my mental health team, and she really got my struggle, but also challenged me a lot when I forgot appointments or did stupid things. I think she really got the whole BPD thing. What is it they say, never judge a book by its cover. It may look like I'm doing okay, turning up for things, catching buses, putting a bit of make-up on, but inside I can feel like I am dying, literally. I wasn't keen on the borderline thing but my treatment changed when they said this is what I have. I did a group called STEPPS which gave me real ways to manage my feelings better. Rather than cut or take drugs I learned to direct myself differently and even to challenge how bad I was thinking I was doing – my filters – that I might not be totally bad inside. Once I got better at managing my feelings, I started to do some therapy so I could learn how to move away from just feeling like I was living in the past. They also gave me an occupational therapist who helped me gain confidence in other life skills and even challenge me to go back to study. I may not see myself as totally fixed – is anyone? – but at least I have let my body heal and allowed my mind to get more peace.

KEY CONCEPTS AND TERMS

- Personality disorder
- Borderline personality disorder
- Attachment theory
- Emotion dysregulation
- Bio-psychosocial integrative formulation
- Mentalisation-based therapy (MBT)
- Systems training in emotion predictability
- and problem solving (STEPPS)
- Dialectical behaviour therapy (DBT)
- Staff containment and self-reflection

LEARNING OUTCOMES

By the end of this chapter you will have:

1 Developed an understanding of how our personality develops over time – and the difficulties we can face as adults when we get stuck in particular patterns of relating because of the personality structures we have developed.
2 Developed an understanding of the controversy and debates over the use of 'personality disorder' as a diagnostic label.
3 Gained an overview of what it means to be diagnosed with a personality disorder and, in particular, to think about the challenges posed by those who present for help with borderline personality disorder (BPD).
4 Grounded this thinking in a bio-psychosocial model of BPD.
5 Gained an ability to critically evaluate different treatment approaches.

SAMPLE ESSAY TITLES

- What are the advantages and disadvantages of diagnosing someone with borderline personality disorder?
- What factors could contribute to the development of borderline personality disorder?
- The clinical psychologist's role is to provide individual psychological therapy for people diagnosed with borderline personality disorder. Discuss.

REFERENCES AND FURTHER READING

Ainsworth, M.D.S., Blehar, M.C., Waters, E. and Wall, S. (1978). *Patterns of Attachment: A psychological study of the strange situation.* Hillsdale, NJ: Erlbaum.

Alwin, N. (2006). The causes of personality disorder. In M.J. Sampson, R.A. McCubbin and P. Tyrer (eds), *Personality Disorder and Community Mental Health Teams.* Chichester: Wiley, ch. 3.

Alwin, N., Blackburn, R., Davidson, K., Hilton, M., Logan, C. and Shine, J. (2006). *Understanding Personality Disorder: A report by the British Psychological Society.* Leicester: BPS.

American Psychiatric Association (2013). *Diagnostic and Statistical Manual of Mental Disorders.* Revised fifth edition. Washington, DC: American Psychiatric Press.

Barrachina, J., Pascual, J.C., Ferrer, M. and Soler, J. (2011). Axis II comorbidity in borderline personality disorder is influenced by sex, age, and clinical severity. *Comprehensive Psychiatry, 52/6,* 725–730.

Bateman, A.W. and Fonagy, P. (2000). Effectiveness of psychotherapeutic treatment of personality disorder. *British Journal of Psychiatry, 177,* 138–143.

—— (2004). *Psychotherapy for Borderline Personality Disorder: Mentalization-based treatment.* Oxford: Oxford University Press.

Blum, N., St. John, D., Pfohl, B., Stuart, S., McCormick, B., Allen, J., Arndt, S. and Black, D.W. (2008). Systems training for emotional predictability and problem solving (STEPPS) for outpatients with borderline personality disorder: A randomised controlled trial and 1-year follow up. *American Journal of Psychiatry, 165,* 468–478.

First, M.B., Gibbon, M., Spitzer, R.L., Williams, J.B.W. and Benjamin, L.B. (1997). Structured Clinical Interview for DSM-IV-R Axis II Personality Disorders (SCID-II). American Psychiatric Publishing. Available at http://www.appi.org.

Haigh, R. (2002). Services for people with personality disorder: The thoughts of service users. Available at Phttp://www_.dh.gov.uk_/en/Publicationsandstatistics_/Publications/PublicationsPolicyAndGuidance_/DH_4009546 (accessed 10 April 2008).

Linehan, M.L. (1993). *Cognitive-behavioural Treatment of Borderline Personality Disorder.* New York: The Guilford Press.

Livesley, W.J. (2004). *Practical Management of Personality Disorder.* New York: The Guilford Press.

Millon, T., Davis, R., Millon, C. and Grossman, S. (2009). The Millon Clinical Multiaxial Inventory-III, Third Edition (MCMI-III). PsychCorp. Available at http://www.millon.net/.

Millon, T., Grossman, S., Millon, C. Meaher, S. and Ramnath, R. (2004). *Personality Disorders in Modern Life* (2nd edn). Hoboken, NJ: Wiley.

Mullins-Sweatt, S.N., Bernstein, D.P. and Widiger, T.A. (2013). Retention or deletion of personality disorder diagnoses for DSM-5: An expert consensus approach. *Journal of Personality Disorders, 26*(5), 689–703.

National Institute for Clinical Excellence (NICE) (2009). Borderline personality disorder: treatment and management. NICE Clinical Guidelines 78. Available at http://www.nice.org.uk/nicemedia/pdf/cg78niceguideline.pdf.

Nysaeter, T.E. and Nordahl, H.M. (2012). Comorbidity of borderline personality disorder with other personality disorders in psychiatric outpatients: How does it look at 2-year follow-up? *Nordic Journal of Psychiatry, 66*(3), 209–214.

Paris, J. (2010). *Treatment of Borderline Personality Disorder: A guide to evidence-based practice*. New York: The Guilford Press.

Treloar, A.J.C. and Lewis, A.J. (2009). Diagnosing borderline personality disorder: Examination of how clinical indicators are used by professionals in the health setting. *Clinical Psychologist, 13*(1), 21–27.

Young, J.E., Klosko, J.S. and Weishaar, M.E. (2003). *Schema Therapy: A practitioner's guide*. New York: The Guilford Press.

10 Working with people with eating disorders

Renate Pantke and Neil Joughin

PETER'S STORY

My eating disorder developed after a series of difficult and troubling personal events. At first I was unaware that I was suffering from anorexia. I sought to justify my sudden and extreme weight loss as something physical, despite my conscious efforts to exercise and restrict my food intake. As my weight loss accelerated over the course of just a few months, so too did the intrusive anorexic mindset; a mindset which became so pervasive that it led to uncomfortable, challenging and overwhelming depressive thoughts. With time the eating disorder caused me to withdraw from friends and family. Social experiences induced intense anxiety, especially when involving food, and as a result it was easier to exclude myself from these occasions rather than face up to my illness. Gradually, as I became weaker and more alone, I realised that life, as a severely anorexic male, was no longer a sustainable or desirable future. Faced with increasing medical evidence from doctors, desperate pleas to seek psychiatric support from my mother and friends, I began to acknowledge that my life was in immediate danger; my organs were at risk of failure and my increasing weakness meant that I was unable to undertake the bare minimum of exertion. I even broke down at the thought of climbing the stairs for bed, given how weak I had become.

SUMMARY

Eating disorders (EDs) are a fascinating area in which to work, combining complex interaction of biological, psychological and social issues. However, many professionals shy away from them perhaps due to the risks they carry or because the skills required are beyond any one profession's core training. As a clinical psychologist, the need for close partnership working with our medical colleagues is essential to good patient care.

This chapter has been written by a psychologist (Renate) and a psychiatrist (Neil), and reflects this partnership approach. We both work with people with severe EDs and find this task immensely challenging yet equally immensely rewarding. In addition to this field being academically interesting, clinically the changes we can see in our patients when they move towards recovery are fantastic, the way in which families mobilise to fight EDs is inspiring, and the courage and stamina of the greatest majority of our patients to keep tackling their disorder day-in-day-out for many years, or, at times, decades, is humbling.

We hope that this chapter will infect you with some of our enthusiasm and interest in EDs. It will describe the features or symptoms that are characteristic of eating disorders and explore how they develop, and the aspects of treatment and management that are key to helping people recover.

INTRODUCTION: WHAT ARE EATING DISORDERS?

Central to the main EDs is a profound over-evaluation of shape and weight, and the control of them as a generator and measure of self-worth. In many this over-evaluation results in major emotional swings between elation and utter despair and terror based on, for example, whether weight has been gained or lost. This leads to behaviours to manage calorie intake and expenditure that have a predictable and profound impact upon a person's physical and psychological well-being.

In binge eating disorder (BED) and bulimia nervosa (BN), a person may eat a much larger amount of food in one go than would be regarded as culturally appropriate with a sense of feeling out of control and associated with negative emotions such as shame or guilt. This 'objective binge episode' may be triggered by interpersonal events and emotional states (anger, frustration, loneliness, boredom, etc.), or may be a consequence of a period of starvation. People with BN attempt to compensate for the binge by vomiting, using laxatives or abusing other medication (e.g. people with Type 1 diabetes may omit insulin). Others exercise excessively. Most commonly they starve themselves. These behaviours are extreme and can result in severe physical problems and even death – without any intention to die.

People with anorexia nervosa (AN) may also binge and/or purge. Often their binge episodes are more subjective than objective, i.e. a normal-sized meal may be experienced as an out-of-control binge. Their weight is significantly low for their height due to insufficient calorie intake and/or excessive exercise as part of an attempt to lose weight or avoidance of weight gain when already low in weight. People with AN often have a cognitive style that is very detailed and rigid. The impact of AN is often described as a 'starvation syndrome'. The body shuts down, the brain shrinks, people who may have always been more anxious than most become even more obsessional, more rigid and less accurate in recognising emotions, etc. Some people with AN have a distorted body image, i.e. they may perceive themselves as 'fat'. Others are ashamed of their emaciation.

Self-esteem issues and heightened anxiety are central to EDs as are issues around perfectionism, attention to detail, rigidity and often obsessionality (especially in AN). Often patients with ED also present with low mood or depression perhaps as a conse-

FOCUS 10.1

Risk

EDs are more likely to result in the death of the patient than any mental health disorder (Fotios *et al.*, 2009). Of those who die, a significant proportion dies of suicide. Others die from the direct consequences of malnutrition. Importantly, even starting to eat after a period of severe malnutrition may result in death. While death may be the extreme risk, the list of other risks is long. Clinical psychologists will have varying roles in managing these risks. However, no professional involved in managing these patients is absolved from the responsibility of knowing how these risks are being addressed. All care sits under the umbrella of risk management.

quence of living with an isolating and debilitating ED often experienced as shameful by the sufferer. They often feel as if they are on an emotional roller-coaster, between numbness in general and extreme emotions when it comes to food or weight. For many, the ED may be a way of regulating emotions or it may have come to be regarded as the only way to improve self-esteem and gain a sense of mastery and control, although at the same time people feel desperately out of control with regard to their ED. They may have social emotion-processing difficulties which can further add to isolation. Fearing the judgement and criticism of others, feeling ashamed, or sometimes superior or special, impacts upon relationships with others with yet more alienation and isolation.

DIAGNOSIS

The American Diagnostic and Statistical Manual (5th edition) DSM-V describes a range of eating disorders (ED). We will give you the edited criteria for just two. Similar disorders that do not fully meet these diagnoses have names such as 'binge eating disorder' (BED) or 'other specified feeding or eating disorders' (e.g. atypical anorexia, etc.).

Anorexia nervosa

A. Restriction of energy intake relative to requirements, leading to a significantly low body weight.
B. Intense fear of gaining weight or of becoming fat, or persistent behaviour that interferes with weight gain, even though at a significantly low weight.
C. Disturbance in the way in which one's body weight or shape is experienced, undue influence of body weight or shape on self-evaluation, or persistent lack of recognition of the seriousness of the current low body weight.

Specify whether this is restricting type or binge-eating/purging type.

Bulimia nervosa

A. Recurrent episodes of binge eating. An episode of binge eating is characterised by both of the following:

1   Eating, within a discrete period of time (e.g. within any two-hour period), an amount of food that is definitely larger than what most individuals would eat during a similar period of time under similar circumstances.

2   A sense of lack of control over eating during the episode (e.g. a feeling that one cannot stop eating or control what or how much one is eating).

B. Recurrent inappropriate compensatory behaviours in order to prevent weight gain such as self-induced vomiting; misuse of laxatives, diuretics or other medications; fasting; or excessive exercise.

C. The binge eating and inappropriate compensatory behaviours both occur, on average, at least once a week for three months.

D. Self-evaluation is unduly influenced by body shape and weight.

E. The disturbance does not occur exclusively during episodes of anorexia nervosa.

FOCUS 10.2

Co-morbidity

'Comorbidity (i.e. having diagnoses other than the ED) is the rule rather than the exception' (Treasure *et al.*, 2010). However, there are some that are particularly important and need to be positively considered within assessment and management.

- EDs are more common in people with diabetes. Manipulation of insulin may be used to control weight and thereby the physical risks are greatly magnified.
- Patients with AN are usually obsessive but also have an increased likelihood of experiencing symptoms of an obsessive compulsive disorder. OCD may be a result of starvation and may disappear as the ED improves but it may also be a problem in its own right.
- Depression may lead to weight loss and low weight in the absence of an ED. However, depression may also be a trigger for the development of an ED as well as the result of a debilitating and isolating ED that is often experienced as shameful by the sufferer.
- Sometimes people with ED meet the diagnostic criteria of emotionally unstable (or borderline) personality disorder. However, many of the features seen in EUPD may be related to the ED and may disappear when the person recovers from their ED. Finding out historical information is essential in order to make this differentiation.
- Particularly when seriously underweight, AN patients show a rigidity of thought and lack of normal emotional responsiveness. This has led to the thought as to whether AN is a – particularly female – manifestation of autistic spectrum disorder (ASD) and what may be learned from the ASD world. Fascinating but as yet inconclusive.

EPIDEMIOLOGY OF EATING DISORDERS

Rightly or wrongly, AN is sometimes called an egosyntonic disorder (acceptable to the person). Therefore people with the syndrome do not all present for help and we are unclear about how common it is. The incidence has been calculated to be 19 in 100,000 per year in females and two in males, rising to 50 in females aged 13 to 19. Despite media reports, the evidence for increasing incidence is weak. The lifetime prevalence of AN in women may be as high as 1.2 to 2.4 per cent. The difference between the incidence and prevalence is one marker of how commonly the disorder can become 'enduring'. Worryingly, despite the severity of the problem, one study suggests that only one-third of people with the disorder are in contact with mental health services.

In community-based studies, the prevalence of BN in young women is usually quoted as 1 per cent. Again, 90 per cent of people diagnosed are female. Even though the symptoms are disliked by the person, it is probable that only 8 per cent of sufferers are in contact with services and wait for very long periods before seeking help. This reflects shame associated with the symptoms compounded by the poor availability of services.

AN and BN together are about as common as EDs that do not fit neatly into these categories (see Diagnosis). For a recent review of these issues see Smink *et al.* (2012).

AETIOLOGY OF EATING DISORDERS

Since the first descriptions of AN in medical papers in the late nineteenth century by William Gull (1873) and in Paris by Dr Laségue (1878), different ideas around the aetiology of EDs have been proposed. Many of these ideas are not supported by current research evidence. Even the validity of the diagnostic categories of EDs as favoured by DSM-V is a matter of debate (see 'Transdiagnostic model' below).

Like so many other mental health diagnoses, we currently understand that the development of an ED requires an interaction between a predisposition, environmental factors and a triggering event. All of these factors would have to be present. No single factor can be causal. There is evidence to support the biological/genetic predisposition hypotheses, ranging from heritability studies showing that the more genetically related a person may be the higher the risk of AN, to observations that people who develop AN are more likely than others to have a very detailed rigid thinking style and a more sensitive temperament from very early on in life (Treasure *et al.*, 2010). Intra-uterine stress, peer group teasing/criticism (especially weight/shape-related) or a family focus on food, weight and shape have been put forward as environmental factors that may contribute to a person's risk of developing an ED.

Most EDs start in adolescence/early adulthood, and are more common in females than in males. This has led researchers to look at the way puberty affects the developing brain, especially in the presence of oestrogen. In addition, there are a great many other developmental challenges during puberty around individuation, separation, physical and identity development, education, etc. Centrally, weight loss for any reason (e.g. due to dieting, physical ill health or mental health issues) needs to be present as a trigger.

Schmidt and Treasure (2006) wonderfully describe how different factors come together in the initial phase of weight loss. The person gains a sense of achievement from their weight loss. This raises their mood and improves their self-esteem. They are likely to receive compliments from others regarding the weight loss, which further improves mood and self-esteem, and motivation to continue with weight loss.

For those who develop BN, starvation is followed by an out-of-control binge, and then compensation for the binge by vomiting or further starvation. All this reinforces the idea that they will need to control their diet and that weight and shape are essential in their emotional and interpersonal experience. For those who develop AN, starvation becomes a greater factor in their life. The 'starvation syndrome' becomes a physical reality with, for example, a heightened sense of fullness due to delayed stomach emptying, impaired ability to plan and regulate behaviour in relation to the bigger picture of the social world and values, increased rigidity, increased preoccupation with food, extreme emotional experience between numbness of being overwhelmed, and social isolation as people may become interpersonally less accurate at recognising others' emotions. Now others become concerned, critical or hostile about the weight loss. All these consequences of starvation promote and maintain AN.

THEORY AND EVIDENCE FOR PSYCHOLOGICAL INTERVENTIONS FOR EATING DISORDERS

According to NICE (2004), the National Institute for Health and Care Excellence, there is moderate evidence for psychological interventions for BN. For AN there is no gold standard evidence base for any type of intervention, including psychological therapy, apart from symptom-focused family work in adolescents. However, the lack of evidence should not deter psychologists from becoming involved with patients with AN.

The starting point for any psychological intervention is the individual formulation of the person's problems, triggers, maintaining factors and their strengths (see Chapter 2). Assessment of their motivation to change is also essential. This formulation then provides guidance on what kind of psychological intervention may be helpful to the individual person at that moment in time.

Recovery from an ED needs to address the biological, the emotional, the cognitive and the interpersonal aspects. Without regular sufficient nutrition a person cannot fully recover from an ED; hence establishing this is an important part of treatment. We speak about 'six a day' (i.e. three meals and three snacks) trying to ensure regular nutrition and avoid starvation. People with EDs will struggle with this, and will require psycho-education and motivational work (Rollnick et al., 2008) in order to understand the impact of the ED upon their life, what keeps them stuck in it and how they can get better.

Initial psychological intervention may be around providing engagement, support, warmth, building trust and may utilise a motivational approach to help the person make some shifts towards getting better. Very malnourished patients may be helped to understand their thinking style and try out being more flexible and move towards being able to see the bigger picture. The problems in managing emotions and relationships often experienced by people with EDs may also be a useful target for intervention.

Early intervention

The concept of 'early intervention' has been developed and implemented into mental health service provision for young people with psychosis across the UK. Best management at an early point can alter the future course of the disorder and evidence in ED research suggests that early effective treatment improves outcome. Complex referral pathways are likely to delay or prevent patients and their families from arriving at early best care. There are arguments for people being able to self-refer to a triage process run by an ED service.

A related issue is the likely age at which people are at most risk of developing schizophrenia or EDs. Service set-up may dictate that patients have to 'transition' their care from adolescent to adult services just as they are engaging in early treatment. There is an argument for all age services.

Cognitive training may help shift negative attention or interpretation biases to more positive biases.

Most patients with eating disorders are ambivalent about engaging in treatment at least at some stage during treatment. The person's position on the 'cycle of change' model (Prochaska and DiClemente, 1982) needs to be kept in mind throughout therapy, as this is likely to alter and as different motivational stages require a different response. A person in the 'ambivalent' stage may benefit from thinking through the costs and benefits of change and of staying with the ED, whereas when a person is in the 'preparation' or 'action' stage they may require support in goal setting and problem solving.

Cognitive-behavioural therapy (CBT) has a moderate evidence base for the treatment of BN and BED. It is best delivered through guided self-help in the first instance. CBT helps the person challenge their thoughts and make behaviour changes. CBT-E (enhanced) developed by Chris Fairburn and colleagues for the treatment of BN and BED additionally tackles ED specific problems such as perfectionism and low self-esteem. Interpersonal psychotherapy (IPT), which adopts a greater focus on the relational aspects of a person's eating disorder, may be equally as helpful as CBT. However, symptom reduction may take a little longer. In cognitive analytic therapy (CAT) patients work collaboratively with their therapist to understand how ED behaviours are embedded in their intra- and interpersonal patterns and coping strategies that may maintain the ED. Diagrammatic and prose reformulation is used to identify exits out of unhelpful coping patterns.

Family therapy focused on symptoms of the ED is supported by NICE as a treatment for adolescents with EDs. Traditionally, this is delivered for individual families. In the past few years a multi-family therapy approach has found increasing popularity where a number of families (patients, parents, siblings and others) work together with professionals. Although there is an absence of evidence base for adults, severe EDs often leave the person functioning at an emotionally younger age than their chronological age. In addition, many people with severe EDs have to rely on the ongoing support of their families. Families are usually desperate to help. Hence helping families develop an understanding of EDs, reduce blame and stigma, and increase skills to support the person with the ED effectively is an important part of intervention for the person with the ED and those around them (see indirect work). It has been shown that carer skills training reduces carer anxiety and depression, and the behaviours that maintain EDs (Goddard *et al.*, 2011), and there are reports that it also improves patient outcome.

CASE STUDY

Aged 22, Anna was pushed by her parents to be referred to mental health services. She was assessed by our eating disorders team. She attended alone and explained that for some years she had weighed 7stone 1lb (44.9kg) at a height of 5ft 8in (1.73m), giving her a body mass index (BMI = weight in kg divided by squared height in m) of 15. She professed to being pleased with her weight but was worried that for the preceding year she had been bingeing and vomiting. 'It's gross – I'm gross.' She said that this loss of control, and the 'huge' weight changes, caused her huge distress. She saw the result as a big drop in her mood and her self-confidence. She felt overpoweringly guilty and had opted out of social contact with her friends, feeling that they would also see her as 'gross'. Her family had been told that her 'body salts', particularly potassium, were very abnormal and might kill her. They were terrified and had good reason to worry that sudden death was a possibility. She seemed unconcerned about this risk and said it would be a happy release. When seen, she said she could see no reason to gain weight but did want help with stopping the binges.

At age 18 she thinks she weighed 9st 7lb, BMI 20, and had quite liked her body. She felt lonely across a summer holiday and began to think that she could be more popular if she lost some weight and took more exercise. She was successful at this. Those around her initially congratulated her, but others soon began to express concern that things were going too far. She remained irritated by their concern and interference.

Our view was that she had developed anorexia nervosa of a binge–purge sub-type. There was a question as to whether she also had a mood disorder or whether her mood was in keeping with the building costs of her eating disorder. Her personality sounded slightly impulsive more than perfectionist, but not markedly so. Alongside this formulation of her problem we had to include recognition of elements of malnutrition and worrying potassium problems. All of these problems needed to be managed.

We decided that it was safe enough to look after her out of an eating disorder unit provided we had in place a monitoring process, agreed with all, to watch her weight, her blood chemistry and ECG (electrical heart recording). Admitting such people to an eating disorder unit is tempting, and at times necessary, because the risks of death are very real. However, the evidence base for admission helping in this circumstance is poor. There are a number of drawbacks. For example, admission results in the service taking control of treatment and there can be difficulties in enabling the patient to take back responsibility for their condition.

Starting off by recognising that she probably saw it differently, we offered Anna our initial understanding of her problem but suggested that she meet with a member of our team to evolve a joint understanding of the mechanisms involved and how we might help, how she might help herself and how her parents might help.

Anna was irritated by the suggestion that her family might be involved, pointing out that she was an adult. Our response was to underline that, in the end, the choice was hers, but that we would recommend the involvement of family whatever the age of the person. We explained that she was not to blame for her problems, but that neither were her family. However, it was probable that her family could be helpful if offered support and direction. On the other side, if not included, there was a risk that their anxiety would make things worse for her. Her irritation was perhaps enhanced by her own belief that events within her family were to blame for her eating disorder.

Part of the initial understanding we offered was a psycho-education package which included the known effects of low weight/starvation on thought and behaviour and normal eating. For Anna in particular this included the process of low weight or dietary restriction making bingeing more likely. Anna's response to the latter was to minimise this information. She could see the implication of the need for eating more regularly and gaining weight. Fear of this led to an avoidant response.

We talked to her about the usefulness of vitamin supplements, potassium supplementation and the role that FLUOXETINE (an antidepressant that reduces appetite) might have but suggested that it would be preferable to begin with a package of psychological care.

Shortly after engaging with us Anna took an overdose and offered a mixed message of saying that everyone would be better off without her, while also saying that nobody took her seriously or they would 'lock me up and stop me stuffing my face'.

Anna did allow her parents to become involved. They would attend review meetings as well as the Family and Friends Support Skills Workshop (see below). With this combination they clearly felt better but the knock-on benefits of less destructive family anxiety and more understanding had a palpable effect on Anna's level of distress.

Individual work blended the input of an eating disorders practitioner (EDP) from our team and a clinical psychologist. It is not easy to draw clear boundaries for 'who is doing what', but the effects can be synergistic. The EDP provided support, ongoing psycho-education and ensured safe physical monitoring. The clinical psychologist worked with Anna to develop a shared understanding of the mechanisms that underpinned her ED based on a bio-psychosocial formulation. They looked at the behaviours such as restriction and bingeing, identified triggers and possible alternative coping strategies. It was important to start the work where Anna felt motivated to make some changes and to get alongside her rather than pushing her to make changes she was not yet ready to contemplate. They saw that Anna has always been extremely sensitive to criticism and often perceived criticism where there was none. Whenever she felt criticised, Anna would feel worthless and frustrated and this would then trigger a binge. Anna and the psychologist worked together to become more aware of this inner critical voice and to challenge it. Over time, Anna learned how to be more compassionate with herself as well as with others (the critical voice had also been directed at those around her, especially her family) and this helped improve Anna's self-esteem, self-care, and her relationship with others.

All of the above sat in the context of practitioners who understand the techniques of motivational interviewing. Through avoiding persistent confrontation regarding the need for weight gain, Anna herself began to see the necessity for this if she was going to move out of the increasingly lonely world of her ED. Sadly, she then made the discovery that she could not eat more and gain weight, and thereby stop bingeing and vomiting. Her belief had been that she 'was in control'. Herself wanting to change these behaviours led her to find out the degree to which the ED controlled her. 'It's an evil illness.'

In concrete terms she could not gain weight. However, she was less blaming of others which moved her from the counterproductive belief that if others had behaved differently in the past she would not now have this problem. She had moved to the more fertile territory of trying to work out what she could change today. Equally she felt understood, and was being offered a model that did not blame her for her problems or failure to improve. In this way her self-esteem improved. Armed with this, she and the professionals were able to look at tangential approaches to her difficulties. She joined a choir. She went on holiday for the first time in years. She began to consider re-engaging in education at the point at which she had left off.

In these circumstances the 'anorexic voice' weakened. She was more able to tolerate weight gain, more able to tolerate 'fear' foods and thereby entered a virtuous circle that eventually enabled her to go off to university to study psychology. At the point of leaving our service her BMI was still only 17.7 and she would still occasionally binge and vomit, but she had been helped to recognise these achievements rather than emphasising what difficulties remained. Her own perception was that she was now armed with tools she could use without ongoing professional involvement.

This process took two years and a lot of expert therapeutic input. It required services to stick with her through a sustained period where she may have been construed as 'not trying'.

Team working/indirect work

The Family and Friends Support Skills Workshops are based on the Maudsley model of collaborative care (see Treasure *et al.*, 2007) and offer a blend of education, training in support skills and support from peers. In the workshop Anna's parents learned – to their initial surprise – that they had no direct control over whether their daughter ate or not, or whether she accepted help or not. What was under their direct control was their behaviour (e.g. how they looked after themselves, what beliefs they had about their role in the development of their daughter's AN and how they responded to the AN). Anna's mother felt that she was the cause of her ED, that if she had been more sensitive to Anna, Anna would be fine. This belief and the corresponding guilt resulted in her trying to compensate by doing anything to help her daughter. This left her exhausted, helpless and even guiltier. On the contrary, Anna's father struggled to understand why Anna could not 'just eat' and often became angry at her, and blamed her for the negative impact her behaviour had upon the family, especially her mother who was close to breaking point. The Maudsley uses animal metaphors. Mum used this to see how she behaved more like a kangaroo (over-caring) and Dad more a rhino (angry, pushing for change). The parents learned that both positions are understandable but neither are helpful. They saw how they could perhaps work together to help Anna get better and in the workshop they began practising some skills to support rather than confront Anna and avoid arguments. Both Mum and Dad felt that they benefited from the workshop. They joined the monthly support group to continue to meet up with others in a similar position and share their struggles and achievements.

CRITICAL ISSUES

Trans-diagnostic model

DSM–V is the mainstay of diagnosis but some professionals are critical of this system (Fairburn and Cooper, 2011). There are two main concerns. First, a significant proportion of patients do not fit into the main categories. If you believe that diagnosis should be helpful in informing a management plan, the category of 'Eating disorder not otherwise specified' is not very useful. Second, ED patients do frequently move between diagnoses. Most commonly restricting AN moves into a more bulimic picture.

Obesity

For reasons explained in the manual, obesity is not included in the DSM–V as a mental disorder. Obesity (excess body fat) results from the long-term excess of energy intake relative to energy expenditure. A range of genetic, physiological, behavioural and environmental factors that vary across individuals contributes to the development of obesity; thus, obesity is not considered a mental disorder. In addition, there is the absence of a known mental health problem in obese people and the very limited evidence for psychological treatments in obesity. It is too easy to think 'but it must work' – despite this lack of evidence.

Starvation syndrome

Chicken or egg? Does abnormal thinking lead to starvation or does starvation create distorted thinking? The answer is that this is a false dichotomy, but the way in which starvation changes thinking is too often ignored in the therapeutic process.

SEVERE AND ENDURING EDs (SEEDs)

Much that is written about EDs focuses on teenage girls. However, people can develop EDs later in life and teenagers who do not recover grow older. The concept of severe and enduring eating disorders has therefore been suggested (Robinson, 2009) to promote modified care models to meet the needs of this group. Overambitious aims will alienate the patient. There will be a greater need for social and financial support.

ADDICTIONS MODELS

It is hard to escape parallels to the world of substance misuse. As a consequence useful concepts such as 'Stages of Change' and motivational interviewing have crossed over to the ED world (Prochaska and DiClemente, 1982; Rollnick *et al.*, 2008). Despite the usefulness it is important to recognise where parallels break down. An example would be the major and early advantages of detoxification from alcohol versus the sustained distress of someone with AN endeavouring to gain weight.

Capacity

A proportion of patients with AN will have a long-term life-ruining illness that has not responded to extensive treatment. Treatment, particularly admission, may be experienced as abusive. Can such patients ever legally refuse life-saving treatment? The current answer is that we do not know, but any such examples will be very rare. The Mental Capacity Act (MCA) gives us a framework for addressing these issues (MCA, 2005; and Tan, 2006, 2012).

CONCLUSION

We hope that we have conveyed the sense that EDs are severe illnesses which can ruin lives but that, while distressing, they provide an interesting and fulfilling area in which to work. It is both anxiety provoking and stimulating to work where there is so much that we do not understand. The management of EDs shows how you cannot extrapolate from effective treatments to cause. For example, we are sure that family dynamics do not cause AN. However, working with the family is our most effective intervention. Uncertainty about cause does not prevent us from helping.

CONCLUSION TO PETER'S STORY

While anorexia nervosa nearly beat me, I have managed to fully recover from my eating disorder. Successful holistic therapy proved invaluable in enabling me to confront and overcome my anorexia. Through a combination of talking therapies, nutritional counselling, antidepressants and a close monitoring of my physical health, the team supporting me helped me transform my future. While sceptical of the value of antidepressants and talking therapies at first, my experience leads me to conclude that these options were critical to my achieving a recovery. I was fortunate to receive excellent medical attention, but the key for me, and other patients whom I encountered, was to acknowledge one's own difficulties and confront these head-on. While fiercely independent, I had to learn to accept the help of others. This was by no means a weakness and now I take great comfort in reaching out and seeking support from those who are closest to me. While recovery was a difficult journey, it was most certainly the right course of action upon which to embark.

KEY CONCEPTS AND TERMS

- Anorexia nervosa
- Bulimia nervosa
- Severe and enduring EDs
- DSM-V
- Trans-diagnostic model

- BMI
- Motivational interviewing
- Family and Friends Support Skills Workshop

- NICE
- Starvation syndrome
- Capacity

LEARNING OUTCOMES

When you have completed this chapter you should be able to:

1. Recognise what features or symptoms are characteristic of anorexia nervosa, bulimia nervosa and other similar types of eating disorders.
2. Have an understanding of the types of psychological difficulties suffered by people with these EDs.
3. Have an understanding of the current evidence base for psychological treatment of these EDs.
4. Have an understanding of the aspects of treatment and management that are likely to be important during the course of the ED.
5. Have an understanding of how clinical psychologists work together with other professions to assess, formulate and treat EDs.

SAMPLE ESSAY TITLES

- What are the important aspects of psychological treatment in EDs?
- When assessing for EDs what factors need to be taken into account?
- What are the areas in need of further research in EDs?
- How do psychologists work together with other professions to help people with EDs?

REFERENCES AND RECOMMENDED READING

American Psychiatric Association (2013). *Diagnostic and Statistical Manual of Mental Disorders* (5th edn). Arlington, VA: American Psychiatric Publishing.

beat – the leading UK charity for people with eating disorders and their families – a very good source of information and useful contact numbers. Available at www.b-eat.co.uk.

BEAT and ProBono Economics Report (2012). Costs of eating disorders in England: Economic impacts of anorexia nervosa, bulimia nervosa and other disorders, focussing on young people. BEAT.

Bryant-Waugh, R. and Lask, B. (2004). *Eating Disorders: A parents' guide*. Hove, Sussex: Brunner-Routledge.

Cooper, P.J. (1993). *Overcoming Bulimia and Binge-eating*. Robinson Publishing.

Fairburn, C.G. (1995). *Overcoming Binge Eating*. New York: The Guilford Press.

—— (2008). *Cognitive Behaviour Therapy and Eating Disorders*. New York: The Guilford Press.

Fairburn, C.G. and Cooper, Z. (2011). Eating disorders, DSM–5 and clinical reality. *The British Journal of Psychiatry, 198*, 8–10.

Fotios, C., Papadopoulos, A.E., Brandt, L. and Ekselius, L. (2009). Excess mortality, causes of death and prognostic factors in anorexia nervosa. *The British Journal of Psychiatry, 194*, 10–17.

Garner, D.M. (1997). Psychoeducational principles in the treatment of eating disorders. In D.M. Garner and P.E. Garfinkel (eds), *Handbook for Treatment of Eating Disorders* (pp. 145–177). New York: The Guilford Press.

Goddard, E., Macdonald, P. and Treasure, J. (2011). An examination of the impact of the Maudsley Collaborative Care Skills Training Workshops on patients with anorexia nervosa: A qualitative study. *European Eating Disorders Review, 19*, 150–161.

Institute of Psychiatry; Eating Disorders Research Site – as described it contains a lot of useful materials for professionals, families and patients. Available at www.eatingresearch.com.

Mental Capacity Act (MCA) (2005). Available at http://www.dca.gov.uk/menincap/legis.htm

Mental Health Act (2007). Available at http://www.legislation.gov.uk/ukpga/2007/12/pdfs/ukpga_20070012_en.pdf.

National Institute for Health and Care Excellence (NICE) (2004 and 2011). *Eating Disorders CG009*. London: National Institute for Health and Care Excellence.

Prochaska, J.O. and DiClemente, C.C. (1982). Transtheoretical therapy: Toward a more integrative model of change. *Psychotherapy: Theory, Research and Practice, 19*(3), 276–288.

Robinson, P. (2009). *Severe and Enduring Eating Disorder (SEED): Management of complex presentations of anorexia and bulimia nervosa*. Oxford: Wiley-Blackwell.

Rollnick, S., Miller, W.R. and, Butler, C.C. (2008). *Motivational Interviewing in Health Care: Helping patients change behaviour*. New York: The Guilford Press.

Royal College of Psychiatrists website – a source of basic information about eating disorders. Available at www.rcpsych.ac.uk/mentalhealthinformation.aspx.

Schmidt, U. and Treasure, J. (1993). *Getting Better Bit(e) by Bit(e)*. Hove, Sussex: Psychology Press.

Schmidt, U. and Treasure, J. (2006). *Anorexia nervosa: Valued and visible*. A cognitive-interpersonal maintenance model and its implications for research and practise. *British Journal of Clinical Psychology, 45*(3), 343–366.

Smink, F.R.E., van Hoeken, D. and Hoek, H.W. (2012). Epidemiology of eating disorders: Incidence, prevalence and mortality rates. *Current Psychiatry Reports, 14*, 406–414.

Tan, J. (2012). Royal College of Psychiatry EDSECT Newsletter. December.

Tan, J., Stewart, A., Fitzpatrick, R., and Hope, R.A. (2006) Competence to make treatment decisions in anorexia nervosa: Thinking processes and values philosophy. *Psychiatry, and Psychology, 13*(4), 267–282.

Treasure, J. (1997). *Anorexia Nervosa; A Survival Guide for Families, Friends and Sufferers*. Hove, Sussex: Psychology Press.

Treasure, J., Smith, G. and Crane, A. (2007). *Skills-based Learning for Caring for a Loved One with an Eating Disorder*. Abingdon, Oxon: Routledge.

Treasure, J., Claudino, A.M. and Zucker, N. (2010) Eating disorders. *Lancet, 375*, 583–593.

Waller, G., Mountford, V., Lawson, R., Gray, E., Cordery, C. and Hinrichsen, H. (2010). *Beating Your Eating Disorder: A cognitive-behavioural self-help guide for adult sufferers and their carers*. Cambridge: Cambridge University Press.

11 Working with people with PTSD and complex trauma

Maeve Crowley and Ines Santos

PETER'S STORY

I am a 35-year-old man, living with my partner and three sons aged between 5 and 11. I am unemployed but previously worked as a plumber. I am one of seven children. My father was a builder and he drank too much and used to beat up us kids. My mother struggled to cope. Life was tough but that's how it was.

Ten years ago after a pub brawl I was beaten and left for dead outside a pub.

Following the attack, my physical recovery from a broken collar bone and broken ribs was slow. From that day on, I lost my confidence and was scared of going out in case I was attacked again as the attackers were never caught; scared that I would lose my rag and end up in prison. I started getting panic attacks and getting easily upset by noise, spending most of the time in my room on my own. I was unable to stop thinking about the beating and it played in my mind almost constantly like a film. Sometimes, I went crazy, I lost the sense of where I was and it felt like the assault was happening all over again – the footsteps behind me, the whack on my head, the sense of falling on my face thinking 'This is it, I'm in for it'. I started smoking cannabis because that was the only way to numb my feelings and get me to sleep but I woke soon after with nightmares of being chased and would wake up shouting and soaked in sweat. My partner got scared when I woke up like that at night.

Ten years on and little has changed. I'm stuck in a rut and don't know how to get out. My life is worthless. I'm a failure for letting this get on top of me. I am failing my partner, I am failing my children. I sometimes wonder if they would be all better off without me.

SUMMARY

In a world where trauma is commonplace, in the form of natural disasters, wars, accidents, violence and abuse, it is important to understand people's reactions to these events and to develop effective clinical treatments. Alongside depression and anxiety, the most common psychological reactions to trauma are post-traumatic stress disorder (PTSD) and complex PTSD (C-PTSD).

Treatment for traumatic stress disorders has a long historical tradition and as early as the First World War soldiers were diagnosed with 'shell-shock'. Early treatments were primitive, based on repressing the memories and experiences (Jones and Wessley, 2006). Our knowledge about PTSD and how to treat it has developed considerably since then.

In this chapter we hope to give you an insight into the experience of having PTSD and C-PTSD, how it can be assessed and treated clinically and also a sense of traumatised individuals' tremendous capacity to heal and grow from their experiences. We also want to give you a sense of how deeply rewarding it can be to work with this client group. We will review some of the psychological theories and models that are relevant to PTSD and complex PTSD and look at how assessment, formulation and intervention techniques are used by psychologists working with traumatised individuals. We will also be highlighting some of the controversies in the field of traumatology and their scientific and clinical implications.

INTRODUCTION: WHAT IS PTSD AND COMPLEX PTSD, AND WHAT ARE THE TYPES OF PSYCHOLOGICAL DIFFICULTIES THAT CAN OCCUR IN THESE DISORDERS?

PTSD

PTSD can occur as a consequence of exposure to exceptionally threatening and distressing events, such as natural disasters, car crashes, sexual assaults, terrorist attacks or war.

A very disturbing feature of PTSD is intrusive memories of the trauma. These memories are accompanied by images, smells and bodily sensations that were experienced at the time of the trauma.

Reminders of the trauma, such as hearing a car braking, lead to intense and prolonged distress (e.g. fear, shame) and are accompanied by physical anxiety similar to a panic reaction.

Sometimes, the person feels as if they are actually reliving the trauma and this is known as a flashback. Flashbacks can be very distressing and people can feel that they are going mad, as they do not understand what is happening to them.

Intrusive memories of the trauma can occur during sleep in the form of nightmares. These intrusive symptoms keep the trauma and the sense of danger very much in the present and thus these individuals are chronically aroused, constantly on the alert for danger (hyper-vigilance). They also startle easily, for example, if there is an unexpected knock at the door. This high level of arousal leads to problems in concentration and sleep, and to people being more irritable and aggressive.

In an attempt to cope with these overwhelming symptoms individuals develop avoidance strategies. For example, people may avoid driving, going out at night or certain television programmes. Avoiding talking about the trauma can make it difficult for people to seek treatment or to give an account of the trauma, for example, to police or lawyers.

Difficulties in mood regulation may include emotional numbing and detachment from others and the world. In addition, they may have negative views of themselves, others and the world, for example, 'I am unlucky' and 'I attract bad people'.

As we can see from this list of symptoms, the effects of PTSD can be far-reaching and have a debilitating impact upon many areas of a person's life such as mental and physical health, relationships, work and school.

Complex PTSD

Complex PTSD was first proposed as a condition by Herman (1992), who observed that exposure to traumas such as prolonged abuse (domestic violence), organised abuse (paedophile gangs, trafficking or torture) was associated with a particular set of clinical symptoms beyond and including those for PTSD. People found it difficult to manage their emotions and urges, sometimes presenting with violent outbursts. Other times they have a tendency towards dissociating when under stress, for example, losing time, seeing themselves as existing outside their bodies, or forgetting important aspects of their past. They often see themselves as worthless, unlovable and weak, and often experience feelings of shame and guilt about what they experienced, witnessed or could not stop. As they were abandoned or betrayed as children they can have difficulty trusting people or find it hard to judge who is trustworthy.

Clients with C-PTSD will often be mislabelled and misunderstood, and so find it hard to access appropriate help.

Diagnosis of PTSD

The Diagnostic and Statistical Manual of Mental Disorders (DSM) is the standard classification of mental disorders used by mental health professionals, and lists which symptoms must be present for each disorder.

DSM-V (APA, 2013) diagnostic criteria for PTSD requires a history of exposure to a traumatic event involving death, threatened death, actual or threatened serious injury, or actual or threatened sexual violence. In addition, symptoms from each of four symptom clusters must be present:

* Intrusion (memories, nightmares, flashbacks, emotional distress and physical anxiety to traumatic reminders) (one symptom required).
* Avoidance (avoidance of thoughts or feelings as well as people, places, conversations, activities, objects or situations related to trauma) (one symptom required).
* Negative alterations in cognitions and mood (two symptoms required).
* Alterations in arousal and reactivity (two symptoms required).

Symptoms must continue for more than one month and cause significant distress and impairment. There is a sub-type of PTSD with dissociative symptoms (depersonalisation or de-realisation) and also a delayed onset sub-type.

Additional symptoms in complex PTSD (Herman, 1992)

An individual who has experienced a prolonged period (months to years) of chronic victimisation and total control by another may also experience difficulties in the following areas:

- *Emotional regulation* (e.g. persistent sadness, suicidal thoughts, explosive anger).
- *Consciousness* (e.g. having episodes in which one feels detached from one's mental processes or body – dissociation).
- *Self-perception* (e.g. a sense of being completely different from other human beings).
- *Distorted perceptions of the perpetrator* (e.g. attributing total power to the perpetrator).
- *Relations with others* (e.g. isolation, distrust).
- *One's system of meanings* (e.g. a sense of hopelessness and despair).

Complex PTSD is not yet a formal psychiatric diagnosis but it is a well-recognised clinical condition. It seems likely that it will be included in the new ICD-11. The symptom pattern being proposed is the core symptoms of PTSD plus persistent and pervasive impairments in affective functioning, self-functioning and relational functioning.

EPIDEMIOLOGY OF PTSD

Epidemiological research of traumatic events in PTSD reveals a number of important points.

First, surveys (e.g. Kessler *et al.*, 1995) reveal that traumatic events are common, with most people (around 60%) experiencing at least one major traumatic event in their life and most having exposure to multiple traumas. Exposure to traumatic events is somewhat higher for men than for women.

Second, these surveys reveal that most people exposed to trauma do not develop PTSD, symptoms developing in only about 10 per cent of cases, suggesting that individual factors play an important role in the aetiology of the disorder.

Third, although only a minority develop PTSD, it is nevertheless a high prevalence disorder, with 7.8 per cent of people having a lifetime history of PTSD, with women twice as likely as men being affected.

Fourth, PTSD tends to be of a chronic nature and requires professional treatment, with a significant minority not recovering even with treatment (NICE, 2005).

Thus, given that only a minority of people develop PTSD after exposure to trauma, what factors determine which people develop the disorder and which do not?

Well, research suggests that it depends on factors such as characteristics of the traumatic events as well as individual risk factors. Rape has the highest trauma impact, with other high-impact events including combat stress, childhood neglect and childhood physical abuse, and physical assaults. Of the individual risk factors, psychiatric history, childhood abuse and family psychiatric history are reliably found to be risk factors for PTSD (Brewin et al., 2000). Cognitive appraisals (i.e. the sense a person makes of the trauma, at the time of trauma and in its aftermath) have also been found to be important predictors of PTSD.

AETIOLOGY OF PTSD

The reasons why someone reacts to a trauma and develops PTSD or C-PTSD are varied, but an understanding of the evolutionary biological basis is essential. A person perceives a threat. It is registered in the part of the brain that is there to raise the alarm (the Amygdala). The system is aroused and prepares for the fight-or-flight response. If this is not possible the body freezes. The neurochemicals released close down the activity of the thinking brain (neocortex) and cortisol shuts down the hippocampus. This means that the experience cannot be processed, time tagged or stored, and as a result may be re-experienced sometime in the future.

Unfortunately, if a trauma memory is not processed it may be re-experienced in a number of ways in the form of intrusions, and this leads to avoidance. This re-triggering is outside the person's conscious control. People who have experienced abuse describe being triggered by certain smells or a look on someone's face and then react as if the past trauma is occurring in the present.

Despite the neurological basis of trauma being central, we also know that different people respond differently to different traumas depending on the resources available to them. For example, a person who has a good experience of parenting (a secure attachment) will manage the effects of a trauma more effectively. People with more effective coping resources, people with greater social support and people without a history of early trauma are more likely to cope better with traumas experienced in adult life.

PSYCHOLOGICAL INTERVENTIONS FOR PTSD

How can an individual be helped to come to terms with a traumatic event? Does trauma therapy really work and what is it like?

In 2005, the NICE (National Institute of Health and Care Excellence) guidelines for treatment for PTSD were published, concluding that trauma-focused cognitive-behavioural therapy (TF-CBT) and eye movement desensitisation and reprocessing (EMDR) are equally effective in the treatment of PTSD and should be offered to all people with PTSD (NICE, 2005).

The fact that these treatments involve some degree of retelling of the trauma narrative is what makes them more effective than other treatments such as relaxation or supportive therapies.

Trauma therapy, like therapy for other conditions, starts with a comprehensive assessment and psycho-education about trauma and trauma symptoms alongside the development of a strong therapeutic relationship.

Trauma-focused CBT

An important element of TF-CBT is exposure to the trauma. There are two types of exposure:

- *Imaginal exposure:* Patients are asked to give a detailed account of the trauma narrative in the present tense, including sights, sounds, smells, emotions and bodily sensations. This is called 'reliving'.
- *In vivo exposure:* This involves exposure to the actual site and triggers of the trauma. Patients may go to the place where the assault happened or to the site of the car crash.

Exposure is hypothesised to lead to an elaboration of the trauma memories, where they become more complete and include extra details, such as 'I could not have seen the car coming because I can't see round corners' or even 'I survived, it's in the past'.

Some TF-CBT treatments, such as *prolonged exposure therapy*, have their main focus on exposure, and have been shown to be very effective, for example, with rape victims (Rothbaum *et al.*, 1992).

With other CBT approaches, such as *cognitive processing therapy*, the focus of therapy is cognitive restructuring; that is, changing how an individual views themselves, the trauma and its consequences (Resick and Schnicke, 1993).

However, most trauma-focused cognitive-behavioural therapies incorporate both exposure and cognitive restructuring. Ehlers and Clark's Cognitive Model of PTSD (Ehlers and Clark, 2000) is the evidence-based CBT model for PTSD. The total duration of TF-CBT therapy is between eight and 20 sessions.

PTSD and CBT (videos)

http://www.youtube.com/watch?v=Tx3KdKDZOS8&list=PLuEO9Uf2A6CXs9J5G1qwvtB8JzZ_Uk1aP.

Eye movement desensitisation and reprocessing (EMDR)

EMDR therapy is based on the Adaptive Information Processing Model (Shapiro, 2001). It postulates that the physiological systems of the brain are no different from body systems. It has a natural tendency to heal and process following a trauma unless there is repeated traumatisation or a block to that healing – as evidenced by the fact that most people do not develop PTSD after exposure to trauma.

According to Shapiro, there is a natural physiological system that is designed to transform disturbing input into an adaptive resolution and a psychologically healthy integration. It will just file it away in the appropriate folder. If there is a blockage in this information processing, it will react to the present as if the individual is in the past, thus experiencing it again. As they are frozen in the past, they cannot freely experience the present. The brain does not discard the maladaptive material and therefore cannot access more adaptive material from the present.

Imagine the exhaustion of constantly experiencing the danger of the past, while trying to experience the present. One can see how it is hard for traumatised people to gain pleasure from good things in the present (family, hobbies, etc.) when there is a movie of the trauma running in the background, often more vivid in response to reminders.

EMDR accesses the target trauma memory and all its emotions, thoughts and physical sensations. As the client has dual attention both on the past memory and the current safety, they process the unprocessed memory and access more adaptive memory networks. This is achieved through bilateral stimulation, activating both hemispheres of the brain, through following the therapist's hand moving from side to side, listening to bilateral sounds, or having bilateral tappers in one's hands.

Getting Past Your Past/Francine Shapiro

YouTube: https://www.youtube.com/watch?v=nylajeG6uFY

Treatments for complex PTSD

The NICE guidelines focused upon PTSD and not upon complex PTSD, acknowledging that individuals who suffered multiple and chronic traumas would need more extensive and comprehensive treatment than that recommended for simple PTSD (NICE, 2005).

For C-PTSD a three-phased approach to treatment involving stabilisation, trauma processing and reintegration is increasingly regarded as the best approach (Cloitre et al., 2012).

*   *Phase 1*: Establishing safety and stability, reducing symptoms and increasing important emotional, social and psychological competencies.
*   *Phase 2*: Processing unresolved trauma memories so that they are integrated into the adaptive representation of self, relationships and the world.
*   *Phase 3*: Consolidation of treatment gains to facilitate transition from the end of treatment to greater engagement with the outside world.

These three phases may be achieved using various evidence-based trauma therapies (EMDR and CBT) and supplemented with other psychological techniques as required.

CASE STUDY 1: TINA

Tina is a 33-year-old woman who was referred to mental health services following a sexual assault in a pub. She presented with severe depression, symptoms of trauma and was at high risk of suicide.

Assessment with a clinical psychologist trauma specialist

Tina had a history of childhood trauma characterised by poor attachments (including separations from both parents at various times and the witnessing of severe domestic violence). She experiences further poor and violent relationships in adulthood.

Assessment revealed severe trauma symptoms following a recent sexual assault, supported by high scores on the Impact of Events Scale Revised (IES-R), and there was evidence of high levels of dissociation, supported by high scores on the Dissociative Experiences Scale (DES).

She reported avoiding going out by herself, which seemed to be due to fears about being attacked again. This was severely affecting her daily functioning, and her ability to continue studying and seek work.

The conclusion from the assessment was that she needed specialist trauma therapy.

Formulation

As the therapist was an EMDR practitioner, this case was formulated using AIP (adaptive information processing).

We hypothesised that unprocessed childhood traumas were reactivated by adult traumas and in particular the recent sexual assault. The sexual attack triggered her feelings of fear, shame and inability to trust others, which were similar to earlier traumatic experiences. The fear network was activated and it generalised to other situations, making her unable to leave the house and function normally.

The goal of therapy was to help her process the past traumas so that she could feel safe again in the present and be able to access more adaptive memory networks and ways of being, such that she had survived, that she was safe and that others could be trustworthy.

Trauma therapy

Tina was treated with EMDR, but trauma-focused CBT would also have been another treatment of choice.

The first phase of trauma therapy is stabilisation. As is always done at the beginning of an EMDR treatment, we developed a calm place, a visualisation of an imagined place – in Tina's case a tropical beach – where she could feel calm, leading to a felt sense of calm and reduced arousal and anxiety. We installed this using bilateral stimulation (in this case through the use of slow eye movements).

The stabilisation was strengthened using Resource Installation, which is an EMDR approach to develop and enhance internal coping in clients with complex presentations and poor emotional regulation skills. We did some work on enabling her to access positive memories – being competent in work situations, being a good mother, feeling safe with her grandfather, again reinforcing this using bilateral stimulation. This resource work enhanced her self-confidence and confidence in her ability to master challenging situations.

The initial focus of trauma processing was the sexual assault, as Tina was clear it was what she wanted to work on and she did not want to delve into the past.

Processing of the sexual assault was done over three sessions. She focused on the worst moment of the assault, the negative belief 'It's my fault' and the sensations in her body, and tracked the therapist's fingers left and right. She then reported what had come up (e.g. 'I can see him coming towards me and I feel sick') and the processing continued for another set, before further feedback was given. Tina accessed the full memory of the assault and how she felt, and experienced a fuller recall, including the fact that she pushed him away, that she got help, that others were sympathetic and helpful, and that the attacker had left the country so she was safe.

Her negative belief of 'It's my fault' changed to 'I did the best I could' and the Subjective Units of Distress (SUDS) reduced from 9/10 to 0/10. She reported that she was no longer disturbed by the memory.

However, she was still afraid to go out. From an AIP perspective this was to be predicted, since the underlying early memories had not been processed. This formulation was again shared with Tina and at this point she was more willing to explore her past.

We were able to identify that a belief that 'I am disgusting' and a high sense of shame, as well as fear, was underlying her avoidance of going out. Using a 'Floatback' technique, we tracked these feelings to early experiences of being treated sexually inappropriately by a step-parent. She had come to blame herself for this and strived to be invisible to keep herself safe. This sexual abuse was in the context of her witnessing severe domestic violence and fearing for her life as well as for the life of her mother and younger sister.

Tina reported that she had not made the link between those traumatic experiences and her current view of herself and her fear of going out.

Using EMDR, we were able to process these earlier traumatic memories and to shift beliefs of 'I am disgusting' and 'I am to blame'. The fear of going out improved, as did the dissociation.

In conclusion, Tina presented with PTSD but in the context of more global C-PTSD. The trauma intervention in this case was EMDR, and involved processing both recent and earlier traumas (sexual abuse, witnessing domestic violence) as these were underlying the current difficulties.

Alongside trauma therapy, Tina was seen regularly by her psychiatrist who took on a very important supportive role, monitored risk on an ongoing basis and enabled her to get on with day-to-day life.

Working alongside another professional who is taking a care coordinating role significantly facilitates the clinical psychologist's role, enabling them to focus on being a therapist as opposed to continuously having to monitor day-to-day functioning and risk, sorting out benefits and liaising with GPs about medical issues.

CASE STUDY 2: LONDON BOMBINGS – A PUBLIC MENTAL HEALTH STRATEGY

On a Thursday morning, 7 July 2005, London was struck by four suicide bombers. Just before nine o'clock, still in rush hour, three bombs went off on underground trains. An hour later the final explosion went off on a double-decker bus. The coordinated attacks killed 52 people and injured more than 770 (BBC News website).

Many of us will remember forever that morning of 7/7, hearing and seeing the unbelievable news. The psychological effect on the population of London was substantial, with about one-third reporting substantial stress, and another one-third reporting fear of travelling on public transport (Rubin *et al.*, 2007). Seven months later, this stress had reduced significantly, though a more negative worldview was common. A significant minority who suffered greater exposure to the bombings remained affected.

The public mental health strategy adopted was to systematically locate and screen individuals directly affected by the bombings and to offer trauma treatment to those in need (Brewin *et al.*, 2010). Contact details of individuals involved in the bombings were obtained from sources such as local NHS services, charities, police, as well as contacting GPs and through a media campaign. The individuals identified were given a screening assessment, including the specially developed Trauma Screening Questionnaire (TSQ) either by letter or phone.

People who scored positive on the screening were invited for a more detailed clinical assessment, to determine whether they had traumatic symptoms that were not resolving on their own. People were referred immediately to treatment or monitored for natural recovery and reassessed at three, six and nine months. In accordance with NICE guidelines, two trauma treatments were offered – TF-CBT or EMDR – across three London trauma services.

Brewin *et al.* (2010) report that in total, 910 people were identified through the Trauma Response Programme as having been directly affected by the terrorist attacks but, given that no official figures exist, many more people could have been affected and remain with unmet needs.

A total of 596 people returned screening questionnaires, of which 57 per cent screened positive and were clinically assessed. The most common diagnosis was PTSD, and almost half had other psychological disorders, including travel phobia, depression and complicated grief.

A total of 304 people (41% of those screened) were found to be in need of treatment. Some did not want therapy and some were referred for therapy near their home, so 248 were taken on for treatment in the programme, of whom 189 completed treatment. The average number of sessions was 12, with some patients receiving as many as 59 sessions. Those requiring greater numbers of sessions had often suffered also from previous prior traumas.

Results showed that therapy led to significant improvement in symptoms of trauma and depression, and these improvements were maintained one year post-treatment.

CRITICAL ISSUES

Dissociation

We all dissociate to a certain extent. We cannot take in every experience around us, but there is a difference between daydreaming through a lecture and losing time from finding yourself in a situation while not knowing how you got there. This is very frightening, overwhelming and risky, especially if you are reliving a traumatic memory.

In their excellent self-help book *Coping with Trauma Related Dissociation*, Boon and colleagues (2011) state:

> Dissociation develops when an experience is too threatening or overwhelming for a person to integrate it. It's spontaneous and adaptive and subsides when the danger has passed. This inability to integrate our traumatic experiences changes our sense of self and our personality.

Van der Hart and colleagues (2006) hypothesise that severe trauma can split the personality into characteristic parts: an apparently normal part (ANP) that continues to adapt to the demands of daily living (working, looking after a family) and an emotional part (EP) that holds the experience of the trauma in the form of reliving (intrusions in the here and now). There is usually a phobic avoidance of the trauma memory held by the EP; hence the need to dissociate. The person who dissociates to this extent is usually frightened and overwhelmed by this experience.

Treatment focuses on first recognising dissociation and learning to stabilise oneself, managing symptoms and keeping oneself safe. Only then can the client go on to process the trauma.

False memory

A false memory is a mental experience that is mistakenly taken to be a true representation of an event from one's personal past. False memories arise from the same encoding, rehearsal and memory attribution processes that produce true memories; some indeed argue that one can never be absolutely sure of the truth of any particular memory.

We know that child sexual abuse is a major societal problem (as evidenced by the high-profile cases in the UK), and children often do not disclose abuse unless specifically asked. The dilemma for applied psychologists and psychological therapists is that we have to balance the need to ask about experiences of childhood trauma, including abuse, in a manner that limits the danger of creating false memories. The British Psychological Society's guidelines are useful to consider in this area (Wright *et al.*, 2006).

Vicarious trauma and burn-out

If you are privileged enough to work with trauma survivors there is a danger that you hear so many distressing and truly traumatic stories that it has a significant effect upon your own well-being. Pearlman (1999) described vicarious traumatisation as the process of how the client's graphic and painful material challenges our cognitive schemas or beliefs, expectations and assumptions about ourselves and others. Through supervision and ensuring we have enriching experiences outside work we can limit the effect of vicarious traumatisation while also marvelling at how people strive to overcome the horrors of traumatic experiences.

Broadening the definition of trauma

There is controversy over the broadening of the definition of trauma, with increasingly more of everyday life being included in the definition of traumatic. McNally (2003) argues that it imposes a medical model upon the human experience while trivialising genuinely traumatic events, and this may shape our culture in ways that undermine our capacity for resilience in the face of adversity. This controversy has been highlighted in the recent changes to DSM-V and the proposed changes to ICD-11.

CONCLUSION

PTSD can be a very disabling and at times chronic condition. Fortunately, once people ask for help, there are two effective evidence-based psychological therapies that are available to help people with the condition. Getting access to help can be difficult, particularly if people are feeling ashamed or if people struggle to come to terms with what they believe will be the implications of asking for help (e.g. members of military). Fortunately, we are now being much more proactive in our attempts to engage people with PTSD in our services to overcome the effects of trauma.

PETER'S STORY: CONCLUSION

My partner saw a programme on TV about PTSD, nightmares and flashbacks and told me that's what I had. She took me to our GP who referred me to a psychology service. I met with a clinical psychologist who spent two hours asking me all sorts of questions and in the end agreed that I had PTSD and gave me the first good news I'd had in years: it was treatable.

I had treatment with EMDR – about 30 sessions of an hour and a half on a weekly basis. It was hard-going initially as I wasn't used to talking about myself and my feelings, it just wasn't how I was brought up. It felt odd. We worked through the assault and the memory changed. It felt more distant, I focused on the fact that I'd survived, that I'd been lucky rather than unlucky. We talked about my childhood and worked through some childhood memories, of being beaten at home and at school, of being humiliated, of having to use my fists to protect myself.

I've stopped smoking cannabis. I spend time with the children and take them to school. I go shopping with my partner. Best of all, I can think through situations now and trust myself to make the right decisions.

KEY CONCEPTS AND TERMS

- Fight, flight and freeze response
- Intrusions, avoidance, hyper-arousal
- Dissociation
- Triggers

- Adaptive information processing
- EMDR
- Targets
- Bilateral stimulation
- Reliving

- Hotspots
- Attachment
- Vicarious traumatisation and burn-out

LEARNING OUTCOMES

When you have completed this chapter you should be able to:

1 Know what features or symptoms are characteristic of PTSD and complex PTSD and to have an awareness of the types of psychological difficulties suffered by people who have experienced these symptoms as the result of exposure to a trauma stressor.
2 Have an understanding of the psychological and societal impact of trauma upon the individual.
3 Have an understanding of the psychological theories or models that are relevant to PTSD and complex PTSD.
4 Have an understanding of the treatment approaches used by clinical psychologists to treat the condition – and the evidence base for these.
5 Have an understanding of how assessment, formulation, intervention and evaluation may be used in a psychologist's work with a specific case.
6 Be able to provide a critical appraisal of the different intervention approaches.

SAMPLE ESSAY TITLES

- What are the factors that impact upon people's processing of a traumatic event?
- What differentiates the theories of PTSD and what do they have in common?
- What issues would you consider when deciding to use either CBT or EMDR?
- What are the current controversies around the diagnosis of PTSD?

FURTHER READING

Briere, J. and Scott, C. (2012). *Principles of Trauma Therapy: A guide to symptoms, evaluation, and treatment* (2nd edn). Thousand Oaks, CA: Sage.

Herman, J.L. (1997). *Trauma and Recovery*. New York: Basic Books.

Van der Kolk, B. *et al.* (2006). *Traumatic Stress: The effects of overwhelming experience on mind, body, and society.* New York: The Guilford Press.

REFERENCES

American Psychiatric Association (2013). *Diagnostic and Statistical Manual of Mental Disorders* (5th edn). Washington, DC: Author.

Boon, S., Steele, K. and Van Der Hart, O. (2011). *Coping with Trauma Related Dissociation.* New York: Norton.

Brewin, C.R., Andrews, B. and Valentine, J.D. (2000). Meta-analysis of risk factors for posttraumatic stress disorder in trauma exposed adults. *Journal of Consulting and Clinical Psychology, 68,* 748–766.

Briere, J. and Scott, C. (2012). *Principles of Trauma Therapy: A guide to symptoms, evaluation, and treatment* (2nd edn). Thousand Oaks, CA: Sage.

Cloitre, M., Courtois, C.A., Ford, J.D., Green, B.L., Alexander, P., Briere, J., Herman, J.L., Lanius, R., Stolbach, B.C., Spinazzola, J., Van der Kolk, B.A. and Van der Hart, O. (2012). *The ISTSS Expert Consensus Treatment Guidelines for Complex PTSD in Adults.* Retrieved from http://www.istss.org.

Ehlers, A. and Clarke, D.M. (2000). A cognitive model of posttraumatic stress disorder. *Behaviour Research and Therapy, 38,* 319–345.

Grey, N., Young, K. and Holmes, E. (2002). Cognitive restructuring within reliving: A treatment for peritraumatic emotional 'hotspots' in posttraumatic stress disorder. *Behavioural and Cognitive Psychotherapy, 30*(1), 37–56.

Herman, J. L. (1992). *Trauma and Recovery: The aftermath of violence from domestic violence to political terrorism.* New York: The Guilford Press.

Jones, E. and Wessley, S. (2006) *Shell Shock to PTSD: Military psychiatry from 1900 to the Gulf War.* Maudsley Series.

Keane, T.M., Brief, D.J., Pratt, E.M. and Miller, M.W. (2007). Assessment of PTSD and its co morbidity in adults. In M.J. Friedman, T.M. Keane and P.A. Resick (eds), *Handbook of PTSD Science and Practice.* New York: The Guilford Press.

Kessler, R.C., Sonnega, A., Bromet, E., Hughes, M.B. and Nelson, C.B. (1995). Posttraumatic Stress Disorder in the National Comorbidity Survey. *Archives General Psychiatry, 52*(12), 1048–1060.

Kilpatrick, D., Resnick, H.S., Milanak, M.E., Miller, M.W., Keyes, K.M. and Friedman, M.J. (2013). *National Estimates of Exposure to Traumatic Events and PTSD Prevalence Using DSM-IV and Proposed DSM-5 Criteria* [Manuscript submitted for publication].

Lab, D., Santos, I. and Zulueta, F. de (2008) Treating post traumatic stress disorder in the 'real world': Evaluation of a specialist trauma service and adaptations to standard treatment approaches. *Psychiatric Bulletin, 32,* 8–12.

McNally, R.J. (2003). Progress and controversy in the study of posttraumatic stress disorder. *Annual Review of Psychology, 54,* 229–252.

NICE (National Institute for Clinical Excellence) (2005). *The Management of PTSD in Adults and Children in Primary and Secondary Care (Vol. 26).* Wiltshire: Cromwell Press.

Pearlman, L.A. (1999) Self-care for trauma therapists: Ameliorating vicarious traumatisation. In B.H. Stamm (ed.), *Secondary Traumatic Stress: Self care for clinicians, researchers and educators* (2nd edn, pp. 51–64). Baltimore, MD: Sidran Press.

Resick, P.A., and Schnicke, M.K. (1993). *Cognitive Processing Therapy for Rape Victims: A treatment manual.* Newbury Park, CA: Sage.

Resick, P., Bovin, M.J., Calloway, A.L., Dick, A.M., King, M.W., Mitchell, K.S. and Wolf, E.J. (2012). A critical evaluation of the complex PTSD literature: Implications for DSM-5. *Journal of Traumatic Stress, 25,* 239–249.

Rothbaum, B.O., Foa, E.B., Riggs, D.S., Murdock, T. and Walsh, W. (1992). A prospective examination of post-traumatic stress disorder in rape victims. *Journal of Traumatic Stress, 5,* 455–475.

Rubin, G.J., Brewin, C.R., Greenberg, N., Hacker Hughes, J., Simpson, J. and Wessely, S. (2007). Enduring consequences of terrorism: 7-month follow-up survey of reactions to the bombings in London on 7 July 2005. *British Journal of Psychiatry, 190,* 350–356.

Shapiro, F. (2001). *Eye Movement Desensitisation and Reprocessing: Basic principles, protocols and procedures* (2nd edn). New York: The Guilford Press.

Van der Hart, O., Nijenhuis, E.R.S. and Steele, K. (2006). *The Haunted self: Structural dissociation and the treatment of chronic traumatisation.* New York: Norton.

Wilson, N., d'Ardenne, P., Scott, C., Fine, H. and Priebe, S. (2012). Survivors of the London Bombings with PTSD: A qualitative study of their accounts during CBT treatment. *Traumatology, 18,* 75–84.

Wright, D., Ost, J. and French, C. (2006). Recovered and false memories. *The Psychologist, 19*(6), 352–355.

4 | Working with people with disabilities and physical health problems

12 Working with people with intellectual disabilities

Jan Burns

JAMES' STORY

My name is James and I am 24 years old. I live with Simon, Colin and Stanley in a house. It is okay, but the others are noisy and shout sometimes. Care staff help us do things like shopping and cleaning the house. I go to the day centre and do things on the computer. I like walking and playing computer games. Mum comes to see me on a Saturday. I have a brother called Harry. Sometimes I get angry and shout. Mum tells me off.

SUMMARY

This chapter looks at why, and how, a clinical psychologist might work with a person with intellectual disabilities. It provides a definition of what intellectual disability is and how it is assessed. The epidemiology and aetiology of intellectual disabilities will also be described. The chapter will explain that clinical psychologists do not see people because they have intellectual disabilities, but as a consequence of the additional challenges faced by people in this group. Having an intellectual disability may bring additional physical and life challenges that most people would find difficult to manage. However, having intellectual disabilities also means that your intellectual capacity is more limited, meaning that dealing with these issues can be even more difficult, leaving you vulnerable to experiencing a greater risk of psychological and behavioural problems. Clinical psychologists are well equipped to help individuals with intellectual disabilities in this situation and may work directly with them, their carers or with wider organisational care and support services. The chapter will describe the types of interventions used and their evidence base, and provide a case example of how such a problem may be assessed, formulated and an intervention developed. Historically, people with intellectual disabilities have been a group that have been excluded and stigmatised and it has been difficult for them collectively to challenge this position. Today, the picture is more positive, with people with intellectual disabilities having more opportunity to voice their concerns and exert their right to access appropriate services; however, as will be explored at the end of the chapter there remains a fine balance between the expression of individual choice and protection by others, which remains one of the most critical issues facing working in this area today.

INTRODUCTION

This chapter will introduce you to the work of the clinical psychologist working with people with intellectual disabilities, their carers and the organisations which support them. Having intellectual disabilities is not a reason alone for being involved with clinical psychology, but it is often the consequences which accompany these disabilities which require intervention. It is important to think of it in terms of intellectual disabilities, not just as an intellectual disability, since individuals will have different profiles in terms of their cognitive limitations, and while they have strengths in one area they will have weaknesses in other areas, and as a consequence of this unique constellation of impairments each person will face different challenges.

Diagnosis of intellectual disability

Intellectual disability (sometimes termed learning disability in the UK) is defined in DSM-V as an impairment of mental abilities which results in a reduced ability to manage everyday life, called adaptive functioning. Three domains or areas of adaptive functioning are described:

1 The conceptual domain which includes skills in language, reading, writing, memory, maths and reasoning.
2 The social domain refers to empathy, social judgement, interpersonal communication skills, the ability to make and retain friendships, and similar capacities.
3 The practical domain includes being able to look after yourself, such as personal care, money management, getting around and managing your time.

The intellectual disability must have occurred during the person's developmental period of growth, and diagnosis is based on the severity of the impact upon adaptive functioning. The disorder is considered chronic and is often co-morbid with other disorders such as autism. Having an intellectual disability is not in itself a psychological problem, but the challenges and stigma attached to the disorder cause significant stress for the individual, placing them more at risk to psychological problems.

FOCUS 12.1

Within this chapter you will learn more about the definition of intellectual disabilities, what causes them, and other issues which frequently co-occur. You will also learn about how the clinical psychologist may work with the person with intellectual disabilities, their carers and the organisations which aim to support them.

WHAT ARE THE TYPES OF PSYCHOLOGICAL DIFFICULTIES THAT MAY OCCUR IN PEOPLE WITH INTELLECTUAL DISABILITIES?

People with intellectual disabilities can suffer the same sorts of psychological problems as anybody else in life. However, the prevalence rates of many psychological problems tend to be higher for people with intellectual disabilities (Taylor and Knapp, 2013). This vulnerability results from both the additive (i.e. the accumulation of additional problems) element of intellectual disabilities and the very nature of the disorder which means that the individual's capacity to manage their situation intellectually is compromised. The additional challenges faced by people with intellectual disabilities fall into three main areas:

1   *Intellectual disability linked disorders.* Generally, people with intellectual disabilities are more likely to have additional physical problems, such as sensory deficits, and mobility and respiratory problems. Some types of intellectual disabilities are a consequence of genetic syndromes which also have accompanying additional disabilities, both physical (e.g. Downs syndrome and hearing loss) and behavioural (e.g. Prader–Willi syndrome and overeating). Some conditions such as autism, epilepsy and cerebral palsy also have a greater likelihood of co-occurrence with intellectual disabilities. The more severe the intellectual disabilities the higher the likelihood of a range of associated disorders. Having additional physical impairments results in increased vulnerability by impacting upon learning opportunities and can lead to increased isolation and reduction of stimulation, causing additional psychological stress.

2   *Common psychological problems.* People with intellectual disabilities may suffer from problems such as anxiety and depression, the same as everyone else; however, they are vulnerable to experiencing this more frequently because of the tough demands of living in our society with intellectual disabilities. Hence, people with intellectual disabilities are more vulnerable to all the accepted setting conditions for common psychological problems such as low income, poor housing, unemployment, poor health and social isolation.

3   *Stigma and prejudice.* Having intellectual disabilities within our society is still stigmatising (i.e. de-valued), which means that people behave in prejudicial and exclusionary ways. This is especially difficult for people with intellectual disabilities as they have fewer psychological resources to manage negative attitudes and are even less able than other disenfranchised groups to fight for their rights. Being in such a socially devalued position brings additional psychological pressures to an already vulnerable group.

Hence, clinical psychologists do not tend to see people *because* they have an intellectual disability, but more usually as a *consequence* of them having an intellectual disability

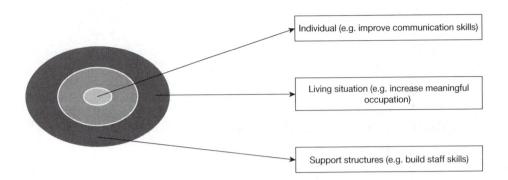

FIGURE 12.1 Points of intervention within an ecological framework surrounding an individual with intellectual disabilities

which has placed them in a more psychologically vulnerable position. It is useful to consider the problems faced by the individual within an ecological framework, which may then require the psychologist to work at a number of different levels to minimise the impact of the impairments caused by the disability. The framework has the individual within the centre surrounded by support or organisational structures, offering a variety of ways in which the psychologist may intervene (see Figure 12.1).

EPIDEMIOLOGY

Obtaining accurate statistics on the epidemiology of intellectual disabilities in the UK is problematic for a number of reasons: first, in terms of identification, second, in terms of different data collection methods across the UK, and third, through changing epidemiological profiles related to changing definitions, medical interventions, health behaviours and demographic profiles. However, a reliable source of information is the *Improving Health and Lives: Intellectual Disabilities Intellectual Disabilities Observatory* (http://www.improvinghealthandlives.org.uk/) which produces regular updates on the current and changing epidemiology.

It is estimated that in 2012 in England 1,144,000 people had learning disabilities, of which 236,000 were children and 908,000 adults (aged 18+). Of the adults 199,000 (22%) are known to GPs as people with intellectual disabilities and 404,000 (44%) were receiving Disability Living Allowance (Emerson *et al.*, 2013). Hence, it is clear from these statistics that a large number of people are living with either no need of being identified as having intellectual disabilities, or in contrast are not receiving the required services.

Of those identified as having intellectual disabilities, the average age of mortality is 24 years (30%) younger than the rest of the population. However, there are important fluctuations in epidemiology to note resulting from changing medical practices, such that there is a lower population over the age of 49, and an increasing population of males under the age of 20. This is because there now tend to be more males born with intellectual disabilities, particularly with severe intellectual disabilities, where improvements have been made in survival rates.

AETIOLOGY

A good place to start to understand the aetiology of intellectual disabilities is from the World Health Organisation's (WHO) *International Classification of Functioning, Disability and Health* (2002), as it provides a useful bio-psychosocial model (see Figure 12.2).

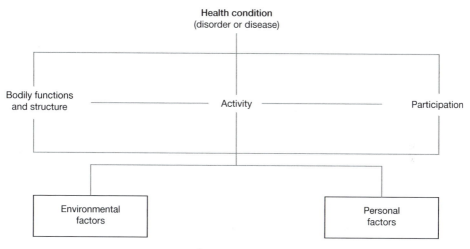

FIGURE 12.2 International Classification of Functioning, Disability and Health

Source: WHO (2002). © 2002 WHO.

If we start at the top of the model we can consider the biological contributions to the aetiology of learning disabilities. These include congenital causes, such as genetic (e.g. Down's syndrome), acquired, both prenatal (e.g. maternal drug abuse), postnatal (e.g. birth trauma), social (e.g. malnutrition) and environmental (e.g. toxins). All of these events may lead to structural and functional negative impacts upon the neurological system. However, even with careful assessment it must be recognised that the biological aetiology remains unknown in over 50 per cent of people with intellectual disabilities (see Smith and Tyler (2009) for further reading on causal factors).

Moving to the middle layer of the diagram we can consider how these biological factors may impact upon body function and structure. Taking the example of an infant with Down's syndrome they are likely to have cognitive deficits, physical differences such as hypotonia (low muscle tone) and sensory problems such as hearing loss, in addition to other issues. Considering their ability to be active, and, like any baby, to explore curiously and play with their environment, without appropriate adjustment their experience will be more limited. Not being able to hear well, and not having the expected cognitive reactions and ability to learn, may then impact upon the interpersonal attachments a person makes and which may further impede their ability to participate in the activities and relationships around them. Participation is important, as it brings richer learning opportunities, and reinforces, encourages and motivates future engagement.

Looking at the bottom of the diagram we can see that we must also consider the environmental and personal factors which will impact upon the outcomes for the individual with intellectual disabilities. Environmentally, just considering the young person with Down's syndrome where their disability is visually recognisable, the reaction of others to this identity will be very important for the self-esteem and inclusion of the person. In addition, the existing knowledge about the condition will have a significant impact upon expectations and importantly what adjustments may need, or not need, to be made to help the person overcome their disabilities. Personal factors include the personality of the individual, their own resilience and coping styles, but also their gender and age, as these will present different challenges during different developmental stages.

The WHO model is helpful, as it moves the focus away from the disability to the more fluid concept of functioning, which is dependent upon the above interrelating set of factors. Such a model suggests a wider range of possibilities in terms of intervention. It also raises the issue that contrary to taking a medical, organic approach to intellectual disabilities, these disabilities could also be conceptualised in terms of a social construction, i.e. something which only exists in this time and place as a consequence of how we structure our society (Rapley, 2004). Clearly, we would not define intellectual disabilities in the same way if we did not have IQ tests with cut-off points, based on purely statistical concepts, or ways of life which demanded high levels of literacy. However, likewise some individuals do have such severe impairments that no matter what their social context was, they would find it impossible to cope. Holding both positions in mind is helpful in ensuring a holistic approach.

THEORY AND EVIDENCE FOR PSYCHOLOGICAL INTERVENTION

Psychological interventions with people with intellectual disabilities have a long history, but mostly within applied behavioural analysis, and less so within the application of 'talking therapies'. This was partly due to emphasis being given to the co-modification of the behaviour of people with intellectual disabilities to 'fit in' with institutional environments, and historical beliefs that their thoughts and feelings were not accessible. These days a more respectful, integrated approach is taken, particularly in terms of managing challenging behaviour, and also the full range of therapeutic modalities are considered as applicable, with appropriate adjustment. The following sections describe a current behavioural approach to managing behaviours which may be seen as challenging, followed by a short review of the types of 'talking therapies' which have been found to be helpful.

Positive behaviour support

There are times when a person's behaviour is seen as 'challenging', and *challenging behaviour* has been defined as follows:

Culturally abnormal behaviour[s] of such an intensity, frequency or duration that the physical safety of the person or others is likely to be placed in serious jeopardy, or behaviour which is likely to seriously limit use of, or result in the person being denied access to, ordinary community facilities.

(Emerson, 2001, p. 3)

Rather than see this as an individual pathology, it is recognised that it is a socially constructed, dynamic concept and where the individual's quality of life and risk management are paramount. The most accepted approach to manage challenging behaviour is positive behaviour support (PBS; Dunlap *et al.*, 2009; Baker and Allen, 2012) which is based on applied behavior analysis (ABA) principles, but set within a clear framework of values. As opposed to pure ABA it is also multi-element, non–linear (i.e. recognising that multiple antecedents and consequences may act upon a behaviour simultaneously) and designed to result in a range of outcomes, which are sustainable and achieved through positive means. PBS has a number of components:

1 Comprehensive functional analysis to try to understand what purpose the behaviour serves for the individual. Then on the basis of this assessment a number of strategies are developed.
2 Ecological strategies: trying to ensure that the environment meets the need of the person as much as possible (e.g. if the individual cannot read, to make sure signage or communication tools use symbols or pictures which they do recognise).
3 Positive programming: teach the person skills to help them control their environment (e.g. using headphones).
4 Focused support strategies: designed to manage the context and reduce the need for reactive strategies (e.g. avoid noisy environment at stressful times).
5 Reactive strategies: designed to gain control of the situation once the behaviour has occurred, and reduce escalation (e.g. help the individual move to a quieter place).

PBS is the most commonly recommended approach with challenging behaviour and there is good evidence for its effectiveness. For example, in a recent review La Vigna and Willis (2012) concluded that by applying the ethical criterion of 'least restrictive intervention' it is effective, open to all involved in managing such behavior and cost-effective. It is recognised that the efficacy of the approach is reliant upon those who need to deliver it which are usually the staff who work directly with the individual on a day-today basis, so McDonald and McGill (2013) conducted a review of the effectiveness of teaching staff this approach. They concluded that there was evidence for a reduction in challenging behaviour, and increases in staff positive attributions and knowledge; however, they recognised that the evidence was limited and no improvement in quality of life has been demonstrated.

Talking therapies

More recently talking therapies have been shown to be effective with people with intellectual disabilities as long as adaptations are made to ensure that the individual can engage with the model. Willner (2005) reviewed the existing literature on the effectiveness of cognitive-behavioural therapy (CBT), cognitive therapy and psychodynamic approaches, and concluded that evidence exists for all three models to be effective with people with mild intellectual disabilities and sometimes effective with people with more severe intellectual disabilities. However, the review recognised that research was very limited and in particular lacked randomised controlled designs, and information on how such models were adapted. Since then a small number of RCTs have been published with positive results, particularly around using CBT for anger management (e.g. Willner *et al.*, 2013), and also other studies on helping people with intellectual disabilities to use CBT (Bruce *et al.*, 2010), and on how simple CBT elements can be adapted for staff for use with their clients (Dodd *et al.*, 2013).

While Willner (2005) concluded there was some limited evidence for the use of psychodynamic psychotherapy with this client group, further evidence for its effectiveness has been slower to follow and the suitability of this model has been increasingly contested. However, more recently evidence has been growing for its potential effectiveness, but with a clear acknowledgement that the practices and procedures used within the application of this modality with this client group requires further description (Beail and Jackson, 2013).

As the use of 'talking therapies' has become more accepted, the breadth of the therapeutic models being used has widened, following the growing evidence base within mainstream work. Hence, a recent book, *Psychological Therapies for Adults with Intellectual Disabilities* (Taylor *et al.*, 2013), also includes mindfulness and acceptance-based approaches.

CASE STUDY

Pat is a 46-year-old woman with Down's syndrome. She has been referred to the community learning disability team, as she has started to get up and wander at night, disturbing other residents of the group home and the sleep-over night staff. She sometimes becomes quite agitated when asked to return to bed, and generally seems down and weepy. When asked what is wrong she seems unable to identify anything.

Assessment

Pat was asked by her key worker if she would like to talk to someone about the problems she has been experiencing. She readily agreed and an appointment was made for her to see the clinical psychologist on the specialist intellectual disabilities team. The clinical psychologist explained that she would like to talk to Pat to see if she could help her, and that it would also help for her to talk to the staff so that she could get a complete picture. Pat consented to this initial assessment. Pat told the psychologist that she was aware she was getting up in the night, that it made her upset and anxious, and that the staff were cross with her, but she did not know why she did it. On talking to staff it was clear that they were concerned, felt that Pat's behaviour had deteriorated generally and wondered if she was starting to show dementia. The night-time disrupted routines were having a bad effect on the other residents and one member of staff thought Pat was doing it to get attention, as

Dementia and Down's syndrome

Down's syndrome (DS) is the most common genetic cause of learning disabilities. Due to better medical intervention in early life, people with DS are now living longer and the higher prevalence rate of dementia for people with Down's syndrome at an earlier expected age has been recognised. Research suggests that co-morbidity is between 10 and 25 per cent in the 40- to 49-year-old group, 20 and 50 per cent in the 50- to 59-year-old group and between 30 and 75 per cent in those aged 60 years or older. There seems to be no relationship between level of learning disability and risk of dementia, but pre-existing cognitive function is related to rate of decline. Behavioural change tends to indicate onset more frequently than functional memory decline. The most common form of dementia co-morbid with DS is of the Alzheimer's type. The link is related to the shared function of the protein Amyloid. Amyloid forms the neural plaques found in Alzheimer's disease and the gene coding for this protein is located on chromosome 21. The majority of people who have DS have the 'trisomy 21' form which means they have an extra copy of this chromosome, disrupting normal Amyloid production. However, not all people with DS develop dementia in later life and the reason for this is unclear.

sometimes she was given a hot chocolate and chat before returning to bed. When asked if anything had changed recently, staff mentioned that Pat's auntie who she was close to had died about six months previously and they had had some work done to the house, which meant that the upstairs bathroom had been out of commission for a couple of weeks, so residents had had to use the downstairs bathroom, but it was all fine now.

It was agreed, given Pat's age and the existence of no previous dementia screening, that she should undergo some psychometric tests, and meanwhile more information would be gathered about Pat's nocturnal behaviour and generally how she was feeling. With Pat's consent *ABC charts* were completed by the night staff over a three-week period; these logged 'Antecedents' (i.e. anything staff noticed before Pat got up in the night), the 'Behaviour' (i.e. what she did and what staff did) and 'Consequences' (i.e. what happened afterwards). The clinical psychologist also agreed with Pat to meet her for six sessions to discuss how she was feeling and to try to understand what led to the nocturnal wandering.

Formulation

It is important in a complex case such as this that a very careful and thorough assessment is made which is based on an initial formulation. As the work progresses it is likely that additional information will come to light which enriches and confirms or rejects ideas present in the initial formulation. The following formulation is an initial formulation which leads to an action plan to gather more information, which will in turn lead to the consolidation of the most appropriate formulation of the problem and continuing action plan.

It seemed clear that something had changed to give rise to these alterations in behaviour which had not been reported before. There may be a number of reasons for this change. Given Pat's age and Down's syndrome she has a 25 to 50 per cent higher chance than those without Down's syndrome of developing dementia which can lead to confusion, anxiety and behavioural change. Down's syndrome and dementia were potential 'predisposing' factors (making Pat more at risk of the current problems), to be investigated further. Pat had also recently experienced the death of someone close to her, and with no other close family this loss was significant. The grieving process is individual but it is likely that Pat was still mourning this loss. At a practical level there had been some work done on the house which may have disrupted her usual routines, and on top of these other factors she was finding it hard to re-establish a routine. These could be termed 'precipitating' factors, as bereavement is a known cause of psychological distress, and having routines disrupted can be particularly upsetting for people with intellectual disabilities, and Pat's behaviour changed quite soon after these events.

Pat was also starting to feel generally quite anxious as she felt staff may be feeling cross with her, which again may disrupt her sleep. This could be seen as a 'perpetuating' factor because it maintains the behaviour, possibly beyond the influence of the initial precipitating events. As Pat becomes more aware of the staff's negative feelings, she becomes more anxious, which in turn disrupts her sleep, and the events continue in a cyclical fashion. Any combination of these factors could have been contributing to this behaviour, so it was important to find out more information before intervening.

Action plan

Comprehensive assessment

- A dementia screening assessment was carried out using the neuropsychological assessment of dementia in adults with intellectual disabilities (NAintellectual disabilities) (Crayton et al., 1998). In addition, to establish a behavioural baseline Pat's adaptive functioning was assessed using the Adaptive Behaviour Assessment System-II (ABAS-II) (Harrison and Oakland, 2003).
- The Glasgow Anxiety Scale for people with an intellectual disability (GAS-intellectual disabilities) was used to assess level of anxiety (Mindham and Espie, 2003). Pat scored 13, which just hit the cut-off of 13 to 15 to be seen as clinically significant.
- The clinical psychologist met with Pat to explore with her in greater depth the anxiety she was experiencing. They also talked in detail about Pat's bedtime

routines. She had felt disrupted by the work on the house, now sometimes forgetting to get a drink of water and going to the toilet before bed. She was also anxious about turning the lights on when she got up in case she woke the night staff, who slept with the door open, but then she ended up going into the wrong room or having to turn the light on, which made her feel cross with herself and embarrassed.

- Ten ABC charts were completed over a three-week time period, showing that Pat did not get up every night, and there was no particular pattern in terms of which days, but that it did tend to happen at around 2 a.m. She then stayed up for variable amounts of time depending on what approach staff took. Some tried to send her back to bed, which tended to make her agitated; others sat up with her for a while and sometimes made a drink. There was only one occasion when she got up more than once.

Reformulation

According to the screening, Pat did not have dementia, but, given this predisposing factor, having a baseline screening follows national guidance. The precipitating factor of bereavement did seem significant, and hence it was appropriate to intervene to resolve some issues and reduce distress about this event. The assessment also illuminated another perpetuating factor: Pat was keeping the light off to reduce disturbance but by doing so she was causing more disturbance and adding to her anxiety levels. The assessment also confirmed that the disruption to routines through building work had perpetuated the situation; hence it was clear that a more standard routine needed to be re-established and agreed with Pat and the staff.

Intervention

- A meeting was held with the staff team to discuss the results of the assessment and action plan. After consulting Pat a procedure was agreed about what should happen if Pat got up, which consisted of two main elements: checking if she wanted to go to the toilet, and going with her to get a drink of water (not a hot drink), then going with her back to her room and settling her in bed. Pat was also to be reassured by staff that they were not cross about her waking. Time was also spent carefully explaining this to Pat's key worker so that she could ensure that all the night staff who could not make the meeting were well informed.
- Pat formed a good rapport with the clinical psychologist and they spent time discussing her deceased auntie, what grief feels like and how things start to feel better. They used a downloadable booklet about grief specifically for people with intellectual disabilities, developed by the NHS North Tyne's Liverpool Care Pathway group (NHS North East, 2012).
- Pat agreed that she still felt very sad about her auntie's death, but felt she could not say this to the staff as she thought they might think 'she was going on' and

'should be over it now', because they never mentioned her auntie now. Pat agreed
that the clinical psychologist could let the rest of the staff team know this and
Pat's key worker suggested that together they could make a photo album
featuring her auntie.
- Night-lights had been installed in the corridor to the bathroom, which made Pat
feel more confident.

Outcome

- The dementia screening did not show any dementia, but it was agreed that Pat
should be assessed on an annual basis.
- Pat had previously scored 13 on the GAS-intellectual disabilities, but when tested
eight weeks later this had reduced to 8, indicating a return to normal levels of
anxiety.
- The staff team stuck to the agreed procedure and after another three-week
period of monitoring with ABC charts there had been only one incident.
- Staff members reported feeling more confident and relieved. They were
especially pleased that they raised the topic of dementia and that they had
followed the guidelines (Royal College of Psychiatry and Division of Clinical
Psychology, 2009), in that they were right to be concerned given Pat's age,
Down's syndrome and change in behaviour (reactive monitoring), and that
Pat was now registered for annual reviews (prospective monitoring). Staff had
found the ABC charts helpful and reported that they would use them again.
They also realised that their anxiety had been noticed by Pat and misinterpreted
by her as them being angry with her, and hence how important it was to check
with Pat what she was thinking.

Team working/indirect work

It was very important to work with the staff team in this case as these were the
people who knew Pat the best and spent long periods of time with her. There was
clearly a communication difficulty in that the staff were genuinely concerned, but
Pat misinterpreted this which made her feel more anxious, exacerbating the
situation. It is not uncommon for seemingly simple and predictable feelings and
interactional dynamics to become confused, so asking both the staff team and the
client what they might feel and how they might behave in the other's situation is a
good way of testing out and challenging these beliefs.

Setting systems in place that are sustainable is very important, as the clinical
psychologist is only likely to be involved for a short period of time and the bulk of the
work will be carried out and continued by the staff team. Hence, their active
engagement is vital. In addition, each clinical intervention is an opportunity to provide
the staff team with more understanding, tools and strategies to help them in their
work and to offer an improving service to their clients. In this case seeking Pat's

approval to talk to the staff team about how she was feeling was vital. It also provided an opportunity to find out how they were feeling and to be able to identify some misunderstandings. It was also important to identify with both the staff and Pat the outcomes they desired. In this situation they were shared outcomes, meaning that we could find strategies to work together for an agreed outcome. When objectives are not shared between the client and staff or even within the same staff team this must be identified and worked upon. It was also important to contextualise the staff's 'hunch' that they 'needed to check for dementia'. Discussing the 'Dementia and People with Learning Disabilities' guidelines with the staff made them feel confident in their decision making, and gave them a resource to draw upon should they have further concerns. Likewise, the ABC chart was a resource they found helpful and could see themselves using again, which may increase their own capacity to problem solve similar situations.

In this case the work of the clinical psychologist was quite contained to Pat and the direct team who worked with her. However, it is not uncommon to involve other members of the multi-disciplinary team such as the speech and language therapist for communication issues, or the team nurse to help manage physical issues. In addition, wider issues may be identified where staff training by the psychologist may be of benefit, or there may be problems with how the team is working where again the clinical psychologist could help.

CRITICAL ISSUES

As the rights of people with intellectual disabilities have been given more attention, the centrality of their voice and choices has also been given more authority. However, with this comes difficult and complex choice making around a vulnerable person's right to be protected and their right to act in the way they choose. Many of the critical issues within the field of psychology and intellectual disabilities currently centre on this dilemma. One particularly contested area of work is around the expression of sexuality, where issues of right to choose, consent, parenthood, protection of self and others, and public prejudice have all had to be addressed.

Historically the sexuality of people with intellectual disabilities has been either denied or tightly controlled. Today it is acknowledged that all people with intellectual disabilities have the same rights to a sex life as everybody else, while acknowledging that this must be within consensual understanding (McCarthy and Thompson, 2010). This may be difficult in two particular circumstances, when the individual(s) concerned lack understanding to give consent, and/or there is such a power imbalance that coercion may be involved. With heterosexual sex comes the possibility of pregnancy, so not only must individuals have the capacity to understand the sexual act, they must also understand that this may lead to conception, and to make the choice to accept this possibility or be able to take precautions. For clinical psychologists these dilemmas have brought not only many invitations to become involved in trying to establish 'capacity for consent', but also to provide assistance in assessment and intervention to help people live sexually fulfilled lives.

Concerning sexual behaviour, this may involve straightforward sex education, to helping staff work through complex issues such as a young man with intellectual disabilities asking a member of staff to show them how to put on a condom. Like the mainstream world some people with intellectual disabilities wish to engage in less normative sexual practices and, for staff concerned about the expression of sexuality anyway, managing a client who wants to cross-dress or has a shoe fetish poses additional challenges. Commonly in such complex, ethically challenging cases clinical psychologists are invited in to assist in helping staff both establish capacity for consent and support staff through the array of complex decisions and actions which may lie before them.

At a more serious edge of transgression lies sexual offending and there has been a rapid growth in forensic psychology with this client group. With rights comes responsibilities, and if people with intellectual disabilities are found to have capacity and make wrong decisions then they have become increasingly involved in the judicial system. Likewise it may not be recognised that offenders have intellectual disabilities and we have seen recognition of a large prison population with unmet needs in this area.

JAMES' STORY: CONCLUSION

I met Amy who is a psychologist. She helped me and told me what to do if I feel angry. We had a house meeting and Amy came too. We agreed some rules about making noise and Amy drew pictures and put them on the wall. If Colin is noisy I point to the picture and he shuts up.

In the morning I go with Jim now and deliver newspapers. It was hard at first but I like it now. People say 'hello James' and I give them their paper.

KEY CONCEPTS AND TERMS

- Learning disabilities
- Intellectual disabilities
- Cognitive functioning
- Autism
- Adaptive behaviour
- Developmental period
- Challenging behaviour
- Down's syndrome
- Positive behavioural support
- Applied behaviour analysis
- Capacity
- Stigma
- Working with staff
- Sexuality
- Dementia

LEARNING OUTCOMES

When you have completed this chapter you should be able to:

1 Know what intellectual disabilities are, what might be some of the causes, and other issues which co-occur.
2 Have an understanding of the sorts of challenges people with intellectual disabilities may face both dealing with their own impairments, but also dealing with the views of society.
3 Be able to position the experience of people with intellectual disabilities within wider psychological theories.
4 Have an understanding of the key psychological approaches in this area, how other treatment approaches might be adapted, and the evidence base for this.
5 Through a case example understand how assessment, formulation, intervention and evaluation are used.
6 Be able to understand how different approaches, at different levels from the individual to the support network, may be integrated to be effective and sustainable.

SAMPLE ESSAY TITLES

- Is 'learning disability' a social construction?
- What is 'challenging behaviour' and how is it best managed?
- How has the acceptance of the sexuality of people with intellectual disabilities changed over the years?
- Do we understand the link between Down's syndrome and dementia?

FURTHER READING

Emerson, E., Hatton, C., Dickson, K., Gone, R. and Caine, A. (eds) (2012). *Clinical Psychology and People with Intellectual Disabilities*. New York: John Wiley & Sons.

Webb, J. (2013). *A Guide to Psychological Understanding of People with Learning Disabilities: Eight domains and three stories*. Abingdon, Oxon: Routledge.

REFERENCES

Baker, P. and Allen, D. (2012). Use of positive behaviour support to tackle challenging behaviour. *Learning Disability Practice, 15*(1), 18–20.

British Psychological Society, Royal College of Psychiatrists, and Royal College of Speech and Language Therapists (2007). *Challenging Behaviour: A Unified Approach*. Leicester: DCP, British Psychological Society.

Brown, M., Duff, H., Karatzias, T. and Horsburgh, D. (2011). A review of the literature relating to psychological interventions and people with intellectual disabilities: Issues for research, policy, education and clinical practice. *Journal of Intellectual Disabilities*, *15*(1), 31–45.

Bruce, M., Collins, S., Langdon, P., Powlitch, S. and Reynolds, S. (2010). Does training improve understanding of core concepts in cognitive behaviour therapy by people with intellectual disabilities? A randomized experiment. *British Journal of Clinical Psychology*, *49*(1), 1–13.

Crayton, L., Oliver, O., Holland, A., Bradbury, J. and Hall, S. (1998). The neuropsychological assessment of age-related cognitive deficits in adults with Down's syndrome. *Journal of Applied Research in Intellectual Disabilities*, 11, 255–272.

Dodd, K., Austin, K., Baxter, L., Jennison, J., Kenny, M., Lippold, T. and Wilcox, E. (2013). Effectiveness of brief training in cognitive behaviour therapy techniques for staff working with people with intellectual disabilities. *Advances in Mental Health and Intellectual Disabilities*, 7(5), 8–8.

Dunlap, G., Sailor, W., Horner, R. and Sugai, G. (2009). Overview and history of positive behavior support. In W. Sailor, G. Dunlap, G. Sugai and R. Horner (eds), *Handbook of Positive Behavior Support*. New York: Springer.

Emerson, 1995, cited in Emerson, E. (2001, 2nd edn). *Challenging Behaviour: Analysis and intervention in people with learning disabilities*. Cambridge: Cambridge University Press.

Emerson, E., Hatton, C., Robertson, J. Baines, S., Christie, A. and Glover, G. (2013). *People with Intellectual Disabilities in England in 2012*. Improving Health and Lives: Intellectual Disabilities Intellectual Disabilities Observatory.

Harrison, P.L. and Oakland, T. (2003). *Adaptive Behaviour Assessment System (ABAS-II)* (2nd edn). New York: The Psychological Corporation.

La Vigna, G. and Willis, T. (2012). The efficacy of positive behavioural support with the most challenging behaviour: The evidence and its implications. *Journal of Intellectual and Developmental Disability*, *37*, 185–195.

MacDonald, A. and McGill, P. (2013). Outcomes of staff training in positive behaviour support: A systematic review. *Journal of Developmental and Physical Disabilities*, *25*(1), 17–33.

McCarthy, M. and Thompson, D. (eds) (2010). *Sexuality and Learning Disabilities: A handbook*. Brighton: Pavilion.

Mindham, J. and Espie, C.A. (2003). Glasgow Anxiety Scale for people with an intellectual disability (GAS-ID): Development and psychometric properties of a new measure for use with people with mild intellectual disability. *Journal of Intellectual Disability Research*, *47*(1), 22–30.

NHS North of Tyne (2012). *Grieving – Easy Read – Supplementary Booklet*. NHS North East. Available online at http://www.cnne.org.uk/end-of-life-care—-the-clinical-network/car eatendoflife (accessed 16 January 2014).

Rapley, M. (2004). *The Social Construction of Intellectual Disability*. Cambridge: Cambridge University Press.

Royal College of Psychiatrists and Division of Clinical Psychology: Faculty for Learning Disabilities (2009). *Dementia and People with Intellectual Disabilities. Intellectual Disabilities Guidance on the assessment, diagnosis, treatment and support of people with intellectual disabilities who develop dementia*. Leicester: British Psychological Society.

Smith, D. and Tyler, N. (2009). *Introduction to Special Education: Making a difference* (7th edn). New Jersey: Pearson.

Taylor, J. and Knapp, M. (2013). Mental health and emotional problems in people with intellectual disabilities. In J. Taylor, W. Lindsay, R. Hastings and C. Hatton (eds), *Psychological Therapies for Adults with Intellectual Disabilities*. New York: Wiley.

Taylor, J., Lindsay, W., Hastings, R. and Hatton, C. (eds) (2013). *Psychological Therapies for Adults with Intellectual Disabilities*. New York: Wiley.

Willner, P. (2005). The effectiveness of psychotherapeutic interventions for people with learning disabilities: A critical overview. *Journal of Intellectual Disability Research, 49*, 73–85.

Willner, P., Rose, J., Jahoda, A., Kroese, B.S., Felce, D., Cohen, D. and Hood, K. (2013). Group-based cognitive-behavioural anger management for people with mild to moderate intellectual disabilities: Cluster randomised controlled trial. *The British Journal of Psychiatry*. doi:10.1192/bjp.bp.112.124529.

World Health Organisation (2002). *Towards a Common Language for Functioning, Disability and Health: ICF – the International Classification of Functioning, Disability and Health*. Geneva: WHO.

13 Working with people with physical health problems

Angela Busuttil, Alesia Moulton-Perkins and Monika Tuite

LIZZIE'S STORY

My name is Lizzie. I am a 57-year-old lady who was diagnosed with Systemic Lupus (SLE) and Sjögren's syndrome in the spring of 2010. Both of these conditions are incurable auto-immune diseases and have had an enormous impact upon my physical and mental well-being.

I left hospital with a diagnosis, detailed literature and a cocktail of drugs, and spent several months in a haze of panic and bewilderment feeling defeated, lonely and scared.

The initial shock and subsequent long-term implications have been unforgiving and changed my life completely.

The symptoms of my illness are constant: immense joint pain and exhaustion, migraine, allergies to food and medication, sensitivity to sunlight, hair loss, muscle spasms, skin rashes, anxiety and depression. I have been left unable to eat or swallow normal everyday foods and have increasing problems with my eyesight. I was overwhelmed by feelings of hopelessness, sadness and isolation. I felt my illness had stolen everything from me, including my identity, my self-confidence, self-esteem, social life and personal appearance.

I became reclusive and self-loathing, lost and frustrated that the 'old me' had gone forever. I mourned my old life. I considered suicide but was prevented by the love of my son, with whom I live. I was referred to the pain management service in 2011 for an assessment and then began one-to-one narrative therapy with a psychologist.

SUMMARY

The part can never be well unless the whole is well.

(Plato 427 BC, Charmides)

Holistic care is not a new concept. Integrating physical and mental health care both conceptually and in service delivery is a challenge with which psychologists working in physical health engage every day. The breadth of this work is significant. The international classification of diseases (ICD 10; WHO, 1992) covers 16 diagnostic categories of which mental disorders is but one. Psychologists working in health potentially work across all 16. Despite presenting considerable challenges, our increasing understanding of the relationship between physical and psychological health means that psychologists are now producing significant health benefits in clinical conditions that were traditionally the domain of physical health experts.

This chapter will describe what clinical health psychology is and what a clinical health psychologist does. It will describe some of the psychological issues that contribute to, are part of, or which follow as a consequence of certain types of physical health problems. It will introduce some of the theoretical models used by clinical psychologists working in physical health settings. It will also give examples of the types of clinical issues that present and describe how a clinical psychologist might work with them in practice using a case example.

INTRODUCTION

Clinical health psychology involves applying our scientific understanding of psychology to the types of psychological difficulties which *contribute* to physical health problems, which *maintain or exacerbate* physical health problems, and which *result* from physical health problems. These psychological factors include health beliefs and behaviours, coping mechanisms and resilience factors, as well as issues relating to mental health such as anxiety, depression and trauma.

Clinical health psychology services are usually provided by clinical psychologists who work in physical health settings, although health and other applied psychologists also undertake some aspects of this work. They usually work with multi-disciplinary teams and deliver psychological interventions to individuals and families, as well as to health care organisations as a whole. They use a bio-psychosocial perspective (integrating medical, psychological and social components of a person's difficulties) and in delivering services across a wide range of physical conditions there is considerable variety in working practice and settings. They may apply their skills on hospital wards, in outpatient teams or in community services.

Areas of service delivery include supporting people with long-term conditions such as diabetes, supporting health-related behaviour change, conducting pre-surgical assessment (e.g. for organ transplantation), and working with people facing end-of-life issues.

THE RELATIONSHIP BETWEEN PSYCHOLOGICAL DIFFICULTIES AND PHYSICAL HEALTH PROBLEMS

Psychological distress can result from many types of physical difficulties, although the level of distress is not always directly related to the severity of the illness. There are a number of factors that, when taken together, will mediate the nature of the relationship between physical health and emotional distress. It is important for a clinical health psychologist to be aware of these mediating factors as they can often suggest how a psychologist may best intervene to help someone in distress. They need to be thought about and understood, and this is a key part of any initial assessment and formulation process. These factors include the following.

The nature of the illness

The illness

The nature of the illness and its prognosis will directly impact upon the physical and psychological challenges presented. Is the illness acute or chronic, or made up of single or multiple conditions? Is it stable or are there periods of exacerbation and remission? Was the patient born with the condition or is it acquired? If genetic, might it be transmitted? How will illness and treatment impact upon quality of life, now and in the future?

With frequently little time to deal with diagnosis before having to consider potentially distressing treatment (Galloway *et al.*, 1997), rapidly unfolding events may lead to feelings of powerlessness with threats to physical and emotional identity, work, role and financial security. With chronic or terminal illness, people often need to review self-concepts, roles and relationships, and grieve for the loss of their anticipated future. All of these variables will impact significantly upon how any one physical problem is experienced and they will need to be assessed and their impact determined in work with any one patient.

Cognitive problems

Cognitive problems (difficulties in doing certain mental tasks) may be associated with certain conditions (e.g. hypertension) or result from the side effects of medication. Coping with cognitive problems can be difficult and leave people more vulnerable to feeling anxious or depressed.

Transdiagnostic difficulties

Sleep problems, weight management, fatigue, sexual concerns and pain can accompany many different types of physical health problem. Each of these difficulties, which occur alongside the physical problem itself, can add a significant additional burden and leave someone more vulnerable to increased levels of distress which can then in turn make these problems worse. The impacts of sleep deprivation and sexual dysfunction are explored further in Focus 13.1 and 13.2.

FOCUS 13.1

The importance of sleep

Sleep is essential for well-being. Persistent poor sleep affects cognitive skills such as attention and memory; it affects mood and energy levels, and impacts upon task performance and relationships. Poor sleep increases the risk of conditions such as high blood pressure, stroke, diabetes and depression, and can negatively affect functioning of the immune system (Robotham *et al.*, 2011).

Sleep problems such as onset insomnia and maintenance insomnia are more common in those with physical health problems and there are many reasons why insomnia is more prevalent. Symptoms such as pain and breathing difficulties, frequency of urination or difficulties associated with taking medication can impact negatively upon sleep.

Organic disease is not always sufficient to account for sleep problems in this group. Psychosocial factors can also play a part. CBT is recommended as a first-line treatment for insomnia (Wilson *et al.*, 2010). In chronic illness it can do more than improve levels of tiredness; it can lead to improvements in the underlying disorder, in the ability of the individual to function and in emotional well-being.

FOCUS 13.2

Talking about sex

Sex and sexuality impact upon quality of life. Sex can increase intimacy in central relationships, affirm self-esteem and be a valuable source of comfort. For people with chronic illness, sexuality can take on added emphasis; being sexual potentially helps people feel 'normal', and arguably this is particularly important for those with physical health problems whose lives may have significantly changed.

Physical health issues may impact upon sexual functioning. This may be for physical reasons, as hormonal, neurological, vascular and pulmonary function impact upon sexual function. Medication, fatigue and pain can also have an impact. Psychological factors such as self-confidence, beliefs about appearance and mood will also affect the expression of sexuality.

Illness may also impact upon sex through changes which occur in the nature of relationships. Couples may struggle to manage shifts from caregiver–patient role to that of lovers. Pre-existing relationship difficulties may be exacerbated by the additional demands imposed in managing illness.

Health care professionals are not always knowledgeable about the impact of illness upon sex and may be uncomfortable raising sex as an issue. McInnes (2003) writes that sexual problems are under-recognised, and under-treated in physical illness as a result.

Personal factors

The following personal characteristics or attributes will also impact upon a person's capacity to live with or adjust to their condition.

Health/illness beliefs

Adopting healthy behaviours and desisting from unhealthy ones involves making the decision to change, implement change and maintain change. Likelihood of change is influenced by: (1) belief that one is at personal risk; (2) outcome expectancy that behavioural change will decrease risk; (3) the belief that one can change and maintain change (Bandura, 1994). The nature of these health beliefs is very important in determining a person's psychological response to a particular physical condition and to their willingness to adopt the treatment regime associated with it.

Coping style

The relationship between physical health problems and psychological distress is also influenced by a person's coping style (Miller *et al.*, 1996). Coping is a dynamic process influenced by individual and environmental factors. 'Acute' illness, where disruption to one's life may be temporary, calls upon different coping responses to that in 'chronic illness' where the goal is to maintain quality of life, manage symptoms and reduce disability. Coping strategies interrelate and may be helpful or unhelpful depending upon the context.

Adjustment

Moos and Holahan (2007) describe the following adaptive tasks in illness and disability:

- managing symptoms and treatment;
- forming relationships with health care professionals;
- managing emotions;
- maintaining self-image;
- relating to family and friends;
- dealing with an uncertain future.

While most people successfully adjust, the process of adjustment is fluid and changing, accompanying changes in either the physical condition or a person's life circumstances. Self-blame can feature if lifestyle choices contributed to the condition. An inability to undertake family or work roles expected by self or society may result in shame and guilt, as this can make adjustment more difficult. Some people may struggle to adapt to changes in their appearance. Positive developments also occur; over a quarter of patients with diabetes reported positive outcomes in at least one area of their lives (Tarkun *et al.*, 2013).

Lifespan issues

The point we are at in our lives can affect our psychological response to illness or disability. Some types of disability may be easier to adjust to later in life than earlier in life, as there can be a cultural expectation of having to manage more complex physical health concerns in later life which can make disability less unexpected. A person with persistent pain may have adapted well but may need to make new adaptations when they have children and find that they cannot undertake expected parental roles. Thus adjustment, particularly to a long-term condition, remains a fluid ongoing process.

Existential issues

Illness confronts patients with the deepest human concerns: death is inevitable, we are essentially alone, we are looking for meaning and, while we have freedom, with that comes responsibility for the decisions we make, including those relating to the consequences of accepting or rejecting treatment. People may differ widely in their capacity to process and make sense of these existential issues. People who can create a sense of meaning from their difficulties tend to adjust better than those who cannot.

Societal factors

The type of society you live in, including cultural beliefs about illness and the types of support available, can also have a significant impact upon how someone copes with their physical illness. These societal factors include the following.

Culture, gender and religious factors

These all affect illness experience. A young male unable to work because of a health condition may experience more stigma than a young female, as it is still more acceptable for a woman to have other roles in society. Culture and religion may affect how an illness is perceived, with some viewing some forms of illness as a punishment and others viewing it as an opportunity for further spiritual development. This obviously has a major impact upon how someone comes to make sense of, and cope with, their illness as well as the amount of support they are likely to get from society, family and friends.

Stigma

Stigma is associated with some types of physical health problems, and the shame that can result from this can further impact upon the distress caused by the condition. For example, lung cancer, obesity and AIDS are all often seen as being self-induced, and people can feel very ashamed about their condition. Stigma may also result if the aetiology of a condition is unclear (Nelson *et al.*, 2012). Concepts such as 'somatisation' and 'functional disorder' can leave patients feeling that health care professionals doubt whether illness and suffering is 'real', adding to illness burden.

EPIDEMIOLOGY OF PSYCHOLOGICAL DISTRESS IN PHYSICAL HEALTH PROBLEMS

Long-term physical health conditions affect approximately one-third of the population (Naylor *et al.*, 2012) and are often associated with mental health concerns. For example, depression is three times more common in people with conditions like diabetes and heart disease (NICE, 2009) than in the general population. Co-morbid depression also increases risk of mortality and morbidity in people with long-term conditions. For example, a person with chronic obstructive pulmonary disease (COPD) and depression is three times more likely to die than someone with COPD alone. This may be partly explained by depression affecting patient treatment adherence and self-care. Some resort to suicide. Druss and Pincus (2000) found that a general medical condition increased the risk of someone making a suicide attempt by 1.6 times and more than one medical illness increased risk 2.4 times. With cancer and asthma, risk was fourfold. Yet physical health clinicians may not always screen for mental health problems. Some patients merely report physical symptoms, perhaps because of shame or considering mood irrelevant. Failing to meet mental health needs associated with physical health is expensive, with estimated increases in health care costs of 45 per cent for each person (Naylor *et al.*, 2012).

Mental health problems including psychological trauma also increase risk of physical health problems (Kendall–Tackett 2009). People with schizophrenia or bipolar disorder die between 16 and 25 years sooner on average than the general population. We still don't fully understand the reasons for this, although modifiable risk factors like smoking or obesity that are associated with patients' attempts to manage distress, and the accompanying side effects of medication, both play a part.

AETIOLOGY OF PSYCHOLOGICAL DISTRESS IN PHYSICAL HEALTH PROBLEMS

Trying to understand the origins of distress among people with physical health difficulties is a little like trying to solve the proverbial 'chicken and egg' paradox. Being physically ill can make you psychologically distressed, but being distressed can also make you physically ill.

Most people would understand why someone might become low or anxious when a long-term physical health problem disrupts relationships or work. It is less obvious why others survive these challenges without serious detriment to their mental health. Clinical health psychologists recognise that psychological factors such as health beliefs and behaviours affect health problems. Lazarus and Folkman's (1984) cognitive stress-coping model suggests that the way in which we appraise adverse events like illness affects how effectively we cope with them. For example, someone who approaches a diagnosis of cancer with an optimistic 'fighting spirit', rather than hopelessness, is more likely to make positive behavioural health choices such as quitting smoking and following treatment recommendations.

Bio-psychosocial theories have gone further than this and seek to explain the two-way nature of physical and mental health. Engel (1977) was one of the first to raise the possibility that our social environment, psychological make-up and biology interact to determine health. In the field of persistent pain, Melzack and Wall's (1967) gate-control theory provided a model to explain how people with similar objective medical findings reported widely differing pain levels. Their model suggested that psychological factors mediate a patient's subjective experience of pain by opening or closing a metaphorical 'gate' in the spinal cord. Positive nerve impulses from the brain, including relaxation, narrow this gate, thus dampening pain signals travelling to the brain where they are processed and perceived as pain. Distress effectively 'opens' the gate, enhancing pain processing.

Recent psychoneuro-immunology (PNI) studies suggest that stress and psychological factors influence a range of disease processes, from cancer to the common cold. Stress affects the hypothalamic–pituitary–adrenal axis (HPA) and sympathetic nervous system, impacting upon the functioning of the immune system. Kiecolt-Glaser *et al.* (2002) cited studies where acute stressors such as taking exams, or chronic stressors like caring for someone with Alzheimer's, delay immune processes like wound healing. Psycho-social factors modify these biological processes. For instance, people with fewer social ties developed more colds, and pessimistic HIV-infected men experienced faster immune decline. Non-infectious diseases are affected also. For example, depression raises heart disease risk by 50 to 100 per cent (Benton *et al.*, 2007). Conversely, during illness the immune system releases certain chemicals which act on the brain and cause the 'sickness response' mimicking depression symptoms such as tiredness, poor appetite and withdrawal behaviours. Inflammatory immune responses may contribute to explaining the increased prevalence of depression in physically ill people (Dantzer *et al.*, 2008).

PSYCHOLOGICAL INTERVENTIONS USED IN PHYSICAL HEALTH CARE SETTINGS

Many psychological approaches are used and adapted in work with people with physical health problems. The assessment will always seek to identify the impact of the various factors already described upon a person's psychological response to their condition. This leads to a theory-based formulation of a person's emotional difficulties and the interaction between their emotional and physical difficulties. The formulation leads to a treatment plan and the choice of treatment approach. The most commonly used treatment approaches include the following.

Cognitive-behavioural therapy approaches

The basic underpinnings of a CBT approach have been described in previous chapters (see especially Chapter 2). It has been shown to be helpful in managing depression in chronic health problems (NICE, 2009) as well as in the treatment of anxiety, depression, and trauma more generally (NICE, 2008).

In people with physical health problems in particular, CBT can help in managing distress, enabling people to maintain a positive but realistic attitude towards their illness. Enhancing communication skills can be helpful in both relationships with family and health care professionals, and also in dealing with stigma. Pacing is a commonly used behavioural intervention where patients manage pain and fatigue levels by breaking up their activities (White, 2001). CBT may also be used in preparing for stressful medical events or in facilitating positive health-related behaviour change.

Systemic or family-based approaches

Because people with chronic physical health problems often require additional caring support from family or other carers, and because the illness can impact negatively upon these relationships, it is recommended that families and carers are included in assessment and clinical intervention, especially when people are suffering from both depression and a physical health problem (NICE, 2009). This may be in the form of family support or may require a formal systemic intervention. Other guidelines including those for chronic fatigue and palliative care similarly acknowledge the value of working with family systems in therapy, as social support is protective for physical and mental health.

Third-wave CBT

Third-wave CBT approaches comprise a heterogeneous group of treatments, including acceptance and commitment therapy (ACT), and mindfulness-based cognitive therapy, that place particular emphasis on compassion, acceptance and the importance of living in the present moment.

ACT is an approach with a growing evidence base (Vowles and Thompson, 2011) and is a particularly useful therapy in health settings. Rather than focus on negative beliefs as in CBT, ACT advocates noticing and accepting thoughts and experiences, including unwanted ones such as pain, without judgement. ACT aims to help the individual clarify their personal values and to take action in line with them, increasing psychological flexibility. It incorporates mindfulness – which emphasises the ability to stay in the moment in an open and non-judgemental way (Dunford and Thompson, 2010) – and is particularly useful in giving patients and therapists the space to sit with existential issues that cannot be fixed.

Integrative therapies

Integrative therapies such as cognitive-analytic therapy (CAT) have been used beneficially in conditions such as diabetes (Fosbury *et al.*, 1997).

Group approaches

Psychologists offer group therapeutic interventions with multi-disciplinary colleagues. Physical, behavioural and medical approaches are considered within a self-management framework (e.g. pain management (Hoffman *et al.*, 2007), cardiac rehabilitation and diabetes self-management groups).

Short-term therapeutic interventions may not meet the needs of those whose conditions are long term and fluctuate. Patient support groups also play an important role.

CASE STUDY

Assessment

Jack, 62 years old, retired, living alone, and with no previous history of mental health problems, presented to one of us with depression and anxiety associated with multiple health conditions. He had a stroke ten years ago but had recovered physically. Mild cognitive problems persisted. He had hypertension, diabetes, persistent pain from arthritis in his neck and concerns about dizziness and numbness. He refused to take prescribed medication because of side effects. He sometimes needed to get to the toilet urgently.

Jack articulated his concerns:

> 'My doctor told me to come though I don't understand what psychology can do. I am not depressed, but I am coping with lots of difficulties. I want my pain and this dizziness to stop. It's frightening; I don't enjoy going out any more. If my tests are normal what's causing this? My wife died last year after 40 years of marriage. She really understood me. I worry my memory isn't what it was and I wish I could do all the things I used to do before I was ill. I fear my son's cancer will return. I can really talk to him but I get tired looking after my grandchildren. I look after myself since my stroke. I attend a gym and practise martial-arts learned in the army. I keep a journal as writing helps me and helps with my memory. I go to church since my wife died. It gives me hope I might see her again one day.'

Interested in self-management, Jack engaged readily. A personal and illness history was taken, including exploration of illness beliefs. One of four brothers, masculinity and athleticism were family values. If Jack fell over, he was told to get up and carry on. This attitude to injury/illness was reinforced in army training with a 'no pain no gain', 'pain is just weakness leaving the body' attitude. After leaving the army Jack had a sedentary job; his weight increased, and his fitness decreased. He used alcohol and smoked tobacco to manage work-related stress. On the day of his stroke he experienced severe headaches but ignored the pain. He collapsed and was rushed to hospital. Extensive rehabilitation followed weeks in intensive care. Jack now feared having another stroke. No longer smoking or drinking, he monitored every symptom 'just in case'.

Jack was asked to keep a CBT thought diary over two weeks noting *when* troubling symptoms occurred, and the *thoughts*, *emotions* and *behaviours* associated with them. His diary reported difficulties with unfamiliar journeys. Previously his wife had compensated for these difficulties by helping him plan. He was hyper-critical of himself for his physical and cognitive difficulties. Before going out Jack worried about potential symptoms. Concerns included: 'Can I find my way there and back? Will I find a toilet in time? Will I feel dizzy or have severe pain? Are these stroke symptoms?' He fasted before going out to avoid needing a toilet. He believed that if he needed help he could not ask strangers, who would view him as an 'old fool'.

Scores on the Hospital Anxiety and Depression Scale (Zigmond and Snaith, 1983) for both anxiety and depression were in the severe range. The Brief Illness Perception Questionnaire (Broadbent *et al.*, 2006) reflected a poor understanding of illness, high concern about conditions and low perception of control. Memory screening was normal.

Formulation

A generic model focusing on the following five areas was used with Jack to formulate his difficulties (Dudley and Kuyken, 2006).

Presenting problems

- Confusion about health problems and how to manage them: dizziness and numbness, pain, bladder and bowel symptoms, anxiety, depression. Symptoms fearfully interpreted as possible sign of stroke.
- Grieving (appropriate).
- Cognitive problems in public cause anxiety.
- Urgency to empty bowel and urinate when out, fasting to avoid going to toilet (affecting diabetes?).

Predisposing problems

- Pre-existing diabetes, hypertension, arthritis, stroke.
- Family narrative about coping response to illness reinforced by army and martial-arts training.
- Mild cognitive deficits following stroke affecting executive function (planning).

Precipitating factors

- Death of wife who had supported him practically and emotionally.
- Negative findings from medical tests (no explanation given for symptoms leading to fear that something is being missed).
- Illness of wife and illness of his son led to preoccupation with health issues.

Perpetuating factors

- Beliefs: all symptoms have a physical cause; asking for help means weakness, self-blame feeds depression.
- Coping behaviours: anxious monitoring of symptoms post-stroke maintains health-related anxiety, not eating exacerbates dizziness.
- Meaning of symptoms: I am perceived by society as vulnerable and weak; I am unsafe.

Protective factors

- Helpful coping: high self-efficacy active engagement in healthy behaviours: good diet, regular exercise.
- Prepared to take an active part in self-managing his problems.
- Good social support.

Jack noted the interplay between physical health issues, cognitive problems and mood. His own health issues, his wife's death and his son's illness had increased awareness of his mortality and vulnerability. Ageing and vulnerability concerns meant he feared going out and feared asking for help. He missed his wife's support in managing his health difficulties.

Drawing upon Folkman and Greer (2000, Figure 13.1), Jack recognised that previous experience of stroke, and believing that physical problems always have a physical cause, resulted in his appraisal of his symptoms as a threat: a sign of a further stroke. This caused anxiety which in turn exacerbated existing physical and cognitive problems. Symptoms he feared might indicate stroke included pain, dizziness, numbness and bladder urgency.

Problem-based coping included dietary restriction. Emotion-based coping included avoiding going out, resulting in not evaluating if his fears were based on fact. Meaning-based coping viewed illness as personal weakness and such self-criticism contributed to depression.

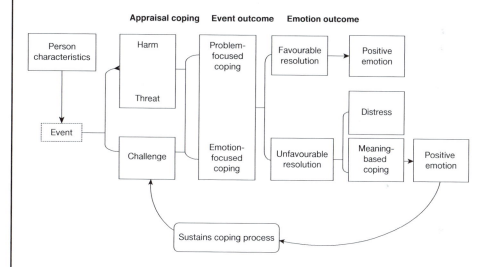

FIGURE 13.1 Coping

Source: From Folkman and Greer (2000). Copyright © 2000 John Wiley & Sons, Ltd.

Action plan

Jack wanted an explanatory framework to make sense of his physical, cognitive and emotional problems; this would be provided through psycho-education. The bio-psychosocial formulation enabled Jack to consider problems as challenges rather than as threats. Jack wanted to learn alternative *coping strategies* which would be effective in managing chronic illness.

CBT, an evidence-based approach for anxiety, depression and health anxiety, which all feature in the formulation, was proposed to explore links between cognitions emotions and behaviour. ACT and compassion-based approaches were included to address both Jack's wish to consider his life-goals at this transition point in his life and his unhelpful self-criticism.

Jack wanted space to reflect on the impact of his wife's death and his son's illness. Jack was grieving appropriately and was comfortable continuing with the support which his church provided to explore existential issues.

Sessions were adapted to allow for Jack's physical and cognitive difficulties by having shorter appointments and providing written summaries.

Intervention

Psycho-education

Jack was given information about anxiety, including hyper-ventilation, and was surprised to learn that symptoms could include dizziness, tingling and numbness in the fingers, as well as bladder/bowel urgency. Jack learned that restricting eating contributed to low blood sugar levels (hypoglycaemia), symptoms of which include anxiety and dizziness.

Looking at the pain-gate model (Melzack and Wall, 1967) enabled Jack to see how psychological factors might exacerbate pain caused by arthritis in his neck.

CBT: cognitive reappraisal

Two possible explanations for Jack's bodily symptoms were considered. The first posited that these might indeed be warning signs of stroke; the second alternative explanation was that anxiety increased existing physical problems and that monitoring symptoms exacerbated anxiety, leading to a vicious cycle (Figure 13.2).

Jack's diary showed that he experienced symptoms daily but had never had a further stroke. Factual information about stroke and anxiety was given. Reading about this material enabled Jack to evaluate the two possibilities using facts. He came to see that his symptoms did not relate to stroke and were either increased by or perhaps in some cases caused by his anxiety response.

Behavioural experiments

Behavioural experiments were designed to test this hypothesis. First, Jack accepted invitations to go out, challenging avoidance coping. He learned to notice, record and then successfully challenge anxiety-related thoughts about stroke using the information material given (see Table 13.1).

Jack began to practise breathing exercises he had learned in martial arts and these controlled hyper-ventilation. Bowel/bladder urgency decreased, enabling him to accept that anxiety contributed to this problem. He experimented with eating before going out with no detrimental effects, and 'dizziness', which may have been exacerbated by low blood sugar and diabetes, improved.

Jack had not understood the implications of post-stroke neuropsychological testing, suggesting that he might have problems planning activity. Understanding

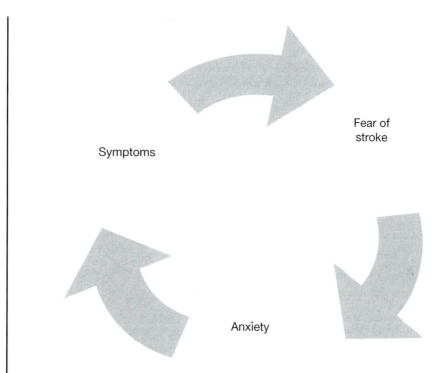

Symptoms

Fear of
stroke

Anxiety

FIGURE 13.2 One explanation for Jack's bodily symptoms

this enabled Jack to effectively use problem- and emotion-focused coping. He
planned new journeys carefully and carried a mobile phone with emergency contact
numbers. Behavioural experiments revealed that when anxious, cognitive problems,
including memory, worsened. Managing anxiety resulted in some cognitive
improvements.

TABLE 13.1 Diary example

Situation	Symptoms	Belief	Alternative	Which belief is more likely
Rushing to martial arts – Late!!	Dizziness, need to empty bladder.	Could be another stroke – shouldn't ignore this.	I am rushing and slightly out of breath. If this is the reason for dizziness, then my symptoms should improve when I slow down.	Symptoms improved so alternative explanation is true. Rushing and anxiety about being late affected my breathing which made me feel a bit dizzy.

Acceptance and commitment therapy (ACT)

Jack's upbringing led him to view himself as worthless if inactive. He often did too much and tiredness increased pain. Mindfulness techniques increased his awareness of self-criticism. He practised being non-judgemental and self-compassionate. This enabled him to give himself permission to use a behavioural technique 'pacing activity' which helped reduce fatigue. Using ACT approaches, Jack identified core personal values, including being a good father/grandfather. He had been supporting his son by providing childcare previously undertaken by his wife, which was physically exhausting. Jack had felt withdrawing would be unsupportive and show weakness. He identified alternatives which would enable him to care for himself, while recognising his core values. Instead of after-school childcare, he agreed to take the children to martial arts and help with homework.

Systemic work

The intervention included a family session which proved helpful. Jack also shared the formulation with his doctors.

Outcome

Jack learned to live with uncertainty about the exact cause of all of his symptoms which had bio-psychosocial components. He found effective ways to cope, reducing both symptoms and distress including anxiety and depression. Re-testing (HADS, BIPQ) confirmed improvements in mood and decreased concerns about illness. Reframing problems as challenges and avoiding self-blame allowed the use of new coping skills with positive outcomes, which in turn sustained positive coping. *'Once I understood what was happening I could see how to cope'.* In accepting his limitations and personal losses he acknowledged that despite ongoing health problems, a good quality of life was achievable.

Team and indirect work

Psychologists in physical health settings are a scarce resource. The New Ways of Working Initiative (BPS, 2007) encourages indirect working so that psychological resources are used efficiently. Indirect activities like consultation, training and supervision empower other health professionals to integrate a psychological perspective in their practice, enhancing patient care without the psychologist necessarily seeing patients directly. Medical staff may consult a psychologist for help in managing patient problems like lack of adherence to treatment recommendations, or helping distressed patients adjust to physical difficulties. Psychologists also provide consultation over staff problems such as disagreement within the team about how best to manage a patient (Hengeveld and Rooymans, 1983). In sharing a psychological formulation the psychologist promotes staff understanding of the patient's emotions and behaviour. This may enable the team to think creatively about alternative ways of managing the patient's problems. Psychological consultation may be informal with psychologists sitting in MDT meetings sharing psychological understandings of patients; or more formal, where medical staff seek advice individually about a patient about whom they have concerns. Psychologists integrated in multi-disciplinary teams may have more opportunities to influence practice than external agents who may only advise.

Psychologists perform an important role in training other professionals to use basic psychological skills with physical health patients. NICE (2004) guidelines on cancer care recommend that all staff receive training in recognising psychological distress and compassionate communication. Designated professionals like nurse specialists may receive further training in using simple screening instruments and basic psychological techniques. By providing regular ongoing supervision following training, clinical psychologists ensure that newly learned psychological skills continue to be applied appropriately.

CRITICAL ISSUES

Psychiatric diagnosis and physical health

The *Diagnostic and Statistical Manual of Mental Disorders* (DSM–V), published in May 2013, had several relevant changes in relation to physical health. One in particular has received significant attention. 'Somatoform disorders' (DSM-IV) are replaced by 'somatic symptom disorders'. Changes in criteria aim to 'better reflect the complex interface between mental and physical health'.

Somatic symptom disorder (SSD) is characterised by somatic symptoms alongside one of the following (APA, 2013, p. 311):

1 Disproportionate and persistent thoughts about the seriousness of symptoms;
2 Persistently high level of anxiety re: health or symptoms;
3 Excessive time and energy devoted to symptoms or health concerns.

DSM–V does not require that the somatic symptoms be 'medically unexplained' as did its predecessor, recognising that psychiatric disorders often occur with physical health problems and that disproportionate or excessive concerns about the somatic symptoms are indicative of psychiatric morbidity. SSD is likened to depression; 'it can occur in the context of a serious medical illness'.

It is argued that these changes promote comprehensive assessment and holistic care, representing a move away from the mind–body separation indicated in DSM-IV.

The introduction of SSD has not been received without controversy. Opponents of the changes highlight the subjective nature of the terms 'disproportionate' and 'excessive', on which diagnosis is based. It is not clear, critics argue, where 'normal' worrying ends and pathological anxiety begins. Similarly, there is no clarity regarding what 'good coping' looks like, and when this becomes 'excessive energy' devoted to symptoms. It is argued that SSD is overly inclusive and will greatly increase the numbers of people with physical health problems diagnosed with psychiatric conditions.

Patient groups have raised concerns that there is greater scope for conditions which are medically unexplained to be seen as 'all in the head' – a diagnosis of SSD in these cases may lead to mental health referral with the exclusion of appropriate medical input – shoring up mind–body dualism rather than dissipating it. At worst, this could lead to misdiagnosis of mental disorder in people with physical health conditions which are difficult to detect and diagnose.

Clinical health psychology has a positive role here. People with physical health problems are vulnerable to distress and mental health problems. Understanding the *context* and *impact* of this are skills which clinical psychologists possess and can harness in client-centred interventions aimed at reducing distress, whatever its label.

OUTCOME: LIZZIE'S STORY

The positive impact of my sessions was invaluable. Through some painful emotive soul searching and honesty I was able to identify areas of my life that were still valuable. I acknowledged the positive things I had managed to retain: my humour, courage, determination and relationship with my son. I accepted that I deserved some happiness and stopped grieving for my past life, and realised that life could still be enjoyable and rewarding in different ways.

It was a joy and relief to see some clarity and take back control of my choices. I reinstalled parts of my life I had locked away and forgotten: lovely clothes, jewellery and lots of creative projects. My sessions provided me with invaluable strategies for regaining self-esteem and pride in myself.

I know my illness is incurable but it no longer dictates my life. I am determined to stride forward in strength and positivity.

CONCLUSION

Clinical health psychologists play a significant role in supporting people to cope with, adjust to, and sometimes overcome, the impact of physical health problems. They teach and support other healthcare staff to use psychological approaches in their work as well as working with families and carers. The health and health economic benefits of this type of work have been demonstrated; the challenge lies in finding the NHS resources to further fund this important area of work.

KEY CONCEPTS AND TERMS

- Bio-psychosocial model
- Psychoneuro-immunology
- Multi-disciplinary working
- Coping
- Self-efficacy
- Locus of control

- Social support
- Adjustment and adaptation
- Self-management approaches
- Long-term conditions (LTCs)
- Medically unexplained symptoms (MUS)

- Quality of life
- Stigma
- Trans-diagnostic health issues
- Existential issues
- Health care system

LEARNING OUTCOMES

When you have completed this chapter you should be able to:

1 Understand the psychological challenges that present within the context of physical health.
2 Have an understanding of the psychological and societal issues which impact upon how an individual lives with a physical health problem.
3 Have an understanding of psychological theories and models relevant to clinical health psychology.
4 Have an understanding of treatment approaches used by clinical psychologists in physical health settings, and the evidence base for these approaches.
5 Understand how assessment, formulation, intervention and evaluation might be used by a psychologist working on a specific case.
6 Be able to provide a critical appraisal of different psychological intervention approaches used in physical health settings.

SAMPLE ESSAY TITLES

- How do psychological factors play a role in physical health conditions?
- What are the similarities and differences between clinical psychology and clinical health psychology?
- What is the role of a clinical health psychologist in a multi-disciplinary team?
- Psychological adjustment is key to positive outcomes in physical health. Discuss.

REFERENCES

Bandura, A. (1994). *Self-efficacy. The exercise of control.* New York: Freeman.

Benton, T., Staab, J. and Evans, D. (2007). Medical co-morbidity in depressive disorders. *Annals of Clinical Psychiatry, 2004*(19), 4.

British Psychological Society (BPS) (2007). *New Ways of Working for Applied Psychologists in Health and Social Care: Working psychologically in teams.* Leicester: British Psychological Society.

Broadbent, E., Petrie, K.J., Main, J. and Weinman, J. (2006). The Brief Illness Perception Questionnaire (BIPQ). *Journal of Psychosomatic Research, 60,* 631–637.

Dantzer, R., O'Connor, J.C., Freund, G.G., Johnson, R.W. and Kelley, K.W. (2008). From inflammation to sickness and depression: When the immune system subjugates the brain. *Nature Reviews Neuroscience, 9*(1), 46–57.

Druss, B. and Pincus, H. (2000). Suicidal ideation and suicide attempts in general medical illnesses. *Archives of Internal Medicine, 160*(10), 15–22.

Dudley, R. and Kuyken, W. (2006). Formulation in cognitive behavioural therapy. In L. Johnstone and R. Dallos (eds), *Formulation in Psychology and Psychotherapy* (pp. 17–46). Abingdon, Oxon: Routledge.

Dunford, E. and Thompson, M. (2010) Relaxation and mindfulness in pain: A review. *Reviews in Pain, 4,* 18. doi: 10.1177/204946371000400105.

Engel, G.L. (1977). The need for a new medical model: A challenge for biomedicine. *Science,* 196, 129–136.

Folkman, S. and Greer, S. (2000). Promoting psychological wellbeing in the face of serious illness; When theory research and practice inform each other. *Psycho-Oncology, 9,* 11–19.

Fosbury, J., Bosley, C., Ryle, A., Sonksen, P. and Judd, S. (1997). A trial of cognitive analytic therapy in poorly controlled type 1 diabetes patients. *Diabetes Care, 20,* 195–203.

Galloway, S., Graydon, J., Harrison, D., Evans-Boyden, B., Palmer-Wickham, S., Burlein-Hall, S., Rich-Van Der Bij, L., West, P. and Blair, A. (1997) Informational needs of women with a recent diagnosis of breast cancer: Development and initial testing of a tool. *Journal of Advanced Nursing, 25*(6), 1175–1183.

Hengeveld, M.W. and Rooymans, H.G. (1983). The relevance of a staff–oriented approach in consultation psychiatry: A preliminary study. *General Hospital Psychiatry, 5,* 259–264.

Hoffman, B.M., Papaps, R.K., Chatkoff, D.K. and Kerns, R.D. (2007). Meta-analysis of psychological interventions for chronic low back pain. *Health Psychology, 26,* 1–9.

Kendall-Tackett, K. (2009). Psychological trauma and physical health: A psychoneuro-immnology approach to aetiology of negative health events and possible intervention. *Psychological Trauma, Theory, Research, Practice and Policy, 1*(1), 35–48.

Kiecolt-Glaser, J.K., McGuire, L., Robles, T.F. and Glaser, R. (2002). Psychoneuro-immunology: Psychological influences on immune function and health. *Journal of Consulting and Clinical Psychology, 70*(3), 537.

Lazarus, R.S., and Folkman, S. (1984). *Stress, Appraisal, and Coping.* New York: Springer.

McInnes, R.A. (2003). Chronic illness and sexuality. *Medical Journal of Australia, 179*(5), 263–266.

Melzack, R. and Wall, P.D. (1967). Pain mechanisms: A new theory. *Survey of Anesthesiology*, *11*(2), 89.

Miller, S.M., Rodoletz, M., Schoreder, C.M., Mangan, C.E. and Sedlacek, T.V. (1996). Applications of the monitoring process model to coping with severe long-term medical threats. *Health Psychology*, *15*(3), 216–225.

Moos, R.H. and Holahan, C.J. (2007). Adaptive tasks and methods of coping with illness and disability. In E. Matz and H. Livneh (eds), *Coping with Chronic Illness and Disability* (pp 107–128). New York: Springer.

National Institute of Clinical Excellence (NICE) (2004). *Improving Supportive and Palliative Care for Adults with Cancer*. London: NICE.

—— (2008). *Cognitive Behavioural Therapy for the Management of Common Mental Health Problems*. Commissioning guide. London: NICE.

—— (2009). *Depression in Adults with a Chronic Physical Health Problem*. London: NICE.

Naylor, C., Parsonage, M., McDaid, D., Knapp, M., Fossey, M. and Galea, A. (2012). *Long-term Conditions and Mental Health: The Cost of Co-morbidities*. London: The King's Fund.

Nelson, S., Baldwin, N. and Taylor, J. (2012). Mental health problems and medically unexplained physical symptoms in adult survivors of childhood sexual abuse: An integrative literature review. *Journal of Psychiatric and Mental Health Nursing*, *19*(3), 211–220.

Robotham, D., Chakkalackal, L. and Cyhlarova, E. (2011). *Sleep Matters: Impact of sleep on health and wellbeing*. London: Mental health Foundation.

Seligman, M.E.P. (1975). *Helplessness: On depression, development, and death*. San Francisco, CA: W.H. Freeman.

Vowles, K.E. and Thompson, M. (2011). Acceptance and commitment therapy for chronic pain. In L.M. McCracken (ed.), *Mindfulness and Acceptance in Behavioural Medicine: Current theory and practice* (pp. 31–60). Oakland: New Harbinger Press.

White, C. (2001). *Cognitive Behaviour Therapy for Chronic Medical Problems. A guide to assessment and treatment in practice*. Chichester: Wiley.

Wilson, S.J., Nutt, D.J. and Alford. C. (2010). British Association for Psychopharmacology consensus statement on evidence-based treatment of insomnia, parasomnias and circadian rhythm disorders. *Journal of Psychopharmacology*, *24*, 1577–1601.

Zigmond, A.S. and Snaith, R.P. (1983). The Hospital Anxiety and Depression Scale. *ActaPsychiatrScand*, *67*(6), 361–370.

14 Working with people with dementia

Jane Shepherd, Sally Stapleton and Maureen Jeal

MAUREEN'S STORY

I am 67 years old and live with my husband Brian. I've always liked to help others. I've always been a worker and I like to keep busy. Alzheimer's stopped me working. When I was first told I had Alzheimer's three or four years ago, I thought, 'don't give in, carry on'. You've got to have a laugh. I like to laugh with the grandchildren. I'm always saying, 'don't ask me, I've got Alzheimer's'. My memory is going fast. I get frustrated when I lose things. Sometimes I don't like being like this, I didn't ask for this. When I get upset with the Alzheimer's, I feel as if I've done something wrong and I'm no good to anyone. But I'm a lot happier than I was. I get on well at the club. They've brought me on a good treat. They appreciate what I do. I'm more like one of the staff. If someone's struggling I'll help them. I set the table, I do the napkins, I help with cooking. I lay the table. I interact with the residents. I help them with their eating. I like to be needed, I like to have purpose. As long as I have the family and Brian, I can cope with the Alzheimer's. Brian helps me remember things. He does the cooking. I help out a bit, with the housework. Brian and my family are fantastic, they've done so much for me. They give me love.

SUMMARY

Maureen's story shows that, with the right care and support, people with dementia can continue to lead active and fulfilling lives. This chapter highlights the role clinical psychologists have in providing psychological interventions that enable people with dementia to live as well as they can with their dementia. As you will see from this chapter, the growing influence of psychological approaches has been crucial in guiding the expansion of practice and research in dementia care. The chapter will cover a range of psychological theories and interventions which focus upon the experiences of people with dementia and their carers/families. The evidence base for these theories and interventions is briefly reviewed. The chapter will also provide case examples to demonstrate how psychologists put their knowledge and skills into practice when working with individuals, families and multi-professional staff teams in care environments. Finally, it will outline the debates and challenges in the shared endeavour of aiming for excellence in dementia care.

INTRODUCTION

The National Dementia Strategy defines 'dementia' as 'a syndrome which may be caused by a number of illnesses in which there is progressive decline in multiple areas of function, including decline in memory, reasoning, communication skills and the ability to carry out daily activities' (Department of Health, 2009, p. 15).

'Dementia' is an umbrella term. There are over 100 conditions which cause dementia (NCCMH, 2007). The most common types are Alzheimer's disease and Vascular dementia. Alzheimer's disease is a condition involving protein 'plaques' and 'tangles' which lead to the death of brain cells. Vascular dementia occurs following damage to the blood-vessels (vascular system) within the brain; for example, following a series of small strokes. Brain cells die due to the lack of oxygen supply. The Alzheimer's Society provides an excellent range of fact sheets on different types of dementia (see www.alzheimers.org.uk).

There is currently no cure for the conditions that cause dementia. However, much can be done to improve the quality of life of people with dementia, from assisting with the diagnostic process, to supporting people at the end of their lives (Department of Health, 2009). Clinical psychologists help us understand the specific experiences of each person with dementia and those who support them. Two people with identical diagnoses may have completely different experiences of living with dementia. Their experiences depend just as much upon factors such as their own life experiences and the quality of support that they receive from others, as it does upon the extent of neurological difficulties.

DIAGNOSIS

DSM–V includes types of dementia under the category of 'Major and mild neuro-cognitive disorders'.

For a diagnosis of a 'major neurocognitive disorder', there needs to be evidence of significant decline in one or more of the following cognitive abilities:

- Complex attention (e.g. keeping focused despite distractions).
- Executive function (e.g. planning and decision making).
- Learning and memory (e.g. remembering recent events).
- Language (e.g. naming, speech production and comprehension).
- Perceptual motor (e.g. object recognition, coordinating actions).
- Social cognition (e.g. considering others' feelings and wishes).

(APA, 2013)

There are specific criteria for different conditions. For example, the criteria of 'Major neurocognitive disorder due to possible Alzheimer's disease' requires clear evidence of a gradual decline in learning and memory and a decline in at least one other cognitive domain.

Evidence of cognitive difficulties from neuropsychological assessment (this involves carrying out a number of standardised tests that tap different aspects of cognitive processing and reasoning) or another 'quantified clinical assessment' is preferable (APA, 2013). Therefore, clinical psychologists (with neuropsychology training) can assist with the diagnostic process.

WHAT ARE THE TYPES OF PSYCHOLOGICAL DIFFICULTIES THAT MAY OCCUR IN DEMENTIA?

Dementia has a profound impact upon the lives of people with dementia and those around them. As you would expect, each person's experience is unique, and people with the same type of dementia and similar brain damage will experience and respond to their dementia in different ways. Dementia can impact directly upon the following factors.

Mood and everyday activities

Maureen described the everyday challenge of being unable to do things the way she used to. Cognitive difficulties such as poor memory and visual perception problems often account for this. She spoke about anxiety and lowered self-esteem and confidence. People with dementia may also experience depression and a range of negative feelings in response to their illness, such as anger and frustration.

Communication and relationships

People with dementia can feel isolated and experience a lack of belonging. This may be as a result of communication difficulties and low confidence but may also be a consequence of how they are perceived and treated by others. There may be difficulties within the caregiving and/or family relationships as the family struggle to adjust to the changes in roles and usual ways of interacting.

Psychological and behavioural distress

As dementia progresses, people with dementia can show distress or engage in behaviours that others find upsetting. One example is being agitated or angry when someone is trying to help with dressing or eating. These episodes can be distressing for the person with dementia and others. The causes of these behaviours are usually complex and often relate to a person's attempts to address an unmet need. Typical causes are pain, boredom and frustration.

Carers and families

Caregiving has been associated with a range of experiences, including high levels of distress, depression and physical ill health as well as positive aspects such as satisfaction and meaning in one's role (Carbonneau *et al.*, 2010).

Families can go through difficult periods of not knowing how best to support the person with dementia. There may be differences of opinion among family members or with professionals about responding to concerns about a person's safety or behaviour. Family members may experience guilt and grief when making difficult decisions in the best interests of the person with dementia and/or the main caregiver, such as going into residential care.

LIVING WELL WITH DEMENTIA

Maureen has maintained her well-being with the loving support of her family, and she has actively developed and has been encouraged to develop positive and valued social roles at the club. She showed awareness of her difficulties and her coping through adopting a positive outlook, using humour and keeping active.

Drawing upon interviews with people with dementia, Clare (2002) provides a useful framework for ways of coping with dementia, on a continuum from *self-maintaining* to *self-adjusting*. Maureen's story illustrates the self-adjusting style of openness and flexibility in adapting to the challenges of dementia through attending a club with people in a similar situation and accepting others' help. Those taking a more self-maintaining position try to maintain their identity and lifestyle as normal and downplay the impact of the dementia. Both positions can be useful in enabling people with dementia to lead meaningful lives.

EPIDEMIOLOGY OF DEMENTIA

The Alzheimer's Society's 2013 report estimated there to be 800,000 people with dementia in the UK. This figure is anticipated to rise to over a million by 2021 and to 1,700,000 by 2051. Dementia is most prevalent in older people but there are 17,000 people with dementia in the UK who are under the age of 65.

The following are the prevalence rates of dementia in different age groups:

- 40 to 64 years: 1 in 1,400
- 65 to 69 years: 1 in 100
- 70 to 79 years: 1 in 25
- 80+ years: 1 in 6.

The proportion of people with dementia doubles for every five-year age group, with one-third of people aged 95 and over experiencing dementia.

At the present time only 44 per cent of individuals with dementia in England, Wales and Northern Ireland receive a diagnosis (Alzheimer's Society, 2013). There is currently a drive to improve dementia care services and research, which includes increasing access to diagnostic services (Department of Health, 2012).

AETIOLOGY OF DEMENTIA

Neurological difficulties do not fully explain the diversity in people's experiences of living with dementia. This section will consider the risk factors for developing dementia and then discuss factors that are related to well-being.

Risk factors

We do not always know why certain individuals develop dementia. Known risk factors include smoking (Ott *et al.*, 1998), excessive alcohol consumption (Saunders *et al.*, 1991), obesity (Kivipelto *et al.*, 2005), diabetes (Biessels *et al.*, 2006), hypertension (Feigin *et al.*, 2005) and raised cholesterol (Jick *et al.*, 2000). A small proportion of people develop dementia due to a genetic-related factor (Morris, 2005), for example, familial autosomal dominant Alzheimer's disease. The full version of the NICE/SCIE Clinical Guideline 42 (NCCMH, 2007) provides an excellent overview of risk factors.

A biopsychosocial model for understanding the experience of living with dementia

How a person with dementia feels, thinks and acts is influenced by a number of biological, psychological and social factors. This is outlined in Figure 14.1.

This model is used by clinical psychologists to formulate an understanding of factors associated with well-being and distress. For example, a staff carer tells you that Raj, a gentleman with dementia, screams and hits out at staff members every time they try to assist him with personal care. It may be thought that Raj's behaviour is the direct result of dementia and that there is nothing that can be done to help. However, drawing upon the bio-psychosocial model (Figure 14.1), we find that Raj has always been shy and private. He may have a *need* to continue to maintain as much privacy as possible but he is unable to tell staff that this is due to language difficulties. Raj's

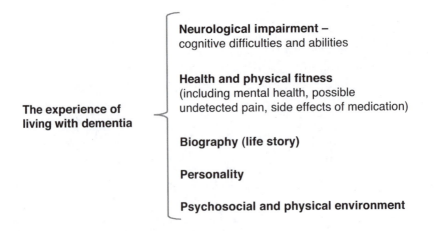

The experience of living with dementia

Neurological impairment –
cognitive difficulties and abilities

Health and physical fitness
(including mental health, possible undetected pain, side effects of medication)

Biography (life story)

Personality

Psychosocial and physical environment

FIGURE 14.1 Bio-psychosocial model of dementia

Source: Kitwood (1997), James (1999), NCCMH (2007).

behaviour in this situation could therefore be formulated as an attempt to communicate an *unmet need*.

Unmet needs and psychological distress

The bio-psychosocial model may be used to identify a person's needs, whether the need relates to neurological difficulties, a health need or a need related to their own personal life experiences. There is a general consensus that psychological distress, often expressed through a person's behaviour, is related to unmet needs (British Psychological Society, 2013).

Models for formulating unmet psychological needs

The bio-psychosocial model has been expanded to formulate factors related to psychological and behavioural distress (James, 2011). Crucially, a care team is encouraged to record a person's vocalisations (thoughts), appearance (feelings) and behaviours, alongside information about what was happening at the time, to help identify triggers. Applying this to Raj, the member of staff might record that the *trigger* for Raj starting to scream was during personal care. At these times he looked frightened in his *appearance*. His *vocalisations* were that he screamed 'no' and his *behaviour* was that he hit a member of staff on the arm when they tried to remove his clothes.

Figure 14.2 outlines the psychological needs for comfort, identity, attachment, occupation and inclusion, with love as a central need (Kitwood, 1997). We can use this model to understand which psychological need may not be being met. For

FIGURE 14.2 The five psychological needs of people with dementia

Source: Kitwood (1997); reproduced with kind permission of the Open University Press/McGraw-Hill Education). Maureen's description of the importance of her family's love validates the central need for love.

example, we might formulate that Raj screamed and hit out at staff members due to his comfort needs not being met. We could therefore formulate that staff members need to help Raj feel safe, secure and comfortable if he needs assistance with personal care.

The potential to support or undermine psychological needs during interactions

People with dementia are greatly affected by how they are treated by others. The terms 'positive' and 'malignant' social psychology have been used to illustrate this (Kitwood, 1997). Examples of malignant social psychology are when an individual experiences depersonalising treatment such as being treated like a 'child' or an 'object'. This can undermine a person's psychological needs. Examples of a positive social psychology are when an individual experiences 'warmth', 'respect' and 'genuineness'. These can help meet an individual's psychological needs (British Standards Institution, 2010).

THEORY AND EVIDENCE FOR PSYCHOLOGICAL INTERVENTIONS IN DEMENTIA CARE

This section will cover the range of psychological and psychosocial approaches for people with dementia and their carers from early through to severe dementia. This is a rapidly growing research field and the interventions described below are recommended in the NICE–SCIE dementia guidance (NCCMH, 2007) and/or the BPS guidance (2013).

Psychologists deliver three main types of interventions:

(1) To support well-being and cognitive abilities in early to moderate dementia and prevent later difficulties.

Psychologists work with people with dementia and their carers to make the most of their remaining cognitive abilities such as memory and language. This work is often based on neuropsychological assessment to explain why the person may be having particular problems with everyday activities such as dressing or understanding what is being said.

Cognitive stimulation therapy is a group intervention to enhance cognitive and social functioning through a range of activities (for example, a review of newspaper stories) and discussion. It also involves reality orientation which focuses on orientation to time, person and place, and reminiscence therapy which focuses on past memories. There is strong evidence for the effectiveness of cognitive stimulation therapy on cognition, mood and behaviours that challenge (e.g. Spector *et al.*, 2010).

Cognitive rehabilitation is an individually tailored approach to achieve everyday activities such as taking tablets at the correct time or walking outside independently. People are encouraged to use learning strategies such as memory aids and reduce the number of errors during learning. Single case studies show positive outcomes with goal performance and satisfaction (Clare, 2010).

Psychologists use life history work such as life reviews and life stories to encourage people to reflect on positive and significant life experiences, often with carers or family. An example of a life review is to ask the person and family to recall how they dealt

FOCUS 14.1

Reduction in inappropriate use of antipsychotic medication: *Time for Action*

Anti-psychotics have been used in dementia to treat behaviours such as 'agitation' and 'aggression' because of their sedative properties. They are also used for delusions and hallucinations. An influential report, *Time for Action* (Banerjee, 2008), found that anti-psychotic medication was often used as a first-line treatment despite evidence that anti-psychotic drugs have limited effect and can cause significant harm to people with dementia, including strokes and death. The government has adopted Banerjee's recommendations for a reduction in the use of anti-psychotics and an increase in the use of alternative non-pharmacological approaches. A recent Alzheimer's Society (2013) report showed a 52 per cent reduction in the number of inappropriate prescriptions for anti-psychotics for people with dementia.

with past difficulties and use their learning and experiences to guide them in their present situation. Life stories can take a number of forms, including conversations, life story-books, collages and reminiscence boxes. Reminiscence therapy is usually delivered as a group intervention for people to share memories and common experiences. Reminiscence and life history work can reinforce the person's sense of self, improve close relationships and promote communication and enjoyable activity (e.g. Woods *et al.*, 2005). See Bruce and Schweitzer (2008) for a comprehensive description of life history work.

Psychologists often work with couples and families in order to improve the communication and interactions in the interests of the person with dementia. From our clinical experience, common themes in this work include facing losses and changes in relationship roles, the impact of family experience of dementia and illness and preparing for the future. There is good evidence that involving carers and families in early interventions can improve the well-being of both the person with dementia and their carer as well as delay later nursing home admissions (e.g. Smits *et al.*, 2007).

(2)   To improve mood disorders for people with dementia and carers.
As described in the psychological difficulties section, people with dementia and carers can also have anxiety and/or depression arising from the experience of dementia or the demands of being in a caregiving role. If so, they may benefit from psychological therapies, including cognitive-behavioural therapy, which is recommended in NICE-SCIE guidance (NCCMH, 2007), with research trials underway (Spector *et al.*, 2012).

(3)   To address psychological and behavioural distress in moderate to severe dementia.
As described above, psychologists use bio–psychosocial assessment and formulation to explain why the distress and behaviours may be occurring in the context of the person's dementia, life history and social and physical environment. There may be a range of

causes including pain, misinterpreting things and people's actions, past trauma and specific interactions with caregivers. Psychologists draw on a range of theories, including neuropsychological, cognitive-behavioural, psychodynamic (especially attachment) and systemic frameworks. Case studies below further illustrate the use of clinical formulation in practice.

There is best practice guidance (BPS, 2013; NCCMH, 2007) and promising research (Moniz-Cook *et al.*, 2012) for individualised psychological formulation-led approaches. An influential RCT study on person–centred interventions in care homes found a significant reduction in the use of anti-psychotic medication with regular input from a trained clinician (Fossey *et al.*, 2006).

Dementia care mapping (DCM) is recommended for improving the well-being of people with dementia within care settings (BPS, 2013). This is a structured observation framework for assessing the factors associated with well-being and distress, including interactions among people with dementia and care staff. DCM has been shown to significantly reduce levels of agitation in a cluster RCT (Chenoweth *et al.*, 2009).

CASE STUDY

Mrs Sylvia Peterson was admitted to an inpatient ward, having become severely distressed following the experience of visual hallucinations. Sylvia and her family reported that they wanted advice and support with the visual hallucinations so that she could return to living at home as soon as possible. I (SS) agreed to meet with Sylvia and her family.

Assessment

I initially met with Sylvia individually to find out more about her as a person, including her life history and strengths. I wanted to explore the emotions she experienced during the hallucinations to see if there were any connections with her life history. I also wanted to explore any potentially unmet psychological needs.

I also met with her husband and son to understand their perspective. I was interested in finding out how they responded to her when she was experiencing hallucinations and distress. I also wanted to find out about their strengths and how they were coping in their relatively new caring roles. I also read Sylvia's health records and talked to members of the care team, as I wanted to obtain as much information as possible about factors that might be relevant to the bio-psychosocial formulation.

Formulation

Neurological impairment

Sylvia told me that she had dementia. Her family said that she had been given a diagnosis of Dementia with Lewy Bodies. In her health records, I saw that a neuropsychological assessment indicated that she had difficulties with memory, visuo-spatial and executive functioning. Her language skills, however, were a strength. Her son told me that people outside of the family would often not realise that she had any difficulties, as she was able to hold a good conversation. This was also my experience.

Health and physical fitness

Sylvia told me that sometimes the hallucinations she experienced were of animals or children and did not worry her too much. However, at other times she saw 'nasty people' who were coming to beat her up. She reported that she thought that they were not real, but it was difficult to know, especially when she was feeling really frightened. On further exploration, she said she was scared of being beaten again, as she experienced this as a child. During her first two weeks on the ward, the nursing team reported that there were times when she looked extremely frightened and would try to hide behind furniture or approach staff members, asking for help and 'clinging' to them. At other times, if alone, she sometimes screamed. These observations were reflected in her scores on the Cohen-Mansfield Agitation scale (CMAI: Cohen-Mansfield et al., 1989).

Sylvia had experienced significant negative side effects of anti-psychotic medication when they were prescribed to treat visual hallucinations in the past. Her family and the care team also told me that she experienced urinary tract infections (UTIs), especially when not drinking enough fluids, and that she sometimes experienced pain due to a previous back injury. The Pain Assessment in Advanced Dementia (PAINAD: Warden et al., 2003) identified that she experienced pain on a regular basis, although she was not always able to report this. Instead staff members were reliant on observing for signs, such as grimacing and holding her back.

Life history

Sylvia told me that she had an unhappy childhood and was badly beaten by her mother when she did something wrong. She met her husband at age 17. They married 18 months later and went on to have a son. She described that they had a happy life together, except for the usual ups and downs, and felt very proud of their son. She worked in a shoe shop for 25 years. Her main interests included gardening and cooking, but she said she liked to 'have a go at anything'. She told me that she liked to be called by her first name.

Personality

Sylvia reported that she liked to keep herself to herself and did not wish to cause any problems for anyone. Her family described her as a kind and caring person who was quite shy.

Psychosocial environment

Sylvia's family described that they did not know what to do when she experienced hallucinations. They had tried telling her that the hallucinations were not real, but this seemed to make things worse. She became more distressed and shouted at them, which made them feel stressed, angry and helpless. They described feeling 'at the end of their tether' but also 'desperately wanting to know what to do to help'.

Her family reported that she had stopped engaging in her interests of gardening and cooking. This was reflected in her scores on the Quality of Life in Alzheimer's Disease Scale (QOL-AD: Logsdon *et al.*, 2002).

Summary of the bio-psychosocial formulation

Sylvia and her family became very distressed when Sylvia experienced hallucinations. She was more at risk of hallucinations due to a diagnosis of Dementia with Lewy Bodies, in addition to her tendency to misperceive objects (visuospatial difficulties). Her hallucinations emerged at the time of her diagnosis, but she was more likely to experience distressing hallucinations when physically unwell or in pain. She did not wish to worry people too much, and so she often would not report if she felt physically unwell or in pain. This led to these difficulties not being treated promptly. Her life history of being beaten as a child by her mother almost certainly influenced her perceptions of the hallucinations she experienced, particularly if she was already distressed. The responses from her family (her psychosocial environment) led to arguments with her, resulting in further distress and anger. Her distress influenced her perception of the hallucinatory experiences. Her quality of life was low due to the impact of the difficulties on her family relationships and her limited engagement in meaningful activities.

Despite these difficulties, Sylvia and her family had a number of strengths. The most striking was their close relationship. Her family described Sylvia as a very kind and caring person who was able to form positive relationships with others. She was also able to talk about her interests and try out new things. As a family, they were all open to thinking together in a psychological way and were open to advice from other members of the care team.

Individual therapeutic sessions

The formulation led me to offer Sylvia some short individual therapeutic sessions on the ward to further explore the links she had started to make between hallucinatory experiences and her childhood experiences. I offered her individual sessions initially, as I was not sure how much she had discussed her childhood experiences with her family. The sessions were based on a simplified cognitive-behavioural framework, as recommended in the NICE-SCIE guideline (NCCMH, 2007) for people with dementia who experience emotional difficulties. The key aim of the sessions was to work towards a joint understanding of her thoughts, feelings and actions when she experienced a hallucination. She engaged very well in the sessions.

Sylvia told me that her family were aware of her childhood experiences and she decided she wanted to include her family within future therapeutic sessions so that together they could find ways of reducing the amount of distress they were all experiencing.

Therapeutic sessions with Sylvia and her family

Sylvia's family were keen to think about the potential links between her past and present experiences. I was therefore hopeful that collaborating on the formulation together, as a family, would help them find useful ways of supporting one another.

A plan of support at times of distress was agreed. This was based on validation therapy (Feil, 1993) whereby a person's feelings take priority. It was agreed that, rather than trying to help her see that she was having a hallucination or pretending that they could see what she was perceiving, they would instead validate her feelings and provide her with a sense of security and comfort. For example, they could say, 'I can see you are really frightened, I'm going to stay with you and make sure that you are safe', or 'It's okay, I'm here with you'. A therapeutic letter was written as a reminder of the discussion.

Work with the care team:

With Sylvia's permission, I agreed to share the key themes of the formulation with the multi-disciplinary team to help identify ways of preventing and responding to times when she was distressed. I also sought the team's advice. The ward doctor prescribed regular paracetamol for pain. The primary nurse gave advice on prevention of recurrent UTIs. The OT advised on meaningful engagement and gentle exercise to reduce back pain and improve her mood. Sylvia was referred to the cognitive stimulation therapy group to further promote quality of life.

Outcome

Sylvia reported feeling less distressed by the hallucinations, although she still reported seeing 'nasty people' at times. Her family reported that they felt much more able to support her during these times. They all reported a shared understanding of the impact of previous abusive experiences and said it made it easier to offer comfort and support.

The ward team reported finding it easier to support Sylvia at times of distress, in addition to feeling more able to support her general well-being on the ward. Her scores on the QOL-AD, CMAI and PAINAD indicated substantial improvements.

TEAM WORKING/INDIRECT WORK

Clinical formulation and consultation

As described above, psychologists work with colleagues and care staff to understand a person's distress and complex behaviour in psychological ways, either as an alternative to or to complement the use of medication. They use clinical formulation to broaden staff members' understanding of communication and behaviour. This can help staff resolve differences of opinion about what is best for the person with dementia and explore ways to respond to distress and behaviour that challenges. The following example illustrates this work:

> Bob was an 84-year-old man in a residential setting. Staff reported him making sexually inappropriate advances towards them when helping him with his washing and dressing. A few staff sometimes told him off and other staff reported that this resulted in 'aggressive behaviour'. During the formulation session, the psychologist helped the staff gather information from Bob's personal history, type of dementia and their interactions with him. The aims were to encourage staff to be curious about what might be causing Bob's behaviour and to reflect on their role in helping to meet his needs in helpful ways. This information sharing revealed that Bob was a happily married man who had been faithful to his wife and so sexual overtures to others was out of character and would normally be embarrassing for him. He was likely to be missing the intimacy with his wife. Due to experiencing 'Frontotemporal dementia' he was more likely to be disinhibited. He might misperceive the close physical contact with staff around personal care as a sexualised act. The staff began to empathise with Bob's situation and a few commented that they might have been 'a bit harsh' with him. The psychologist helped them devise a range of interventions; they reflected on whether they might talk with Bob about missing his wife, they discussed ways of addressing boredom and inactivity, and they identified the best ways of approaching and communicating with him during personal care tasks.

Staff and service development

Clinical psychologists working in dementia services support staff learning and development, drawing upon psychological perspectives and clinical research. Topics include assessment of cognitive functioning, neurological causes of behaviour that challenges and working with families. They also advise on service design and evaluation which includes specific interventions and clinical outcomes.

CRITICAL ISSUES

Responding to the increasing numbers of people with dementia

Dementia is both a national and international priority owing to growth in ageing populations and the related significant increase in the prevalence of dementia. The G8 Dementia Summit in 2013 sent a global message about the need for collaborative action on research and treatments. It set an ambitious target of identifying a cure or disease-modifying therapy by 2025. The UK government pledged to double research funding by 2025. The hopes for people to 'live well with dementia' need to be backed up by properly funded and resourced services. Research into both 'cure' and 'care' is seriously underfunded, with the UK government currently investing eight times less in dementia than in cancer research (Alzheimer's Society, 2013b).

Public awareness

There is greater recognition that society can make a difference to the lives of people with dementia through dementia-friendly communities (Alzheimer's Society, 2013a). Loneliness and social isolation are real issues for people living on their own, with 62 per cent of 500 people with dementia surveyed reporting feeling lonely (Alzheimer's Society, 2013a). There is also the risk of double discrimination within services and society due to negative attitudes about both ageing and dementia. Real progress will be made when people with dementia are enabled to maintain their involvement and contribution to their community (NICE, 2013).

Earlier diagnosis and support

Dementia diagnosis rates are shockingly low (Alzheimer's Society, 2013a). Less than half of the 800,000 people living with dementia in the UK have a diagnosis. Without this, they are denied access to support, information and potential treatments that can help them to live as best they can with dementia.

Quality of care

While there are many excellent services around the country, provision is patchy and there are real challenges in driving up the quality of care from acute hospitals through to people's homes. Attention needs to be given to those with more severe dementia and complex needs as well as those with early dementia. Guidance such as the National Dementia Strategy (Department of Health, 2009) have recognised the challenges facing services to meet the full range of needs of people with dementia and their carers. One key way of improving quality is to increase the involvement of people with dementia and their carers in the delivery and evaluation of services.

Support for carers

There is a serious problem of inadequate recognition and support for people who care for people with dementia. Two-thirds of people with dementia live in the community and it is estimated that family carers contribute work to the value of £8 billion (Alzheimer's Society, 2013a); yet much of the caring is hidden and unpaid carers can struggle on their own with insufficient help.

Abuse and poor practice

There have been shocking reports of poor care and abuse of older people in some hospitals and care homes. Strong leadership is required to address the staff and organisational barriers to good care. Research highlights barriers to good care such as poor leadership, high staff turnover, low pay and staffing levels, and lack of supervision (Bowers, 2008).

CONCLUSION

One of the greatest challenges of our time is what I'd call the quiet crisis, one that steals lives and tears at the hearts of families, but that relative to its impact is hardly acknowledged.

This statement by Prime Minister David Cameron at the G8 Summit in 2013 is a powerful invitation to focus upon the needs of people living with dementia and their families. We hope this chapter has shown that, despite the lack of a cure, psychologists can play a key role in spearheading best practice interventions and models of care that can make significant improvements to the quality of life of people with dementia, as well as their families and carers.

CONCLUSION TO MAUREEN'S STORY

Experience of psychological intervention as told by Kate, Maureen's daughter.

'Mum was a bit anxious about seeing you (JS) at first. She is not one to come out with how she feels. She didn't want to cry or feel anxious. We were surprised at how much she said. She let her emotions out talking to you. You were trying to get her to understand how she feels, how her worry about the Alzheimer's affected her stomach pain. We wanted advice on whether we were doing what we should be doing. We got so much from it. We understood that it was okay for Mum to feel low about having Alzheimer's. I spoke to the club about how they could help Mum. They got her helping out and got her a task sheet. We got a daily checklist together to assist Dad with housekeeping. The grandchildren made a nice photo album. Everything we talked about with you we discussed as a family. We all support each other.'

KEY CONCEPTS AND TERMS

- Dementia
- Carer/caregiver
- Person-centred care
- Bio-psychosocial model
- Unmet psychological needs
- Alzheimer's Society
- National Dementia Strategy
- Dementia-friendly communities
- Psychological and behavioural distress
- Neuropsychology

LEARNING OUTCOMES

When you have completed this chapter you should have an understanding of:

1   The range of difficulties that may be experienced by people with dementia and their families/carers.
2   The bio-psychosocial models that are used to inform our understanding of the experiences of people with dementia.
3   The evidence base for interventions used to increase well-being and quality of life in people with dementia and their families/carers.
4   The work of clinical psychologists in their use of assessment, formulation, intervention and evaluation with people with dementia, their families and care staff.
5   The key issues relating to the well-being of people with dementia and their family/carers and the challenges of driving up the quality of dementia care in services.

SAMPLE ESSAY TITLES

- Can people with dementia benefit from psychological interventions?
- How can helping carers help people with dementia?
- What are 'good outcomes' for people with dementia?
- How can clinical psychologists help care staff resolve difficulties that relate to the behaviour of a person with dementia?

REFERENCES

Alzheimer's Society (2013a). *Dementia 2013: The hidden voice of loneliness*. London: Alzheimer's Society

—— (2013b). Website available at: http://www.alzheimers.org.uk/site/scripts/documents_info.php?documentID=1111(accessed 27 August 2013).

American Psychiatric Association (APA) (2013). *Diagnostic and Statistical Manual of Mental Disorders Fifth Edition DSM-5*. Arlington, VA: American Psychiatric Association.

Banerjee, S. (2008). The use of antipsychotic medication for people with dementia: Time for Action.

Biessels, G.J., Staekenborg, S. and Brunner, E. (2006). Risk of dementia in diabetes mellitus: A systematic review. *Lancet Neurology*, 5, 64–74.

Bowers, B. (2008). A trained and supported workforce. In M. Downs and B. Bowers (eds), *Excellence in Dementia Care; Research into practice*. Maidenhead: Open University Press.

British Psychological Society (2013). *Alternatives to Antipsychotic Medication: Psychological approaches in managing psychological and behavioural distress in people with dementia.* Leicester: British Psychological Society.

British Standards Institution (2010). *PAS 800: 2010. Use of dementia care mapping for improved person-centred care in a care provider organisation – guide.* London: British Standards Institution.

Bruce, E. and Schweitzer, P. (2008). Working with life history. In M. Downs and B. Bowers (eds), *Excellence in Dementia Care; Research into practice.* Maidenhead: Open University Press.

Carbonneau, H., Caron, C. and Desrosiers, J. (2010). Development of a conceptual framework of positive aspects of caregiving in dementia. *Dementia, 9*(3), 327–353.

Chenoweth, L., King, M.T., Jeon, Y.H., Brodaty, H., Stein-Parbur, J., Norman, R.M., Haas, M. and Luscombe, G. (2009). Caring for aged dementia care resident sudy (CADRES) of person-centred care, dementia-care mapping, and usual care in dementia: A cluster-randomised trial. *Lancet Neurology, 8,* 317–325.

Clare, L. (2002). We'll fight it as long as we can: Coping with the onset of Alzheimer's disease. *Aging and Mental Health,* 6, 139–148.

—— (2010). Goal-oriented cognitive rehabilitation for people with early stage Alzheimer disease: A single blind randomized controlled trial of clinical efficacy. *American Journal of Geriatric Psychiatry, 18,* 928–939.

Cohen-Mansfield, J., Marx, M.S. and Rosenthal, A.S. (1989). A description of agitation in a nursing home. *Journal of Gerontology: Medical Sciences, 44*(3), 77–84.

Department of Health (2009). *Living Well with Dementia: A national dementia strategy.* London: Department of Health.

—— (2012). *Prime Minister's Challenge on Dementia: Delivering major improvements in dementia care and research by 2015.* London: Department of Health.

Feigin, V., Ratnasabapathy, Y. and Anderson, C. (2005). Does blood pressure lowering treatment prevent dementia or cognitive decline in patients with cardiovascular and cerebrovascular disease? *Journal of the Neurological Sciences, 229–230,* 151–155.

Feil, N. (1993). *The Validation Breakthrough.* Cleveland: Health Professions Press.

Fossey, J., Ballard, C., Jusczak, E., James, I., Alder, N., Jacoby, R. and Howard, R. (2006). Effect of enhanced psychosocial care and antipsychotic use in nursing home residents with severe dementia: A cluster randomised trial. *British Medical Journal, 23 March.*

James, I.A. (1999). Using a cognitive rationale to conceptualise anxiety in people with dementia. *Behavioural and Cognitive Psychotherapy, 27*(4), 345–351.

—— (2011). *Understanding Behaviour in Dementia that Challenges: A guide to assessment and treatment.* London: Jessica Kingsley.

Jick, H., Zornberg, G.L., Jick, S.S. and Seshadri, S. (2000). Statins and the risk of dementia. *The Lancet, 356,* 1627–1631.

Kitwood, T. (1997). *Dementia Reconsidered: The person comes first.* Buckingham: Open University Press.

Kivipelto, M., Ngandu, T. and Fratiglioni, L. (2005). Obesity and vascular risk factors at midlife and the risk of dementia and Alzheimer disease. *Archives of Neurology, 62,* 1556–1560.

Logsdon, R.G., Gibbons, L.E., McCurry, S.M. and Teri, L. (2002). Assessing quality of life in older adults with cognitive impairment. *Psychosomatic Medicine, 64,* 510–519.

Moniz-Cook, E., Swift, K., James, I., Malouf, R., De Vugt, M. and Verhey, F. (2012). Function analysis-based interventions for challenging behaviour in dementia. *Cochrane Library, 2.* Retrieved from http://onlinelibrary.wiley.com/doi/10.1002/14651858.CD006929.pub2.

Morris, J.C. (2005). Dementia update 2005. *Alzheimer Disease and Associated Disorders, 19,* 100–117.

National Collaborating Centre for Mental Health (NCCMH) (2007). *Dementia: The NICE-SCIE Guideline on supporting people with dementia and their carers in health and social care (Full Guidance).* London: National Institute for Health and Clinical Excellence.

—— (2013). *QS30 Supporting People to Live Well with Dementia: Quality standard.* Issued April.

Ott, A., Slooter, A.J. and Hofman, A. (1998). Smoking and risk of dementia and Alzheimer's disease in a population-based cohort study: The Rotterdam Study. *The Lancet, 351,* 1840–1843.

Saunders, P.A., Copeland, J.R. and Dewey, M.E. (1991). Heavy drinking as a risk factor for depression and dementia in elderly men. Findings from the Liverpool longitudinal community study. *British Journal of Psychiatry, 159,* 213–216.

Smits, C.H., de Lange, J., Droes, R.M., Meiland, F., Vernooij-Dassen, M. and Pot, A.M. (2007). Effects of combined intervention programmes for people with dementia living at home and their caregivers: A systematic review. *International Journal of Geriatric Psychiatry, 22*(12), 1181–1193.

Spector, A., Orrell, M. and Woods, B. (2010). Cognitive Stimulation Therapy (CST): Effects on different areas of cognitive function for people with dementia. *International Journal of Geriatric Psychiatry, 25*(12), 1253–1258.

Spector, A., Orrell, M., Lattimer, M., Hoe, J., King, M., Harwood, K., Qazi, A. and Charlesworth, G. (2012). *Cognitive Behavioural Therapy (CBT) for Anxiety in People with Dementia: Study protocol for a randomised controlled trial.* Trials, 13.

Warden, V., Hurley, A.C. and Volicer, L. (2003). Development and psychometric evaluation of the Pain Assessment in Advanced Dementia (PAINAD) scale. *Journal of the American Medical Directors Association,4*(1), 9–15.

Woods, B., Spector, A.E., Jones, C.A., Orrell, M. and Davies, S.P. (2005). Reminiscence therapy for dementia. *Cochrane Database of Systematic Reviews* 2005, Issue 2. Art. No.: CD001120. DOI: 10.1002/14651858.CD001120.pub2.

15 Working in neuropsychology

*Angela Reason, Anna Healey
and Jan Rich*

JAN'S STORY

I am 70 and retired at 63 to help look after my mother. My working life started at a very early age when I worked at a local riding school. I loved every minute of it, getting the ponies in before I went to school. I have worked in retail and a charity, all in management positions. My hobbies are varied; I love gardening and have an allotment. I also do quite a lot of sewing.

During the last year I have found myself to be very forgetful, i.e. deciding what we were going to have for our evening meal, and completely forgotten by lunchtime; going into town shopping to get something specific, forgotten by the time I get there, particularly if the list has been left at home! The wake-up call to the problem really began when I found myself driving along a local road, not having a clue why I was there. Also my husband was getting cross and would say, 'you know we decided on dinner this morning'; yes, we had, but I had completely forgotten. I have always been a person that writes lists. I had to when I had a lot of staff to organise and needed rotas, so that we all knew what was happening. I also keep a FiloFax and a list of what is happening daily at home, but even these were getting muddled up.

Having decided something was wrong and I must do something about it, I first went to my doctor who was very helpful. She sent me for blood tests galore (I felt like Tony Hancock when I came out, no blood left). The results couldn't really find much wrong. She referred me to the Memory Assessment Service where I was sent for a scan and more tests.

SUMMARY

Neuropsychology makes a difference to people's lives at times of great vulnerability and change, by helping with understanding what is happening to them, and by helping people and their families adapt to a change in their situation which may be sudden (as with a stroke) or more gradual (as with a dementia). Neuropsychology draws upon the knowledge gained more generally from clinical psychology, coupled with neuroscience. This work takes place in a range of different settings, from the very medical (e.g. supporting neuro-surgery) to working with a patient in their home. The role may be either exclusively assessment focused (e.g. in a diagnostic service, which may assess whether a person has a dementia) or focused on working with the often devastating effects of having a neurological condition (such as a brain injury caused by an accident), offering psychological support around adjustment and cognitive rehabilitation. This chapter aims to describe this role in more detail, highlighting some of the settings and work that a neuropsychologist might do, with examples illustrating the curious way in which our lives can be affected by changes in our brains, and how neuropsychology can help when this happens.

INTRODUCTION

> '*Neuropsychology*': The branch of psychology that deals with the relationship between the nervous system, especially the brain, and cerebral or mental functions such as language, memory, and perception.
>
> (www.thefreedictionary.com)

Neuropsychology offers a fascinating insight into the amazing functions of the brain, and indeed the distressing effects on people when aspects cease to work efficiently. For example, the accountant who can no longer do a simple arithmetic task, the teacher who has forgotten how to write her name, the woman who draws only the right side of a house and says it's complete, the man who is shown a picture of a scarecrow but only sees the grass on which it stands, the previously law-abiding woman who now parks in the middle of roundabouts. All of these examples are real and represent significant changes from the person's previous abilities. They present new and frustrating challenges for the person and their loved ones and one of the jobs of a neuropsychologist can be to support people in understanding and adjusting to these issues. In many cases the cause of such difficulties may be obvious, for example, after a stroke or after a head injury, but at other times the neuropsychologist may play an important part in determining the diagnosis, alongside neuroimaging (brain scans) and other investigations, for example, in a dementia. Thus the neuropsychologist may need to offer support to an individual and their family at a very upsetting time. However, this can also be an enormously rewarding and humbling aspect of the job.

Background to the field

When we look back at the origins of this specialty, neuropsychology is, relatively speaking, one of the newer branches within psychology, although references pertaining to discovery in the field date back to ancient Egypt (Finger, 2000). For many centuries the brain was not seen as important and was often thrown away at autopsy when other organs were kept.

Learning about the brain has ranged from the less credible theories (e.g. the study of 'phrenology' (Franz Gall, 1758–1828) where lumps and bumps on the skull were

---

FOCUS 15.1

Metal rod that changed a man's personality

Phineas Gage was a young man injured in the mid-nineteenth century whilst working on a railroad in Vermont. He was packing explosive powder with a tamping iron when a spark from the iron ignited the powder and sent it straight through his skull and brain. He survived the injury but his family and colleagues reported subsequent dramatic changes in personality.

> His contractors, who regarded him as the most efficient and capable foreman in their employ previous to his injury, considered the change in his mind so marked that they could not give him his place again. He is fitful, irreverent, indulging at times in the grossest profanity.
>
> (Harlow, 1848)

This case was important in developing our understanding of the role of behaviour and personality associated with the frontal lobes.

---

thought to represent people's mental and moral faculties), to more robust findings such as Pierre Paul Broca's (1824–1880) theory of regions in the brain responsible for expressive speech which still stand strong today.

This latter discovery came about from the study of a man who could only say one word ('Tan'). The learning that has been gained through real-life examples is perhaps one of the most interesting areas and shows the powerful effect of damage to the brain on functioning.

AREAS OF NEUROPSYCHOLOLOGICAL PRACTICE

A neuropsychologist's role can be extremely varied and is certainly not confined to being stuck in a room mechanically 'testing' someone. Even if assessment is a large part of the role, every individual comes with a unique and fascinating narrative and profile of functioning which makes the role both diverse and appealing.

It provides opportunity to work across a range of settings and with a variety of patient groups. This may be in a specialist neurological service where the neuro-psychologist may assist the neurosurgeons in monitoring functions such as speech during a surgical procedure, or working alongside neurologists to clarify diagnosis or areas affected by a neurological condition. For example, Gill, a 45-year-old nurse, diagnosed with a type of brain tumour called an astrocytoma, was assessed by the neuropsychologist to see what aspects of her brain functioning were affected and to try to pinpoint more specifically in which areas of the brain the difficulties arose. A specialist neurological service may be in a hospital where patients are either inpatients or come in as outpatients, or it may be within the community, for example, a community neuro-rehabilitation team which endeavours to support people in reaching their own goals for recovery.

Another area for work may be within a mental health service. The neuro-psychologist may be asked to investigate whether a patient's difficulties are due to psychological factors or due to a neurological condition. Many neuro-degenerative conditions can present with mood/psychiatric factors early in the course of the condition and may thus be misdiagnosed. Conversely, some psychiatric/psychological conditions may initially be mistaken for neurological conditions (for example, non-epileptic seizures). There may also be lifestyle factors that affect the brain which need exploring and understanding. For example, Ben, a 19-year-old university student, had previously shown promise at school and been an A-grade student. Following a period of heavy illicit drug and alcohol use he was struggling with his course and had to drop out. He could not concentrate or remember aspects of his course work. The neuropsychologist offered an assessment to review whether there was significant cognitive impairment and to consider what strategies may support him to return to further education.

Neuropsychologists may also work privately, for example, providing expert opinions during legal processes, such as if there appears to be impairment following a road traffic accident, or on capacity issues, such as if a person has the mental capacity to make a decision about their finances.

Table 15.1 highlights some of the types of clinical conditions one might come across in different settings.

Thus you can see that the neuropsychologist needs a broad understanding of the effects many different conditions can have on the brain and on behaviour.

TABLE 15.1 Types of problems with which neuropsychologists work

Category	Examples of conditions (not an exhaustive list)
Acquired brain injury	Stroke, hypoxia, head injury
Progressive/degenerative	Dementia, Parkinson's disease, Huntington's disease, Multiple Sclerosis, Motor Neurone Disease
Medical	Seizures, cardiovascular, liver disease, respiratory disorders
Neuro-oncology	Brain tumours
Psychiatric	Psychosis, Bipolar disorder
Toxic	Alcohol-related brain damage, drug use, exposure to neurotoxins
Inflammatory	Encephalitis, Meningitis
Neuro-developmental	Learning disabilities, Autistic Spectrum disorders
Other	Medically unexplained symptoms

FOCUS 15.2

Clinical psychology and clinical neuropsychology

Clinical psychologists have a basic introduction to neuropsychology through their core training and may conduct cognitive assessments with a range of client groups, including those in neurological settings.

Clinical neuropsychologists have undergone further specialist training in clinical neuropsychology and thus have a more specialist role in this field.

NEUROPSYCHOLOGY IN ACTION

Neuropsychology involves both assessment and contributing to rehabilitation. This section outlines the various ways in which neuropsychological assessment may be used to make a difference by answering particular questions about a person's situation, including what may be causing their difficulties, and whether they have the capacity to make particular decisions. It then outlines the contribution that neuropsychologists can make to helping people adapt to their changed situation following a neurological event such as a brain injury.

Neuropsychology and assessment

The image of a neuropsychologist conducting assessment probably conjures up one of sitting in a bare room with a range of tests and a stopwatch. In many ways this image is correct, as the neuropsychologist needs to ensure the test results are not affected by other distractions, are based on standardised measures, and are a true reflection of the person's abilities. However, the work is far more engaging and intriguing than this image portrays.

Formal tests are only one aspect of a neuropsychological assessment as we also need to obtain a formal history of the presenting problems from the patient and ideally from other people who know the patient well. As with clinical psychology more generally, the patient's story is crucial to understanding the problem.

Once the patient/relative has been able to provide a narrative of the issues, assessment can take many forms. Most typically the neuropsychologist attempts to 'measure' aspects of brain functioning according to 'cognitive domains'. Effectively this is a little like visualising a world globe (the brain) and travelling around the different continents (the lobes) and countries (more specific brain areas), seeing what works well and what doesn't (the domains). Domains include the following:

- Orientation
- Attention and concentration
- Memory
- Language
- Visual perception and visual spatial skills
- Executive function
- Speed of processing
- Praxis.

However, formal testing may not always be possible. Sometimes neuropsychologists have to think on their feet and draw on different resources. For example, Graham, a 52-year-old engineer, was not able to complete the tests brought for their session due to difficulties in understanding visual information. The neuropsychologist resorted instead to rummaging in her bag and pulling out a variety of items, including a pen, a mobile phone, a hair clip and some coins. They then looked at whether Graham was able to identify and name the items and whether he could recognise the value of the individual coins. This allowed for informal assessment of the domains of visual perception and language in a format with which Graham could engage.

Equally, if a patient is not able to attend a clinic for assessment for any reason, the neuropsychologist may need to conduct an assessment in other settings. This can be challenging given that the reliability of testing is heavily dependent on the tests being given in a structured and specific way. However, a neuropsychologist may need to try to do the best possible in such a situation. This may mean administering a test on a busy hospital ward, or in a patient's home with the cat on their lap. One strange assessment situation involved a patient constructing a makeshift testing table in their studio out of an amp and a guitar box while seated on a drum-kit stool. It was surprisingly sturdy!

We will now consider more specific ways in which neuropsychological assessment is used.

Assessment for diagnosis: what's wrong?

In a diagnostic setting the work often feels like being a detective. The patient is referred to the service with some unexplained symptoms and the team get to work in trying to solve the riddle, using a variety of tests and investigations of which neuropsychology is one part. Many conditions may be determined easily (e.g. presence of a brain tumour visible on a scan), although assessment is still useful in finding out its effects on cognition; but with rarer conditions the diagnostic process can be a real puzzle and some conditions such as dementia still cannot be definitively confirmed until autopsy (which is a little late!).

As we saw with Jan, blood tests didn't reveal any problems and she was referred to the Memory Service with the cause of her problems unknown. She had a brain scan which was also inconclusive and so the neuropsychological assessment was an essential component in trying to establish what was happening to her. Part of the work was also in preparing her for what might be found (often referred to as *pre-diagnostic counselling*).

In some cases testing will reveal problems immediately and the clinical picture will be clear. However, in other cases the assessment may be diagnostically inconclusive but it will be useful in profiling someone's strengths and weaknesses at that time point (a 'baseline') and allow for measurement of change over time (e.g. the assessment may be repeated some months later to see whether decline or recovery has occurred).

Diagnostic work may be conducted in both inpatient or community settings, for example, in an acute hospital, in a specialist neurological centre, or within community services such as memory assessment teams, dementia services or mental health teams.

Examples of typical referral questions are as follows:

- 'This lady appears to have some progressive cognitive impairment. Please could you assess whether this lady may have an early stage dementia?'
- 'Please assess this lady to help clarify whether her dementia is of Alzheimer's type or a vascular dementia.'

Assessment for profiling function: what works well and what areas are damaged?

Neuropsychologists may still need to conduct assessments even when the diagnosis is clear. The aim of this is to gain a clearer picture or profile of the damage to the brain affecting an individual's behaviour and thinking. As we saw in the example of Gill, the woman with an astrocytoma tumour, assessment may aim to clarify in which areas of the brain the impairments are found.

Assessment is also very helpful in providing personalised information on an individual's abilities (strengths and difficulties) specifically to inform care plans or rehabilitation programmes. For example, with the accountant who wishes to return to work but is now unable to calculate simple arithmetic tasks, the assessment may reveal that he can still perform the task under certain conditions. For example, he may be able to do the work successfully when calculations are broken down into step-by-step stages and when he has a pen and paper to write things down, as opposed to trying to do them in his head. Knowledge of these details may be the difference between him returning to work or not.

An example of a typical referral question is as follows:

- 'Please could you undertake a cognitive assessment of this 26-year-old man who has sustained a head injury but also has had epilepsy since he was young, to help understand what cognitive difficulties have been caused by his more recent head injury?'

Assessment for capacity: is the person able to make an informed decision?

When people have cognitive difficulties, questions about their 'capacity' are often asked. In these situations, assessment attempts to discover whether an individual is capable of making an informed decision on a specific matter and whether they fully understand the related implications. The Mental Capacity Act (2005) is aimed at supporting the rights of people who lack the capacity to make decisions for themselves. Assessment for capacity is in relation to a specific query, for example, whether someone has the capacity to make particular financial decisions or to decide where they want to live. Assessment may include a comprehensive interview with the patient and possibly the use of formal tests.

Neuropsychologists, among other health professionals, may be asked to comment on capacity issues. The neuropsychologist may offer advice about how to support a patient's capacity to make a decision, such as provision of written information for someone with memory difficulties.

Examples of typical referral questions are as follows:

- 'Please assess to see if this lady has the capacity to make a decision about remaining in her own home.'
- 'Does this gentleman have the capacity to make an informed choice about refusing his treatment?'

Assessment for formulation: what factors might explain these difficulties?

Psychological and neurological factors may overlap, and unpicking which is which can be tricky. In reality, people don't fit neatly into the theoretical boxes we often read about. Developing a formulation involves wearing your clinical psychology and your neuropsychology 'hat' and a touch of intuition. The art of collating all the information about a patient into a coherent understanding of their presenting difficulty is key. This may involve reviewing a range of factors, for example:

- Your observations of the person.
- The person's past and current situation and feelings.
- The person's family context and other psychosocial factors.
- Knowledge of neurological disorders and how they present.
- Knowledge of psychiatric/psychological disorders or factors and how they present.
- Neuropsychological test results.
- Other clinical information (e.g. brain scan results, medical history).

On consideration of these variables, one needs to then consider how they may interact for a specific patient. Figure 15.1 attempts to illustrate these components. For example, a patient who has been diagnosed with multiple sclerosis (MS) (*biology*) may be experiencing anxiety about future deterioration (*psychology*) and now relates to her family differently for fear of worrying them about her problems (*social*). She may be worrying about her memory, and so it is necessary to understand how worry and the MS can influence the efficiency of memory (*mechanism*), understand how it manifests (*symptoms*), and also what goals she wants to achieve, for example, wanting to stay in work for as long as possible (*everyday functioning*) which is currently not possible due to her problems with forgetting to do things (*limitation*). A neuropsychologist's job is to help the patient understand this process, how each of these factors interacts and how they can then use this information to make changes to their situation. For example, introducing electronic memory aids on a smart phone may help reduce worry about memory and enable the patient to carry on working.

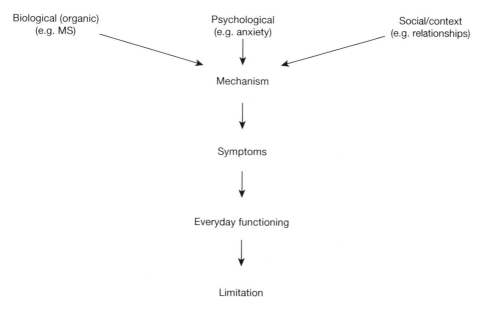

FIGURE 15.1 Example diagram of overall formulation

Thus, a neuropsychologist's role is like any clinical psychologist's; that is, to be flexible and thoughtful, always considering the patients within the context of their everyday life and as a person; not just the brain damage.

Examples of typical referral questions are as follows:

- 'Please assess this 46–year–old lady who experienced a traumatic brain injury last year. She has subsequently separated from her partner and finds it difficult to maintain a job.'
- 'Please could you assess this 61–year–old gentleman who has recently lost his job? He found the process of redundancy stressful and found it difficult to process orders for the company and complained of memory problems.'

In summary, the role of assessment in neuropsychology is wide and varied. Table 15.2 summarises the main purposes of assessment.

Neuropsychology and rehabilitation

We have so far described the varied role of assessment in neuropsychology, but another key area in which neuropsychologists work is rehabilitation. This work occurs largely, but not exclusively, with people who have suffered an acquired brain injury (ABI). ABI refers to injury to the brain which has occurred after birth and is not accounted for by neurodegenerative changes in the brain. Conditions may include traumatic brain injury (e.g. resulting from a road traffic accident), stroke, anoxic injury (e.g. brain starved of oxygen following near-drowning), and injury from infections affecting the brain (e.g. from meningitis or encephalitis). There is also a growing interest in the use of neuropsychological rehabilitation approaches with people with other types of neurological conditions such as dementia (Clare, 2008).

Rehabilitation for patients is described as 'a process aimed at enabling them to reach and maintain their optimal, physical, sensory, intellectual, psychological and social functional levels' (World Health Organisation, www.who.int).

A neuropsychologist supporting a person with an acquired brain injury in rehabilitation may take on a variety of roles across numerous settings, including hospital, stroke or head injury units, in community rehabilitation teams, in regional neuroscience centres or in specialist services such as neuro-rehabilitation centres, vocational services or services for children with acquired brain injury and services for people in minimally conscious/vegetative states.

Once again the neuropsychologist is usually part of a wider rehabilitation team, all of whom play their part in the rehabilitation process. For example, John, 62, suffered with language problems and weakness down one side of his body following a stroke. The physiotherapist focused on helping him with his mobility, the speech and language therapist assessed the degree and nature of his language difficulties and practised techniques with him to help him speak again, the occupational therapist helped him with aspects of daily living, for example, how to make an evening meal, and the neuropsychologist assessed him and found problems with memory function, and considered memory strategies that might be helpful to him.

The emphasis in neuropsychological rehabilitation over the years has developed from an impairment-led focus to a more holistic approach which focuses on everyday skills

TABLE 15.2 Summary of main purposes of assessment in neuropsychology

Purpose of assessment	Clinical example
To determine a baseline. This means establishing a person's level of functioning in order to then compare results at a later time point.	To determine if someone with Down's syndrome may be developing a dementia.
To determine whether a person has cognitive difficulties and if so, to what degree/severity.	Assessing someone following a head injury.
To determine change in ability, i.e. if cognitive decline is present.	Assessing someone with a diagnosis of mild cognitive impairment to see whether they have progressed to a diagnosis of dementia.
To contribute to a diagnosis.	Testing someone and offering a view on the cognitive profile to assist diagnosis (e.g. does the person have dementia with Lewy Bodies or dementia of Alzheimer's type?).
Establishing the impact or effects of a specific treatment such as neurosurgery or radiotherapy.	Testing someone's language function during epilepsy surgery.
To explore if a person's cognitive difficulties are organic (in the brain) or psychological in origin.	Assessing to see whether someone's memory problems may be related to depression.
To determine effort levels in a patient.	Exploring whether someone's test performance may be influenced by conscious or unconscious lack of effort.
To influence a patient's care plan, cognitive intervention or rehabilitation programme.	Testing to determine how to help a patient adapt to difficulties through individual cognitive rehabilitation.
To validate a patient's experience.	Testing a patient who is experiencing subjective change to their memory even if other investigations are normal.
To assess for capacity-related issues.	To determine whether a patient with Huntington's disease is able to manage their own finances.

and roles relevant to the individual (Wilson, 2001). The use of goal setting is common and allows intervention to be focused on what is important to the patient. For example, Julie, 32, was a successful advertising consultant and mother of two, who developed viral encephalitis. She made a fairly good recovery initially but was left with some memory problems. Her family assumed her 'goal' for rehabilitation was to return to the job she loved, but for Julie, her focus was to be able to develop reminders and memory aids to enable her to take her daughters to and from school successfully.

In rehabilitation work, a neuropsychologist may advise on compensatory strategies, engaging the person and family in understanding their difficulties following injury. For example, a patient with memory difficulties may benefit from a rehabilitation programme focusing on learning to use systems to support their memory (e.g. smart phones, calendars, diaries, etc.). In addition, the neuropsychologist may have more of a therapeutically focused role, helping the person and their family to adjust to the injury/illness, which in ABI, usually by its nature, happens suddenly. This is likely to include adapting therapeutic interventions such as cognitive-behavioural therapy (CBT) and systemic therapies to minimise the impact of cognitive difficulties, for example, by providing written summaries, having short sessions if fatigue or concentration is an issue, and working with family.

Other interventions may include working on reducing the impact of changes in behaviour which are common following brain injury and which can impact upon an individual's social participation and challenge others (Wilson *et al.*, 2003). A *functional analysis* of behaviour which helps understand the triggers or consequences of behaviour can help formulate an understanding of the behaviour and guide intervention.

Examples of typical referral questions are as follows:

- 'Please could you see this 70–year-old man who, since he has experienced a head injury following a road traffic accident, is fearful of going out?'
- 'Please could you assess this 65–year-old lady who has had a stroke as she is having trouble finding her way around the rehabilitation unit?'

CASE STUDY

Background

Jason, a 40-year-old married man and father of two young children, worked full time as a web designer and was the main earner in his family. His wife worked as a part-time nursery assistant. They lived in a mortgaged property. In his spare time Jason loved family life, especially taking his son to football at weekends. He enjoyed running, having recently achieved a half-marathon, and having the odd game of pool at his local pub on a Friday night. He was also a keen motorcyclist and often relied on this means of transport to get him to work.

The accident

One wet Wednesday morning Jason was travelling to work on his motorbike when he was hit by a car and thrown off his bike. He was knocked unconscious at the scene. He was rushed to hospital and once stabilised was given a brain scan which showed he had sustained a head injury, which had mainly affected the front part of his brain (his frontal lobes). He had also broken his right leg. He remained in hospital for the next three months.

After hospital

Once discharged, Jason was transferred to the Community Neuro-rehabilitation Team who carried out an assessment of his rehabilitation needs.

Medically, Jason had made a good recovery but there appeared to be some cognitive difficulties evident and his family reported some changes in his personality, saying he appeared more irritable, unreliable and unmotivated. His wife described him as 'uncaring and disinterested' in her and the children and said, 'he has become lazy – I need to prompt him to do something or he just sits there'. This meant she had to pick up more duties at home. His children struggled to understand the changes and were concerned about whether they had caused the problem: 'I was naughty yesterday and daddy got really cross with me. He never used to so I must have been really naughty.'

Following discussion with Jason and his family the neuropsychologist met with him to conduct a neuropsychological assessment. Jason completed a series of tests and the assessment was able to shed light on areas of brain functioning that remained intact and functions that were now impaired compared to how he was previously. In particular it showed that he struggled with thinking skills such as planning, organisation, initiation and attention which are all functions typically implicated with the frontal lobes, as well as having some memory problems. An assessment of mood indicated he was moderately depressed.

Formulation

The assessment results concurred with the brain scan findings and helped the team formulate how Jason's accident had contributed to the changes reported. It was clear from his wife's description of Jason prior to the accident that he was hard-working and enjoyed social interaction, so his current malaise and lack of motivation was unlikely to be due to factors explained by his previous (often referred to as 'pre-morbid') personality. It is also known that the problems the family described were typical features following injury to the frontal lobes. Thus – if we refer back to our model in Figure 15.1 – this was a likely biological explanation. However, Jason was also showing signs of depression. He had discussed with the neuropsychologist how he was aware he 'felt different' now and got 'more grumpy with the kids'. He was also missing work (he had not been able to return to work as yet) and felt 'useless'. This was having a notable effect on his mood. Thus it was possible that some of his apparent apathy and lack of motivation was due to psychological factors (see Figure 15.1). Furthermore, the changes to the family's situation were also having a more systemic effect, for example, on their finances and on his relationships which was further impacting upon his mood.

Intervention

The formulation enabled the neuropsychologist, along with the team, to consider a care plan for Jason and his family. First, she felt that some psycho-education would be helpful in supporting Jason and his family in their understanding of the difficulties to help shift the explanation away from 'laziness' to understand the changes as a consequence of his brain injury. She believed this psycho-education might also help so that the children could stop blaming themselves unnecessarily for any difficulties.

Jason, the neuropsychologist and the team's occupational therapist then worked together on implementing some strategies to help increase his independence. Jason's personal goal was to get back to taking his son to football at the weekend (hampered by problems of getting started with things – known as *initiation*). Jason was previously keen on technology and used a smart phone, so assistive technology aids were recommended. Jason set up reminder alerts which activated at 9 a.m. on Saturday mornings, and comprised a checklist of tasks he had to do in order to take his son out (e.g. 'book taxi', 'pack season ticket', etc.). Over a few weeks this increase in independence had a notable effect on his mood and improved his relationship with his son.

In addition, the family were able to attend some family support sessions to help them reflect on the changes, such as his wife having to return to full-time work to be able to support them financially. His children drew pictures to help them express their views of changes to their dad.

Jason was also invited to a men's group which focused on adjustment to brain injury. Jason was able to talk in this group about his frustrations at not working but also about changes in his family relationships. Other members in the group said they related to the problems he raised. They also helped him think about practical solutions to some of his goals, based on their own experience of overcoming problems associated with brain injury. For example, one man told Jason to 'count to ten when you see the red mist [anger]' which helped Jason control his irritability towards his children. This may appear a simple technique but, coming from another member in the group who had experienced something similar, it held a lot of power.

Outcome

Jason remained with the neuro-rehabilitation team for a few weeks. Over this period he developed a greater understanding of his difficulties, helping him to reframe some of the unhelpful ideas he had developed about himself. Although many of his cognitive difficulties remained, he was able to find alternative ways around some of these difficulties and this meant he did not have to feel so reliant on his wife, which in turn gave him a greater sense of well-being. He remarked that he realised he had actually been quite depressed, which had resulted in some of the irritability and lack of motivation. The men's group had been a great source of support to him and given him a sense of shared experience.

His family also felt more tolerant of the changes once they understood them as being a result of his injuries and began to adapt to a new and different way of family life.

Jason was discharged from the neuro-rehabilitation team after some follow-up visits. His longer term goal was to return to his job.

TEAM WORKING/INDIRECT WORK

The neuropsychologist rarely works alone and is usually part of a wider clinical team, even if indirectly. The brain is complex; we still have a lot to learn, so pulling together and offering assessment and intervention from a holistic multi-professional approach is crucial. The effects of brain injury or neurological illness are far-reaching. The work can be both humbling and emotional, but maintaining an appropriate sense of humour is also important for all. Teams must work together not only to support the person and their loved ones, but also each other.

CRITICAL ISSUES

With a developing field such as neuroscience, 'hot' issues change and evolve all the time. One issue to date for neuropsychology has been between the use of a 'fixed battery' approach to assessment (common in North America), which involves administering a large and set number of tasks covering a wide breadth of cognitive domains (time-consuming but thorough), versus that of the 'flexible battery' or 'hypothesis-led' approach (common in the UK) which aims to test only specific areas according to the hypothesis or referral question (time-efficient but may miss something). There are ongoing debates about which is the preferred approach, with arguments on both sides.

Another area is the utility of tests across different cultural groups. This includes considering what 'normative' sample test data is based on and how transferable tests are across cultures and when English is not a person's first language.

Finally, one area that is likely to be pertinent for the next generation of neuropsychologists is the improvements made to neuroimaging in the future and what this will mean for the future of the specialty – will neuropsychological testing become redundant at some point and the focus move entirely to rehabilitation?

CONCLUSIONS

In conclusion, neuropsychology is a branch of clinical psychology that focuses more specifically on the way the brain works, and how it affects cognition, emotion and behaviour. It is diverse, fascinating, and at times challenging, both practically and emotionally. However, it is also immensely rewarding. It allows you to help people and their families at a really vulnerable time in their life which is an enormous privilege.

CONCLUSION TO JAN'S STORY

Eventually I was sent to see a psychologist and met a very helpful lady; she was friendly, but explained everything in great detail as we went along. If she wasn't sure I had understood she would go through it all again before starting the test. I felt very much at ease with her, which helped a great deal, as I had found it a very big step to admit anything was wrong.

I found the whole experience very rewarding, some of the tests more difficult than others, but that just proves to me that I was right to be concerned.

I do try to put as many of the things the tests taught me into my everyday work as possible. I think the whole procedure was an excellent wake-up call, and I would recommend it to anyone with the same or similar problems.

KEY CONCEPTS AND TERMS

- Neuropsychology
- Psychometrics
- Cognitive
- Domains
- Acquired brain injury
- Rehabilitation
- Capacity
- Pre-morbid

LEARNING OUTCOMES

When you have completed this chapter you will have gained:

1 Foundation knowledge of the field of neuropsychology.
2 An awareness of the different types of work and different settings in which a neuropsychologist might work.
3 A flavour of some of the conditions with which neuropsychologists work.
4 An introduction to what a neuropsychological assessment and intervention may involve.

SAMPLE ESSAY TITLES

- How can neuropsychological testing help patients?
- Describe three areas in which a neuropsychologist might work, describing briefly what they might be asked to do.
- Discuss the areas a typical neuropsychological assessment would cover and how it may guide rehabilitation.

REFERENCES

Clare, L. (2008). *Neuropsychological Rehabilitation and People with Dementia.* Hove and New York: Psychology Press.

Finger, S. (2000). *Minds Behind the Brain: A history of the pioneers and their discoveries.* New York: Oxford University Press.

Harlow, J.M. (1848). Passage of an iron rod through the head. *Boston Medical and Surgical Journal, 39*, 389–393.

The Free Dictionary. Available online at www.thefreedictionary.com.

The Mental Capacity Act. Available online at www.direct.gov.uk.

Wilson, B.A. (2001). Towards a comprehensive model of cognitive rehabilitation. *Neuropsychological Rehabilitation, 12*(2), 97–110.

Wilson, B.A., Herbert, C.M. and Shiel, A. (2003). *Behavioural Approaches in Neuropsychological Rehabilitation: Optimising rehabilitation procedures*. Hove and New York: Psychology Press.

World Health Organisation. Available online at www.who.int.

5 | Current professional issues in clinical psychology

16 Clinical psychology: past, present, future

Adrian Whittington and Nick Lake

SUMMARY

Clinical psychology is a relatively new profession, but it has become a popular career choice with fierce competition for postgraduate training places. Interest in the profession has grown quickly and there are a number of high-profile clinical psychologists both in the media and portrayed as characters in television and film. The status of the profession is strong and public awareness high.

Despite this, the profession of clinical psychology had humble beginnings. This chapter will provide a brief history of the development of clinical psychology within the UK, highlighting how clinical psychologists have moved from a role based largely on psychometric testing and research in the 1950s, to their role as behavioural practitioners in the 1960s and 1970s, to the 1980s where practitioners began to integrate a wide variety of psychological perspectives and clinical models in practice and apply their knowledge as trainers, consultants and leaders, as well as therapists. We will aim to bring this history to life by describing a typical working day of a clinical psychologist during each of these periods. We will look at the role of the clinical psychologist in the current NHS, highlighting some of the challenges and new opportunities that the profession faces. We will also project ourselves forward over the next ten years to look at how we think the profession will need to adapt and develop to meet the new demands of health care as the twenty-first century unfolds.

INTRODUCTION

The profession of clinical psychology has grown rapidly in the UK. From its origin in research labs, and as psychological technicians, you will now find clinical psychologists occupying senior leadership positions in health care, as well as having an increasing influence in other sectors such as recruitment, consultancy and leadership development. As a profession grounded in the clinical application of the science of psychology, clinical psychology has the potential also to expand into many other fields in health and social care, including a greater role in physical health care and public health agendas such as enhancing well-being in the general population (making people and society happier and healthier).

In the early twenty-first century, the expansion of psychological therapy services in the NHS, often now provided by other professionals who cost less to train and pay, has placed clinical psychology at a new crossroads. For some this is perceived as a threat to the role of clinical psychologists in the NHS. We regard it as an opportunity. The ability to apply psychological knowledge, and the breadth and depth of the clinical psychologist's training, will always be important when dealing with the more complex cases and more challenging contexts faced in clinical practice. However, clinical psychology also occupies a unique role in offering an applied science of the human psyche, which is different to both psychiatric medicine and to a model or a series of models of therapy. This is not only important in further developing our understanding of how to work best with individuals through integrating separate fields of theoretical and research development (e.g. attachment research with research on cognition), but it should also enable us to develop a greater understanding of how to work with psychological distress across communities, services and teams. We believe that providing psychological interventions that impact upon more than just the individual will be increasingly important in health care, as the focus turns to developing more psychologically healthy teams, communities and societies, not just more psychologically healthy individuals.

As you will see, clinical psychology and clinical psychology training has adapted rapidly over the past 60 years, flexing to the changing demands being faced and to the new understandings and knowledge that the science of psychology has brought us. However, we cannot stop adapting. We will argue that clinical psychology training needs to adapt further, offering depth in specific fields of practice to complement the breadth of theory, practice and research skills development which it currently offers. We also need to strengthen further the training in leadership, ensuring that clinical psychologists can act as architects of more psychologically informed mental and physical health care, as well as more psychologically healthy communities as a whole.

A BRIEF HISTORY OF CLINICAL PSYCHOLOGY IN THE UK

Psychometrics and research

Psychology as an academic field appeared around the turn of the twentieth century, bringing together medics, philosophers and other academics. The Psychological Society was founded in London in 1901, defining psychology as a distinct and scientific discipline. Interest in the application of psychological science grew, particularly in relation to stress and industrial production, the impact of combat in the First World War, and in applications to education.

The birth of the profession of clinical psychology may be associated largely with the launch of the new National Health Service in 1948. Psychology graduates found a place in the new service, typically assisting psychiatrists with diagnoses through psychometric testing. This position was upheld by one of the most influential psychologists in the field at the time, Hans Eysenck, who wrote: 'the psychiatrist is responsible for carrying out therapy. The psychologist for diagnostic help and research design, and the social worker for investigating social conditions in as far as they affect the case' (Eysenck, 1949, p.174). This was a very different emphasis from that appearing in the United States, where clinical psychologists were embracing psychotherapy (at this time in the form of psychoanalysis) as a core component of their role.

Eysenck positioned psychologists in the UK as scientist-practitioners who should not be concerned with psychotherapy and should not let social need drive their activities, but rather focus on advancing psychological knowledge through research. Based largely on this approach, the first UK training course in clinical psychology was established in 1957 at the Maudsley Hospital, London. This course was highly influential, training many early leaders in the field.

Behaviourism and psychotherapy

From the 1950s, significant steps were taken towards the use of behavioural methodologies (see Chapter 2) based on the work of B.F. Skinner, Stanley Rachman and others. These methods were applied to address psychiatric difficulties including anxiety and phobias and to shape behaviour in institutional environments, including the widespread long-stay mental hospitals of the time (Baum, 2005). These methodologies were incorporated by clinical psychologists hungry to expand their roles and took root as part of the curriculum in the growing number of clinical psychology training courses across the UK. Clinical psychologists took up positions in a wider variety of services, including leading roles in services for people with intellectual disabilities.

In 1976, Aaron Beck published *Cognitive Therapy and the Emotional Disorders* (Beck, 1976), launching what was to become a very influential approach to psychotherapy. Beck was a psychiatrist and psychoanalyst who had begun to question some accepted psychoanalytic principles after exposing them to testing. Cognitive therapy, in contrast to psychoanalysis, was located firmly within a scientific paradigm, which made it attractive for UK clinical psychologists to adopt. It built upon their existing behavioural traditions.

THE DAY OF A CLINICAL PSYCHOLOGIST IN 1960

James spends the morning doing assessments for Dr Willett on Ward 4 of a large psychiatric hospital. He produces a brief assessment report on two of the patients to show the current severity of schizophrenia, having administered psychometric measures. Hopefully this will influence their care. James isn't convinced that one of the patients has any active symptoms of schizophrenia, but may simply be showing behaviours that are the effects of being in hospital for several years. In the afternoon, James continues his research into the effects of the token reward system that has been introduced on Ward 2. The nurses have been using tokens to reward patients for attending to their personal hygiene. Tokens buy cigarettes and sweets at the end of the week. James has been collating records of the changes in behaviour over the past three months to see whether there has been an increase in frequency of bathing and teeth cleaning.

As training numbers grew over this period, clinical psychologists diversified, also taking on a role in applying other psychotherapies in NHS contexts, including family therapy and psychodynamic therapy.

Redefinition and team working

In 1979 a Conservative government under Margaret Thatcher set out to exert greater control over costs of the NHS, introducing a stronger role for health service management. Reviews of the NHS workforce were undertaken to seek greater efficiencies. Community care was replacing long-stay institutions as the primary means of delivering mental health care at this time. Community multi-disciplinary teams were established which brought together different professional groups in the task of providing community services. In this atmosphere of change and threat, the profession of clinical psychology, represented by the British Psychological Society Division of Clinical Psychology, sought an independent review of the role of the clinical psychologist. The result was the 1989 Manpower Advisory Service (MAS) report (Management Advisory Service, 1989). While never fully adopted, the recommendations of this report have proved highly relevant. The MAS report identified three levels of psychological skills:

Level 1: Communication skills and basic counselling.
Level 2: Defined psychological intervention skills (e.g. anxiety management groups, behaviour modification).
Level 3: Skills in the use of multiple psychological theories to develop individually tailored and adapted interventions to address difficulties at individual and organisational levels.

Of these, the report suggested that all mental health professionals should have level 1 skills, that many would have level 2 skills, but that clinical psychologists were unique in their level 3 skills. The report recommended an expansion of clinical psychology training to deploy more of these skills into the NHS.

THE DAY OF A CLINICAL PSYCHOLOGIST IN 1980

Julie starts her day by doing two detailed assessments, helping to prepare for the closure of the mental handicap hospital. The psychiatrist would be making a decision about the next group to move out into a community group home, and has asked for Julie's opinion, so they are going to meet to discuss this. She is not looking forward to it – they have quite different views and the psychiatrist thinks the most severely disabled will never be able to manage in the community. Julie spends the afternoon on Dolphin ward, where the nurses have asked for help with stopping a young client slapping himself. Julie plans to complete a functional analysis of the behaviour and produce a new care plan. At the end of the day she finds a few minutes to read about a relatively new therapy approach: cognitive therapy. She is very interested in learning more and in exploring whether this might be adaptable to her work context.

Expansion and improving access

Although the MAS report was not directly acted upon by the government, the growing profession of clinical psychology continued to prove its worth in teams. Greater evidence of the effectiveness of psychological therapies started to emerge in the 1980s and the public expressed a demand for talking therapies to be provided on the NHS. Expanded numbers of posts continued to be developed but through the 1990s it was typical for a proportion of these posts to remain vacant for long periods owing to a shortage of trained clinical psychologists to fill them. It was hard for training programmes to keep pace with the need for expansion owing to the limited capacity of supervisors for the desired numbers of trainees. The incoming Labour government in 1997 heralded a period of significantly increased health service spending and this resulted in the continued expansion of clinical psychology training to meet workforce demand. Total numbers of clinical psychologists grew from 2,500 in 1992 to 6,900 in 2010 (Pilgrim and Treacher, 1992; Centre for Workforce Intelligence, 2012).

The early twenty-first century saw the unprecedented expansion of psychological therapies under the Improving Access to Psychological Therapies (IAPT) initiative. Richard Layard, a health economist, successfully argued that if services were expanded to treat depression and anxiety disorders with CBT, this investment would pay for itself through savings to the exchequer because a portion of those successfully treated would return to work and stop claiming welfare benefits (Centre for Economic Performance, 2006). On the back of this argument, £170 million was invested over three years in training and employing new therapists, representing a doubling of

---

THE DAY OF A CLINICAL PSYCHOLOGIST IN 2000

Sally arrives at work at her Community Mental Health Team where she is the only psychologist in the team. She attends the multi-disciplinary team (MDT) referrals meeting. She has a year-long waiting list and colleagues at the meeting tell her they are frustrated about this because they want their patients to have better access to therapy. In the team formulation meeting (which involved all staff, including the psychiatrist) that follows the MDT meeting, Sally facilitates an exploration of what was going on for one of the clients who was causing the team the most difficulty. Sally draws upon systemic, psychodynamic and cognitive knowledge and theory in helping the team develop a bio-psychosocial formulation of what was going on for that client. This helped the team adjust their treatment plan and agree how they might better manage the client's self-harming behaviour. In the afternoon, Sally visits one client at home, and then goes over to the central Psychology Department where she sees another two clients for individual sessions in her consulting room. Sally catches up briefly with her trainee clinical psychologist who had a potentially difficult session to manage today (they had discussed the details in supervision the day before). The session went well. Sally is also pleased to hear that they are continuing to expand the local training course to train more psychologists for the NHS.

investment in psychological services. Some of these new therapists have been clinical psychologists, but the majority have been drawn from other professional backgrounds, including mental health nursing and counselling. Cognitive-behavioural Therapy has been the core of this expansion, but other psychological therapies that appear in NICE guidance have been incorporated in the later stages. The IAPT services have operated a 'stepped-care' model, with additional staff trained specifically to deliver 'low-intensity' guided self-help interventions based on CBT principles. While psychologists have played a key role in leading the new psychological therapy services, these services have represented a move away from clinical psychology as the most numerous professional supplier of psychological health care to the NHS.

THE PRESENT: CLINICAL PSYCHOLOGY AT A CROSSROADS (AGAIN)

The psychological therapies revolution

The expansion in resources attached to talking therapies in the period since 2007, under strong central control from the Department of Health in the early stages, has had a dramatic impact on the landscape of psychological care:

- It has raised public awareness and coincided with increased public desire for CBT and other talking therapies.
- It has introduced a greatly expanded workforce of psychological therapists who are not clinical psychologists.
- It has led to increased attention and routine collection of data on the outcomes of therapy.
- It has led to an increased focus on the delivery of specified individual treatments that appear in NICE guidance for specific diagnoses.

Proponents of the IAPT programme highlight that over a million additional people received psychological therapy in the first three years of the new services, addressing the previous scandal of a lack of access to talking therapy that had shown benefit in research trials. Others have critiqued the focus of the new services on individual, diagnostically driven interventions, when much human distress is known to be associated with social and economic factors. For clinical psychology, the new services highlight that effective therapies, particularly in primary care service settings, can be provided by staff who are cheaper to employ than most clinical psychologists.

Cost pressures

Cost pressures in the period since 2010 have added to concerns and in some areas there have for the first time been programmes of redundancies and reorganisation, resulting in reduced pay for some clinical psychologists. Overall, workforce data show little change over this period in the numbers of clinical psychologists, but the expansion has certainly come to an end for now. The cost pressures of this period are reminiscent of the1980s and the MAS report findings may have renewed relevance.

Partnerships of care

Since 2010 health policy has focused on increased localism – with local clinical commissioning groups, led by general practitioners, responsible for the majority of the NHS budget and a reduced role for strategic regional and national bodies within the NHS. At the same time, the service-user movement has taken on new momentum, with the users of services finding a voice in the design and delivery of health care. The result is an environment that favours locally focused delivery of psychological care involving both smaller and larger organisations, including charities, service-user groups, NHS Trusts and private companies. Larger statutory organisations are increasingly partnering with smaller third sector organisations, offering benefits to both parties.

Demographic changes

The population in the UK is ageing, with the projected numbers of people over 85 years in England due to rise from 1.1 million in 2009 to 2.6 million in 2032. This change will see a rising need for health services, in particular for long-term physical health conditions (e.g. diabetes, stroke or heart disease) and dementia. About 50 per cent of all GP consultations and 70 per cent of hospital bed use are for long-term conditions and the probability of mental health problems rises with the number of long-term conditions that a person suffers from. Numbers of people with dementia are due to double, from 700,000 in the UK in 2009, to 1.4 million in 2039. These changes are likely to require a fundamental shift in how health and social care is provided, with a need for more home-based care, a greater reliance on unpaid and family carers, and the use of new technologies to enable access to support. (Ham *et al.*, 2012).

FUTURE DIRECTIONS: AN INTEGRATED APPLIED SCIENCE OF PSYCHOLOGY

As we move into an environment shaped by an expansion of psychological therapies, cost pressures, new organisational arrangements and demographic changes, clinical psychology faces both challenges and opportunities. Clinical psychologists will need to demonstrate explicitly their value beyond providing a single model of therapy and have the opportunity to be architects of psychological care across physical as well as mental health services. We illustrate this section with brief case studies of clinical psychologists taking hold of this opportunity and reflect upon the implications for clinical psychology training.

Moving beyond a model of therapy

Providing therapies is likely to continue to be an important part of the role for clinical psychologists. In practice, clinical psychologists are trusted as team members competent to achieve good therapy results with the most complex cases, often integrating methods and ideas from more than one model of therapy. However, they currently face two challenges as providers of therapy. First, they risk being seen as expensive therapists who are not guaranteed to have recognised levels of competence in 'approved' single modality therapies as defined by the national bodies offering accreditation in these therapies. This can be addressed by individual practitioners and training programmes working to ensure that defined standards of competence are met in specific therapies that they offer. Second, while many hold that the integration of different therapy models is a core feature of being a clinical psychologist and provides added benefit in therapy (Hollanders and McLeod, 1999), research efforts have not been focused sufficiently in this area to fully evaluate this claim. This sort of research into the flexible application of therapy models with people with multiple and complex difficulties is bound to be challenging, but requires further investment.

Clinical psychology can also offer much more in addition to providing psychological therapy. Psychology is a broad field of knowledge, and the application of psychology in clinical practice offers myriad ways in which this changing field of knowledge may be brought to bear on human distress (Gilbert, 2009). The application of broader psychological science continues to be needed across numerous areas in the current health and social care system. These applications include acting to:

- Understand and support communities.
- Help grow healthy organisations (including through leadership).
- Enable teams and networks to pursue psychological well-being.
- Recognise and work with the crucial role of families and attachment in creating emotionally healthy individuals and emotionally healthy communities.
- Work therapeutically with individuals, groups and families whose emotional difficulties do not fall easily into current diagnostic categories.
- Work with people with complex mental health difficulties who haven't responded to psychological therapy.
- Develop service initiatives to support the growing proportion of the population affected by long-term physical and neurological conditions, and their carers.
- Design supervision and reflective practice systems to allow services to remain compassionate when they are themselves under threat.
- Produce research and training to help others advance knowledge of, and capacity to intervene in, all of the above.

To be true to the broader field of psychology, the profession now needs to reassert its broader role. This is not to set itself up in opposition to the defined psychological therapies. Many psychologists have been working for years to increase access to these therapies. Yet, in addition to acting as therapists, clinical psychologists should be leading on initiatives to address human distress from many different angles.

Integrating the biological, the psychological and the social

Divisions continue in the provision of mental health care, with biological, psychological and social models upheld by different individuals within teams. Because of their broad training, clinical psychologists are well placed to break down these barriers and to promote an explicitly biopsychosocial model of mental health care.

There is also increasing awareness of the role of psychological factors in aspects of health care traditionally delivered according to a biomedical model, including long-term physical and neurological conditions (such as diabetes, heart disease, pulmonary

> ### CASE STUDY: SARAH AND THE NEW CONSULTATION SERVICE
>
> Sarah is a newly qualified clinical psychologist who has just joined a community learning disability team. The consultant psychologist in the area intends to redesign their way of working to offer brief formal psychological consultation sessions to people with intellectual disabilities, together with their family members, care staff and professionals in the wider system of health and social care. Sarah contributes to the design and delivery of the new consultation service by reviewing the relevant literature and research evidence. As a result, they define a five-stage consultation model based on established family therapy practices and Edgar Schein's work on process consultation (Martin and Milton, 2005; Schein, 1999). The psychologists start to work in pairs to elicit different perspectives on referred problems from all in the system at an initial consultation meeting, then offer structured reflections on the issues raised. They also collaborate with the system to design solutions. This sort of work had not been formally evaluated in intellectual disability services before. Sarah researches potential methods of measuring outcomes for the consultations, and the team of clinical psychologists agree on a feedback process and follow-up questionnaires so that they can evaluate the impact of the service.

disease, stroke, dementia and chronic pain). There are often good health economic reasons to address physical health with a more integrated model of care, as psychological factors play such an important role in how people manage long-term health conditions and adjust to physical decline or loss. Put simply, psychologically effective health care may reduce the need for some repeat consultations and expensive medical intervention. With an ageing population and projections of massively increased demand on NHS services, this economic argument may open up significant new roles for clinical psychologists to implement psychological health care in what have traditionally been physical health care settings.

Clinical psychologists as clinical leaders and the architects of psychological care

Increasingly clinical psychologists are taking up leadership in teams and NHS organisations. Some leadership positions occupied by clinical psychologists are formal leadership posts leading the whole clinical team, or leading psychology in a team. Clinical psychologists are also directors of NHS Trusts, taking up roles at board level or leading on areas such as research, education, or across a large clinical field. For many, however, leadership is not clearly defined within a specific job, but is still required (for example, leading on specific service development or research projects). Clinical psychologists are well placed to offer leadership, being a highly selected group trained to postgraduate level, and with some training coverage of leadership and organisational psychology. There is increasing recognition currently that clinical staff can offer

---

CASE STUDY: JASON AND THE NEURO-BEHAVIOURAL CLINIC

Jason is a clinical psychologist with five years' experience since qualification working in a pain management clinic with people with long-term health conditions. There is a specialist neuro-behavioural assessment service locally which assesses children and adults suspected of suffering with neuro-behavioural conditions such as Tourette's syndrome (characterised by involuntary tics and vocal expression) and attention deficit and hyperactivity disorder (characterised by high levels of distractibility). Both conditions can lead to significant social and occupational difficulty but there is currently no psychological input available locally. Jason is invited to design a psychological intervention service to attach to the clinic, including the main empirically supported treatments – Habit Reversal Training for Tourette's (Piacentini and Chang, 2006) and a specific form of CBT for ADHD (Ramsay and Rostain, 2007). Jason designs a service plan based on group and individual interventions, and the service wins a bid to the local commissioners to pilot it. As a result Jason and a CBT therapist are employed to deliver the service.

---

aspects of leadership that non–clinical managers may struggle to offer – implementing a vision of health care in a manner that is directly informed by clinical practice. This offers a great opportunity for clinical psychologists to become influential by taking up formal and informal roles as leaders, and by doing so to advance the quality of psychological health care.

Clinical psychologists can legitimately see themselves as architects of psychological care. The increased programme of building psychological therapy services in recent years does not threaten the need for new psychological service architecture and design but embeds its importance. As architects, clinical psychologists have always, and always will, find themselves involved in new projects, implementing change and delivering psychological aspects of care in new ways. By taking up roles of influence at all levels of organisations they can continue to drive forward psychologically informed health care to face the challenges ahead.

Implications for clinical psychology training

There are a number of implications of this analysis for the future of clinical psychology training. Clinical psychologists are increasingly positioning themselves as leaders and architects of psychological health care. The breadth of their training across different theoretical and empirical aspects of psychology provides essential equipment to do this. However, to lead in services that increasingly deliver specific defined interventions, training must also equip clinical psychologists with the depth in these approaches, such as CBT or systemic psychotherapy. This will enhance credibility and the potential to shape future services.

CASE STUDY: JAMILA AND THE PATHWAY FOR PSYCHOLOGICAL CARE FOR CHILDREN AND FAMILIES

Jamila is a consultant clinical psychologist who is the psychology and psychological therapies lead for a large children and young people's mental health team covering a population area of 100,000. Jamila is aware of a national push to increase the use of evidence-based psychological therapies for children, under the children and young people's IAPT programme. She works with service managers to make a successful bid for some national monies to train three nurses and a social worker in the team to deliver CBT for children. Aware of the evidence for multiple forms of therapy for children, she also convenes a group including the team manager, a senior family therapist, art therapist and child psychotherapist to design an integrated psychological pathway of care so that children and families entering the service receive a form of help targeted at their particular difficulties, based on the NICE-based evidence and professional consensus. This pathway proves a success, and outcome measures demonstrate that all the forms of therapy are proving helpful to children in the service. As a result the pathway is adopted by other teams in the locality.

The development of multiple entry routes to psychological therapy practice has also highlighted the haphazard nature of current training pathways. Some clinical psychologists train in a specific psychological therapy before undertaking their doctorate, others afterwards, others not at all. Meanwhile 10,000 psychology students are graduating each year, and often find it difficult to gain a foothold in any training pathway to enable them to work in mental health. New attention to designing integrated training pathways could help ensure that clinical psychologists arrive at the completion of their doctorate training with in-depth training in one or more methods of psychological intervention as well as a broad-based training and all of the benefits that this brings. For example, new roles for psychology graduates within services, with training attached, could ensure this. Finally, with clinical leadership emerging as an important role for clinical psychologists, it will be important for this to feature as an explicit and significant component of doctorate training, preparing clinical psychologists to lead in multi-professional services earlier in their careers than has been the case in the past.

CONCLUSION

The profession of clinical psychology in the UK has grown in a dramatic way in terms of both numbers of practitioners, and in the range of work and activities they do, since the 1950s. The influence of the profession has grown, and a qualification in clinical psychology will open many doors in many fields. However, the profession will need to continue to adapt and develop, as it has always done, to meet the ever-expanding

THE DAY OF A CLINICAL PSYCHOLOGIST IN 2025?

Fahima splits her working week between her role as a private therapist and her role as a leader of a new 'Sussex Dementia Care Alliance'. She starts the day by sending two video tweets from her home office, ensuring she follows the current Royal College of Clinical Psychology's guidance on the use of psychosocial media. Fahima is reluctant to move to the open online visual forums that people are constantly connected to through their Apple eye glasses and feels that Twitter, although a largely obsolete medium, is still the best way of connecting to her followers. One of the tweets is for 2,000 community dementia care volunteers. There are a couple of direct messages on her account from carers in crisis and she takes time to respond to these.

After this she completes two Skype therapy sessions. She is pleased that both clients have made good progress on their online outcome measures, which means she is eligible for a small bonus payment this month from the clients' NHS insurance schemes.

In the afternoon, Fahima attends a leadership meeting for the Dementia Care Alliance. Her co-leader is a local carer of someone with dementia, and the partnership includes representatives from the local council, two charities and Seaview Health, a private company providing all NHS-funded primary care mental health services in the region. The partnership are using today's meeting to look at the outcome data assessing the ongoing programme of activities aimed at enhancing the well-being of carers of people with dementia as assessed by online data provided by these carers. They are also reviewing data evaluating the improvements to emotional well-being being experienced by the dementia care volunteers as a consequence of the voluntary work they are undertaking. Through a strong government-driven public health campaign over the past five years, giving back to your community in some formal way is now seen as important for everyone in contributing to a 'well' society. However, dementia care is often seen as one of the less attractive options available, and struggles to attract people's interest. Fahima and the other members of the alliance are working to challenge the stigma that they believe may be contributing to this view, looking to demonstrate the positive psychological impact (upon well-being and self-esteem) that caring for people with dementia can have for these volunteers.

Fahima sees two more clients in the evening in the 'emotional fitness' section of her local gym.

---

challenges and opportunities of psychological and physical health care in the twenty-first century. We hope that this chapter has given you some sense of what these key challenges and opportunities might be. For the aspiring clinical psychologist, the increasing recognition of the benefits of developing more psychologically healthy individuals, teams, organisations and communities means that there are good prospects for an increasing range of interesting and innovative work that will require your skills.

KEY CONCEPTS AND TERMS

- Psychometrics
- Behaviourism
- Cognitive therapy
- Workforce

- Improving access to psychological therapies (IAPT)

- Talking therapies
- Clinical leadership

LEARNING OUTCOMES

When you have completed this chapter you should be able to:

1. Describe the history of clinical psychology in the UK.
2. Understand how the current context may influence the future role of clinical psychology.
3. Understand ways in which clinical psychology could draw further upon core psychological science and apply this to enhancing well-being.

SAMPLE ESSAY TITLES

- How has the role of the clinical psychologist changed since 1950, and what roles can clinical psychologists expect to take up in the next ten years?
- What are the main similarities and differences in the roles of psychological therapist and clinical psychologist?
- Why are clinical psychologists seemingly always re-inventing their role in the NHS?

REFERENCES

Baum, W.M. (2005). *Understanding Behaviourism: Behaviour, culture and evolution*. Malden, MA: Blackwell.

Beck, A.T. (1976). *Cognitive Therapy and the Emotional Disorders*. New York: Meridian.

Centre for Economic Performance (2006). *The Depression Report: A new deal for depression and anxiety disorders*. London School of Economics and Political Science. Available online at http://cep.lse.ac.uk/textonly/research/mentalhealth/DEPRESSION_REPORT_LAYARD2.pdf (accessed 23 November 2013).

Centre for Workforce Intelligence (2012). Workforce risks and opportunities: Clinical psychologists, psychological therapists and related applied psychology divisions. Education Commissioning Risks Summary. Available online at http://www.cfwi.org.uk/publications/applied-psychologists-workforce-risks-and-opportunities-2013-education-commissioning-risks-summary-from-2012/@@publication-detail (accessed 4 January 2014).

Eysenck, H.J. (1949). Training in clinical psychology: An English point of view. *American Psychologist, 4,* 173–176.

Gilbert, P. (2009). Moving beyond cognitive behavioural therapy. *The Psychologist, 22*(5), 400–403. Available online at http://www.thepsychologist.org.uk/archive/archive_home. cfm?volumeID=22&editionID=175&ArticleID=1505 (accessed 23 November 2013).

Ham, C., Dixon, A. and Brooke, B. (2012). *Transforming the Delivery of Health and Social Care: The case for fundamental change.* London: The Kings Fund. Available online at http://www. kingsfund.org.uk/sites/files/kf/field/field_publication_file/transforming-the-delivery-of-health-and-social-care-the-kings-fund-sep-2012.pdf (accessed 4 January 2014).

Hollanders, H. and McLeod, J. (1999). Theoretical orientation and reported practice: A survey of eclecticism among counsellors in Britain. *British Journal of Guidance and Counselling, 27*(3), 405–414.

Management Advisory Service (1989). Review of Clinical Psychology Services. Available online at http://www.mas.org.uk/uploads/articles/MAS%20Review%201989.pdf (accessed 23 November 2013).

Martin, E. and Milton, A. (2005). Working systemically with staff working in a residential home. *Context: The magazine for family therapy and systemic practice, Special Edition, Grey Matters: Ageing in the Family, 77,* 37–39.

Piacentini, J. and Chang, S. (2006). Behavioral treatments for tic suppression: Habit reversal training. *Advances in Neurology, 99,* 227–233.

Pilgrim, D. and Treacher, A. (1992). *Clinical Psychology Observed.* London: Routledge.

Ramsay, R. and Rostain, A. (2007). *Cognitive-behavioural Therapy for Adult ADHD: An integrative psychosocial and medical approach.* New York: Routledge.

Schein, E.H. (1999). *Process Consultation Revisited: Building the helping relationship.* Boston, MA: Addison-Wesley.

17 Moving forward into clinical psychology

Clara Strauss and Mary John

SUMMARY

The aim of this chapter is to help you consider how you may want to apply what you have learned from your psychology degree in your future career. Clinical psychology can offer an excellent career path to make a real difference to people's lives using psychology in practice, high levels of job satisfaction and a relatively good income in the health sector. However, it is certainly not the right choice for everyone and there is a range of related career options. In this chapter we overview a number of career choices for psychology graduates in health and social care, then focus in detail on clinical psychology training. We provide information and advice about what clinical psychology training involves, and what you will need to do to secure a place. Overall this chapter can help you consider whether or not this is the right career choice for you and, if it is, enable you to move forward towards this goal.

INTRODUCTION

It is important to understand in detail what being a clinical psychologist involves as part of your career decision making. Other parts of this book can help with this. Before reading this chapter you will find it helpful to first read Chapters 1, 2 and 3. Chapter 1 provides you with an insight into the working life of a clinical psychologist and Chapter 2 outlines the principles on which the profession of clinical psychology are based and how these principles are applied in practice. Chapter 3 focuses on the opportunities and challenges of working in multi-disciplinary teams, and includes an overview of the roles of the different disciplines in the health and social care sector. This chapter focuses on career choice and in particular training to become a clinical psychologist. It provides information to help you decide whether or not this is the right profession for you and, if so, what you will need to do to realise your aspiration. For further information on the role of the clinical psychologist see Hall and Llewelyn (2006) or Beinart *et al.* (2009).

Completing an undergraduate or conversion degree in psychology provides a really sound platform for a number of careers within the health and social care sector. The degree offers you an opportunity to blend your approach to inquiry through both the humanities and the sciences; the former through the provision of experiences to think critically and articulate thoughts through essays and reports and the latter through opportunities to develop hypotheses and then the consequential testing of these hypotheses. Alongside these core skills the degree facilitates the process of acquiring an understanding and knowledge of fundamental psychological processes and principles from, for example, information processing, neuropsychology, cognition, memory, developmental and social psychology perspectives to, at a more fine-tuned level, the developmental trajectory of the emergent self. In addition, the degree provides opportunities to consider the application of these principles to all walks of life including in health and societal contexts. Communication and critical thinking skills are central to the degree with an emphasis on being able to understand the underlying theories as well as their application to daily life with the appreciation of the impact of cognitive biases on what is heard and digested and relayed.

I HAVE A PSYCHOLOGY DEGREE: HOW CAN I USE IT WITHIN THE HEALTH AND SOCIAL CARE SECTOR?

There are a wide range of roles in health and social care that are opened up if you have a degree in psychology, some of which are as follows:

- Clinical psychology
- Academic research and teaching
- Psychological therapy
- Nursing
- Occupational therapy
- Social work
- Medicine
- Management and finance
- Human resources.

The careers that psychology graduates choose to enter are highly varied, as highlighted in the list above. The skills attained at undergraduate level are evident in the competences of the front-line health and social care professions (e.g. psychotherapy, nursing, occupational therapy, social work and medicine). They all require critical analysis, the understanding and use of research as well as person–centred skills such as those required to communicate effectively whether orally or in written form. Support services, such as human resources within organisations, also use these skills to enable and maintain the effective functioning of the wider organisation.

A career in applied psychology draws upon the entire undergraduate syllabus as this is the foundation for the necessary postgraduate skills and competences. Within the applied psychology career pathway the application and translation of psychological theory into real-life predicaments for individuals and their social networks are central to the process of understanding the emotional lives of individuals across the lifespan and offering helpful interventions. Within postgraduate courses there is emphasis on developing advanced research skills so that the evidence base can be contributed to and so that evidence-based practice can be adopted and implemented effectively.

WHICH OF THESE CAREERS SHOULD I CHOOSE?

Making the choice of career may seem daunting as the thought of spending an entire life time engaged in one form of activity can be inconceivable. This can be more overwhelming if leaving university with little experience of the working environment. To help in this decision-making process it is advisable to try to gain as much information as you can from a variety of sources so that you have an unbiased and clear picture of what will be required and what the longer term opportunities are within that sector. Books can help (e.g. McDonald and Das, 2008), but taking the initiative in seeking out people who are doing the job is a really helpful way of gaining a more grounded understanding of what a day in the life of an individual undertaking this career may be like. This direct contact will enable you to grasp the core aspects of the job that you will enjoy, as well as the less wonderful but nevertheless important aspects which you may find difficult, boring, demanding or emotionally distressing. Building on this with visits to career advisers and shadowing someone adds to the richness of your understanding. At some universities the psychology degree is offered with an additional placement year, typically taken in the third year. This can provide an in-depth opportunity to explore your chosen field as well as specific aspects of it, for example, working with adults with psychosis or with young people. Securing a placement in the health care sector while being supervised by a member of the discipline is invaluable and for many undergraduates this experience clarifies that the current career is worth pursuing, while for others it helpfully determines that there is a need to focus attention elsewhere. You may wish to consult the NHS careers website (www.nhscareers.nhs.uk) which provides a link to all the NHS jobs and training courses, and the Clinical Psychology Clearing House (www.leeds.ac.uk/chpccp) which provides information on all the clinical psychology training programmes in the UK.

AM I SURE THAT I WANT TO BE A CLINICAL PSYCHOLOGIST?

The allure of becoming a clinical psychologist can organise individuals' lives for a number of years. The path of obtaining at least a 2.1 degree, experience of working within an applied psychology context to obtain skills and knowledge followed by the application process can take between five and eight years to achieve. The competition is strong with about six candidates for every clinical psychology training place across the country and some courses having fiercer competition. To commence on this pathway when there are other interesting career opportunities for people with a psychology degree needs careful thought, as this time is precious in terms of personal and professional development. To this end it is worth examining one's motivations for wanting to become a clinical psychologist. Does the career sit easily with your personal values and goals, and do the NHS and other health care providers also rest easily with these values? There can be a misperception about what the job entails and a lack of regard for the mental and physical robustness needed to attend to the emotional distress of others. There is a real expectation that trainees and qualified practitioners need to be able to multi-task, switching activities quickly, and being able to apply knowledge laterally and creatively. For many this level of creativity is part of the draw; for others it is daunting.

When considering this career there is a need to self-reflect and consider objectively one's personal strengths, learning needs and, importantly, limitations. Given the demands of the profession and the use of 'self' in the therapeutic endeavour, personal emotional well-being needs particular consideration. This does not mean that someone who has experienced a mental health problem should not join the profession. In fact, this can be an important source of values and insight. However, we all need to be committed to understanding ourselves, what triggers exist for personal distress and how we can effectively manage in an environment that may elicit strong and difficult feelings in ourselves. Without this self-knowledge, training can become very challenging. In particular, the training experience can be deskilling at first, as previous ways of thinking are challenged and new skills have to be acquired. The emphasis on being evaluated by supervisors and others may be particularly challenging to some individuals who do not feel sure about their own identity, and it is not unusual for trainees to experience anxieties or low mood at times. Some choose to undertake personal therapy or other self-development activities before or during training to help with these issues.

A further issue to consider is that of timing. When applying to undertake a challenging course it is worth considering whether this is the right time. Are family and friends supportive and will they be able to help you when life challenges present? Is there an appreciation of what the course entails regarding the time commitments?

Finally, choosing the right course; the programmes across the country provide many similar experiences but they also have some unique differences. To this end it is worth really exploring which programme offers the optimal experiences in terms of your specific learning needs and also holds a philosophy that you can appreciate and want to uphold. The programme websites as well as the Clearing House Handbook and the Alternative Handbook are all valuable sources of information.

There is no appropriate set of motivations for training as a clinical psychologist but there are some that can be less helpful, for example, pursuing a career to try to resolve one's own or other family members' ongoing emotional difficulties. In terms of reflecting, it may be helpful to consider what you want from the role. Most individuals who enter the profession do so at least partly for altruistic reasons, to try to make a difference in the lives of others. However, this altruism needs to be moderated by ensuring that helping is undertaken in collaboration, rather than being 'done to' or 'done for' the person being helped. For some, the rewards will be experienced through seeing clients directly or supervising others, while for others a clinical academic career provides the vehicle to effect change, either through the development of novel research, translating this research into action, or training others in the application of these techniques and processes.

I DO WANT TO BE A CLINICAL PSYCHOLOGIST: WHAT DO I NEED TO DO NOW?

Clinical psychology training courses

The Clearing House for Postgraduate Training in Clinical Psychology, based at the University of Leeds, administers applications for clinical psychology training in the UK (www.leeds.ac.uk/chpccp). There are currently 30 clinical psychology training courses in the UK, with courses spread fairly evenly across the country. In 2012 there were 3,875 application forms for 586 places, meaning that approximately 15 per cent of applicants were offered a place on a course.

Courses are three-year, full-time postgraduate doctoral programmes. They are accredited by the Health and Care and Professions Council (HCPC) and by the British Psychological Society (BPS). This means that while courses differ from each other in terms of emphasis, there are common elements across all courses. Requirements are that trainees undertake clinical practice placements in a range of settings (typically working-age adult mental health, child and adolescent mental health, learning disability services and older people's mental health services), and there is often the opportunity also to undertake a specialist clinical placement. Each placement lasts six months to a year and is linked to a qualified clinical psychologist who provides weekly supervision and often joint or observed practice.

Training is divided between placement, teaching and study time, with approximately 50 per cent of time spent on placement, with the other 50 per cent split between teaching and study. Most courses will organise this through having two teaching or study days and two to three placement days each week. Some courses, particularly those in rural areas, provide teaching blocks with full-time placements in between these blocks.

Teaching will cover a range of psychological theories, models and related practice approaches. All courses will teach at least two psychological therapy approaches (one of which must be cognitive-behavioural therapy (CBT)) with different courses emphasising different approaches. Clinical psychologists are often involved in offering a range of contributions to teams in addition to psychological therapy once they have qualified, and teaching on courses reflects this. Teaching is likely to be offered on supervision and consultation as well as on leadership, with clinical psychologists being prepared to take on leadership positions in the NHS and other health settings. As this is a doctoral-level programme, courses will provide teaching to equip trainees with the necessary knowledge and skills to undertake research.

Assignments will include written case reports, service evaluation projects and a major research project. As this is a doctoral training programme the assignments are expected to be of doctoral (Ph.D.) standard with the major research project to make a novel, theoretically important contribution to the clinical literature.

Courses based in large cities may offer placements within a small geographical area, whereas courses in more rural areas are likely to offer placements across a wide area. This may involve travelling for an hour or more each day to and from placement, and this is worth considering before applying.

Funding

At the time of writing, the NHS pays the tuition fees for clinical psychology training and provides a salary for trainees. However, this arrangement has periodically come under review and it is not certain that this will continue in its current form in the years to come. The Clearing House website provides up-to-date information on funding arrangements.

Entry requirements

Graduate Basis for Chartership and academic qualifications

Courses require entrants to have an undergraduate psychology degree that has BPS Graduate Basis for Chartership (GBC), meaning sufficient coverage of a psychology curriculum and meeting defined standards of teaching. Many, but not all, UK undergraduate psychology degrees confer GBC and so it is worth checking that your undergraduate degree is eligible for GBC. If not it may be necessary to undertake a further degree that does confer GBC.

Almost all courses will require an undergraduate psychology degree grade at a 2.1 or first. Some courses will consider a 2.2 but usually only with subsequent academic qualifications such as a Master's degree. In addition to having a 2.1 or first, many successful applicants have Master's degree qualifications and some also have Ph.D.s.

Relevant clinical experience

Courses also require entrants to have gained relevant experience in working in the kinds of settings in which clinical psychologists work. This may involve working in NHS settings, social services organisations or in the voluntary sector. Positions may be voluntary or paid and may include psychology assistant or research assistant posts, or a range of other relevant posts such as nursing assistant, support worker, mental health practitioner or clinical associate in applied psychology. Some courses prefer applicants to have held psychology assistant or research assistant posts, while other courses welcome applicants with a broader range of relevant experience. What is important is that the relevant experience positions have provided an opportunity to apply psychological theories and models in practice, and it can be particularly helpful to have had some supervision from a clinical psychologist. Work experience in the NHS is not required by most courses but knowledge of the NHS and of the latest NHS structures and policies is expected.

There are a number of ways of finding relevant clinical experience. The NHS will advertise posts for research assistants, psychology assistants, support workers and other relevant posts through their jobs website (www.jobs.nhs.uk), and research assistant posts will be advertised through the university jobs site (www.jobs.ac.uk). You can sign up for email alerts on both of these sites for jobs that may be of interest. Posts are also advertised on the BPS job website (www.bps.org.uk/jobs/jobs) and it is worth contacting NHS Trusts, charities, voluntary sector organisations and private providers of health care directly for job opportunities. Although it is not a financial option for everyone, some people gain voluntary experience, for example, through volunteer internships. For further advice on gaining relevant experience see Knight (2002).

Courses vary in the amount of relevant experience needed before applying and it is important to consult websites from individual courses first. Some will require several months of relevant experience while others will require several years.

Research skills and experience

Research skills and experience are also required. Many successful applicants have postgraduate research qualifications such as Master's degrees or Ph.D.s, and many have held research assistant posts. Having at least one peer-reviewed publication can be an advantage as this can be one way of demonstrating research skills and experience (see Hall, 2012).

Personal qualities

In addition to the entry requirements outlined above, courses will also be looking for certain personal qualities. Clinical psychology is a profession that involves working with people who may be experiencing a great deal of distress or who may be vulnerable, and so personal values are important. As well as applying psychological theory in clinical practice clinical psychologists are also expected to be able to reflect thoughtfully upon their own experiences and backgrounds and will be encouraged through supervision to develop a greater self-awareness. Clinical psychologists are just the same as everyone else and can experience high levels of distress in response to the work or in response to events in their own lives. Clinical psychologists need to have a degree of resilience and to be able to manage difficulties and seek appropriate support for themselves. For further ideas on developing reflective capacity, see Thompson and Thompson (2008).

Equal opportunities and clinical psychology training

The clinical psychology training community is committed to continuing to improve the diversity of the profession and welcomes applicants from a broad range of backgrounds. Diversity is important because a helping profession such as clinical psychology should aim to reflect all the members of the society that it serves.

At the time of writing, approximately 85 per cent of applicants and successful candidates are women (Clearing House for Postgraduate Courses in Clinical Psychology [CHPCCP], 2013). The majority of applicants are in their twenties, although applications are received from people in their thirties and forties, and they are no less likely to be successful than younger candidates (CHPCCP, 2013). In 2012 (the latest year for which figures are available), 10 per cent of candidates were from black and minority ethnic (BME) backgrounds and 5 per cent described their sexual orientation as gay, lesbian or bisexual (CHPCCP, 2013).

The profession therefore could be doing better to reflect the communities that it serves. It seems that the challenge lies in A level (Guardian News and Media Limited, 2013) and university (Trapp et al., 2011) choices made whilst at school, rather than a bias in the selection process for postgraduate training. For instance, the fact that the vast majority of successful applicants are women reflects the fact that the vast majority of applicants are women, which in turn reflects the fact that most undergraduate psychology students are women (Trapp et al., 2011). In response to this, many courses are proactively encouraging more men to choose psychology at undergraduate level and to then apply for clinical psychology training. Many training courses also proactively seek BME applicants and host pre-application selection events targeted at

ROUTES TO TRAINING: YASMIN

I graduated from Loughborough University in 2006 with a first in B.Sc. Psychology. After graduation, I gained a place on a graduate scheme in a FTSE 30 company. As a graduate manager, I led and managed a range of projects in various parts of the organisation. I loved working with teams and the fast pace of my job but also felt that my work was not particularly interesting or meaningful, and I began to feel that there was something missing in what I was doing. So I wondered if I could apply my personal and professional skills to something more satisfying.

I attended a talk about the PsychD programme at the University of Surrey. I previously thought a clinical psychologist was just a therapist but I realised at the talk that the role entailed so much more, which was attractive to me. I also realised that as well as my personal skills, my business skills would be an advantage rather than a hindrance, given that leadership was a key competence of a clinical psychologist.

I gained just under four years of relevant clinical experience before I got a place on training. I think I applied for over 100+ NHS posts to begin with and did not get a single interview, so I started applying for roles outside the NHS. Eventually, I managed to get a psychology assistant post with the Prison Service. I then managed to get a foot in the door in the NHS, volunteering as an assistant psychologist for one day a week around support worker shifts. Once I was in the NHS, I started getting interviews for paid assistant psychologist posts and did two assistant psychologist posts before getting a place on training, one in a forensic setting and another in Child and Adolescent Mental Health Services.

I secured a place on clinical training on my third application. I saw my first application as a way to become familiar with the application process and learn from the experience. To my surprise, I got an interview and although it did not turn into a place, the feedback was invaluable and it spurred me on.

I think my two assistant psychologist roles were crucial to gaining a place on training due mainly to access to the network of support and contacts. As well as developing my clinical skills in these roles, I had the opportunity to see successful applications, discuss my application with psychologists and have a mock interview.

On my second application I managed to get two interviews, one of which turned into a reserve offer. I remember feeling very disheartened and upset about not getting a place, especially after all the preparation and anxiety of going through the process. However, I applied once more the following year. I got three interviews and accepted a place.

Getting a place on clinical training felt amazing. I think I was floating for about a month! I felt so relieved that the effort was all worth it and I was actually going to be a clinical psychologist.

Starting training felt like a continuation of my journey to qualify as a clinical psychologist. Looking back, I feel grateful for all of my work experiences prior to starting training as I feel they prepared me for some of the challenges of being a trainee. Clinical training is demanding and the workload is high. I sometimes feel out of my depth, particularly with academic assignments, since it has been seven years since I graduated with my Bachelor's degree. However, it is also incredibly rewarding and satisfying, and there is plenty of support from the course team as well as 27 other people going through it with you.

CASE HISTORY ROUTES TO TRAINING: CHRIS

Between 2002 and 2005, I completed my B.Sc. in Psychology (Hons.) and Human Biology at the University of Plymouth and achieved an upper 2.1. In 2008 I started a part-time M.Sc. in Developmental Psychopathology at Reading University and finished in the summer of 2010 with a credit, gaining the Graduate Basis for Chartership with the BPS. I began clinical training in 2010.

After finishing my first degree, I took on three jobs. I worked as a care assistant in a residential home for older adults diagnosed with dementia. My role here was to provide care for their physical and psychological needs. Meeting their psychological needs included life story and reminiscence work. At the same time, I completed training with the Samaritans and worked voluntarily as a Samaritans listener. Towards the end of my first degree I also applied for a volunteer assistant psychology job in a primary care setting, which would now most probably be called an Improving Access to Psychological Therapies (IAPT) service. One day a week I was involved in supporting adults with depression and anxiety to make use of computerised CBT and guided self-help. In late 2006, after nearly 18 months of juggling jobs, I decided to shift my focus back towards working with adolescents, which had always been of clinical interest to me. Between late 2006 and 2009 I was employed by Connexions as a youth worker, offering support and guidance to young people who had been excluded from secondary school for emotional and behavioural difficulties. In 2009, I transferred to a local CAMHS service and provided this support to young people with more severe mental health difficulties.

When I applied in 2009 I did not seriously think that I would secure a place on clinical training the first time. I treated the application as a practice. I applied to the University of Surrey, Royal Holloway, UCL and the Institute of Psychiatry. I remember expecting to be asked to take the entrance exam as I met the criteria. Although the exam was tough in the sense of time management, I was in the process of writing up my M.Sc. dissertation, so research design and statistics were at the forefront of my thinking, which certainly helped. Although I was certainly nervous on the day of the interview, I do also remember a feeling of being put at ease. The situational interview was what I expected. I was, however, surprised by the personal suitability interview, which felt more like a chat. I have always been a very reflective person and having this ability felt like a very important part of selection.

As I come to the end of training, I have definitely changed in terms of my thinking and practice. The key components that the training at Surrey has provided me with are the emphasis on reflection and the importance of working within the scientist-practitioner model. I do not think I was expecting such a commitment to developing research skills, but in order to make sense of research in terms of clinical practice, this is vital. I have enjoyed and felt challenged in the process of developing my therapeutic skills and have been pleased with opportunities to make use of training and supervision to develop other competences of being a clinical psychologist such as consultation and leadership.

BME undergraduate psychology students. All courses welcome applications from all candidates, irrespective of background.

Work permits and English language proficiency

Applicants must be allowed to work in the UK and, if relevant, to have a UK work permit. Applicants who do not speak English as a first language will be required to have an International English Language Testing System (IELTS) certificate at level 7 or above.

I THINK I AM READY TO APPLY FOR CLINICAL PSYCHOLOGY TRAINING: WHAT DO I NEED TO DO?

1   The first thing to do is to look at the Clearing House website (www.leeds.ac.uk/chpccp) to check that you meet all the currently relevant criteria, as these may have changed since this book was published.

2   Decide which four courses you would like to apply to. Not all courses are the same and so you will want to carefully consider which courses are right for you. The Clearing House website provides links to all the individual course websites where you can find out more information about each course, its specific entry requirements, and its ethos, content and structure. The Alternative Handbook is produced by the Division of Clinical Psychology and presents the views and experiences of trainees on each of the 30 courses. You can download the latest copy of the handbook from the British Psychological Society online shop by searching for 'Alternative Handbook' at http://shop.bps.org.uk/publications.html.

3   Applications are made online through the Clearing House website. The site opens for new applications in September each year with the deadline for applying at the beginning of December, but make sure that you check the deadline, as these can change from year to year.

4   The application form will ask you to provide details of your qualifications and relevant experience as well as to provide a personal statement. A guideline document for completing the application form is available on the Clearing House website. You will also be asked to name two referees, one to provide an academic reference and the other to provide a relevant experience reference.

5   Some courses have a written or screening test and these occur between the beginning of February and mid-March each year.

6   All courses interview potential trainees with interviews occurring between mid-March and mid-May. Most applicants will not be offered an interview owing to the large number of applications. Courses apply robust criteria to screen applicants for interview based on the application form and, where relevant, based on performance on the written or screening test.

7   Following interview, courses will offer places to successful candidates and offer a selection of other candidates a place on their reserve list. Most courses interview many more candidates than they have available places, so it is likely that the majority of interview candidates will not be offered a place.

8   Candidates are required to accept an offered place by the beginning of June and any remaining places will be offered to candidates on the reserve list.

9   Courses start in September or October.

It is important to remember that only 15 per cent of applicants in 2012 were offered a place on a course. The majority of applicants have a strong academic record, plenty of relevant experience and good references. This means that not being successful in obtaining a place does not necessarily mean that you will not make an excellent clinical psychologist one day and many people apply several times before being successful.

WHAT HAPPENS IF I AM NOT SUCCESSFUL OR IF I HAVE CHANGED MY MIND ABOUT BEING A CLINICAL PSYCHOLOGIST?

As outlined earlier, there are many routes to working in the health and social care sector. Clinical psychology involves applying psychological theories to real-life, everyday situations, often when people are feeling distressed or vulnerable, and using these theories in practice to help people move forward in their lives. However, clinical psychologists are increasingly moving away from spending most of their time providing direct therapeutic support and towards training and supervising others to provide therapy, and towards taking on leadership roles in the health care and other sectors (See Skinner and Toogood, 2010).

For those interested in a career as a psychological therapist there are a number of routes and organisations whose role is to support this: the British Association of Behavioural and Cognitive Psychotherapists (BABCP) can direct you if you wish to become a cognitive-behavioural therapist (www.babcp.com), the United Kingdom Council for Psychotherapy if you want to train in another form of psychotherapy (UKCP; www.psychotherapy.org.uk), and the British Association for Counselling Psychotherapists (BACP; www.bacp.co.uk) will direct you if you wish to become a counsellor.

If research particularly appeals to you then perhaps a career in a university setting would be of interest. Following an undergraduate degree many people undertake a Masters degree and then a Ph.D. before moving on to post-doctoral positions and then on to a lectureship (See Phillips and Pugh, 2010). Ph.D. positions are often advertised on the www.jobs.ac.uk website where you can sign up for email alerts, and individual universities will often advertise Ph.D. opportunities on their websites.

Many people with an undergraduate psychology degree go on to train as nurses, including as mental health nurses (see www.nhscareers.nhs.uk). This profession opens up plenty of opportunities to work with people experiencing mental health difficulties and to gain further training, for example, as a cognitive-behavioural therapist (see www.babcp.com).

FINAL THOUGHTS

This chapter has provided a detailed overview of what is entailed when training as a clinical psychologist and the processes involved when applying for training. This chapter has provided you with some important questions to consider about your future career and whether or not clinical psychology is the right choice for you. Whatever you decide, we wish you well.

KEY CONCEPTS AND TERMS

- Clinical psychology
- Training
- Careers
- Psychotherapy

- Supervision and consultation
- Research
- Resilience

- Self-reflection
- Leadership
- Support networks

LEARNING OUTCOMES

When you have completed this chapter you should be able to:

1. Consider the range of career options open to graduate psychologists in health and social care.
2. Consider the right career direction for you.
3. Understand ways of gaining relevant experience for a career in clinical psychology.
4. Navigate the system for applying for postgraduate training in clinical psychology in the UK.
5. Cope better with whatever happens!

REFERENCES AND FURTHER READING

Careers information

NHS careers website: www.nhscareers.nhs.uk.

Clearing House for Postgraduate Courses in Clinical Psychology: www.leeds.ac.uk/chpccp.

Division of Clinical Psychology (BPS): dcp.bps.org.uk.

British Association of Behavioural and Cognitive Psychotherapists: www.babcp.com.

United Kingdom Council for Psychotherapy: www.psychotherapy.org.uk.

British Association for Counselling Psychotherapists: www.bacp.co.uk.

Job advertisements

NHS jobs: www.jobs.nhs.uk.

University-based jobs: www.jobs.ac.uk.

British Psychological Society jobs website: www.bps.org.uk/jobs/jobs.

Equal opportunities in clinical psychology

Clearing House for Postgraduate Courses in Clinical Psychology (2013). *Equal Opportunities Numbers: 2012 Entry*. Retrieved from: http://www.leeds.ac.uk/chpccp/BasicEqualopps2012.html.

Guardian News and Media Limited (2013). *A Level Results 2012: Breakdown by subject, gender and region*. Retrieved from: http://www.theguardian.com/news/datablog/2012/aug/16/a-level-results-data-gender-region-subject#data.

Trapp, A., Banister, P., Ellis, J., Latto, R., Miell, D. and Upton, D. (2011). *The Future of Undergraduate Psychology in the United Kingdom*. York: Higher Education Academy Psychology Network.

Books

Beinart, H., Kennedy, P. and Llewelyn, S. (2009). *Clinical Psychology in Practice*. Chichester: BPS Blackwell.

Hall, G.M. (ed.) (2012). *How to Write a Paper*. Chichester: Wiley Blackwell.

Hall, J. and Llewelyn, S. (eds) (2006). *What is Clinical Psychology?* Oxford: Oxford University Press.

Knight, A. (2002). *How to Become a Clinical Psychologist: Getting a foot in the door*. Hove: Brunner-Routledge.

McDonald, M. and Das, S. (2008). *What to do with your Psychology Degree*. Maidenhead: Open University Press.

Phillips, E.M. and Pugh, D.S. (2010). *How to Get a PhD: A handbook for students and their supervisors* (5th edn). Maidenhead: Open University Press.

Skinner, P. and Toogood, R. (2010). *Clinical Psychology Leadership Development Framework.* Leicester: Division of Clinical Psychology.

Thompson, S. and Thompson, N. (2008). *The Critically Reflective Practitioner.* Basingstoke: Palgrave Macmillan.

Index

Note: Page numbers in **bold** are for figures, those in *italics* are for tables.